내신
백신

고등 기출문제집

Common 1
English

민병천

⚜ Preface ⚜

Learning is not attained by chance,
It must be sought for with ardor
And attended with diligence.

배움은 우연히 얻어지는 것이 아니라
열성을 다해 갈구하고
부지런히 집중해야 얻을 수 있는 것입니다.

-Abigail Adams-

이 책의 **구성과 특징**

Words

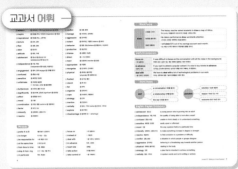

교과서 어휘

교과서 어휘 익히기

교과서에 제시된 주요 단어와 숙어를 정리하고, 기본 다지기와 실력 다지기 문제를 통해 어휘를 연습할 수 있습니다.

Functions

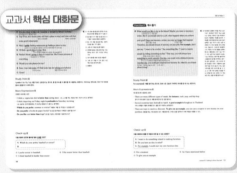
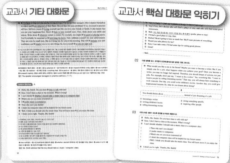

교과서 핵심 및 기타 대화문

교과서 핵심 대화문 익히기

교과서 대화문의 해석과 해설을 보며 익히고, 교과서 핵심 대화문 익히기를 통해 학습한 내용을 확인할 수 있습니다.

Grammar

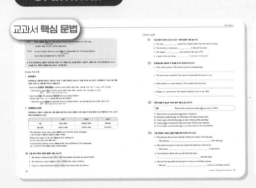
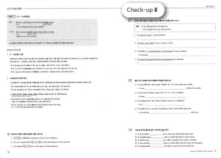

교과서 핵심 문법 / Check-up

단원별 핵심 문법 사항을 정리하고, Check-up 문제를 통해 연습할 수 있습니다.

Reading

교과서 본문 분석

교과서 본문 익히기

교과서 본문 외 지문 분석

교과서 본문에 대한 첨삭식 해설을 통해 문장을 정확히 익히고, 빈칸 완성하기, 옳은 어법·어휘 고르기, 틀린 부분 고치기 등의 활동을 통해 연습할 수 있습니다.

내신 1등급 공략

내신 1등급 어휘 공략

내신 1등급 어법 공략

교과서 지문을 이용하여 수능 어휘와 어법 문제 유형을 집중 연습할 수 있도록 구성하였습니다.

내신 1등급 실전 1회~3회

실제 학교 내신 기출 문제에서 엄선한 내신 기출 문제와 내신 시험에 나올 확률이 높은 문제들로 구성된 내신 1등급 실전 문제를 통해 풍부한 실전 경험을 쌓을 수 있습니다.

내신 1등급 수능형 고난도

내신 1등급 서술형

교과서 변형 지문을 활용하여 수능형 고난도 문제를 훈련하고, 다양한 서술형 문항도 대비할 수 있도록 구성하였습니다.

중간고사, 기말고사

중간고사, 기말고사

최종 점검 중간고사와 기말고사를 통해 학교 내신 1등급에 완벽하게 대비할 수 있습니다.

이 책의 차례

01

Getting to Know Yourself

Functions

▶ 선호 표현하기
I prefer finding restaurants **to** finding a place to stay.

▶ 예시 들기
For example, don't just say, "I want to be a writer."

Grammar

▶ In your brain, there is *a part* **that** is responsible for solving problems.

▶ **It** is natural **to feel** angry from time to time.

교과서 어휘

Words

☐ achieve	⑧ 성취하다, 이루다 (achievement ⑲ 성취)
☐ inspire	⑧ 영감을 주다, 격려하다 (inspiration ⑲ 영감)
☐ inspirational	⑲ 영감을 주는, 고무적인
☐ lecture	⑲ 강의, 강연
☐ flaw	⑲ 결함, 결점
☐ slam	⑧ 쾅 닫다
☐ attitude	⑲ 태도, 자세
☐ adolescent	⑲ 청소년 ⑲ 청소년기의 (adolescence ⑲ 청소년기)
☐ independence	⑲ 자립, 독립 (independent ⑲ 독립된, 독립적인)
☐ engagement	⑲ 참여, 관계 (engage ⑧ 관계를 맺다)
☐ confused	⑲ 혼란스러운
☐ sensitive	⑲ 예민한, 민감한
☐ unfairness	⑲ 부당함, 불공평 (↔ fairness, unfair ⑲ 불공평한)
☐ furthermore	⑨ 더욱이, 뿐만 아니라
☐ significantly	⑨ 중요하게, 상당히 (significant ⑲ 중요한)
☐ affect	⑧ 영향을 미치다
☐ mood	⑲ 기분
☐ combination	⑲ 조합, 결합 (combine ⑧ 결합하다)
☐ factor	⑲ 요인, 요소
☐ intensify	⑧ 강화하다, 심화시키다
☐ resolve	⑧ 해결하다
☐ conflict	⑲ 갈등, 분쟁
☐ manage	⑧ 처리하다, 관리하다
☐ aggressive	⑲ 공격적인
☐ violent	⑲ 폭력적인, 격렬한 (violence ⑲ 폭력)
☐ behavior	⑲ 행동, 행실 (behave ⑧ 행동하다, 처신하다)
☐ productive	⑲ 생산적인
☐ intense	⑲ 강렬한, 극심한
☐ direct	⑧ ~으로 향하다
☐ react	⑧ 반응하다 (reaction ⑲ 반응)
☐ appropriate	⑲ 적절한
☐ recognize	⑧ 인지하다, 인식하다
☐ physical	⑲ 육체의, 물리적인 (physically ⑨ 육체적으로)
☐ flushed	⑲ 상기된, 빨간
☐ clench	⑧ 꽉 쥐다
☐ fist	⑲ 주먹
☐ organize	⑧ 정리하다
☐ cope	⑧ 대처하다, 대응하다
☐ strategy	⑲ 전략
☐ mention	⑧ 언급하다
☐ verbally	⑨ 말로, 구두로 (verbal ⑲ 언어의, 구두의)
☐ explore	⑧ 탐구하다
☐ disadvantage	⑲ 불리한 점 (↔ advantage)

Phrases

☐ prefer A to B	A를 B보다 선호하다
☐ no longer	더 이상 ~ 않는
☐ be responsible for	~에 책임이 있다
☐ at the same time	(그와) 동시에
☐ from time to time	가끔, 때때로
☐ stop A from -ing	A가 ~하는 것을 막다
☐ in particular	특히, 특별히
☐ focus on	~에 집중하다
☐ instead of	~ 대신에
☐ deal with	~을 다루다, 처리하다
☐ in advance	미리, 사전에
☐ heart rate	심박동
☐ take action	조치를 취하다
☐ take control of	~을 지배하다

Word Focus

draw	(그림을) 그리다	The history teacher asked students to **draw** a map of Africa. 역사 교사는 학생들에게 아프리카의 지도를 그리라고 했다.
	(반응을) 끌어내다	His dance performance **drew** worldwide attention. 그의 댄스 공연은 세계적인 관심을 끌었다.
	(돈을) 인출하다	I will **draw** $70 out of my savings account each month. 나는 매달 내 저축 계좌에서 70달러를 인출할 것이다.

Useful Expressions

focus on ~에 집중하다	It was difficult to **focus on** the conversation with all the noise in the background. 주변에 온갖 소음이 있는 채로 대화에 집중하는 것은 어려웠다.
in advance 사전에, 미리	If you want to attend a popular concert, it's wise to buy tickets **in advance**. 인기있는 콘서트에 참석하고 싶다면 티켓을 미리 구매하는 게 현명하다.
deal with ~을 다루다, 처리하다	We have to **deal with** a lot of technological problems in our work. 우리는 업무에서 많은 기술적 문제들을 다뤄야 한다.

Word Mates

end
- a conversation 대화를 끝내다
- a relationship 관계를 끝내다
- the war 전쟁을 끝내다

possible
- solution 가능한 해결책
- reason 가능성 있는 이유
- outcome 발생 가능한 결과

English-English Dictionary

- **adolescent** 청소년   a young person who is growing into an adult
- **independence** 자립, 독립   the quality of being able to look after oneself
- **confused** 혼란스러운   unable to think clearly or to understand something
- **sensitive** 예민한, 민감한   easily upset or offended
- **mood** 기분   the way a person feels at a particular time
- **intensify** 강화하다, 심화시키다   to make something increase in degree or strength
- **resolve** 해결하다   to find a solution to a problem or difficulty
- **conflict** 갈등, 분쟁   a situation in which people or groups disagree
- **aggressive** 공격적인   behaving in a threatening way towards another person
- **physical** 육체의, 물리적인   relating to the body
- **strategy** 전략   a plan that is intended to achieve something
- **verbally** 말로, 구두로   in spoken words and not in writing or actions

교과서 어휘 익히기

✤ 다음 영어는 우리말로, 우리말은 영어로 쓰시오.

01 inspire	동 _____	25 명 강의, 강연	_____
02 flaw	명 _____	26 명 태도, 자세	_____
03 Prefer A to B	_____	27 동 쾅 닫다	_____
04 mood	명 _____	28 형 공격적인	_____
05 confused	형 _____	29 명 자립, 독립	_____
06 conflict	명 _____	30 형 적절한	_____
07 combination	명 _____	31 가끔, 때때로	_____
08 deal with	_____	32 형 생산적인	_____
09 affect	동 _____	33 명 주먹	_____
10 engagement	명 _____	34 ~ 대신에	_____
11 significantly	부 _____	35 부 말로, 구두로	_____
12 achieve	동 _____	36 명 전략	_____
13 intensify	동 _____	37 형 육체의, 물리적인	_____
14 resolve	동 _____	38 형 폭력적인, 격렬한	_____
15 unfairness	명 _____	39 동 인지하다, 인식하다	_____
16 direct	동 _____	40 형 강렬한, 극심한	_____
17 inspirational	형 _____	41 동 언급하다	_____
18 in particular	_____	42 형 예민한, 민감한	_____
19 factor	명 _____	43 미리, 사전에	_____
20 clench	동 _____	44 명 행동, 행실	_____
21 be responsible for	_____	45 ~에 집중하다	_____
22 organize	동 _____	46 더 이상 ~ 않는	_____
23 disadvantage	명 _____	47 형 상기된, 빨간	_____
24 cope	동 _____	48 명 청소년 형 청소년기의	_____

A 다음 밑줄 친 부분과 바꿔 쓸 수 있는 것을 보기에서 골라 기호를 쓰시오.

> 보기   ⓐ attract   ⓑ paint   ⓒ withdraw

01 Baseball games in this city draw large audiences. (   )

02 She tried to draw $5,000 from her account, but a bank teller stopped her. (   )

B 빈칸에 들어갈 말로 알맞은 것을 고르시오.

01 My grandparents taught me how to deal _____ life's challenges.

ⓐ by   ⓑ in   ⓒ with

02 He tried to _____ on his driving, but the heavy rain made it difficult.

ⓐ care   ⓑ focus   ⓒ abide

03 Pack your bag in _____ to avoid forgetting any important items.

ⓐ advance   ⓑ before   ⓒ progress

C 네모 안에서 알맞은 말을 골라 문장을 완성하시오.

01 One able / possible reason for the flight delay could be the weather conditions.

02 A failure to communicate can sometimes end / stop a relationship.

D 다음 밑줄 친 부분의 영어 뜻풀이로 알맞은 것을 보기에서 골라 기호를 쓰시오.

> 보기   ⓐ to find a solution to a problem or difficulty
>   ⓑ in spoken words and not in writing or actions
>   ⓒ the quality of being able to look after oneself

01 The changes in your brain lead you toward independence, social engagement, and creativity.

(   )

02 An angry but open conversation can resolve a conflict between friends. (   )

03 Without the right coping skills, you may find yourself becoming verbally or even physically aggressive. (   )

교과서 핵심 대화문

선호 표현하기

B Are you ready to plan our vacation to Jeonju for Mom's birthday?
  be ready to -V: ~할 준비가 되다
G Yep! First, let's decide [who will find a place to stay] and [who will find
                         목적어 1 (간접의문문)   목적어 2 (간접의문문)
  some good restaurants].

B Well, **I prefer** finding restaurants **to** finding a place to stay.
        prefer A to B: A를 B보다 선호하다, A와 B의 자리에 동명사가 쓰이고 있음
G I'll find a good place to stay, then.
                    └─── 형용사 역할을 하는 to부정사. 앞의 place를 수식
B Perfect! Mom's going to have so much fun. She'll want pictures of
          be going to -V: ~할 것이다
  everything.

G Would you take photos for her?

B Sure, I can take some. I'll find some tips for taking good photos.
                   = some photos   동명사 (전치사의 목적어)
G Great!

《 B: 너는 엄마 생신을 맞아 전주로 떠나는 우리 휴가를 계획할 준비가 되었니?

G: 응! 일단 누가 묵을 장소를 찾고 누가 좋은 식당을 찾을지 결정하자.

B: 음, 나는 묵을 장소를 찾는 것보다 식당을 찾는 게 더 좋아.

G: 그럼 내가 묵을 장소를 찾을게.

B: 완벽해! 엄마는 정말 즐거우실 거야. 엄마는 모든 것의 사진을 원하실 거야.

G: 네가 엄마를 위해 사진을 찍을래?

B: 그래, 내가 찍을 수 있어. 좋은 사진 찍는 팁을 찾아봐야겠다.

G: 훌륭해!

Study Point ✖

I prefer X to Y는 '나는 X를 Y보다 선호한다'는 뜻으로, 둘 중 하나를 더 좋아할 때 사용하는 표현이다. 이때 to는 전치사로, X와 Y의 자리에 명사나 동명사가 쓰여야 한다.

More Expressions ✖

선호를 나타내는 표현

· I think a vegetarian diet **is better than** eating meat. 나는 고기를 먹는 것보다 채식 식단이 낫다고 생각한다.

· I think departing on Friday night **is preferable to** Saturday morning.
  나는 금요일 저녁에 출발하는 게 토요일 아침보다 더 좋다고 생각한다.

· **Which do you prefer**, summer or winter? 여름과 겨울 중 무엇을 더 선호합니까?

· **Do you prefer** e-books **to** paper books? 당신은 종이책보다 이북을 더 좋아합니까?

· **Do you like** cats **better than** dogs? 당신은 개보다 고양이를 더 좋아하나요?

Check-up ✖

다음 대화의 빈칸에 들어갈 말로 어색한 것은?

A Which do your prefer, baseball or soccer?

B _____

ⓐ I prefer soccer to baseball.
ⓑ I like soccer better than baseball.
ⓒ I think baseball is harder than soccer.

Function 2 예시 들기

W What <u>would you like to do</u> in the future? Maybe you want to become a
_{would like to -V: ~하고 싶다}
writer. But if you simply aim for a job, what happens when you achieve

your goal? <u>Once</u> you become a writer, you may <u>no longer</u> feel inspired.
_{접속사 (일단 ~하면)}   _{더 이상 ~ 않다}
Therefore, you should dream of actions, not just jobs. **For example,** don't

just say, "I want to be a writer." Say something like, "I want to inspire

people <u>by</u> telling interesting stories." That way, you will always have
_{수단을 나타내는 전치사 (~함으로써)}
something to work towards. One day, you could write children's stories.
_{to부정사의 형용사적 용법 (something 수식)}
<u>Another day</u>, you could give inspirational lectures. So, what do you dream
_{one day, ... another day: 어느 날은 ···, 또 어느 날은 ~}
about doing?

W: 여러분은 장래에 무엇을 하고 싶은 가요? 여러분은 작가가 되고 싶을 수도 있어요. 하지만 만일 여러분이 단순히 직업에만 목표를 둔다면 그 목표를 이루었을 때 무슨 일이 일어날까요? 일단 작가가 되고 나면 여러분은 더 이상 영감을 받지 못할 수도 있습니다. 그러므로 여러분은 그저 직업이 아니라 행동을 꿈꿔야 합니다. 예를 들어, 단지 "나는 작가가 되고 싶어."라고 말하지 마세요. "나는 재미있는 이야기를 들려주어 사람들에게 동기를 부여하고 싶어."와 같이 말하세요. 그런 식으로 하면 여러분은 언제나 지향하며 일할 무언가를 가지게 됩니다. 어느 날은 어린이를 위한 이야기를 쓸 수 있고, 또 다른 어떤 날에는 영감을 주는 강연을 할 수도 있어요. 자, 여러분은 무슨 일을 하기를 꿈꾸나요?

Study Point ☙

For example은 '예를 들어'라는 뜻으로, 앞에 나온 진술의 구체적인 예시를 들 때 쓰는 표현이다.

More Expressions ☙

예시를 들 때 사용하는 표현

- There are many different types of music, **for instance**, rock, pop, and hip-hop.
  음악의 여러 종류가 있는데, 예를 들자면 록, 팝, 힙합 등이다.
- Several countries have festivals in April. **A good example is** Songkran in Thailand.
  여러 나라들이 4월에 축제를 연다. 좋은 예가 태국의 송크란이다.
- There are ways to receive a discount. **To give you an example**, you can use a coupon to save money on your
  purchase. 할인을 받는 여러 방법이 있다. 예를 들자면, 구매시 돈을 절약하기 위해 쿠폰을 사용할 수 있다.

Check-up ☙

다음 대화에서 밑줄 친 부분과 바꿔 쓸 수 있는 표현은?

> **A** I want to do something related to making furniture.
> **B** Do you have an idea in mind?
> **A** For example, I could start my own furniture line.

ⓐ For a moment   ⓑ As I have mentioned before
ⓒ To give you an example

교과서 **기타 대화문**

Watch and Communicate A. Watch

M ❶ <u>I've been</u> an inspirational speaker for many years. I've learned that teenagers often compare themselves to others and ❷ <u>are ashamed of</u> their flaws. Do you have the same problems? If so, you need to practice self-love. Self-love means ❸ <u>loving</u> yourself just like you love your friends or family. It also means that you put your happiness first. Here's ❹ <u>how to love</u> yourself more. First, think about your skills and talents. Write down ❺ <u>whatever</u> comes to mind. For example, you might ❻ <u>be good at playing</u> sports. You'll probably be surprised at ❼ <u>how long the list is</u>. Next, celebrate yourself for your achievements. They can even be small ones, like not being late for school this morning. This will ❽ <u>increase</u> your self-confidence and ❽ <u>inspire</u> you to try new things. So, love yourself ❾ <u>as you are right now</u>.

M: 저는 수년간 동기 부여 강연자였습니다. 저는 십 대들이 자주 그들 스스로를 다른 사람들과 비교하고 그들의 결점을 부끄러워한다는 것을 알게 되었습니다. 여러분도 같은 문제를 가지고 있나요? 만약 그렇다면, 여러분은 자기애를 연습할 필요가 있습니다. 자기애는 여러분이 여러분의 친구나 가족들을 사랑하는 것과 같이 여러분 스스로를 사랑하는 것을 의미합니다. 그것은 또한 여러분의 행복을 1순위로 두는 것을 의미합니다. 여러분 스스로를 더 사랑하는 방법을 알려 드리고자 합니다. 첫 번째로, 여러분의 기술과 재능에 대해 생각해 보세요. 마음에 떠오르는 것이 무엇이든 적어 보세요. 예를 들어, 여러분은 스포츠에 능할지도 모릅니다. 여러분은 아마도 그 목록이 얼마나 긴지 보면 놀랄 것입니다. 다음으로, 여러분의 성취에 대해 여러분 스스로를 축하해 주세요. 그것들은 오늘 아침 학교에 늦지 않은 것과 같이 작은 것도 가능합니다. 이것은 여러분의 자신감을 높여 주고 여러분이 새로운 일을 시도하도록 영감을 줄 것입니다. 그러니까, 바로 지금의 여러분 모습 그대로 스스로를 사랑하세요.

❶ 현재완료의 계속적 용법: ~해 왔다 ❷ be ashamed of: ~을 부끄러워 하다 ❸ 동사 means의 목적어로 쓰이는 동명사 ❹ how+to부정사: ~하는 방법 ❺ whatever: ~한 어떤 것이든 (=anything that) ❻ be good at: ~을 잘하다. 뒤에 명사나 동명사가 옴 ❼ 전치사 at의 목적어 ❽ increase와 inspire는 조동사 will에 걸리는 표현으로, 접속사 and로 연결된 병렬 관계 ❾ as you are right now: 지금의 당신 모습 그대로

Q1 The speaker encourages teenagers to practice self-love. (T / F)

Lesson Review A

B Hello, Ms. Smith. Do you have ❶ <u>time to talk</u> with me?
W Sure, I don't have a class at the moment. What's wrong?
B I can't decide ❷ <u>whether I should take a music class or a computer class</u>.
W Which one are you more interested in?
B I ❸ <u>prefer music to computers</u>.
W Then why can't you decide?
B I think the computer class will be helpful for my future career.
W Well, I think you should take the music class. You will learn more ❹ <u>if</u> you enjoy the class.
B I think you're right. Thanks, Ms. Smith!

B: 안녕하세요, Smith 선생님. 저와 얘기 나눌 시간 있으신가요?
W: 물론, 지금은 수업이 없어. 무슨 문제니?
B: 제가 음악 수업을 들어야 할지 컴퓨터 수업을 들어야 할지 결정하지 못하겠어요.
W: 너는 무엇에 더 관심이 있는데?
B: 저는 음악을 컴퓨터보다 더 좋아해요.
W: 그런데 왜 결정을 할 수 없는 거지?
B: 제 진로에 컴퓨터 수업이 더 도움이 될 것 같아서요.
W: 음, 내 생각에는 네가 음악 수업을 들어야 해. 수업을 즐기면 더 많은 걸 배울 거야.
B: 선생님 말씀이 맞아요. 감사해요, Smith 선생님.

❶ time+to부정사: ~할 시간 (to부정사의 형용사적 용법) ❷ whether: decide의 목적어로 쓰인 명사절을 이끄는 접속사 ❸ prefer A to B: A를 B보다 더 좋아하다 ❹ 조건의 부사절을 이끄는 접속사

Q2 Ms. Smith advices that the boy should take a (music / computer) class.

교고서 **핵심 대화문 익히기**

01 다음 대화의 밑줄 친 우리말과 일치하도록 주어진 말을 활용하여 문장을 완성하시오.

> B Are you ready to plan our vacation to Jeonju for Mom's birthday?
>
> G Yep! First, let's decide who will find a place to stay and who will find some good restaurants.
>
> B Well, 나는 묵을 장소를 찾는 것보다 식당을 찾는 게 더 좋아. (prefer, place to stay)
>
> G I'll find a good place to stay, then.
>
> B Perfect! Mom's going to have so much fun. She'll want pictures of everything.
>
> G Would you take photos for her?
>
> B Sure, I can take some. I'll find some tips for taking good photos.
>
> G Great!

→ Well, _____.

02 다음 담화를 읽고, 요약문의 빈칸에 들어갈 말로 알맞은 것을 고르시오.

> W What would you like to do in the future? Maybe you want to become a writer. But if you simply aim for a job, what happens when you achieve your goal? Once you become a writer, you may no longer feel inspired. Therefore, you should dream of actions, not just jobs. For example, don't just say, "I want to be a writer." Say something like, "I want to inspire people by telling interesting stories." That way, you will always have something to work towards. One day, you could write children's stories. Another day, you could give inspirational lectures. So, what do you dream about doing?

↓

> You should dream about _____ instead of just dreaming of a job.

① becoming a writer
② doing something specific
③ writing children's books
④ inspiring other people
⑤ telling interesting stories

03 자연스러운 대화가 되도록 문장을 순서대로 배열하시오.

> B Hello, Ms. Smith. Do you have time to talk with me?
>
> W Sure, I don't have a class at the moment. What's wrong?
>
> B I can't decide whether I should take a music class or a computer class.
>
> (   ) Then why can't you decide?
>
> (   ) I prefer music to computers.
>
> (   ) Which one are you more interested in?
>
> (   ) I think the computer class will be helpful for my future career.
>
> (   ) Well, I think you should take the music class. You will learn more if you enjoy the class.
>
> B I think you're right. Thanks, Ms. Smith!

POINT 1) 주격 관계대명사

예제	*The runner* **who** has the fastest record will be chosen for the race. 주격 관계대명사 가장 빠른 기록을 가진 주자가 경주에 선발될 것이다.
교과서	In your brain, there is *a part* **that** is responsible for solving problems. 주격 관계대명사 당신의 뇌에는 문제 해결을 담당하는 부분이 있다.

▶ 주격 관계대명사는 선행사가 관계사절 내에서 주어 역할을 하는 경우를 말한다. 선행사가 사람일 때는 주격 관계대명사로 who나 that을 쓰고, 사물이나 동물일 때는 which나 that을 쓴다.

Study Point ✿

1 관계대명사

관계대명사는 선행사를 대신하는 대명사의 기능과 두 절을 연결하는 접속사의 기능을 동시에 하는 말이다. 관계대명사가 이끄는 절은 형용사절로, 앞에 쓰인 선행사를 꾸며주는 역할을 한다.

- Jason has a sister. The sister is twelve years older than him. Jason은 누나가 있다. 그 누나는 그보다 12살 많다.
  → Jason has *a sister* **who** is twelve years older than him. Jason은 그보다 12살 많은 누나가 있다.
    선행사   선행사가 사람인 주격 관계대명사(=that)
- Jason has a cat. He adopted the cat from an animal shelter.
  Jason은 고양이가 있다. 그는 그 고양이를 동물 보호소에서 입양했다.
  → Jason has *a cat* **which** he adopted from an animal shelter. Jason은 동물 보호소에서 입양한 고양이가 있다.
    선행사   선행사가 동물인 목적격 관계대명사(=that)

2 관계대명사의 종류

관계대명사는 선행사가 사람일 때와 사물·동물일 때에 따라 다르게 사용한다. 또한 선행사가 관계사절에서 하는 역할에 따라 주격, 소유격, 목적격 관계대명사로 나뉜다.

	주격	목적격	소유격
사람	who, that	whom, that	whose
사물, 동물	which, that	which, that	of which

- The musician wrote *some songs* **which** were loved by many teenagers.
  그 음악가는 많은 십 대들에게 사랑받은 노래들을 작곡했다.
- What is the name of *the girl* **whom** you're talking to?
  네가 얘기 나누고 있던 소녀의 이름이 뭐니?
- I interviewed *a famous writer* **whose** book was published in five languages.
  나는 그의 책이 5개 국어로 출판된 유명한 작가를 인터뷰했다.

Q 다음 네모 안에서 어법상 알맞은 것을 고르시오.

1 She keeps a balanced diet who / that has helped maintain her good health.

2 Mr. Brown is a nice neighbor who / which who owns a bakery.

3 I have to return the books whom / that I borrowed from the library.

Check-up ⚇

01 다음 문장의 빈칸에 who와 which 가운데 알맞은 것을 넣으시오.

(1) The man _____ caused the accident didn't have his driver's license.

(2) Tim works at a restaurant _____ is famous for pasta.

(3) The subject _____ most students like best is P.E.

(4) I need to buy new shoes _____ I can wear to the party.

02 관계대명사를 사용하여 두 문장을 하나의 문장으로 만드시오.

(1) They need a person. The person is good at programming.

→ _____

(2) The movie was wonderful. My uncle recommended the movie to me.

→ _____

(3) Helen Keller is a social educator. Dora admires her the most.

→ _____

(4) Megan is a veterinarian. Her animal hospital is next to my office.

→ _____

03 보기의 밑줄 친 that과 쓰임이 같은 것을 두 개 고르시오.

> 보기   We provide various pie recipes <u>that</u> are easy to follow.

① They lived in an apartment <u>that</u> had no elevators.
② Scientists predicted <u>that</u> AI technology will replace human jobs.
③ I don't agree with the idea <u>that</u> we must reduce public spending.
④ Anyone <u>that</u> is interested in hip-hop music will love the musician.
⑤ It is strongly recommended <u>that</u> we eat less meat for the environment.

04 다음 문장에서 어법상 어색한 부분을 찾아 바르게 고쳐 쓰시오.

(1) The pictures that you are looking at them were taken a few days ago.

→ The pictures _____ a few days ago.

(2) The award was given to the actor played the detective in the movie.

→ The award _____ in the movie.

(3) I'm looking for shoes who go well with this dress.

→ _____ with this dress.

(4) She lost the ring which he had given it to her as a birthday present.

→ She lost _____ to her as a birthday present.

POINT 2 It ~ to부정사

예제　**It** was a challenge for the kid **to keep** calm.
　　　가주어　　　　　　　　　　　　　to부정사구: 진주어
　　　그 아이가 평정심을 유지하는 것은 도전이었다.

교과서　**It** is natural **to feel** angry from time to time.
　　　가주어　　　　　to부정사구: 진주어
　　　때때로 화가 나는 것은 자연스럽다.

▶ to부정사가 문장의 주어로 쓰일 때, 주어 자리에 가주어 it을 쓰고 to부정사구는 문장의 뒤로 보낸다.

Study Point 🍅

1 It ~ to부정사 구문

to부정사구가 문장의 주어로 쓰일 때 주어가 길어지는 것을 피하기 위해 보통 가주어 it을 주어 자리에 대신 쓰고, 진주어인 to부정사구는 뒤로 보내서 「it ~ to부정사」 구조로 쓴다. 이때 it은 형식적인 주어이므로 뜻을 갖지 않는다.

- **It** is dangerous **to swim** in the sea at night. 밤에 바다에서 수영하는 것은 위험하다.
- **It** is not easy **to maintain** your balance on one leg. 한 쪽 다리로 균형을 잡는 것은 쉽지 않다.
- **It** is a great achievement **to finish** a marathon. 마라톤을 완주하는 것은 위대한 성과이다.

2 to부정사의 의미상 주어

(1) to부정사구가 나타내는 동작의 주체를 밝힐 때 「for+목적격」을 써서 앞에 나타내는데, 이를 to부정사의 의미상 주어라고 한다.

- **It** is impossible *for me* **to work out** every day. 내가 매일 운동하는 것은 불가능하다.
- **It** was necessary *for Daisy* **to travel** alone. Daisy는 홀로 여행하는 것이 필요했다.

(2) 사람의 성격이나 성질을 나타내는 형용사 뒤에서는 의미상 주어로 「of+목적격」을 쓴다.
　　kind, nice, honest, polite, careful 등

- **It** is kind *of them* **to provide** shelter for abandoned animals.
  그들이 유기된 동물들에게 보호소를 제공하는 것은 친절한 일이다.
- **It** was careless *of you* **to share** all the details about the issue.
  네가 그 이슈에 관한 모든 것을 공유한 것은 경솔했다.

Q 다음 네모 안에서 어법상 알맞은 것을 고르시오.

1 |It / That| is difficult to speak in front of an audience.

2 It is not a good idea |rely / to rely| on the information on the internet.

3 It is natural |for / of| her to feel upset in that situation.

Check-up ♀

01 보기와 같이 밑줄 친 부분에 가주어 It을 써서 문장을 바꿔 쓰시오.

> 보기 To go hiking alone is dangerous.
> → It is dangerous to go hiking alone.

(1) <u>To walk my dog</u> is a great pleasure.

→ _____

(2) <u>To learn a new skill</u> is never a waste of time.

→ _____

(3) Nowadays, <u>to communicate via cell phones</u> is more common.

→ Nowadays, _____ .

(4) <u>To watch the sunset from the mountaintop</u> was amazing.

→ _____

02 괄호 안의 단어를 바르게 배열하여 문장을 완성하시오.

(1) It was (difficult / the project / finish / for / to / us) within two weeks.

→ It was _____ within two weeks.

(2) It was (your mother's ring / lose / of / to / you / careless).

→ It was _____ .

(3) It is (important / for / from / failure / learn / to / children)

→ It is _____ .

(4) It would be (to / around / wonderful / travel / the world) with you.

→ It would be _____ with you.

03 다음 중 빈칸에 들어갈 말이 나머지와 다른 것은?

① It was foolish _____ me to waste my time before the exam.
② It is frightening _____ him to watch the horror movie alone.
③ It will be easy _____ us to talk to people from other countries.
④ It was exciting _____ them to watch their favorite team win the game.
⑤ It is impossible _____ the kids to save the cat from the tree.

교과서 본문 분석

Don't Let Anger Be Your Boss
화가 주도권을 갖게 하지 마라

01
Do you ever find yourself suddenly feeling angry?
　　　　　　　　　목적어 (재귀대명사)　　목적격보어 (현재분사)

당신은 갑자기 화가 나는 경우가 있는가?

02
One moment you're fine, and the next moment you're slamming doors or rolling your eyes at your
　　　　　　　　　　　　　　　　　　　　　　　　　　　　병렬 연결
　　　　　　　　　　　　　　　　　　　　　　　　　(진행형을 나타내는 현재분사)
parents.

한순간 당신은 괜찮다가도, 다음 순간에 문을 쾅 닫거나 부모님께 눈을 치켜뜨기도 한다.

03
　　　　　　　　　　　　　　(that)　　　　　　　　　　　　　(you)
Some people may think [you just have a bad attitude or are getting too upset about a small
　　　　　　　　　　　명사절 (think의 목적어)
problem].

어떤 사람들은 당신이 그저 태도가 나쁘거나 작은 문제에 너무 화를 낸다고 생각할지도 모른다.

04
　　　　　　　　　갑자기 화가 나는 감정들
However, these feelings don't simply come from stress [about everyday life].
　　　　　　　　　　　　　　　　　　　　　　　　　　　전치사구

그러나 이러한 감정들은 단순히 일상생활에 대한 스트레스에서 오는 것이 아니다.

Where does adolescent anger come from?
청소년기의 화는 어디서부터 오는가?

05
As a teen, you may feel like an adult, but your brain is still growing.
전치사 (~로서)　　~일지 모른다　　　　　　　　　　　현재진행형

십 대로서, 당신은 어른인 것처럼 느낄지도 모르지만 당신의 뇌는 여전히 자라고 있다.

06
　　　　　　　　　　　　　　　　　　　　　　　　(for의 목적어로 쓰이는 동명사)
　　　　　　　　　　　　　　　　　　　　　　　　병렬 연결
In your brain, there is a part [that is responsible for solving problems and controlling your
　　　　　　　　　　　　선행사 a part를 수식하는 주격 관계대명사
emotions].

당신의 뇌에는 문제 해결과 감정 조절을 담당하는 부분이 있다.

07
　　　　　　　　　문제 해결과 감정 조절을 담당하는 부분
In your teen years, this part is still in development.
　　　　　　　　　　　　　　　　　　전치사 (~ 중인)

십 대 때에 이 부분은 여전히 발달하고 있다.

08

주어

The changes [in your brain] lead you toward independence, social engagement, and creativity.

동사

전치사구

뇌의 변화는 당신을 독립성, 사회적 참여, 그리고 창의성으로 이끈다.

09

At the same time, however, you may feel confused about [who you are].

동시에

보어 (과거분사)

간접의문문 (about의 목적어)

그러나 동시에 당신은 당신이 누구인지에 대해 혼란스럽게 느낄지도 모른다.

10

You may also be more sensitive to unfairness.

비교급

당신은 또한 불공정에 더욱 민감할 수도 있다.

11

Furthermore, your body is flowing with hormones.

게다가

게다가 당신의 신체는 호르몬으로 넘쳐나고 있다.

12

This significantly affects your mood.

앞문장의 내용 (신체에 호르몬이 넘쳐나는 것)

이것은 당신의 기분에 상당히 영향을 미친다.

13

주어

동사 (수의 일치)

The combination [of these factors] intensifies your strong emotions.

전치사구

이러한 요인들의 조합은 당신의 강한 감정을 강화한다.

Getting to Know Your Anger
당신의 화를 알아보기

14

(that)

명사절 (mean의 목적어)

It is natural [to feel angry from time to time]; it doesn't mean [there is something wrong with you].

가주어

진주어 (to부정사구)

가끔, 때때로

때때로 화가 나는 것은 자연스러우며 그것은 당신에게 문제가 있다는 것을 뜻하지 않는다.

15

Anger can sometimes be a useful tool.

빈도부사 (때때로)

화는 가끔 쓸모 있는 도구가 될 수 있다.

16 For example, an angry but open conversation can resolve a conflict [between friends].
예를 들어   └─ 병렬 연결 ─┘   ↑   └ 전치사구

예를 들어, 격양되지만 진솔한 대화는 친구들 사이의 갈등을 해결할 수 있다.

17 The important thing is [to manage your anger so that it does not turn into aggressive or violent behavior].
                          └ to부정사의 명사적 용법 (보어)   ~하도록 (목적)   └── 병렬 연결 ──┘

= your anger
~으로 변하다

중요한 것은 당신의 화가 공격적이거나 폭력적인 행동으로 변하지 않도록 조절하는 것이다.

18 This does not mean [that you should stop yourself from feeling angry].
명사절 (mean의 목적어)   stop + 목적어 + from + V-ing: ~가 …하는 것을 막다

이는 당신이 화를 내지 말아야 한다는 것을 의미하지 않는다.

19 Rather, you should express it in a productive way.
오히려   = your anger

오히려 당신은 화를 생산적인 방식으로 표현해야 한다.

20 Ask yourself some questions [about your angry feelings].
간접목적어   직접목적어   ↑   └ 전치사구

당신의 성난 감정에 대해 스스로에게 몇 가지 질문을 해 봐라.

21 This can help you to better understand your anger.
앞문장 전체
        help + 목적어 + (to)동사원형: ~가 …하는 것을 돕다

이는 당신의 화를 더 잘 이해하는 데 도움이 될 수 있다.

Questions to Ask Yourself
스스로에게 물어볼 질문

22 How often do I feel angry?

나는 얼마나 자주 화가 나는가?

23 What situations make me feel the most intense anger?
최상급
        사역동사(make) + 목적어 + 동사원형: ~가 …하게 하다

어떤 상황이 나에게 가장 극심한 화를 느끼게 하는가?

24   Is my anger directed at anyone or anything <u>in particular</u>?
특히

나의 화는 특히 어떤 사람 혹은 어떤 것을 향해 있는가?

25   Do I <u>focus on</u> the causes of my anger <u>instead of</u> solutions?
～에 집중하다   ～대신에

나는 해결책보다는 내 화의 원인에 초점을 두는가?

26   Can I control my emotions <u>when</u> I get angry?
접속사 (～할 때에)

화가 날 때 나는 내 감정을 조절할 수 있는가?

27   How do I react and behave when I get angry?

화가 날 때 나는 어떻게 반응하고 행동하는가?

First Aid to Calm Yourself Down
스스로를 진정시키기 위한 응급 처치

28   You need to learn <u>how to deal</u> with anger [in a socially appropriate way].
how to -V: ～하는 방법   전치사구 (부사구)

당신은 사회적으로 적절한 방식으로 화를 다스리는 방법을 배워야 한다.

29   Remember: anger is a feeling, <u>but</u> behavior is a choice.
접속사 (역접 관계)

기억하라. 화는 감정이지만 행동은 선택이다.

30   The first step is [recognizing the physical signs of anger].
동명사구 (is의 보어)

첫 번째 단계는 화의 신체적 징후를 알아차리는 것이다.

31   <u>It</u> is possible [to recognize those signs in advance].
가주어   진주어 (to부정사구)   미리

그러한 징후를 미리 알아차리는 것은 가능하다.

32   They include an increased heart rate, a flushed face, and the clenching of your fists.
과거분사   과거분사

그것들은 증가한 심박수, 빨개진 얼굴, 그리고 주먹을 꽉 쥐는 것을 포함한다.

33   When these things happen, take action to reduce your anger.
to부정사의 부사적 용법 (목적)

이러한 것들이 발생할 때 당신의 화를 줄이기 위해 조치를 취해라.

예를 들어   동명사구 1   동명사구 2

34   For example, you could try [taking a break to organize your thoughts] or [ending a conversation
try V-ing: 한번 ~해보다   to부정사의 부사적 용법 (목적)
before it gets too intense].
~하기 전에   =the conversation
(접속사)

예를 들어, 당신의 생각을 정리하기 위해 휴식을 취하거나 대화가 너무 격해지기 전에 중단하는 것을 시도해 볼 수 있다.

Finding Proper Coping Skills
적절한 대처 기술 찾기

과거분사구

35   In some cases, the strategies [mentioned above] may not be enough, so you may need to find
접속사 (그래서)
proper coping skills [for your personal situation].
전치사구

어떤 경우에는 위에 언급한 전략이 충분하지 않을 수 있으므로 당신의 개인 상황에 맞는 적절한 대처 기술을 찾아야 할지도 모른다.

전치사 (~이 없다면)

36   Without the right coping skills, you may find yourself becoming verbally or even physically
동사   목적어   목적격 보어
(재귀대명사) (현재분사)
aggressive.

올바른 대처 기술이 없다면 당신은 스스로가 언어적으로 혹은 심지어 신체적으로 공격적이 되는 것을 발견할지도 모른다.

to부정사의 부사적 용법 (목적)   동명사구 1   동명사구 2

37   Explore various strategies to discover [what is best for you], such as [taking a walk], [drawing a
간접의문문 (discover의 목적어)   such as A, B, or C (A, B, C가 동명사구)
picture], or [writing down things (that come to your mind)].
동명사구 3   주격 관계대명사절

무엇이 당신에게 가장 좋은지 찾기 위해 산책하기, 그림 그리기, 혹은 마음에 떠오르는 것들을 적기와 같은 다양한 전략을 탐구해라.

to부정사의 명사적 용법 (try의 목적어)   (try to)

38   You can also try to find possible solutions [to a problem] and then compare the advantages and
전치사구
disadvantages of each one.
=solution

당신은 또한 문제에 대한 가능한 해결책들을 찾고 각각의 장점과 단점을 비교하려고 노력할 수 있다.

39 By developing problem-solving skills, you will learn [that there are many ways (to solve a problem
by+동명사: ~함으로써   명사절 (learn의 목적어)   +to부정사의 형용사적 용법
without getting angry)].
동명사구 (without의 목적어)

문제 해결 능력을 발전시킴으로써 당신은 화를 내지 않고 문제를 해결할 많은 방법이 있다는 것을 알게 될 것이다.

40 Anger is an emotion [that we all experience].
목적격 관계대명사절

화는 우리 모두가 겪는 감정이다.

by+동명사: ~함으로써
41 By managing your anger properly, you can be the boss of your feelings, not the other way around.
~가 아니라   반대 상황

화를 적절하게 다룸으로써 당신은 그 반대가 아니라 (화가 주도권을 갖는 게 아니라) 당신이 감정의 주도권을 가질 수 있다.

동명사구 1   동명사구 2
42 This is an important step in [finding your true self] and [taking control of your life].
병렬 연결
(in의 목적어)

이것은 진정한 자아를 찾고 당신의 삶을 주도하는 데 있어 중요한 단계이다.

♣ 다음 빈칸에 알맞은 말을 쓰시오.

01 Do you ever _____ angry?
당신은 갑자기 화가 나는 경우가 있는가?

02 One moment you're fine, and _____ you're slamming doors or
_____ your parents.
한순간 당신은 괜찮다가도, 다음 순간에 문을 꽝 닫거나 부모님께 눈을 치켜뜨기도 한다.

03 Some people may think you just have a bad attitude or _____ about a small
problem.
어떤 사람들은 당신이 그저 태도가 나쁘거나 작은 문제에 너무 화를 낸다고 생각할지도 모른다.

04 However, these feelings don't simply come from _____.
그러나 이러한 감정들은 단순히 일상생활에 대한 스트레스에서 오는 것이 아니다.

05 _____, you may feel like an adult, but your brain is still growing.
십 대로서, 당신은 어른인 것처럼 느낄지도 모르지만 당신의 뇌는 여전히 자라고 있다.

06 In your brain, there is _____ solving problems and controlling your emotions.
당신의 뇌에는 문제 해결과 감정 조절을 담당하는 부분이 있다.

07 In your teen years, this part is still _____.
십 대 때에 이 부분은 여전히 발달하고 있다.

08 The changes in your brain _____, social engagement, and creativity.
뇌의 변화는 당신을 독립성, 사회적 참여, 그리고 창의성으로 이끈다.

09 _____, however, you may feel confused about _____.
그러나 동시에 당신은 당신이 누구인지에 대해 혼란스럽게 느낄지도 모른다.

10 You may also be _____.
당신은 또한 불공정에 더욱 민감할 수도 있다.

11 Furthermore, your body is flowing _____.
게다가 당신의 신체는 호르몬으로 넘쳐나고 있다.

12 This _____ your mood.
이것은 당신의 기분에 상당히 영향을 미친다.

13 The combination of these factors _____.
이러한 요인들의 조합은 당신의 강한 감정을 강화한다.

14 _____ to feel angry from time to time; it doesn't mean
_____ with you.
때때로 화가 나는 것은 자연스러우며 그것은 당신에게 문제가 있다는 것을 뜻하지 않는다.

15 _____ sometimes be a useful tool.

화는 가끔 쓸모 있는 도구가 될 수 있다.

16 For example, an _____ can resolve a conflict between friends.

예를 들어, 격앙되지만 진솔한 대화는 친구들 사이의 갈등을 해결할 수 있다.

17 The important thing is to manage your anger _____ aggressive or violent behavior.

중요한 것은 당신의 화가 공격적이거나 폭력적인 행동으로 변하지 않도록 조절하는 것이다.

18 This does not mean that you should _____ feeling angry.

이는 당신이 화를 내지 말아야 한다는 것을 의미하지 않는다.

19 Rather, you should express it _____.

오히려 당신은 화를 생산적인 방식으로 표현해야 한다.

20 _____ some questions about your angry feelings.

당신의 성난 감정에 대해 스스로에게 몇 가지 질문을 해 봐라.

21 This can help you to _____ your anger.

이는 당신의 화를 더 잘 이해하는 데 도움이 될 수 있다.

22 _____ do I feel angry?

나는 얼마나 자주 화가 나는가?

23 What situations make me _____ anger?

어떤 상황이 나에게 가장 극심한 화를 느끼게 하는가?

24 Is my anger directed at anyone or _____?

나의 화는 특히 어떤 사람 혹은 어떤 것을 향해 있는가?

25 Do I _____ of my anger instead of solutions?

나는 해결책보다는 내 화의 원인에 초점을 두는가?

26 Can I _____ when I get angry?

화가 날 때 나는 내 감정을 조절할 수 있는가?

27 How do I _____ when I get angry?

화가 날 때 나는 어떻게 반응하고 행동하는가?

28 You need to learn _____ in a socially appropriate way.

당신은 사회적으로 적절한 방식으로 화를 다스리는 방법을 배워야 한다.

29 Remember: anger is a feeling, but _____.

기억하라. 화는 감정이지만 행동은 선택이다.

30 _____ recognizing the physical signs of anger.

첫 번째 단계는 화의 신체적 징후를 알아차리는 것이다.

31 _____ to recognize those signs in advance.

그러한 징후를 미리 알아차리는 것은 가능하다.

32 They include an _____, a flushed face, and the clenching of your fists.

그것들은 증가한 심박수, 빨개진 얼굴, 그리고 주먹을 꽉 쥐는 것을 포함한다.

33 When these things happen, _____.

이러한 것들이 발생할 때 당신의 화를 줄이기 위해 조치를 취해라.

34 _____, you could try taking a break to organize your thoughts or ending a conversation _____.

예를 들어, 당신의 생각을 정리하기 위해 휴식을 취하거나 대화가 너무 격해지기 전에 중단하는 것을 시도해 볼 수 있다.

35 In some cases, the _____ may not be enough, so you may need to find _____ your personal situation.

어떤 경우에는 위에 언급한 전략이 충분하지 않을 수 있으므로 당신의 개인 상황에 맞는 적절한 대처 기술을 찾아야 할지도 모른다.

36 _____, you may find yourself becoming verbally or even physically aggressive.

올바른 대처 기술이 없다면 당신은 스스로가 언어적으로 혹은 심지어 신체적으로 공격적이 되는 것을 발견할지도 모른다.

37 Explore various strategies to discover _____, such as taking a walk, drawing a picture, or writing down things _____.

무엇이 당신에게 가장 좋은지 찾기 위해 산책하기, 그림 그리기, 혹은 마음에 떠오르는 것들을 적기와 같은 다양한 전략을 탐구해라.

38 You can also try to find possible solutions to a problem and then compare the _____ of each one.

당신은 또한 문제에 대한 가능한 해결책들을 찾고 각각의 장점과 단점을 비교하려고 노력할 수 있다.

39 By developing problem-solving skills, you will learn that there are _____ without getting angry.

문제 해결 능력을 발전시킴으로써 당신은 화를 내지 않고 문제를 해결할 많은 방법이 있다는 것을 알게 될 것이다.

40 Anger is an emotion _____.

화는 우리 모두가 겪는 감정이다.

41 _____ properly, you can be the boss of your feelings, _____.

화를 적절하게 다룸으로써 당신은 그 반대가 아니라 (화가 주도권을 갖는 게 아니라) 당신이 감정의 주도권을 가질 수 있다.

42 This is an important step in _____ and taking control of your life.

이것은 진정한 자아를 찾고 당신의 삶을 주도하는 데 있어 중요한 단계이다.

교과서 본문 익히기 ❷ 옳은 어법·어휘 고르기

♣ 다음 네모 안에서 옳은 것을 고르시오.

01 Do you ever find yourself suddenly feeling / to feel angry?

02 One moment you're fine, and the next moment you're slamming doors or roll / rolling your eyes at your parents.

03 Some people may think you just have a bad attitude or are getting too relaxed / upset about a small problem.

04 However, these feelings don't simply come from stress about everyday / always life.

05 As a teen, you may feel as / like an adult, but your brain is still growing.

06 In your brain, there is a part that / what is responsible for solving problems and control / controlling your emotions.

07 In your teen years, this part is still in development / improvement .

08 The changes in your brain lead / leads you toward independence, social engagement, and creativity.

09 At the same time, however, you may feel confused about who you are / who are you .

10 You may also be more sensitive / sensitively to unfairness.

11 Furthermore, your body is flowing / flowed with hormones.

12 This significantly affects / effects your mood.

13 The combination of these factors intensify / intensifies your strong emotions.

14 It is natural feeling / to feel angry from time to time; it doesn't mean there is something wrong with you.

15   Anger can sometimes be a [harmful / useful] tool.

16   For example, an angry but open conversation can [resolve / resort] a conflict between friends.

17   The important thing is to manage your anger [so that / so as to] it does not turn into aggressive or violent behavior.

18   This does not mean that you should stop [you / yourself] from feeling angry.

19   Rather, you should express it in a [progressive / productive] way.

20   Ask yourself some [favors / questions] about your angry feelings.

21   This can help you to [better / best] understand your anger.

22   How [much / often] do I feel angry?

23   What situations make me [feel / to feel] the most intense anger?

24   Is my anger [direct / directed] at anyone or anything in particular?

25   Do I focus on the causes of my anger [instead / instead of] solutions?

26   Can I [control / collect] my emotions when I get angry?

27   [How / What] do I react and behave when I get angry?

28   You need to learn how to deal with anger in a [social / socially] appropriate way.

29   Remember: anger is a feeling, but behavir is a [choice / choose].

30   The first step is recognizing the mental / physical signs of anger.

31   It is possible to recognize those signs for / in advance.

32   They include an decreased / increased heart rate, a flushed face, and the clenching of your fists.

33   When these things happen, take action to enhance / reduce your anger.

34   For example, you could try taking a break to organize your thoughts or end / ending a conversation before it gets too intense.

35   In some cases, the strategies mentioning / mentioned above may not be enough, so you may need to find proper coping skills for your personal situation.

36   With / Without the right coping skills, you may find yourself becoming verbally or even physically aggressive.

37   Explore various strategies to discover that / what is best for you, such as taking a walk, drawing a picture, or write / writing down things that come to your mind.

38   You can also try to find possible situations / solutions to a problem and then compare the advantages and disadvantages of each one.

39   By developing problem-solving skills, you will learn that there are many ways solving / to solve a problem without getting angry.

40   Anger is an emotion that / whom we all experience.

41   By managing your anger properly, you can be the boss / staff of your feelings, not the other way around.

42   This is an important step in finding your true self and take / taking control of your life.

♣ 다음 밑줄 친 부분을 바르게 고쳐 쓰시오.

01   Do you ever find <u>you</u> suddenly feeling angry?

02   One moment you're fine, and the next moment you're <u>slam</u> doors or rolling your eyes at your parents.

03   Some people may think you just have a bad attitude or <u>getting</u> too upset about a small problem.

04   In your brain, there is a part <u>what</u> is responsible for solving problems and <u>controll</u> your emotions.

05   In your teen years, this part is still <u>to</u> development.

06   The changes in your brain <u>leads</u> you toward independence, social engagement, and <u>creative</u>.

07   At the same time, however, you may feel <u>confusing</u> about who you are.

08   You may also be <u>sensitiver</u> to unfairness.

09   The combination of these factors <u>intensifiy</u> your strong emotions.

10   It is natural <u>feel</u> angry from time to time; it doesn't mean there is <u>nothing</u> wrong with you.

11   Anger can be <u>sometime</u> a useful tool.

12   For example, an angry <u>and</u> open conversation can resolve a conflict <u>in</u> friends.

13   The important thing <u>is to managing</u> your anger so that it <u>does</u> turn into aggressive or violent behavior.

14   This does not mean that you should stop yourself <u>to feel</u> angry.

15   <u>Therefore</u>, you should express it in a productive way.

16   Ask <u>you</u> some questions about your angry feelings.

17   This can help you to <u>better understanding</u> your anger.

18   What situations make me <u>to feel</u> the most intense anger?

19   Do I focus on the causes of my anger <u>instead</u> solutions?

20   You need to learn <u>how</u> deal with anger in a socially appropriate way.

21   <u>First</u> step is recognizing the physical signs of anger.

22   <u>That</u> is possible to recognize those signs in advance.

23   They include an increased heart rate, a <u>flushing</u> face, and the clenching of your fists.

24   When these things happen, <u>make action</u> to reduce your anger.

25   For example, you could try taking a break to organize your thoughts or <u>end</u> a conversation before it gets too intense.

26   In some cases, the strategies mentioned above <u>may</u> be enough, so you may need <u>finding</u> proper coping skills for your personal situation.

27   Without the right coping skills, you may find yourself <u>to become</u> verbally or even physically aggressive.

28   Explore various strategies to discover what is best for you, such as <u>take</u> a walk, <u>draw</u> a picture, or writing down things <u>what</u> come to your mind.

29   You can also try to find possible solutions to a problem and then <u>comparing</u> the advantages and disadvantages of each one.

30   By developing problem-solving skills, you will learn that there are many ways <u>solving</u> a problem without <u>get</u> angry.

31   Anger is an emotion <u>what</u> we all experience.

32   <u>In</u> managing your anger properly, you can be the boss of your feelings, <u>no</u> the other way around.

33   This is an important step in finding your true self and <u>to take</u> control of your life.

교과서 본문 외 지문 분석

Think and Write ❣ 교과서 25쪽

❶<u>What Makes Me Unique</u>
  There are a few things ❷<u>that</u> make me unique. Firstly, my interests make me unique. ❸<u>I'm interested in</u> music, and I sometimes compose songs for my friends. My daily habits also make me unique. For example, I write about my feelings in a journal every evening. This ❹<u>helps me reduce</u> my stress. Lastly, I have a special talent ❺<u>that</u> makes me unique. I ❻<u>am good at</u> telling jokes. I can always ❼<u>make my classmates laugh</u>.

나를 특별하게 만드는 것

나를 특별하게 만드는 것들이 몇 가지 있다. 첫째, 나의 관심사는 나를 특별하게 만든다. 나는 음악에 관심이 있고, 가끔 친구들을 위해 노래를 작곡한다. 나의 일상 습관 또한 나를 특별하게 만든다. 예를 들어, 나는 매일 저녁 일기에 내 감정에 대해 적는다. 이것은 내 스트레스를 줄이는 데 도움이 된다. 마지막으로, 나는 나를 특별하게 만드는 특이한 재능이 있다. 나는 농담을 잘한다. 나는 항상 우리 반 친구들을 웃게 만들 수 있다.

❶ what: '~하는 것'이라는 뜻의 관계대명사 ❷ that: 앞의 things를 수식하는 주격 관계대명사절을 이끄는 관계대명사 ❸ be interested in: ~에 관심이 있다 ❹ help(준사역동사)+목적어(me)+원형부정사(reduce) ❺ that: 선행사 talent를 꾸며 주는 관계대명사절을 이끈다. ❻ be good at: ~을 잘하다, at 뒤에 동명사(telling)가 쓰였다. ❼ 사역동사 make가 쓰여 「사역동사+목적어+동사원형」의 형태를 이룬다.

Q What is the writer's special talent that makes the writer unique?

Check-up ❣

다음 빈칸에 알맞은 말을 쓰시오.

01 There are a few things that _____.
    나를 특별하게 만드는 것들이 몇 가지 있다.

02 Firstly, _____ make me unique.
    첫째, 나의 관심사는 나를 특별하게 만든다.

03 I'm _____ music, and I sometimes compose songs for my friends.
    나는 음악에 관심이 있고, 가끔 친구들을 위해 노래를 작곡한다.

04 _____ also make me unique.
    나의 일상 습관 또한 나를 특별하게 만든다.

05 For example, I _____ in a journal every evening.
    예를 들어, 나는 매일 저녁 일기에 내 감정에 대해 적는다.

06 This _____ my stress.
    이것은 내 스트레스를 줄이는 데 도움이 된다.

07 Lastly, I _____ that makes me unique.
    마지막으로, 나는 나를 특별하게 만드는 특이한 재능이 있다.

08 I am _____ jokes.
    나는 농담을 잘한다.

09 I can always _____.
    나는 항상 우리 반 친구들을 웃게 만들 수 있다.

01 (A), (B), (C)의 각 네모 안에서 문맥에 맞는 낱말로 가장 적절한 것은?

What would you like to do in the future? Maybe you want to become a writer. But if you simply aim for a job, what happens when you achieve your goal? (A) Once / Since you become a writer, you may no longer feel inspired. Therefore, you should dream of actions, not just jobs. For example, don't just say, "I want to be a writer." Say something like, "I want to (B) inspire / perspire people by telling interesting stories." That way, you will always have something to work towards. One day, you could write children's stories. (C) Another / Other day, you could give inspirational lectures. So, what do you dream about doing?

	(A)	(B)	(C)
①	Once	⋯ inspire	⋯ Another
②	Once	⋯ perspire	⋯ Another
③	Since	⋯ inspire	⋯ Another
④	Since	⋯ perspire	⋯ Other
⑤	Since	⋯ inspire	⋯ Other

02 밑줄 친 부분 중, 문맥상 낱말의 쓰임이 적절하지 않은 것은?

Self-love means loving yourself just ① like you love your friends or family. Here's how to love yourself more. First, think about your skills and talents. Write down ② whatever comes to mind. For example, you might be good at playing sports. You'll ③ probably be surprised at how long the list is. Next, celebrate yourself for your ④ achievements. They can even be small ones, like not being late for school this morning. This will ⑤ decrease your self-confidence and inspire you to try new things. So, love yourself as you are right now.

①   ②   ③   ④   ⑤

03 밑줄 친 부분 중, 문맥상 낱말의 쓰임이 적절하지 않은 것은?

As a teen, you may feel like an adult, but your brain is still growing. In your brain, there is a part that is ① responsible for solving problems and controlling your emotions. In your teen years, this part is still in development. The changes in your brain lead you toward ② dependence, social engagement, and creativity. At the same time, however, you may feel ③ confused about who you are. You may also be more sensitive to ④ unfairness. Furthermore, your body is flowing with hormones. This significantly ⑤ affects your mood. The combination of these factors intensifies your strong emotions.

①   ②   ③   ④   ⑤

04 (A), (B), (C)의 각 네모 안에서 문맥에 맞는 낱말로 가장 적절한 것은?

It is natural to feel angry (A) by / from time to time; it doesn't mean there is something wrong with you. Anger can sometimes be a useful tool. For example, an angry but open conversation can (B) resolve / dissolve a conflict between friends. The important thing is to manage your anger so that it does not turn into aggressive or violent behavior. This does not mean that you should stop yourself from feeling angry. Rather, you should express it in a (C) productive / progressive way.

	(A)	(B)	(C)
①	by	⋯ resolve	⋯ productive
②	by	⋯ dissolve	⋯ productive
③	from	⋯ resolve	⋯ productive
④	from	⋯ dissolve	⋯ progressive
⑤	from	⋯ resolve	⋯ progressive

05 (A), (B), (C)의 각 네모 안에서 문맥에 맞는 낱말로 가장 적절한 것은?

> **Questions to Ask Yourself**
> ✓ How often do I feel angry?
> ✓ What situations make me feel the most (A) instant / intense anger?
> ✓ Is my anger directed at anyone or anything in particular?
> ✓ Do I focus on the (B) causes / effects of my anger instead of solutions?
> ✓ Can I control my emotions when I get angry?
> ✓ How do I react and (C) behave / behalf when I get angry?

	(A)	(B)	(C)
①	instant	causes	behave
②	instant	effects	behave
③	intense	causes	behave
④	intense	effects	behalf
⑤	intense	causes	behalf

06 밑줄 친 부분 중, 문맥상 낱말의 쓰임이 적절하지 <u>않은</u> 것은?

> You need to learn how to deal with anger in a ① <u>socially</u> appropriate way. Remember: anger is a feeling, but behavior is a choice. The first step is recognizing the ② <u>mental</u> signs of anger. It is possible to recognize those signs in advance. They include an increased heart rate, a ③ <u>flushed</u> face, and the clenching of your fists. When these things happen, take action to ④ <u>reduce</u> your anger. For example, you could try taking a break to organize your thoughts or ⑤ <u>ending</u> a conversation before it gets too intense.

①   ②   ③   ④   ⑤

07 밑줄 친 부분 중, 문맥상 낱말의 쓰임이 적절하지 <u>않은</u> 것은?

> In some cases, the strategies mentioned above may not be enough, so you may need to find proper coping skills for your personal situation. Without the right coping skills, you may find yourself becoming ① <u>verbally</u> or even physically aggressive. ② <u>Explore</u> various strategies to discover what is best for you, such as taking a walk, drawing a picture, or writing down things that come to your mind. You can also try to find ③ <u>able</u> solutions to a problem and then compare the advantages and ④ <u>disadvantages</u> of each one. By developing problem-solving skills, you will learn that there are many ways to solve a problem ⑤ <u>without</u> getting angry.

①   ②   ③   ④   ⑤

08 (A), (B), (C)의 각 네모 안에서 문맥에 맞는 낱말로 가장 적절한 것은?

> There are a few things that make me unique. Firstly, my interests make me unique. I'm interested in music, and I sometimes (A) compose / comprise songs for my friends. My daily habits also make me unique. For example, I write about my feelings in a (B) journal / journey every evening. This helps me reduce my stress. Lastly, I have a (C) special / specific talent that makes me unique. I am good at telling jokes. I can always make my classmates laugh.

	(A)	(B)	(C)
①	compose	journal	special
②	compose	journey	special
③	comprise	journal	special
④	comprise	journey	specific
⑤	comprise	journal	specific

01 다음 글의 밑줄 친 부분 중, 어법상 틀린 것은?

There are a few things ① that makes me unique. Firstly, my interests make me unique. I'm interested in music, and I sometimes compose songs for my friends. My daily habits also ② make me unique. For example, I write about my feelings in a journal every evening. This ③ helps me reduce my stress. Lastly, I have a special talent that makes me unique. I am ④ good at telling jokes. I can always make ⑤ my classmates laugh.

①   ②   ③   ④   ⑤

02 (A), (B), (C)의 각 네모 안에서 어법에 맞는 표현으로 가장 적절한 것은?

I've been an inspirational speaker (A) for / since many years. I've learned that teenagers often compare themselves to others and are ashamed of their flaws. Do you have the same problems? If so, you need to practice self-love. Self-love means loving (B) you / yourself just like you love your friends or family. It also means that you put your happiness first. Here's how to love yourself more. First, think about your skills and talents. Next, celebrate yourself for your achievements. They can even be small ones, like not being late for school this morning. This will increase your self-confidence and inspire you (C) try / to try new things.

	(A)		(B)		(C)
①	for	⋯	you	⋯	try
②	since	⋯	you	⋯	try
③	for	⋯	you	⋯	to try
④	since	⋯	yourself	⋯	to try
⑤	for	⋯	yourself	⋯	to try

03 (A), (B), (C)의 각 네모 안에서 어법에 맞는 표현으로 가장 적절한 것은?

As a teen, you may feel like an adult, but your brain is still growing. In your brain, there is a part (A) which / who is responsible for solving problems and controlling your emotions. In your teen years, this part is still in development. The changes in your brain lead you toward independence, social engagement, and (B) creative / creativity. At the same time, however, you may feel confused about who you are. You may also be more sensitive to unfairness. Furthermore, your body is flowing with hormones. This significantly affects your mood. The combination of these factors (C) intensify / intensifies your strong emotions.

	(A)		(B)		(C)
①	which	⋯	creative	⋯	intensify
②	who	⋯	creative	⋯	intensify
③	which	⋯	creativity	⋯	intensify
④	who	⋯	creativity	⋯	intensifies
⑤	which	⋯	creativity	⋯	intensifies

04 다음 글의 밑줄 친 부분 중, 어법상 틀린 것은?

It is natural ① feeling angry from time to time; it doesn't mean there is ② something wrong with you. Anger can sometimes be a useful tool. For example, an angry but open conversation can resolve a conflict between friends. The important thing is ③ to manage your anger so that it does not turn into aggressive or violent behavior. This does not mean that you should stop yourself ④ from feeling angry. Rather, you should express it in a productive way. Ask yourself some questions about your angry feelings. This can help you ⑤ to better understand your anger.

①   ②   ③   ④   ⑤

05 다음 글의 밑줄 친 부분 중, 어법상 틀린 것은?

You need to learn ① how to deal with anger in a socially appropriate way. Remember: anger is a feeling, but behavior is a choice. The first step is ② recognizing the physical signs of anger. ③ That is possible to recognize those signs in advance. They include an increased heart rate, ④ a flushed face, and the clenching of your fists. When these things happen, take action to reduce your anger. For example, you could ⑤ try taking a break to organize your thoughts or ending a conversation before it gets too intense.

①   ②   ③   ④   ⑤

06 (A), (B), (C)의 각 네모 안에서 어법에 맞는 표현으로 가장 적절한 것은?

Without the right coping skills, you may find yourself (A) become / becoming verbally or even physically aggressive. Explore various strategies to discover (B) that / what is best for you, such as taking a walk, drawing a picture, or writing down things that come to your mind. You can also try to find possible solutions to a problem and then compare the advantages and disadvantages of each one. By developing problem-solving skills, you will learn that there are many ways to solve a problem without (C) get / getting angry.

	(A)	(B)	(C)
①	become	that	get
②	become	what	get
③	become	that	getting
④	becoming	what	getting
⑤	becoming	that	getting

07 (A), (B), (C)의 각 네모 안에서 어법에 맞는 표현으로 가장 적절한 것은?

Anger is an emotion (A) that / whom we all experience. By (B) manage / managing your anger properly, you can be the boss of your feelings, not the other way around. This is an important step in finding your true self and (C) take / taking control of your life.

	(A)	(B)	(C)
①	that	manage	take
②	whom	manage	take
③	that	manage	taking
④	whom	managing	taking
⑤	that	managing	taking

08 다음 글의 밑줄 친 부분 중, 어법상 틀린 것은?

What would you like to do in the future? Maybe you want to become a writer. But if you simply aim for a job, what happens ① when you achieve your goal? Once you become a writer, you may no longer ② feel inspiring. Therefore, you should dream of actions, ③ not just jobs. For example, don't just say, "I want to be a writer." Say something like, "I want to inspire people ④ by telling interesting stories." That way, you will always have something ⑤ to work towards. One day, you could write children's stories. Another day, you could give inspirational lectures. So, what do you dream about doing?

①   ②   ③   ④   ⑤

[01~02] 다음 대화를 읽고, 물음에 답하시오.

> **B** Are you ready to plan our vacation to Jeonju for Mom's birthday?
>
> **G** Yep! First, let's decide who will find a place to stay and who will find some good restaurants.
>
> **B** Well, I prefer _____ to finding a place to stay.
>
> **G** I'll find a good place to stay, then.
>
> **B** Perfect! Mom's going to have so much fun. She'll want pictures of everything.
>
> **G** Would you take photos for her?
>
> **B** Sure, I can take some. I'll find some tips for taking good photos.
>
> **G** Great!

01 위 대화를 읽고 유추할 수 있는 내용이 <u>아닌</u> 것은?

① The boy is the girl's brother.
② They are planning their trip to Jeonju.
③ They will celebrate their mom's birthday.
④ The girl is going to search for accommodations.
⑤ Their mom is good at taking pictures.

02 위 대화의 빈칸에 알맞은 말을 <u>두 단어</u>로 쓰시오.

> Well, I prefer _____ to finding a place to stay.

[03~04] 다음 글을 읽고, 물음에 답하시오.

> I've been an inspirational speaker for many years. I've learned that teenagers often compare themselves to others and ① are ashamed of their flaws. Do you have the same problems? If so, you need to practice self-love. (A) Self-love means ② loving yourself just like you love your friends or family. (B) Here's how to love yourself more. (C) First, think about your skills and talents. (D) Write down ③ whatever comes to mind. (E) For example, you might be good at playing sports. You'll probably be surprised at how long ④ the list is. Next, celebrate yourself for your achievements. They can even be small ones, like ⑤ not be late for school this morning. This will increase your self-confidence and inspire you to try new things. So, love yourself as you are right now.

03 글의 흐름으로 보아, 주어진 문장이 들어가기에 가장 적절한 곳은?

> It also means that you put your happiness first.

① (A)   ② (B)   ③ (C)   ④ (D)   ⑤ (E)

04 윗글의 밑줄 친 부분 중, 어법상 <u>틀린</u> 것은?

①   ②   ③   ④   ⑤

05 주어진 글 다음에 이어질 글의 순서로 가장 적절한 것은?

What would you like to do in the future? Maybe you want to become a writer.

(A) That way, you will always have something to work towards. One day, you could write children's stories. Another day, you could give inspirational lectures.

(B) But if you simply aim for a job, what happens when you achieve your goal? Once you become a writer, you may no longer feel inspired.

(C) Therefore, you should dream of actions, not just jobs. For example, don't just say, "I want to be a writer." Say something like, "I want to inspire people by telling interesting stories."

① (A) – (B) – (C)   ② (A) – (C) – (B)
③ (B) – (A) – (C)   ④ (B) – (C) – (A)
⑤ (C) – (B) – (A)

06 (A), (B), (C)의 각 네모 안에서 문맥에 맞는 낱말로 가장 적절한 것은?

Do you ever find (A) oneself / yourself suddenly feeling angry? One moment you're fine, and the (B) next / other moment you're slamming doors or rolling your eyes at your parents. Some people may think you just have a bad attitude or are getting too (C) excited / upset about a small problem. However, these feelings don't simply come from stress about everyday life.

	(A)	(B)	(C)
①	oneself	… next	… excited
②	oneself	… other	… excited
③	yourself	… next	… excited
④	yourself	… other	… upset
⑤	yourself	… next	… upset

[07~08] 다음 글을 읽고, 물음에 답하시오.

As a teen, you may feel like an adult, but your brain is still growing. In your brain, there is a part that is responsible for solving problems and controlling your emotions. In your teen years, this part is still in development. The changes in your brain lead you toward independence, social engagement, and creativity. At the same time, however, you may feel confused about who you are. You may also be more sensitive to unfairness. Furthermore, your body is flowing with hormones. This significantly affects your mood. The combination of these factors intensifies your strong emotions.

07 윗글의 주제로 가장 적절한 것은?

① when the brain develops the most
② the parts of the brain that control emotions
③ how adolescents can cope with troubles
④ the effects of stress on the body
⑤ why adolescents have strong emotions

08 윗글의 밑줄 친 that과 쓰임이 같은 것은?

① Nobody believes that she lost the tennis match.
② We heard the news that the trees in the mountain were cut down.
③ There is a concern that the project will pollute the river.
④ They need a solution that is acceptable to all.
⑤ Daisy was so tired that she went to bed early.

[09~10] 다음 글을 읽고, 물음에 답하시오.

ⓐ It is natural to feel angry from time to time; it doesn't mean there is something wrong with you. Anger can sometimes be a useful tool. For example, an angry but open conversation can resolve a conflict between friends. The important thing is to manage your anger so that ⓑ it does not turn into aggressive or violent behavior. This does not mean that you should stop yourself from feeling angry. Rather, you should _____. Ask yourself some questions about your angry feelings. This can help you to better understand your anger.

09 윗글의 빈칸에 들어갈 말로 가장 적절한 것은?

① burst into anger
② change your anger into hatred
③ tell yourself your anger is not real
④ express your anger in a productive way
⑤ practice open communication with friends

10 윗글의 밑줄 친 ⓐ와 ⓑ가 각각 가리키는 것을 찾아 쓰시오.

ⓐ It → _____

ⓑ it → _____

[11~12] 다음 글을 읽고, 물음에 답하시오.

You need to learn how ⓐ to deal with anger in a socially appropriate way. Remember: anger is a feeling, but behavior is ⓑ a choice. The first step is recognizing the physical signs of anger. It is possible ⓒ to recognize those signs in advance. They include an increased heart rate, a flushed face, and the clenching of your fists. When these things happen, take action ⓓ to reduce your anger. For example, you could try taking a break to organize your thoughts or ending a conversation before it gets ⓔ too intense.

11 윗글의 내용을 요약할 때, 빈칸 (A), (B)에 들어갈 말로 가장 적절한 것은?

To deal with your anger, you should first ____(A)____ the physical signs and then take ____(B)____ to reduce it.

	(A)		(B)
①	recognize	⋯	action
②	reduce	⋯	steps
③	relieve	⋯	consideration
④	release	⋯	recognition
⑤	increase	⋯	account

12 윗글의 밑줄 친 ⓐ~ⓔ와 바꿔 쓸 수 있는 표현이 아닌 것은?

① ⓐ to manage
② ⓑ a decision
③ ⓒ to notice
④ ⓓ to intensify
⑤ ⓔ too fierce

In some cases, the strategies mentioned above may not be enough, so you may need to find proper coping skills for your personal situation.   (A)   the right coping skills, you may find yourself becoming verbally or even physically aggressive. Explore various strategies to discover what is best for you, such as taking a walk, drawing a picture, or writing down things that come   (B)   your mind. You can also try to find possible solutions to a problem and then compare the advantages and disadvantages of each one.   (C)   developing problem-solving skills, you will learn that there are many ways to solve a problem without getting angry.

Anger is an emotion that we all experience. By managing your anger properly, you can be the boss of your feelings, not the other way around. This is an important step in finding your true self and taking control of your life.

13 윗글의 내용과 일치하지 <u>않는</u> 것은?

① 분노를 조절하는 적절한 방법을 찾지 못하면 공격적으로 행동하기 쉽다.
② 분노를 조절하는 좋은 방법으로는 그림 그리기나 글 쓰기가 있다.
③ 여러 방법 중 자신에게 맞는 방법을 찾는 것이 중요하다.
④ 분노를 더 자주 느끼는 성향의 사람들이 있다.
⑤ 분노를 통제할 수 있어야 삶을 통제할 수 있다.

14 윗글의 빈칸 (A), (B), (C)에 들어갈 말이 바르게 연결된 것은?

	(A)		(B)		(C)
①	With	⋯	to	⋯	By
②	Without	⋯	on	⋯	For
③	By	⋯	in	⋯	With
④	With	⋯	in	⋯	For
⑤	Without	⋯	to	⋯	By

15 (A), (B), (C)의 각 네모 안에서 어법에 맞는 표현으로 가장 적절한 것은"?

There are a few things (A) that / what make me unique. Firstly, my interests make me unique. I'm interested in music, and I sometimes compose songs for my friends. My daily habits also make me unique. For example, I write about my feelings in a journal every evening. This helps me (B) reduce / reducing my stress. Lastly, I have a special talent that makes me unique. I am good at (C) telling / to tell jokes. I can always make my classmates laugh.

	(A)		(B)		(C)
①	that	⋯	reduce	⋯	telling
②	that	⋯	reducing	⋯	telling
③	that	⋯	reduce	⋯	to tell
④	what	⋯	reducing	⋯	to tell
⑤	what	⋯	reduce	⋯	to tell

[01~02] 다음 글을 읽고, 물음에 답하시오.

What would you like to do in the future? Maybe you want to become a writer. But if you simply aim for a job, what happens when you achieve your goal? Once you become a writer, you may no longer feel inspired.   (A)   , you should dream of actions, not just jobs.   (B)   , don't just say, "I want to be a writer." Say something like, "I want to inspire people by telling interesting stories." That way, you will always have something to work towards. One day, you could write children's stories. Another day, you could give inspirational lectures. So, what do you dream about doing?

01 윗글의 제목으로 가장 적절한 것은?

① What Should You Do to Be a Good Writer?
② A Variety of Jobs Are Waiting for You
③ Keep Going to Achieve Your Goal
④ Inspire People, Inspire the World
⑤ Dream in Verbs, Not in Nouns

02 윗글의 빈칸 (A)와 (B)에 들어갈 말이 바르게 짝지어진 것은?

	(A)		(B)
①	However	…	On the contrary
②	Therefore	…	For example
③	So	…	On the other hand
④	Moreover	…	For instance
⑤	Furthermore	…	In other words

[03~04] 다음 글을 읽고, 물음에 답하시오.

I've been an inspirational speaker for many years. I've learned that teenagers often compare themselves to others and are ashamed of their flaws. Do you have the same problems? If so, you need to practice self-love. Self-love means loving yourself just like you love your friends or family. ⓐ It also means that you put your happiness first. Here's how to love yourself more. First, think about your skills and talents. Write down whatever comes to mind. For example, you might be good at playing sports. You'll probably be surprised at how long the list is. Next, celebrate yourself for your achievements. ⓑ They can even be small ones, like not being late for school this morning. This will increase your self-confidence and inspire you to try new things. So, love yourself as you are right now.

03 윗글의 밑줄 친 how to love yourself more를 잘못 이해한 사람은?

① Jongmin: I am the best soccer player in my class.
② Becky: I can fix anything in my house.
③ Sora: I'm good at programming.
④ Dean: I'm proud that I practiced the guitar really hard today.
⑤ Minji: I want to become a great dancer.

04 윗글의 밑줄 친 ⓐ와 ⓑ가 각각 가리키는 것을 찾아 쓰시오.

ⓐ It   → _____
ⓑ They → _____

[05~06] 다음 글을 읽고, 물음에 답하시오.

As a teen, you may feel like an adult, but your brain is still growing. In your brain, there is a part that is (A) responsible / irresponsible for solving problems and controlling your emotions. In your teen years, this part is still in development. The changes in your brain lead you (B) from / toward independence, social engagement, and creativity. At the same time, however, you may feel confused about who you are. You may also be more sensitive to unfairness. Furthermore, your body is flowing with hormones. This significantly (C) affects / effects your mood. The combination of these factors intensifies your strong emotions.

05 (A), (B), (C)의 각 네모 안에서 문맥에 맞는 낱말로 가장 적절한 것은?

	(A)	(B)	(C)
①	responsible	⋯ from	⋯ affects
②	irresponsible	⋯ from	⋯ affects
③	responsible	⋯ toward	⋯ affects
④	irresponsible	⋯ toward	⋯ effects
⑤	responsible	⋯ toward	⋯ effects

06 윗글의 밑줄 친 these factors로 글에서 언급되지 않은 것은?

① 독립적이고 창의적인 사고가 늘어난다.
② 자신의 정체성에 관한 질문이 많아진다.
③ 부당하다고 느끼는 것에 민감하게 반응한다.
④ 신체에서 호르몬의 활동이 왕성해진다.
⑤ 자신의 감정을 통제할 수 있다는 믿음이 생긴다.

[07~08] 다음 글을 읽고, 물음에 답하시오.

It is natural ① that feel angry from time to time; it doesn't mean there is ② something wrong with you. Anger can sometimes be a useful tool. For example, an angry but open conversation can resolve a conflict between friends. The important thing is to manage your anger ③ so that it does not turn into aggressive or violent behavior. This does not mean that you should stop yourself ④ from feeling angry. Rather, you should express it in a productive way. Ask yourself some questions about your angry feelings. This can help you to ⑤ better understand your anger.

07 윗글 다음에 이어질 내용으로 가장 적절한 것은?

① tips to manage your anger well
② questions to ask yourself about your anger
③ effects that angry feelings have on you
④ signs on your body when you get angry
⑤ the difference between expressing and managing your anger

08 윗글의 밑줄 친 부분 중, 어법상 틀린 것은?

①   ②   ③   ④   ⑤

09 다음 글에 제시된 질문에 대한 대답으로 적절하지 <u>않은</u> 것은?

> **Questions to Ask Yourself**
> ✓ How often do I feel angry?
> ✓ What situations make me feel the most intense anger?
> ✓ Is my anger directed at anyone or anything in particular?
> ✓ Do I focus on the causes of my anger instead of solutions?
> ✓ Can I control my emotions when I get angry?
> ✓ How do I react and behave when I get angry?

① I think I feel angry every day.
② I feel angry especially when people don't keep their word.
③ I often get angry with my little brother.
④ I feel less angry after talking to a friend.
⑤ I often walk away from a situation when I'm angry.

10 다음 글의 밑줄 친 표현이 의미하는 바로 가장 적절한 것은?

> Anger is an emotion that we all experience. By managing your anger properly, you can be the boss of your feelings, not <u>the other way around</u>. This is an important step in finding your true self and taking control of your life.

① your feelings are completely under your control
② you can manage your emotions well
③ your emotions rule your life
④ you are not overwhelmed by anger
⑤ you can stop yourself from easily getting upset

[11~12] 다음 글을 읽고, 물음에 답하시오.

> You need to learn how to deal with anger in a socially appropriate way. (A) Remember: anger is a feeling, but behavior is a choice. (B) It is possible to recognize those signs in advance. (C) They include an increased heart rate, a flushed face, and the clenching of your fists. (D) When these things happen, take action to reduce your anger. (E) For example, you could try taking a break to organize your thoughts or ending a conversation before _____.

11 글의 흐름으로 보아, 주어진 문장이 들어가기에 가장 적절한 곳은?

> The first step is recognizing the physical signs of anger.

① (A)   ② (B)   ③ (C)   ④ (D)   ⑤ (E)

12 윗글의 빈칸에 들어갈 말로 어색한 것은?

① it gets too intense
② you get too furious
③ you lose your temper
④ it turns into a conflict
⑤ an agreement is reached

13 (A), (B), (C)의 각 네모 안에서 어법에 맞는 표현으로 가장 적절한 것은?

In some cases, the strategies (A) ⎢mentioning / mentioned⎢ above may not be enough, so you may need to find proper coping skills for your personal situation. Without the right coping skills, you may find yourself (B) ⎢becoming / to become⎢ verbally or even physically aggressive. Explore various strategies to discover what is best for you, such as taking a walk, drawing a picture, or (C) ⎢write / writing⎢ down things that come to your mind. You can also try to find possible solutions to a problem and then compare the advantages and disadvantages of each one. By developing problem-solving skills, you will learn that there are many ways to solve a problem without getting angry.

	(A)		(B)		(C)
①	mentioning	⋯	becoming	⋯	write
②	mentioning	⋯	to become	⋯	write
③	mentioned	⋯	becoming	⋯	write
④	mentioned	⋯	to become	⋯	writing
⑤	mentioned	⋯	becoming	⋯	writing

[14~15] 다음 글을 읽고, 물음에 답하시오.

There are ① few things that make me unique. Firstly, my interests make me unique. I'm ② interested in music, and I sometimes compose songs for my friends. My ③ daily habits also make me unique. For example, I write about my feelings in a journal every evening. This helps me ④ reduce my stress. Lastly, I have a special talent that makes me unique. I am good at telling jokes. I can ⑤ always make my classmates laugh.

14 윗글의 주제로 가장 적절한 것은?

① things that make me unique
② my special talent that makes me happy
③ the importance of keeping a journal
④ my unique way of relieving stress
⑤ music and mental health

15 윗글의 밑줄 친 부분 중, 문맥상 낱말의 쓰임이 적절하지 <u>않은</u> 것은?

①   ②   ③   ④   ⑤

[01~02] 다음 대화를 읽고, 물음에 답하시오.

B Hello, Ms. Smith. Do you have time to talk with me?

W Sure, I don't have a class at the moment. What's wrong?

B I can't decide whether I should take a music class or a computer class. (A)

W Which one are you more interested in?

B I prefer music to computers. (B)

W Then why can't you decide? (C)

B I think the computer class will be helpful for my future career. (D)

W Well, I think you should take the music class. (E)

B I think you're right. Thanks, Ms. Smith!

01 대화의 흐름으로 보아 주어진 말이 들어갈 위치로 가장 적절한 곳은?

You will learn more if you enjoy the class.

① (A)   ② (B)   ③ (C)   ④ (D)   ⑤ (E)

02 위 대화의 내용과 일치하지 <u>않는</u> 것은?

① The boy wants to talk to Ms. Smith.
② The boy must choose between music and computer class.
③ The boy is more interested in music than computers.
④ The boy is thinking of becoming a musician.
⑤ Ms. Smith recommends the boy take the music class.

[03~04] 다음 글을 읽고, 물음에 답하시오.

What would you like to do in the future? Maybe you want to become a writer. But if you simply ① aim for a job, what happens when you achieve your goal? Once you become a writer, you may ② no longer feel inspired. Therefore, you should _____.

For example, don't just say, "I want to be a writer." Say something like, "I want to ③ inspire people by telling interesting stories." That way, you will always have something to ④ work with. One day, you could write children's stories. Another day, you could give inspirational lectures. So, what do you ⑤ dream about doing?

03 윗글의 빈칸에 들어갈 말로 가장 적절한 것은?

① dream of actions, not just jobs
② think of a more detailed job title
③ make plans to switch careers
④ start dreaming as early as possible
⑤ read many books to become a writer

04 윗글의 밑줄 친 부분 중, 문맥상 어구의 쓰임이 적절하지 <u>않은</u> 것은?

①   ②   ③   ④   ⑤

[05~06] 다음 글을 읽고, 물음에 답하시오.

I've been an inspirational speaker for many years. I've learned that teenagers often compare themselves to others and are ashamed of their flaws. Do you have the same problems? If so, you need to practice self-love. Self-love means loving yourself just like you love your friends or family. It also means that you put your happiness first. Here's how to love yourself more. First, think about your skills and talents. 마음에 떠오르는 것은 무엇이든 기록하라. For example, you might be good at playing sports. You'll probably be surprised at how long the list is. Next, celebrate yourself for your achievements. They can even be small ones, like not being late for school this morning. This will increase your self-confidence and inspire you to try new things. So, love yourself as you are right now.

05 윗글의 내용과 일치하지 <u>않는</u> 것은?

① 십 대들은 종종 남과 비교하며 자신의 약점을 부끄러워한다.
② 자기애는 가족과 친구를 사랑하듯 스스로를 사랑하는 것을 의미한다.
③ 자신의 행복과 타인의 행복을 함께 고려하는 것이 중요하다.
④ 자신을 더 사랑하기 위해 자신이 가진 기술과 재능을 떠올려 보는 게 좋다.
⑤ 자신이 이룬 성과를 축하하는 것이 자존감을 키워준다.

06 윗글의 밑줄 친 우리말과 일치하도록 주어진 표현을 활용하여 문장을 완성하시오.

마음에 떠오르는 것은 무엇이든 기록하라.
(whatever, come to mind)

→ _____

[07~08] 다음 글을 읽고, 물음에 답하시오.

Do you ever find yourself suddenly feeling angry? One moment you're fine, and the next moment you're slamming doors or _____. Some people may think you just have a bad attitude or are getting too upset about a small problem. However, these feelings don't simply come from stress about everyday life.

As a teen, you may feel like an adult, but your brain is still growing. In your brain, there is a part that is responsible for solving problems and controlling your emotions. In your teen years, this part is still in development. The changes in your brain lead you toward independence, social engagement, and creativity. At the same time,   (A)   , you may feel confused about who you are. You may also be more sensitive to unfairness.   (B)   , your body is flowing with hormones. This significantly affects your mood. The combination of these factors intensifies your strong emotions.

07 윗글의 빈칸에 들어갈 말로 <u>어색한</u> 것은?

① bursting into anger
② throwing books at the floor
③ rolling your eyes at your parents
④ shouting at your brother or sister
⑤ counting numbers in your head

08 윗글의 빈칸 (A)와 (B)에 들어갈 말이 바르게 짝지어진 것은?

	(A)		(B)
①	however	···	Furthermore
②	thus	···	In addition
③	therefore	···	Nevertheless
④	in consequence	···	On the other hand
⑤	unfortunately	···	In short

[09~10] 다음 글을 읽고, 물음에 답하시오.

It is natural to feel angry _____ time to time; it doesn't mean there is something wrong with you. Anger can sometimes be a useful tool. For example, an angry but open conversation can resolve a conflict between friends. The important thing is to manage your anger so that it does not turn into aggressive or violent behavior. This does not mean that you should stop yourself _____ feeling angry. Rather, you should express it in a productive way. Ask yourself some questions about your angry feelings. This can help you to better understand your anger.

09 윗글의 요지로 가장 적절한 것은?

① Asking yourself many questions about your anger is important.
② It's okay to feel angry, but it's important to express your anger in a healthy way.
③ Anger can be a powerful way to communicate with friends.
④ Controlling your anger is the first step toward better mental health.
⑤ Anger is a normal human emotion that must not be managed in any way.

10 윗글의 빈칸에 공통으로 들어갈 말로 적절한 것은?

① at   ② for   ③ from
④ with   ⑤ into

[11~12] 다음 글을 읽고, 물음에 답하시오.

You need to learn how to deal with anger in a (A) social / socially appropriate way. Remember: anger is a feeling, but behavior is a choice. The first step is recognizing the physical signs of anger. It is possible (B) recognize / to recognize those signs in advance. They include an increased heart rate, a flushed face, and the clenching of your fists. When these things happen, take action to reduce your anger. For example, you could try taking a break to organize your thoughts or (C) end / ending a conversation before it gets too intense.

11 윗글의 어조로 가장 적절한 것은?

① instructive   ② sympathetic
③ skeptical   ④ festive
⑤ optimistic

12 (A), (B), (C)의 각 네모 안에서 어법에 맞는 표현으로 가장 적절한 것은?

	(A)	(B)	(C)
①	social	… recognize	… end
②	social	… to recognize	… end
③	socially	… recognize	… end
④	socially	… to recognize	… ending
⑤	socially	… recognize	… ending

[13~14] 다음 글을 읽고, 물음에 답하시오.

In some cases, the strategies mentioned above may not be enough, so you may need to find proper coping skills for your personal situation. Without the right coping skills, you may find ① yourself becoming verbally or even physically aggressive. Explore various strategies to discover what is best for you, such as taking a walk, drawing a picture, or writing down things ② what come to your mind. You can also try to find possible solutions to a problem and then compare the advantages and disadvantages of each one. ③ By developing problem-solving skills, you will learn that there are many ways to solve a problem without getting angry.

Anger is ④ an emotion that we all experience. By managing your anger properly, you can be the boss of your feelings, not the other way around. This is an important step in finding your true self and ⑤ taking control of your life.

13 윗글의 앞에 언급되었을 내용으로 가장 적절한 것은?

① factors that cause anger during adolescence
② methods to calm down your anger
③ benefits of getting angry
④ physical signs that mean you are angry
⑤ the importance of managing your emotions

14 윗글의 밑줄 친 부분 중, 어법상 틀린 것은?

①   ②   ③   ④   ⑤

15 다음 글의 내용을 요약할 때, 빈칸에 알맞은 말을 글에서 찾아 쓰시오.

There are a few things that make me unique. Firstly, my interests make me unique. I'm interested in music, and I sometimes compose songs for my friends. My daily habits also make me unique. For example, I write about my feelings in a journal every evening. This helps me reduce my stress. Lastly, I have a special talent that makes me unique. I am good at telling jokes. I can always make my classmates laugh.

↓

Three things that make me (1) _____ are my interest in music, my daily habit of keeping a journal, and my (2) _____ to tell a joke.

[01~02] 다음 글을 읽고, 물음에 답하시오.

What do you dream of doing? Perhaps you dream of becoming a writer. However, focusing solely on a job title can lead to a sense of emptiness once that goal is (A) achieved / arrived . Instead, dream of the impact you want to make. For example, instead of saying, "I want to be a writer," say, "I want to inspire others (B) though / through telling stories." This approach ensures a continuous sense of purpose. One day, you could write children's books, and another day, give (C) monotonous / motivational speeches. So, what are your dreams?

01 윗글의 주제로 가장 적절한 것은?

① setting goals that focus on purpose
② the importance of having dreams
③ writing inspirational stories for children
④ how to choose the best job
⑤ tips for getting over the sense of emptiness

02 (A), (B), (C)의 각 네모 안에서 문맥에 맞는 낱말로 가장 적절한 것은?

	(A)		(B)		(C)
①	achieved	⋯	though	⋯	monotonous
②	arrived	⋯	though	⋯	monotonous
③	achieved	⋯	though	⋯	motivational
④	arrived	⋯	through	⋯	motivational
⑤	achieved	⋯	through	⋯	motivational

[03~04] 다음 글을 읽고, 물음에 답하시오.

As an inspirational speaker, I've noticed that teenagers often compare themselves to others and ① feel ashamed of their imperfections. Do you have the same problem? If so, ② that's important to practice self-love. This means valuing yourself ③ as much as you value your loved ones and puttting your happiness first. Here's how to cultivate self-love: First, reflect on your skills and talents. You'll likely be surprised by _____. Second, celebrate your accomplishments, big or small. This can boost your self-confidence and encourage you ④ to take risks. Remember, self-love means accepting yourself ⑤ as you are.

03 윗글의 밑줄 친 부분 중 어법상 틀린 것은?

①   ②   ③   ④   ⑤

04 윗글의 빈칸에 들어갈 말로 가장 적절한 것은?

① how many skills and talents you have
② why you didn't develop any skills or talents
③ which skills and talents to develop
④ how you should enhance your skills and talents
⑤ where you can learn new skills and talents

[05~06] 다음 글을 읽고, 물음에 답하시오.

As a teenager, you may feel mature, but your brain is still developing. During your teenage years, the part (A) that / what is responsible for solving problems and controlling emotions is still maturing. These brain changes foster independence, social engagement, and creativity. However, they can also make you feel confused about your identity and increase your (B) sensitive / sensitivity to unfairness. Additionally, hormonal fluctuations can significantly impact your mood. The combination of these factors (C) intensify / intensifies your strong emotions.

05 윗글에서 언급된 십 대의 특징과 일치하지 않는 것은?

① 스스로 성숙하다고 느끼기 시작한다.
② 감정 통제에 관여하는 뇌 부위의 성장이 완료된다.
③ 자신의 정체성에 관해 혼란스럽게 느낀다.
④ 공정하지 않은 것에 민감하게 반응한다.
⑤ 호르몬 변화가 감정 변화에 영향을 미친다.

06 (A), (B), (C)의 각 네모 안에서 어법에 맞는 표현으로 가장 적절한 것은?

	(A)		(B)		(C)
①	that	⋯	sensitive	⋯	intensify
②	what	⋯	sensitive	⋯	intensify
③	that	⋯	sensitivity	⋯	intensify
④	what	⋯	sensitivity	⋯	intensifies
⑤	that	⋯	sensitivity	⋯	intensifies

[07~08] 다음 글을 읽고, 물음에 답하시오.

_____ It does not indicate any personal flaws. In some cases, anger can bring about positive methods, such as open communication, to resolve conflicts. The key is to manage your anger to prevent it from turning into aggression or violence. This doesn't mean that you must suppress your anger. Instead, express it constructively. Reflect on your feelings to gain a better understanding of your anger.

07 윗글의 빈칸에 들어갈 말로 어색한 것은?

① You may feel angry from time to time.
② Experiencing anger is normal.
③ It is important to control anger.
④ It is natural to become angry.
⑤ It is not unusual for you to feel angry.

08 윗글의 내용을 요약할 때 빈칸 (A), (B)에 들어갈 말로 가장 적절한 것은?

Anger is a(n) ____(A)____ human emotion, and it is important to manage your anger to ____(B)____ it from turning into someting harmful.

	(A)		(B)
①	personal	⋯	protect
②	negative	⋯	avoid
③	productive	⋯	stop
④	natural	⋯	prevent
⑤	inevitable	⋯	control

[09~10] 다음 글을 읽고, 물음에 답하시오.

Ask yourself questions about your anger, which help you understand it.

Questions to Ask Yourself

✓ How frequently do I experience anger?

✓ Under what circumstances do I feel the most furious?

✓ Is there a specific person or thing that I am angry at?

✓ Do I concentrate on the reasons for my anger rather than solutions?

✓ Am I able to manage my feelings when I become angry?

✓ How do I act when I am angry?

09 윗글의 목적으로 가장 적절한 것은?

① to explain positive aspects of getting angry

② to guide individuals toward mental wellness

③ to help individuals understand and manage their anger

④ to suggest various ways of controlling emotional problems

⑤ to introduce specific parts of the brain that trigger intense emotions

10 윗글의 질문이 파악하고자 하는 내용과 관계가 <u>없는</u> 것은?

① 분노의 빈도

② 분노를 유발하는 상황

③ 분노가 향하는 곳

④ 분노의 강도

⑤ 분노의 조절 여부

[11~12] 다음 글을 읽고, 물음에 답하시오.

It's important ① to learn how to express anger in a socially acceptable manner. Remember, anger is a feeling, but your actions are a choice.

(A) When you notice these signs, you can take further steps ② to manage your anger.

(B) The first step is recognizing the physical reactions to anger, ③ that can often be identified beforehand.

(C) For instance, you could take a break to gather your thoughts or ④ end a conversation before it escalates.

(D) These include ⑤ an increased heart rate, a flushed face, and clenched fists.

11 주어진 글 다음에 이어질 글의 순서로 가장 적절한 것은?

① (A) – (B) – (D) – (C)

② (B) – (A) – (C) – (D)

③ (B) – (D) – (A) – (C)

④ (C) – (A) – (B) – (D)

⑤ (C) – (B) – (D) – (A)

12 윗글의 밑줄 친 부분 중 어법상 <u>틀린</u> 것은?

①　　　　②　　　　③　　　　④　　　　⑤

Sometimes, the strategies mentioned above may not be sufficient, so you'll need to find coping skills for your ① specific situation. Without effective coping skills, you might resort to verbal or even ② mental aggression. Explore various strategies to discover what works best for you, such as going for a walk, drawing, or keeping a journal. You can also try ③ brainstorming solutions to problems and evaluating their pros and cons. By developing problem-solving skills, you'll realize there are many ways to ④ address issues without resorting to anger.

Anger is a universal emotion. By effectively managing your anger, you can take control of your feelings rather than letting them ⑤ control you. This is a crucial step in self-discovery and taking charge of your life.

13 윗글의 요지로 가장 적절한 것은?

① Finding your own anger-managing skills is important.
② Aggressive words and actions are harmful.
③ There are many skills that help you control anger.
④ Outdoor activities are a good way to control your anger.
⑤ Maintain good relationships for your mental health.

14 윗글의 밑줄 친 부분 중 문맥상 낱말의 쓰임이 적절하지 않은 것은?

①　　②　　③　　④　　⑤

15 다음 글의 ①~⑤ 중 전체 흐름과 관계 없는 문장은?

I have a few unique qualities. ① My interests, such as composing music for my friends, set me apart from others. ② There are some AI programs that can compose music. ③ My daily habits, like writing about my feelings in a journal, also make me unique. ④ This helps me manage my stress. ⑤ In addition, my ability to tell jokes and make others laugh is a special talent that distinguishes me from others.

①　　②　　③　　④　　⑤

[01~02] 다음 글을 읽고, 물음에 답하시오.

What would you like to do in the future? Maybe you want to become a writer. But if you simply aim for a job, what happens when you achieve your goal? Once you become a writer, you may no longer feel ⓐ <u>inspire</u>. Therefore, you should dream of actions, not just jobs. For example, don't just say, "I want to be a writer." Say something like, ⓑ <u>"나는 재미있는 이야기를 들려주며 사람들에게 영감을 주고 싶다."</u> That way, you will always have something to work towards. One day, you could write children's stories. Another day, you could give inspirational lectures. So, what do you dream about ⓒ <u>do</u>?

01 윗글의 밑줄 친 ⓐ와 ⓒ를 알맞은 형태로 바꿔 쓰시오.

ⓐ inspire → _____

ⓒ do → _____

02 윗글의 밑줄 친 ⓑ의 우리말과 일치하도록 조건에 맞게 영작하시오.

조건
1. 전치사 by를 사용할 것
2. 다음 표현을 사용할 것: inspire, interesting

나는 재미있는 이야기를 들려주며 사람들에게 영감을 주고 싶다.

→ _____
_____

[03~04] 다음 글을 읽고, 물음에 답하시오.

I've been an inspirational speaker for many years. I've learned that teenagers often compare themselves to others and are ashamed of their flaws. Do you have the same problems? If so, you need to practice self-love. Self-love means loving yourself just like you love your friends or family. It also means that you put your happiness first. Here's how to love yourself more. First, think about your skills and talents. Write down ⓐ <u>whatever that comes to mind</u>. For example, you might be good at playing sports. You'll probably be surprised at ⓑ <u>how long is the list</u>. Next, celebrate yourself for your achievements. They can even be small ones, like ⓒ <u>not be late for school</u> this morning. This will increase your self-confidence and inspire you to try new things. So, love yourself as you are right now.

03 윗글의 내용과 일치하도록 다음 질문에 알맞은 답을 조건에 맞게 완성하여 쓰시오.

조건
1. 본문에 사용된 표현을 활용하여 쓸 것
2. 동명사를 사용할 것

What is self-love?

→ It means _____
and _____.

04 윗글의 밑줄 친 ⓐ~ⓒ에서 어법상 틀린 부분을 찾아 바르게 고쳐 쓰시오.

ⓐ → _____

ⓑ → _____

ⓒ → _____

[05~06] 다음 글을 읽고, 물음에 답하시오.

As a teen, you may feel like an adult, but your brain is still growing. In your brain, <u>there is a part that are responsible for solving problems and control your emotions</u>. In your teen years, this part is still in development. The changes in your brain lead you toward ____(A)____, social engagement, and creativity. At the same time, however, you may feel confused about who you are. You may also be more ____(B)____ to unfairness. Furthermore, your body is flowing with hormones. This significantly affects your mood. The combination of these factors ____(C)____ your strong emotions.

05 윗글의 밑줄 친 부분에서 어법상 틀린 곳을 두 개 찾아 바르게 고쳐 쓰시오.

there is a part that are responsible for solving problems and control your emotions

→ there _____

_____

06 윗글의 빈칸 (A)~(C)에 들어갈 말을 다음 영어 뜻풀이를 참고하여 주어진 철자로 시작하여 쓰시오. (문맥에 맞게 변형할 것)

(A) the quality of being able to look after oneself
(B) easily upset or offended
(C) to make something increase in degree or strength

(A) i_____
(B) s_____
(C) i_____

[07~09] 다음 글을 읽고, 물음에 답하시오.

ⓐ To feel angry from time to time is natural; it doesn't mean there is something wrong with you. Anger can sometimes be a useful tool. For example, an angry but open conversation can resolve a conflict between friends. The important thing is to manage your anger so that it does not turn into aggressive or violent behavior. This does not mean that you should stop yourself from feeling angry. Rather, you should express ⓑ it in a productive way. Ask yourself some questions about your angry feelings. This can help you to better understand your anger.

Questions to Ask Yourself
✓ How often do I feel angry?
✓ What situations make me feel the most intense anger?
✓ _____
✓ Do I focus on the causes of my anger instead of solutions?
✓ Can I control my emotions when I get angry?
✓ How do I react and behave when I get angry?

07 윗글의 밑줄 친 ⓐ를 가주어 It을 사용하여 바꿔 쓰시오.

To feel angry from time to time is natural

→ It _____

08 윗글의 밑줄 친 ⓑ it이 가리키는 것을 찾아 쓰시오.

ⓑ It → _____

09 윗글의 빈칸에 알맞은 질문을 보기의 말을 바르게 배열하여 쓰시오.

보기
my anger / at / in particular / is / anyone or anything / directed

→ _____

_____

[10~11] 다음 글을 읽고, 물음에 답하시오.

> You need to learn how to deal __(A)__ anger in a socially appropriate way. Remember: anger is a feeling, but behavior is a choice. The first step is recognizing the physical signs of anger. It is possible to recognize those signs __(B)__ advance. They include an increased heart rate, a flushed face, and the clenching of your fists. When these things happen, take action to reduce your anger. For example, you could try taking a break to organize your thoughts or ending a conversation before it gets too intense.

10 윗글의 빈칸 (A)와 (B)에 알맞은 말을 쓰시오.

(A) _____

(B) _____

11 윗글의 밑줄 친 the physical signs 세 가지를 글에서 찾아 쓰시오.

(1) _____

(2) _____

(3) _____

12 다음 글의 밑줄 친 ⓐ~ⓕ 중 어법상 틀린 것을 두 개 찾아 기호를 쓰고, 바르게 고쳐 쓰시오.

> There are ⓐ a few things ⓑ who make me unique. Firstly, my interests make me unique. I'm interested in music, and I sometimes compose songs for my friends. My daily habits also ⓒ make me unique. For example, I write about my feelings in a journal every evening. This helps me ⓓ reduce my stress. Lastly, I have a special talent that ⓔ makes me unique. I am good at telling jokes. I can always make my classmates ⓕ to laugh.

(1) _____ → _____

(2) _____ → _____

[13~14] 다음 글을 읽고, 물음에 답하시오.

> In some cases, the strategies mentioned above may not be enough, so you may need to find proper coping skills for your personal situation. Without the right coping skills, you may find yourself becoming verbally or even physically aggressive. Explore various strategies to discover what is best for you, such as taking a walk, drawing a picture, or writing down things ⓐ 당신의 마음에 떠오르는. You can also try to find possible solutions to a problem and then compare the advantages and disadvantages of each one. By developing problem-solving skills, you will learn that there are many ways to solve a problem without getting angry.
>
> Anger is an emotion ⓑ 우리 모두가 경험하는. By managing your anger properly, you can be the boss of your feelings, not the other way around. This is an important step in finding your true self and taking control of your life.

13 윗글의 내용을 요약할 때 빈칸에 알맞은 말을 글에서 찾아 쓰시오. (필요시 형태를 바꿀 것)

> Anger is a normal emotion, but it's important to manage it effectively. (1) _____ skills, like taking walks or writing, can help you deal with anger in healthy ways. By (2) _____ problem-solving skills, you can find solutions without resorting to aggression.

14 윗글의 밑줄 친 우리말 ⓐ, ⓑ와 일치하도록 조건에 맞게 영작하시오.

> 조건
> 1. 관계대명사를 사용할 것
> 2. 다음 표현을 사용할 것: come to mind, experience

ⓐ 당신의 마음에 떠오르는

→ _____

ⓑ 우리 모두가 경험하는

→ _____

02

—

Caring Hearts

Functions

▶ 공감 표현하기
I agree with you.

▶ 제안·권유하기
How about volunteering with me?

Grammar

▶ We could reward the investors **by sending** them jars of organic jam!

▶ This video **allows** investors **to learn** about your product.

교과서 어휘

□ volunteer	몡 자원봉사자 ⑧ 자원하다	□ thrilled	혱 신이 난, 아주 기쁜
□ opportunity	몡 기회	□ production	몡 생산 (produce ⑧ 생산하다)
□ facility	몡 시설	□ potential	혱 잠재적인, 가능성 있는
□ disability	몡 장애	□ fulfill	⑧ 충족하다, 만족시키다
□ install	⑧ 설치하다	□ amount	몡 총액, 양
□ access	⑧ 접근하다, 입장하다	□ calculation	몡 계산 (calculate ⑧ 계산하다)
□ blind	혱 눈이 먼	□ approximately	뷔 거의, 대략 (=around, about)
□ replace	⑧ 바꾸다, 교체하다	□ harvest	몡 수확
□ vision	몡 시력	□ cover	⑧ (충분한 돈을) 대다
□ shelter	몡 보호소	□ launch	⑧ 시작하다, 개시하다
□ abandon	⑧ 유기하다	□ application	몡 지원서, 신청서
□ adopt	⑧ 입양하다 (adoption 몡 입양)	□ promotion	몡 홍보 (promote ⑧ 홍보하다)
□ organic	혱 유기농의	□ update	몡 최신 정보
□ stare	⑧ 응시하다, 빤히 보다	□ request	몡 요청, 요구 ⑧ 요청하다
□ greenhouse	몡 온실	□ track	⑧ (진행을) 추적하다
□ immediately	뷔 즉시 (immediate 혱 즉각적인)	□ progress	몡 진행, 과정
□ crowdfunding	몡 크라우드펀딩	□ impression	몡 인상 (impress ⑧ 인상을 주다)
□ raise	⑧ (자금을) 모으다	□ highlight	⑧ 강조하다
□ charity	몡 자선단체	□ chemical	몡 화학물질
□ advantageous	혱 유리한, 이로운 (advantage 몡 유리한 점)	□ clip	몡 짧은 영상
□ individual	몡 개인	□ ingredient	몡 재료
□ attract	⑧ 끌어들이다	□ edit	⑧ 편집하다 (edition 몡 편집)
□ investor	몡 투자자 (invest ⑧ 투자하다)	□ post	⑧ 게시하다
□ reward	몡 보상	□ spread	⑧ 퍼지다, 확산하다
□ contribution	몡 기여, 이바지 (contribute ⑧ 기여하다)	□ commit	⑧ 약속하다

□ lost and found	분실물 보관소	□ decide on	~으로 정하다
□ voice guidance	음성 안내	□ turn A into B	A를 B로 바꾸다
□ stare at	~을 응시하다	□ fill out	(서식을) 작성하다
□ figure out	알아내다, 생각해 내다	□ be eager to	~하고 싶어 하다
□ fill A with B	A를 B로 채우다		

raise	(위로) 들어 올리다	You can **raise** your hand and ask a question. 손을 들고 질문을 해도 된다.
	(자금을) 모으다	We had a garage sale to **raise** money for people in need. 우리는 도움이 필요한 사람들을 위한 돈을 모으기 위해 창고 세일을 열었다.
	(가축, 작물을) 기르다	I have been **raising** farm animals for three years now. 나는 지금까지 3년째 가축을 사육하고 있다.

Useful Expressions

figure out 알아내다, 생각해 내다	He is smart enough to **figure out** what to do. 그는 무엇을 해야 할지 알아낼 만큼 영리하다.
be eager to ~하고 싶어 하다	The students **were eager to** learn about the new topic. 학생들은 새로운 주제에 관해 학습하고 싶어 했다.
fill out (서식을) 작성하다	He didn't **fill out** the application form properly. 그는 지원서를 알맞게 작성하지 않았다.

Word Mates

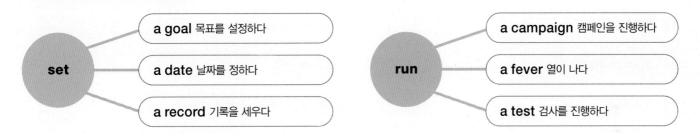

set — a goal 목표를 설정하다
set — a date 날짜를 정하다
set — a record 기록을 세우다

run — a campaign 캠페인을 진행하다
run — a fever 열이 나다
run — a test 검사를 진행하다

English-English Dictionary

☐ **organic** 유기농의   without using artificial chemicals when growing plants for food

☐ **charity** 자선단체   an official organization for helping those in need

☐ **advantageous** 유리한, 이로운   helping to make you more successful

☐ **contribution** 기여, 이바지   an action or service that helps the achievement of something

☐ **potential** 잠재적인, 가능성 있는   having the qualities to develop into something

☐ **calculation** 계산   the process of using numbers to determine an amount

☐ **harvest** 수확   the time when the crops are gathered

☐ **launch** 시작하다, 개시하다   to begin an important activity

☐ **promotion** 홍보   activities done in order to increase the sales of a product

☐ **highlight** 강조하다   to emphasize something or make people notice something

☐ **clip** 짧은 영상   a short part of a film or video that is shown on its own

☐ **commit** 약속하다   to promise your time, effort, or money to something or someone

교과서 어휘 익히기 ─────────────

♣ 다음 영어는 우리말로, 우리말은 영어로 쓰시오.

01	replace	동 _____	25	분실물 보관소	_____
02	launch	동 _____	26	형 유기농의	_____
03	reward	명 _____	27	동 접근하다, 입장하다	_____
04	figure out	_____	28	명 기회	_____
05	stare	동 _____	29	명 장애	_____
06	highlight	동 _____	30	명 투자자	_____
07	install	동 _____	31	~하고 싶어 하다	_____
08	shelter	명 _____	32	명 수확	_____
09	thrilled	형 _____	33	부 즉시	_____
10	amount	명 _____	34	명 자선단체	_____
11	commit	동 _____	35	명 요청, 요구 동 요청하다	_____
12	fill A with B	_____	36	명 기여, 이바지	_____
13	approximately	부 _____	37	명 재료	_____
14	attract	동 _____	38	형 잠재적인, 가능성 있는	_____
15	clip	명 _____	39	동 (자금을) 모으다	_____
16	turn A into B	_____	40	명 홍보	_____
17	fulfill	동 _____	41	동 편집하다	_____
18	abandon	동 _____	42	형 유리한, 이로운	_____
19	track	동 _____	43	명 개인	_____
20	adopt	동 _____	44	동 게시하다	_____
21	impression	명 _____	45	명 지원서, 신청서	_____
22	spread	동 _____	46	명 계산	_____
23	update	명 _____	47	명 진행, 과정	_____
24	fill out	_____	48	명 크라우드펀딩	_____

A 다음 밑줄 친 부분과 바꿔 쓸 수 있는 것을 보기 에서 골라 기호를 쓰시오.

> 보기   ⓐ collect   ⓑ cultivate   ⓒ lift

01 The farmers raise various types of crops on the land. (   )

02 Raise your arm over your head and hold it there for three minutes. (   )

B 빈칸에 들어갈 말로 알맞은 것을 고르시오.

01 When the boys found the secret passage, they were _____ to explore it.

ⓐ busy   ⓑ eager   ⓒ enthusiastic

02 The participants need to _____ a survey after watching the video.

ⓐ fill out   ⓑ take in   ⓒ work out

03 Scientists are trying to _____ the best protection against the disease.

ⓐ check in   ⓑ figure out   ⓒ make off

C 네모 안에서 알맞은 말을 골라 문장을 완성하시오.

01 The runner built / set a world record in the marathon.

02 The charity plans to run / set a campaign to promote their fundraising events.

D 다음 밑줄 친 부분의 영어 뜻풀이로 알맞은 것을 보기 에서 골라 기호를 쓰시오.

> 보기   ⓐ to begin an important activity
> ⓑ to promise your time, effort, or money to something or someone
> ⓒ without using artificial chemicals when growing plants for food

01 My grandparents sell their delicious organic jam at the local market every weekend. (   )

02 I was really excited when I filled out the form to launch the campaign. (   )

03 When the first investor committed to supporting us, I almost jumped for joy. (   )

교과서 핵심 대화문

M Excuse me. Do you need help?

W I think I lost my cell phone.
        (that)

M You can use mine to call your phone.
                    ~하기 위해 (목적을 나타내는 to부정사)

W Thank you. ... Nobody is answering it.

M I think you should check with lost and found.
                                    분실물 보관소

W **I agree with you.** Can you tell me where it is?
    동의하는 표현   간접의문문 (「의문사+주어+동사」의 어순)

M It is near the information center.

W Oh, is it between the roller coaster and the gift shop?
            between A and B: A와 B 사이에

M Yes. That's right.

≪ M: 실례합니다. 도움이 필요하신가요?

W: 제 휴대전화를 잃어버린 것 같아요.

M: 당신 전화기에 전화를 걸기 위해 제 전화기를 이용하실 수 있어요.

W: 감사합니다. … 아무도 전화를 받지 않네요.

M: 제 생각에는 분실물 보관소에 확인 해 보셔야겠어요.

W: 저도 동의해요. 그곳이 어디에 있는 지 알려주시겠어요?

M: 안내소 인근에 있어요.

W: 롤러코스터와 기념품 가게 사이에 있나요?

M: 네, 맞아요.

Study Point ❦

I agree with you.는 '나도 동의해.'라는 뜻으로, 상대의 의견에 동의하거나 공감을 나타내는 표현이다.

More Expressions ❦

동의하거나 동의 여부를 묻는 표현

상대의 의견에 동의하거나 공감할 때에는 That's right. 또는 That's a good idea.라고 말한다. 상대의 동의를 구할 때에는 Do you agree with me?라고 묻는다. 참고로, 상대의 의견에 동의하지 않을 때에는 I don't think so. 또는 I don't agree with you.라고 말한다.

· A We should reduce meat consumption for the environment.
    우리는 환경을 위해 육류 소비를 줄여야 해.

B **That's right.** It can help fight the climate crisis.
    네 말이 맞아. 그것은 기후 위기와 싸우는 데 도움이 돼.

· A I think everybody must be able to use their cell phones during class. **Do you agree with me?**
    나는 수업 시간에 모두가 휴대전화를 사용할 수 있어야 한다고 생각해. 내 의견에 동의하니?

B I don't agree with you. 나는 동의하지 않아.

Check-up ❦

다음 대화의 빈칸에 들어갈 말로 어색한 것은?

> A I think we can help others in our everyday lives.
>
> B _____ We can help others even when we go into a building.

ⓐ That's right.   ⓑ I agree with you.   ⓒ I don't think so.

Function 2 제안·권유하기

G Hey, Michael! The community center is looking for <u>volunteers to teach</u>

<u>children</u>.
형용사적 용법의 to부정사 (명사 수식)

B <u>Teaching children</u> <u>sounds</u> fun.
주어로 쓰인 동명사   이때 동사는 단수 (sounds)

G **How about** volunteering with me? It would be a great opportunity.
How about + 동명사?: ~하는 게 어때?

B Okay. What do you want to teach?

G Painting, of course. You know I love to paint.
(that)   명사적 용법의 to부정사 (love의 목적어)

B Hmm... I don't know <u>what I can teach</u>, though.
목적어로 쓰인 간접의문문 (의문사 + 주어 + 동사)

G You can <u>teach basketball to the children</u>. You're good at <u>it</u>.
= teach the children basketball   = basketball

B You're right! I'll do that.

≪ G: Michael! 주민센터에서 어린이들을 가르칠 자원봉사자를 찾고 있어.

B: 아이들을 가르치는 건 재미있겠다.

G: 나와 함께 자원봉사하는 거 어때? 좋은 기회가 될 거야.

B: 좋아. 너는 뭘 가르치고 싶어?

G: 물론 그림 그리기지. 내가 그림 그리기 좋아하는 거 알잖니.

B: 음, 그런데 나는 뭘 가르칠 수 있는지 잘 모르겠어.

G: 너는 아이들에게 농구를 가르칠 수 있어. 너 농구 잘하잖아.

B: 네 말이 맞네. 그걸 해야겠어.

Study Point ❧

How about ~?은 '~ 하는 게 어때?'라는 의미로, 상대방에게 제안이나 권유할 때 쓰는 표현이다.

More Expressions ❧

제안이나 권유하는 표현

상대방에게 제안이나 권유할 때는 Why don't we/you ~? 또는 I suggest (that) ~.라고 말한다. 제안이나 권유에 답하는 표현으로는, 제안을 수용할 때 (That) sounds good. 또는 (That's) a good idea.라고 말하고, 거절할 때 I'm afraid I can't.라고 말하며 보통 거절의 이유를 덧붙인다.

· A **Why don't we** go the ball park this Saturday?
이번주 토요일에 야구장에 가는 게 어때?

B **I'm afraid I can't**. I have to watch a movie for the science project.
어려울 것 같아. 나는 과학 프로젝트로 영화를 봐야 해.

· A **I suggest that** we create a website to promote our product.
웹사이트를 개설해 우리 제품을 홍보할 것을 제안합니다.

B **That's a good idea**. 그거 좋은 생각이다.

Check-up ❧

다음 대화에서 밑줄 친 말의 의도로 가장 알맞은 것은?

A There is no traffic lights at the crosswalk. We need to do something about it.

B <u>How about asking the government to install traffic lights?</u>

A Sounds great.

ⓐ 설득하기   ⓑ 제안하기   ⓒ 동의하기

교과서 기타 대화문

Watch and Communicate A. Watch

G Good morning, students of Happyville High School! My name is Lucy, and I'm in grade 11. Today, I want to ❶ <u>tell everyone an important message</u>. We need to improve our school's facilities for ❷ <u>people with disabilities</u>. This is important ❸ <u>so that</u> everyone can reach all the areas in our school. So, what can we do? First, we ❹ <u>need to</u> install an elevator for people with physical disabilities. This will ❺ <u>make all areas of our school easier</u> ❻ <u>to access</u>. Second, all signs should be improved for blind people. Signs with voice guidance would be especially helpful. Lastly, we should replace all blackboards with greenboards. They ❼ <u>make words easier to see</u>, especially for people ❽ <u>with low vision</u>. Let's work together ❾ <u>to make</u> these changes. With your help, Happyville High School can become a welcoming place for everyone!

G: 좋은 아침입니다. Happyville 고등학교 학생 여러분! 저는 11학년 Lucy입니다. 오늘, 저는 모두에게 중요한 메시지를 전하고 싶습니다. 우리는 장애인들을 위해 학교 시설을 개선할 필요가 있습니다. 이것은 모든 사람이 우리 학교의 모든 영역에 도달할 수 있게 하기 위해 중요합니다. 그래서, 우리가 무엇을 할 수 있을까요? 첫 번째로, 우리는 신체장애가 있는 사람들을 위해 엘리베이터를 설치할 필요가 있습니다. 이는 우리 학교의 모든 공간에 접근하기 쉽게 만들 것입니다. 두 번째, 시각장애인들을 위해 모든 표지판이 개선되어야 합니다. 음성 안내가 동반된 표지판은 특히 도움이 될 것입니다. 마지막으로, 우리는 모든 흑색 칠판을 녹색 칠판으로 바꿔야 합니다. 녹색 칠판은 특히 저시력을 가진 사람들이 글자를 더 쉽게 볼 수 있게 합니다. 이런 변화를 만들기 위해 함께 노력합시다. 여러분들의 도움이 있다면, Happyville 고등학교는 모두를 위한 안락한 공간이 될 것입니다!

❶ tell + 간접목적어 + 직접목적어: ~에게 …을 말하다 ❷ 장애를 가진 사람들 (= the disabled) ❸ so that: ~할 수 있도록 ❹ need to: ~해야 한다 (must보다는 약한 의무를 나타내는 조동사) ❺ make + 목적어(all areas of our school) + 목적격 보어(easier to access) ❻ to access: 부사적 용법의 to부정사 (앞에 있는 easier 수식) ❼ make + 목적어(words) + 목적격 보어(easier to see) ❽ with low vision: 낮은 시력을 가진 ❾ to make: 부사적 용법의 to부정사 (목적)

Q1 Lucy says Happyville High School should install facilities such as a(n) _____, signs with voice guidance, and greenboards.

Lesson Review A

G Brian, is everything okay?

B Well, I'm a little upset. I just can't believe this news story from the local animal shelter.

G What is it?

B According to the shelter, many pets ❶ <u>are abandoned</u> by their owners when ❷ <u>they</u> go on vacation.

G That's terrible.

B I don't understand those people. Pets are not toys.

G ❸ <u>I agree with you.</u> Didn't you adopt your dog from the shelter?

B ❹ <u>I did.</u> After that, several of my friends also adopted pets.

G ❺ <u>Look on the bright side.</u> You're already making a difference.

B You're right. Maybe everyone's small actions can ❻ <u>help solve</u> the problem someday.

G: Brian, 괜찮니?
B: 음, 난 조금 화가 나. 지역 동물 보호소에서의 소식을 믿을 수가 없어.
G: 무슨 소식인데?
B: 보호소에 따르면, 많은 동물들이 주인이 휴가를 떠날 때 버려진대.
G: 끔찍해.
B: 그런 사람들을 이해할 수가 없어. 반려동물은 장난감이 아니야.

G: 나도 그렇게 생각해. 네 개를 보호소에서 입양하지 않았니?
B: 그랬지. 그 후로 내 친구 여러 명도 반려동물을 입양했어.
G: 긍정적으로 생각해. 너는 이미 변화를 만들고 있어.
B: 네 말이 맞아. 아마도 모두의 작은 행동이 언젠가는 문제를 해결하는 데 도움이 될 거야.

❶ be abandoned: 유기되다 ❷ they = the owners ❸ I agree with you.: 동의를 나타내는 표현 ❹ I did. = I adopted my dog from the shelter. ❺ Look on the bright side.: 긍정적인 면을 봐. ❻ help + (to) 동사원형: ~하는 것을 돕다

Q2 Brian's friends adopted their pets from the animal shelter. (T / F)

교고서 핵심 대화문 익히기

01 다음 대화의 빈칸에 들어갈 말로 가장 알맞은 것을 고르시오.

> M Excuse me. Do you need help?
> W I think I lost my cell phone.
> M You can use mine to call your phone.
> W Thank you. ... Nobody is answering it.
> M I think you should _____.
> W I agree with you. Can you tell me where it is?
> M It is near the information center.
> W Oh, is it between the roller coaster and the gift shop?
> M Yes. That's right.

① borrow a phone   ② call your phone again

③ answer the phone immediately   ④ check with lost and found

⑤ buy a new phone

02 자연스러운 대화가 되도록 문장을 순서대로 배열하시오.

> G Hey, Michael! The community center is looking for volunteers to teach children.
> B Teaching children sounds fun.
> G How about volunteering with me? It would be a great opportunity.
>
> (   ) You're right! I'll do that.
> (   ) What do you want to teach?
> (   ) Hmm... I don't know what I can teach, though.
> (   ) Painting, of course. You know I love to paint.
> (   ) You can teach basketball to the children. You're good at it.

03 다음 대화의 내용과 일치하도록 빈칸에 알맞은 말을 쓰시오.

> G Brian, is everything okay?
> B Well, I'm a little upset. I just can't believe this news story from the local animal shelter.
> G What is it?
> B According to the shelter, many pets are abandoned by their owners when they go on vacation.
> G That's terrible.
> B I don't understand those people. Pets are not toys.
> G I agree with you. Didn't you adopt your dog from the shelter?
> B I did. After that, several of my friends also adopted pets.
> G Look on the bright side. You're already making a difference.
> B You're right. Maybe everyone's small actions can help solve the problem someday.

→ Brian _____ his dog from the local animal _____.

교과서 핵심 문법

POINT 1 전치사 + 동명사

예제 We are looking forward **to watching** the baseball game.
전치사 + 동명사
우리는 야구 경기 보기를 고대하고 있다.

교과서 We could reward the investors **by sending** them jars of organic jam.
전치사 + 동명사
우리는 투자자들에게 유기농 잼 병을 보냄으로써 그들에게 보상을 할 수 있었다.

▶ 전치사 뒤에 오는 목적어는 명사나 대명사 형태가 되어야 한다. 따라서 동사(구)가 전치사의 목적어로 오기 위해서는 동명사 형태로 쓰여야 한다.

Study Point 🏅

1 동명사의 역할

동명사는 문장에서 주어, 보어, 동사의 목적어, 전치사의 목적어 역할을 한다.

· **Taking pictures** is not allowed in this art gallery. 이 미술관에서는 사진을 찍는 것이 허락되지 않는다.
· One of the best ways to stay healthy is **getting enough sleep**.
건강을 유지하는 가장 좋은 방법 중 하나는 충분한 수면을 취하는 것이다.
· I'm considering **taking a trip to Busan** during summer vacation.
나는 여름방학에 부산으로 여행 가는 것을 고려 중이다.
· The sisters were interested in **reading sci-fi novels**. 그 자매는 공상과학 소설을 읽는 데 흥미가 있었다.
→ 전치사의 목적어

2 before/after + 동명사

before와 after는 전치사로도 쓰이고 접속사로도 쓰이는 말이다. 전치사로 쓰일 때는 「before/after + 동명사」 형태로 나타내고, 접속사로 쓰일 때는 「before/after + 주어 + 동사」의 형태로 나타낸다.

· **Before beginning** your campaign, be sure to plan all the production details. [전치사 + 동명사]
= Before you begin your campaign, be sure to plan all the production details. [접속사 + 절]
당신의 캠페인을 시작하기 전, 모든 생산 세부 사항을 계획해라.

3 동명사 vs. 현재분사

· **Taking a walk** in the park is part of Mr. Powell's morning routine. [동명사]
공원에서 산책하는 것은 Powell씨의 아침 일과 중 일부이다.
· Mr. Powell is **taking a walk** in the park with his wife. [현재분사]
Powell씨가 부인과 같이 공원에서 산책하고 있다.

Q 다음 네모 안에서 어법상 알맞은 것을 고르시오.

1 Timmy is afraid of make / making close friends.

2 Work / Working out regularly can help relieve your stress.

3 Before travel / traveling to Spain, she learned Spanish.

Check-up ✿

01 괄호 안의 동사를 알맞은 형태로 바꿔 빈칸에 넣으시오.

(1) Without _____ to anyone, Tony sat in silence. (talk)

(2) _____ to music is a good way to relax. (listen)

(3) Jessie is thinking about _____ for the manager position. (apply)

(4) You should avoid _____ high-fat foods. (eat)

(5) Thank you for _____ care of my dog. (take)

02 다음 문장과 같은 의미가 되도록 동명사를 사용하여 문장을 바꿔 쓰시오.

(1) Before you leave for the airport, make sure you bring your passport.

→ _____ for the airport, make sure you bring your passport.

(2) Every morning, Emily has breakfast after she does yoga.

→ Every morning, Emily has breakfast _____.

03 다음 문장에서 어법상 <u>어색한</u> 부분을 찾아 바르게 고쳐 쓰시오.

(1) Doing jigsaw puzzles are one of my favorite hobbies.

→ Doing jigsaw puzzles _____.

(2) Julie is interested in learn a new language.

→ Julie _____.

(3) They look forward to move to a new city.

→ They look _____.

(4) After we beginning our project, we must make every effort to finish it.

→ _____, we must make every effort to finish it.

(5) The orchestra members were proud of to perform at Carnegie Hall.

→ The orchestra members _____ at Carnegie Hall.

(POINT 2) 목적격 보어로 쓰이는 to부정사

예제   My friends **expect** me **to join** their trip to Busan.
       　　　　　동사　　　　+to부정사 (목적격 보어)
       나의 친구들은 내가 그들의 부산 여행에 함께 하기를 기대하고 있다.

교과서 This video **allows** investors **to learn** about your product.
       　　　　동사　　　　　　　　+to부정사 (목적격 보어)
       이 비디오는 투자자들이 당신의 제품에 관해 배울 수 있게 한다.

▶ to부정사가 목적격 보어로 쓰여 「동사＋목적어＋목적격 보어」 구문을 이룬다.

Study Point 🍎

1 동사＋목적어＋to부정사

「주어＋동사＋목적어＋목적격 보어」 형태의 5형식 문장에서 ask, want, allow 등의 동사가 쓰이면 목적격 보어로 to부정사가 온다.

> 「동사＋목적어＋to부정사」 구문에 자주 쓰이는 동사
> allow(허락하다), advise(충고하다), ask(요청하다), cause(야기하다), encourage(독려하다), persuade(설득하다), enable(가능하게 하다), want(원하다), expect(기대하다), tell(말하다), order(지시하다)

· The manager **wanted** her staff **to be** nice to the customers. 매니저는 직원이 고객들에게 친절하기를 원했다.
· He tried to **encourage** his students **to challenge** themselves. 그는 자신의 학생들에게 도전하라고 격려하려 애썼다.
· We never **expected** our soccer team **to win** the championship. 우리는 우리 축구팀이 우승할 거라 전혀 기대하지 않았다.
· The support from her friends **enabled** her **to focus** on her work. 친구들의 지지는 그녀가 작업에 집중할 수 있도록 했다.

2 지각동사/사역동사＋목적어＋동사원형

지각동사(see, watch, hear, feel 등)와 사역동사(let, make, have) 뒤에는 목적격 보어로 동사원형(원형부정사)을 쓴다.

· She **watched** her son **cross** the street to the school. 그녀는 아들이 길을 건너 학교에 가는 것을 지켜보았다.
　　　　　　　　　　지각동사의 목적격 보어로는 현재분사(crossing)를 쓸 수도 있다.
· Everybody in the town **heard** the wind **blow** hard last night.
마을 사람들 모두가 지난밤 바람이 세차게 부는 것을 들었다.
· Ms. Swift didn't **let** her students **contact** her after 9:00 p.m.
Swift 선생님은 학생들이 밤 9시 이후에는 그녀에게 연락하지 못하게 했다.
· Having an ice cream cone always **makes** me **feel** happy. 아이스크림콘을 먹는 것은 항상 나를 행복하게 만든다.
· My friends **helped** me **(to) find** my cell phone. 내 친구들이 내 휴대전화 찾는 것을 도와주었다.
　　　　　　　　　　help는 준사역동사로, 목적격 보어 자리에 동사원형이나 to부정사 모두 올 수 있다.

Q 다음 네모 안에서 어법상 알맞은 것을 고르시오.

1 My brother asked me help / to help solve the math problem.

2 They saw their kids perform / to perform a wonderful dance on the stage.

3 The coach persuaded the team believe / to believe in their own abilities.

Check-up ♉

01 괄호 안의 동사를 알맞은 형태로 바꿔 빈칸에 넣으시오.

(1) I expect the company _____ my proposal. (accept)

(2) He heard his dad _____ his name on the street. (call)

(3) The vet advised her _____ her dog twice a day. (walk)

(4) The test results made Susie _____ frustrated. (feel)

(5) Her love of books inspired her _____ a librarian. (be)

02 우리말과 일치하도록 괄호 안에 주어진 말을 이용하여 문장을 완성하시오.

(1) 너는 Steve가 우리에게 손을 흔드는 게 보이니? (wave)

→ Can you see Steve _____ at us?

(2) 그의 부주의가 인기 영화배우로서의 그의 명성을 잃게 했다. (cause, lose)

→ His carelessness _____ as a movie star.

(3) 많은 사람들은 지난밤 땅이 흔들리는 것을 느꼈다. (feel, shake)

→ Many people _____ last night.

(4) 그 앱은 내가 영어를 좀 더 유창하게 말하도록 도와주었다. (help, speak)

→ The app _____ more fluently.

(5) 그 NGO는 사람들에게 환경을 위해 에너지를 절약하라고 설득했다. (persuade, save)

→ The NGO _____ for the environment.

03 괄호 안의 동사를 알맞은 형태로 바꿔 빈칸에 넣으시오.

(1) • He had his twin daughters _____ their room every day. (clean)

• He got his twin daughters _____ their room every day. (clean)

(2) • My parents won't allow me _____ alone. (travel)

• My parents won't let me _____ alone. (travel)

(3) • His joke made everyone in the room _____ into laughter. (burst)

• His joke caused everyone in the room _____ into laughter. (burst)

Turning Ideas into Reality
생각을 현실로 바꾸기

01 My grandparents sell their delicious organic jam at the local market every weekend.
주말마다

나의 조부모님은 주말마다 지역 시장에서 맛있는 유기농 잼을 판매하신다.

02 I went to help them last weekend.
그들을 돕기 위해 (목적을 나타내는 to부정사)

나는 지난 주말에 그들을 돕기 위해 갔다.

03 However, they had already sold all of their jam!
과거완료 (대과거)

그러나 조부모님은 잼을 이미 모두 다 팔았다!

04 They didn't have enough strawberries to make any more jam.
enough ~ to-V: …하기에 충분한 ~
to부정사의 형용사적 용법

그들에게는 더 이상의 잼을 만들 충분한 딸기가 없었다.

05 That evening, I sat by the window and stared out at the empty field [behind their house].
전치사 (~ 옆에)   stare at: ~을 응시하다   전치사구

그날 저녁, 나는 창가에 앉아 조부모님 집 뒤쪽의 빈 들판을 바라보았다.

06 Suddenly, I got an idea.

갑자기, 나에게 생각이 떠올랐다.

07 The field would be the perfect place for a larger greenhouse.
전치사 (~을 위한)

그 들판은 더 큰 온실을 위한 완벽한 장소가 될 것이었다.

08 Then they could grow more strawberries!
= my grandparents

그러면 그들은 더 많은 딸기를 기를 수 있을 것이다!

09 I immediately started searching for a way, and I found the perfect solution.
started의 목적어로 쓰인 동명사 (= to search)

나는 즉시 방법을 찾기 시작했고 완벽한 해결책을 찾았다.

10 I would start a crowdfunding campaign!

나는 크라우드펀딩 캠페인을 시작할 것이다!

What Is Crowdfunding?
크라우드펀딩은 무엇인가?

11 Crowdfunding is a way of [raising money for a product, company, or charity].
전치사 of의 목적어로 쓰인 동명사구

크라우드펀딩은 제품, 회사, 자선 단체를 위해 돈을 모금하는 방식이다.

12 These days, people can use crowdfunding websites to collect money.
오늘날   to부정사의 부사적 용법 (목적)

오늘날, 사람들은 돈을 모금하기 위해 크라우드펀딩 사이트를 이용할 수 있다.

13 Crowdfunding is especially advantageous for individuals or small companies [that can't attract big investors].
관계대명사절

크라우드펀딩은 큰 투자자를 끌어들일 수 없는 개인이나 작은 회사에 특히 유리하다.

14 If the campaign is successful, the investors receive direct rewards for their contribution.
조건의 접속사 (~하면)

캠페인이 성공적이면 투자자들은 그들의 기여에 직접적인 보상을 받는다.

15 My grandparents were thrilled when I told them my idea.
아주 흥분했다   tell + 간접목적어 + 직접목적어

내 생각을 나의 조부모님께 말씀드렸을 때 그들은 아주 기뻐하셨다.

16 비교급 강조
With the help of investors, we could build a large greenhouse and grow a lot more strawberries.
병렬 연결

투자자들의 도움으로 우리는 큰 온실을 짓고 훨씬 더 많은 딸기를 재배할 수 있을 것이었다.

17 = the investors
Moreover, we could reward the investors for their help by [sending them jars of organic jam]!
게다가   by의 목적어로 쓰인 동명사구   send + 간접목적어 + 직접목적어

게다가 우리는 투자자들에게 유기농 잼 병을 보냄으로써 그들의 도움에 대해 그들에게 보상을 할 수 있을 것이었다!

18 With this plan in mind, the next step was [to figure out the details].
with + 목적어 + 전치사구: ~을 … 한 채로   to부정사의 명사적 용법 (보어)

이 계획을 염두에 두고, 그 다음 단계는 세부 사항을 생각해내는 것이었다.

Campaign Details
캠페인 세부 사항

19 Before [beginning your campaign], be sure to plan all the production details.

before의 목적어로 쓰인 동명사구

전치사 (~ 전에)   be sure to -V: 반드시 ~하라

당신의 캠페인을 시작하기 전에 반드시 생산 세부 사항을 계획해라.

20 How many products will you make?

how many + 셀 수 있는 명사: 얼마나 많은 ~

얼마나 많은 제품을 만들 것인가?

21 How long will it take [to make the product]?

it take + 시간 + to부정사: ~하는 데에 (시간)이 걸리다

그 제품을 만드는 데 얼마나 오래 걸릴 것인가?

22 This planning is important because your potential investors will want to see a clear schedule.

접속사 (~ 때문에)

이 계획은 중요한데, 당신의 잠재적인 투자자들이 명확한 일정을 보고 싶어 할 것이기 때문이다.

23 Once your plan is complete, remember to set your funding goal.

접속사 (일단 ~하면)   remember + to-V: ~할 것을 기억하다

일단 당신의 계획이 완료되면 재정 목표를 세울 것을 기억해라.

24 It should be enough to complete the project and fulfill the rewards for the investors.

= Your funding goal   병렬 연결

enough to-V: ~할 만큼 충분한   (to)

재정 목표는 프로젝트를 완료하고 투자자들을 위한 보상을 충족시킬 정도로 충분해야 한다.

25 Consider all the necessary costs before [deciding on the amount].

before의 목적어로 쓰인 동명사구

명령문 (~해라)

총액을 결정하기 전에 모든 필요한 비용을 고려해라.

26 After [doing some calculations], we decided on an 8-by-12-foot greenhouse.

after의 목적어로 쓰인 동명사구

전치사 (~ 후에)   ~으로 정하다   가로 8피트, 세로 12피트

몇 가지 계산을 한 이후에 우리는 가로 8피트에 세로 12피트 크기의 온실로 결정했다.

27 We thought [it would cost approximately $4,000].

명사절 (thought의 목적어)

(that)

우리는 그것이 대략 4,000달러의 비용이 들 것으로 생각했다.

28 Once it was built, we could fill it with strawberry plants and expect a harvest within about four months.

접속사 (일단 ~하면)   병렬 연결

fill A with B: A를 B로 채우다   전치사 (~ 이내에)

그것이 지어진다면 우리는 그것을 딸기 모종으로 채우고 약 4개월 이내에 수확을 기대할 수 있을 것이었다.

29

turn A into B: A를 B로 바꾸다

Then it would take a few weeks [to turn the strawberries into delicious jam].

it take + 시간 + to부정사: ~하는 데에 (시간)이 걸리다

그러고 나서 딸기를 맛있는 잼으로 만드는 데 몇 주가 걸릴 것이었다.

30

We decided [to set our funding goal at $5,000] to cover all the costs.

to부정사의 명사적 용법 (목적어)   to부정사의 부사적 용법 (목적)

우리는 모든 비용을 감당하기 위해 5,000달러로 재정 목표를 세우기로 결정했다.

31

Also, we planned [to run the campaign for three months].

to부정사의 명사적 용법 (목적어)

또한 우리는 캠페인을 3개월 동안 운영하기로 계획했다.

32

I was really excited when I filled out the form [to launch the campaign].

to부정사의 부사적 용법 (목적)

나는 캠페인을 시작하기 위해 양식을 작성할 때 정말 신이 났다.

33

In less than a week, our application was accepted and funding began!

수동태 (be동사 + p.p.)

일주일이 안 되어 우리의 지원서가 받아들여졌고 모금이 시작되었다!

Campaign Promotion and Communication
캠페인 홍보와 의사소통

34

For a successful crowdfunding campaign, [promoting it] is necessary.

동명사 주어   단수 동사

성공적인 크라우드펀딩 캠페인을 위해 그것을 홍보하는 것이 필요하다.

35

You should consider [making a video].

동명사구 (consider의 목적어)

당신은 영상을 만드는 것을 고려해야 한다.

36

병렬 연결

This allows investors to get to know you and learn about your product.

allow + 목적어 + to부정사: ~가 …하게 하다   (to)

이것은 투자자들이 당신에 대해 알게 하고 당신의 제품에 대해 배울 수 있게 한다.

37

In the video, describe your situation clearly and show your product.

병렬 연결

영상에서는 당신의 상황을 명확히 설명하고 당신의 제품을 보여 주어라.

38

You also need to express [how important the product is to you].
간접의문 (express의 목적어): 「주어 + 동사」 어순

당신은 또한 그 제품이 당신에게 얼마나 중요한지 표현해야 한다.

39

Don't forget to include a direct request for support at the end.
forget + to-V: (미래에) ~할 것을 잊다

마지막에는 지원에 대한 직접적인 요청을 포함하는 것을 잊지 마라.

40

가주어   진주어

During a campaign, it is important [to send investors updates every week].
전치사 (~ 동안)   send + 간접목적어 + 직접목적어

캠페인를 하는 동안, 매주 투자사들에게 최신 정보를 보내는 것은 중요하다.

41

Through the update, the investors will be able to track the progress of the campaign.
전치사 (~을 통해)   be able to-V: ~할 수 있다

최신 정보를 통해 투자자들은 캠페인의 진행 상황을 따라갈 수 있을 것이다.

42

After our application was accepted, I was eager to make a good first impression with our investors.
접속사 (~한 후에)   수동태   be eager to-V: ~하기를 열망하다   첫인상

우리의 지원서가 받아들여진 후 나는 우리의 투자자들에게 좋은 첫인상을 남기고 싶었다.

43

[To achieve this], I made a video [about my grandparents and their jam].
to부정사의 부사적 용법 (목적)   전치사구

이를 성취하기 위해서 나는 조부모님과 그들의 잼에 관한 영상을 만들었다.

44

without의 목적어로 쓰인 동명사구

In the video, I highlighted [how the strawberries were grown without using chemicals].
간접의문 (highlighted의 목적어)

영상에서 나는 딸기가 어떻게 화학 약품을 사용하지 않고 재배되는지를 강조했다.

45

I also included clips [of my grandparents].
전치사구

나는 또한 조부모님의 짧은 영상을 포함시켰다.

46

In the clips, they were making the jam with all-natural ingredients.
과거진행형

그 영상에서 조부모님은 모두 천연으로 된 재료로 잼을 만들고 계셨다.

병렬 연결

47

Finally, I explained [where I wanted to put the new greenhouse] and asked for support.
간접의문 (explained의 목적어)   ~을 요청하다

마지막으로 나는 새 온실을 어디에 짓고 싶은지 설명했고 지원을 요청했다.

48   After some editing, I posted the video [on many social media sites].
전치사구 (부사구)

약간의 편집을 거친 후, 나는 영상을 여러 소셜 미디어 사이트에 게시했다.

49   to부정사의 의미상 주어

It didn't take long [for word of our campaign to spread].
it take + 시간 + to부정사: ~하는 데에 (시간)이 걸리다

우리 캠페인에 대한 소식이 퍼지는 데는 오래 걸리지 않았다.

50   [Funding for our campaign] started slowly.
동명사구 (주어)

우리 캠페인을 위한 모금은 느리게 시작했다.

51   to의 목적어로 쓰인 동명사구

When the first investor committed to supporting us, I almost jumped for joy.

첫 투자자가 우리를 지원할 것을 약속했을 때 나는 기뻐서 거의 뛰어올랐다.

52   Now, after six weeks, we have raised almost $2,500.
현재완료 (완료)

이제 6주가 지났고 우리는 거의 2,500달러를 모았다.

53   It seems like we might make our funding goal!
~인 것 같다   조동사 (불확실한 추측)

우리는 아마 재정 목표를 달성할 수도 있을 것 같다!

❖ 다음 빈칸에 알맞은 말을 쓰시오.

01   My grandparents sell their delicious organic jam _____.
      나의 조부모님은 주말마다 지역 시장에서 맛있는 유기농 잼을 판매하신다.

02   I went _____ last weekend.
      나는 지난 주말에 그들을 돕기 위해 갔다.

03   However, they _____ all of their jam!
      그러나 조부모님은 잼을 이미 모두 다 팔았다!

04   They didn't have enough strawberries _____.
      그들에게는 더 이상의 잼을 만들 충분한 딸기가 없었다.

05   That evening, I sat by the window and _____ behind their house.
      그날 저녁, 나는 창가에 앉아 조부모님 집 뒤쪽의 빈 들판을 바라보았다.

06   The field would be _____ a larger greenhouse.
      그 들판은 더 큰 온실을 위한 완벽한 장소가 될 것이었다.

07   Then they _____ strawberries!
      그러면 그들은 더 많은 딸기를 기를 수 있을 것이다!

08   I immediately started _____, and I found the perfect solution.
      나는 즉시 방법을 찾기 시작했고 완벽한 해결책을 찾았다.

09   Crowdfunding is _____ for a product, company, or charity.
      크라우드펀딩은 제품, 회사, 자선 단체를 위해 돈을 모금하는 방식이다.

10   These days, people can use crowdfunding websites _____.
      오늘날, 사람들은 돈을 모금하기 위해 크라우드펀딩 사이트를 이용할 수 있다.

11   Crowdfunding is _____ for individuals or small companies that
      _____.
      크라우드펀딩은 큰 투자자를 끌어들일 수 없는 개인이나 작은 회사에 특히 유리하다.

12   If the campaign is successful, the investors receive _____.
      캠페인이 성공적이면 투자자들은 그들의 기여에 직접적인 보상을 받는다.

13   My grandparents _____ when I told them my idea.
      내 생각을 나의 조부모님께 말씀드렸을 때 그들은 아주 기뻐하셨다.

14   _____, we could build a large greenhouse and grow
      _____.
      투자자들의 도움으로 우리는 큰 온실을 짓고 훨씬 더 많은 딸기를 재배할 수 있을 것이었다.

15   Moreover, we could reward the investors for their help _____!
      게다가 우리는 투자자들에게 유기농 잼 병을 보냄으로써 그들의 도움에 대해 그들에게 보상을 할 수 있을 것이었다!

16 With _____ , the next step was _____ the details.

이 계획을 염두에 두고, 그 다음 단계는 세부 사항을 생각해내는 것이었다.

17 _____ , be sure to plan all the production details.

당신의 캠페인을 시작하기 전에 반드시 생산 세부 사항을 계획해라.

18 How long _____ the product?

그 제품을 만드는 데 얼마나 오래 걸릴 것인가?

19 This planning is important _____ will want to see a clear schedule.

이 계획은 중요한데, 당신의 잠재적인 투자자들이 명확한 일정을 보고 싶어 할 것이기 때문이다.

20 _____ , remember to set your funding goal.

일단 당신의 계획이 완료되면 재정 목표를 세울 것을 기억해라.

21 It should be _____ the project and fulfill the rewards for the investors.

재정 목표는 프로젝트를 완료하고 투자자들을 위한 보상을 충족시킬 정도로 충분해야 한다.

22 Consider all the necessary costs before _____ .

총액을 결정하기 전에 모든 필요한 비용을 고려해라.

23 After doing some calculations, we decided on an _____ greenhouse.

몇 가지 계산을 한 이후에 우리는 가로 8피트에 세로 12피트 크기의 온실로 결정했다.

24 We thought it would _____ $4,000.

우리는 그것이 대략 4,000달러의 비용이 들 것으로 생각했다.

25 _____ , we could fill it with strawberry plants and expect a harvest _____ .

그것이 지어진다면 우리는 그것을 딸기 모종으로 채우고 약 4개월 이내에 수확을 기대할 수 있을 것이었다.

26 Then it would take a few weeks _____ delicious jam.

그리고 나서 딸기를 맛있는 잼으로 만드는 데 몇 주가 걸릴 것이었다.

27 We decided to set our funding goal at $5,000 _____ .

우리는 모든 비용을 감당하기 위해 5,000달러로 재정 목표를 세우기로 결정했다.

28 Also, we _____ for three months.

또한 우리는 캠페인을 3개월 동안 운영하기로 계획했다.

29 I was really excited _____ to launch the campaign.

나는 캠페인을 시작하기 위해 양식을 작성할 때 정말 신이 났다.

30 _____ , our application was accepted and funding began!

일주일이 안 되어 우리의 지원서가 받아들여졌고 모금이 시작되었다!

31 _____ campaign, promoting it is necessary.

성공적인 크라우드펀딩 캠페인을 위해 그것을 홍보하는 것이 필요하다.

32 You should _____ a video.

당신은 영상을 만드는 것을 고려해야 한다.

33 This allows investors _____ and learn about your product.

이것은 투자자들이 당신에 대해 알게 하고 당신의 제품에 대해 배울 수 있게 한다.

34 In the video, _____ clearly and show your product.

영상에서는 당신의 상황을 명확히 설명하고 당신의 제품을 보여 주어라.

35 You also need to express _____ to you.

당신은 또한 그 제품이 당신에게 얼마나 중요한지 표현해야 한다.

36 _____ a direct request for support at the end.

마지막에는 지원에 대한 직접적인 요청을 포함하는 것을 잊지 마라.

37 During a campaign, _____ investors updates every week.

캠페인을 하는 동안, 매주 투자자들에게 최신 정보를 보내는 것은 중요하다.

38 Through the update, the investors _____ the progress of the campaign.

최신 정보를 통해 투자자들은 캠페인의 진행 상황을 따라갈 수 있을 것이다.

39 After our application was accepted, _____ a good first impression with our investors.

우리의 지원서가 받아들여진 후 나는 우리의 투자자들에게 좋은 첫인상을 남기고 싶었다.

40 _____, I made a video about my grandparents and their jam.

이를 성취하기 위해서 나는 조부모님과 그들의 잼에 관한 영상을 만들었다.

41 In the video, I highlighted _____ without using chemicals.

영상에서 나는 딸기가 어떻게 화학 약품을 사용하지 않고 재배되는지를 강조했다.

42 In the clips, they were making the jam _____.

그 영상에서 조부모님은 모두 천연으로 된 재료로 잼을 만들고 계셨다.

43 Finally, I explained _____ the new greenhouse and asked for support.

마지막으로 나는 새 온실을 어디에 짓고 싶은지 설명했고 지원을 요청했다.

44 After some editing, I posted the video _____.

약간의 편집을 거친 후, 나는 영상을 여러 소셜 미디어 사이트에 게시했다.

45 It didn't take long _____ to spread.

우리 캠페인에 대한 소식이 퍼지는 데는 오래 걸리지 않았다.

46 When the first investor _____, I almost jumped for joy.

첫 투자자가 우리를 지원할 것을 약속했을 때 나는 기뻐서 거의 뛰어올랐다.

47 Now, after six weeks, _____ $2,500.

이제 6주가 지났고 우리는 거의 2,500달러를 모았다.

48 It _____ our funding goal!

우리는 아마 재정 목표를 달성할 수도 있을 것 같다!

교과서 본문 익히기 ❷ 옳은 어법·어휘 고르기

♣ 다음 네모 안에서 옳은 것을 고르시오.

01 My grandparents sell their delicious organic / natural jam at the local market every weekend.

02 I went to help them last / the last weekend.

03 However, they have / had already sold all of their jam!

04 They didn't have enough strawberries to make any many / more jam.

05 That evening, I sat by / on the window and stared out at / to the empty field behind their house.

06 The field would be the complete / perfect place for a larger greenhouse.

07 I immediately finished / started searching for a way, and I found the perfect solution.

08 Crowdfunding is a way of giving / raising money for a product, company, or charity.

09 These / Those days, people can use crowdfunding websites to collect money.

10 Crowdfunding is especially advantageous / disadvantageous for individuals or small companies that can / can't attract big investors.

11 If the campaign is successful, the investors receive direct forwards / rewards for their contribution.

12 My grandparents were thrilled / thrilling when I told them my idea.

13 With / Without the help of investors, we could build a large greenhouse and grow / grew a lot more strawberries.

14 Moreover, we could reward the investors for their help by / on sending them jars of organic jam!

15   With this plan in mind, next / the next step was to figure out the details.

16   Before beginning your campaign, be sure planning / to plan all the production details.

17   How long it will / will it take to make the product?

18   This planning is important because your able / potential investors will want to see a clear schedule.

19   Once your plan is complete, remember setting / to set your funding goal.

20   It should be enough to complete the project and fulfill / fulfilling the rewards for the investors.

21   Consider all the necessary costs / prices before deciding on the amount.

22   After doing some calculations, we decided on an 8-by-12- foot / feet greenhouse.

23   As / Once it was built, we could fill it with strawberry plants and expect a harvest for / within about four
      months.

24   Then it would take a few weeks turning / to turn the strawberries into delicious jam.

25   We decided to get / set our funding goal at $5,000 to cover all the costs.

26   Also, we planned to have / run the campaign for three months.

27   I was really excited / exciting when I filled out the form to lunch / launch the campaign.

28   In less than a week, our application was accepted / received and funding began!

29   You should consider making / to make a video.

30 This allows investors [get / to get] to know you and learn about your product.

31 In the video, [describe / describing] your situation clearly and show your product.

32 You also need to express [how / what] important the product is to you.

33 Don't forget [including / to include] a direct request for support at the end.

34 During a campaign, it is important to send investors [dates / updates] every week.

35 [Though / Through] the update, the investors will be able to [track / trick] the progress of the campaign.

36 After our application was [accepted / rejected], I was eager to make a good first [expression / impression] with our investors.

37 In the video, I highlighted [how / if] the strawberries were grown without using chemicals.

38 In the clips, they were making the jam with all-natural [chemicals / ingredients].

39 Finally, I explained where [I wanted / did I want] to put the new greenhouse and asked for support.

40 After some editing, I [posed / posted] the video on many social media sites.

41 It didn't take long [for / of] word of our campaign to spread.

42 When the first investor committed to [support / supporting] us, I almost jumped for joy.

43 Now, after six weeks, we have [risen / raised] almost $2,500.

44 It seems like we [might / should] make our funding goal!

♣ 다음 밑줄 친 부분을 바르게 고쳐 쓰시오.

01   My grandparents sell <u>his</u> delicious organic jam at the local market every <u>weekends</u>.

02   However, they had <u>sold already</u> all of their jam!

03   They didn't have enough strawberries <u>making</u> any more jam.

04   That evening, I sat by the window and <u>stare</u> out at the empty field behind their house.

05   The field would be the perfect place <u>to</u> a larger greenhouse.

06   I immediately started <u>searching</u> a way, and I found the perfect solution.

07   Crowdfunding is a way of <u>rising</u> money for a product, company, or charity.

08   These days, people can use crowdfunding websites to <u>collecting</u> money.

09   Crowdfunding is especially <u>advantage</u> for individuals or small companies <u>who</u> can't attract big investors.

10   If the campaign is successful, the investors <u>received</u> direct rewards for their contribution.

11   My grandparents were thrilled when I told <u>to them</u> my idea.

12   With the help of investors, we could build a large greenhouse and grow <u>very</u> more strawberries.

13   Moreover, we could reward the investors for their help <u>by send for them</u> jars of organic jam!

14   <u>By</u> this plan in mind, the next step was to <u>figure of</u> the details.

15   Before <u>begin</u> your campaign, be sure to plan all the production details.

16   How long <u>it will take</u> to make the product?

17　This planning is important <u>if</u> your potential investors will want to see a clear schedule.

18　Once your plan is complete, remember <u>setting</u> your funding goal.

19　It should be enough to complete the project and <u>fulfilled</u> the rewards for the investors.

20　Consider all the necessary costs <u>after</u> deciding on the amount.

21　After doing some calculations, we decided on an 8-<u>to</u>-12-foot greenhouse.

22　Once it was built, we could fill it <u>of</u> strawberry plants and expect a harvest <u>about within</u> four months.

23　Then it would take <u>few</u> weeks to turn the strawberries <u>of</u> delicious jam.

24　We decided to set our funding goal at $5,000 to <u>recover</u> all the costs.

25　Also, we planned <u>running</u> the campaign for three months.

26　In less than a week, our application <u>accepted</u> and funding began!

27　For a successful crowdfunding campaign, promoting it <u>necessary</u>.

28　You should consider <u>to make</u> a video.

29　This <u>lets</u> investors to get to know you and <u>learns</u> about your product.

30　You also need to express <u>how important is the product</u> to you.

31　Don't forget <u>including</u> a direct request for support at the end.

32　During a campaign, it is important <u>sending</u> investors updates every week.

33　Through the update, the investors will be able <u>track</u> the progress of the campaign.

34   After our application was accepted, I <u>eager</u> to make a good first impression with our investors.

35   In the video, I highlighted <u>how were the strawberries</u> grown without using chemicals.

36   In the clips, they were making the jam <u>without</u> all-natural ingredients.

37   Finally, I explained <u>which</u> I wanted to put the new greenhouse and <u>ask</u> for support.

38   After some editing, I posted the video on many social media <u>sights</u>.

39   It didn't take long for word of our campaign <u>spread</u>.

40   <u>Fund</u> for our campaign started slowly.

41   When the first investor committed to <u>support</u> us, I almost jumped for joy.

42   Now, after six weeks, we <u>had raised</u> almost $2,500.

43   It <u>seem</u> like we might make our funding goal!

교과서 **본문 외 지문 분석**

Think and Write ✿ 교과서 45쪽

Helping Our Community

  Last weekend, I went to a local park ❶<u>to participate</u> in an event ❷<u>called Help Our Park</u> with my brother. ❸<u>During</u> the event, we painted old playground equipment. After that, we planted some flowers around the pond in the park. I felt proud that I ❹<u>had contributed</u> to my community. I think events like this ❺<u>make our town a better place</u>.

우리 공동체 돕기

  지난 주말, 나는 남동생과 함께 '우리 공원 돕기'라는 행사에 참여하기 위해 지역 공원에 다녀왔다. 행사 중에, 우리는 놀이터의 낡은 기구들을 칠했다. 그 이후에, 우리는 공원 내 연못 주변에 꽃을 심었다. 나는 내가 우리 지역 공동체에 기여했다는 것에 자부심을 느꼈다. 나는 이런 행사들이 우리 동네를 더 나은 공간으로 만든다고 생각한다.

❶ to participate: 목적을 나타내는 to부정사의 부사적 용법 (참가하기 위해) ❷ 명사 an event를 뒤에서 꾸며 주는 과거분사구 ❸ During: 전치사 (~하는 동안) ❹ 과거보다 앞선 때의 일을 나타내므로 과거완료(had+p.p.) 형태, contribute to: ~에 기여하다 ❺ 동사(make)+목적어(our town)+목적격 보어(a better place)

Q At Help Our Park event, the writer planted some trees. (T / F)

Check-up ✿

다음 빈칸에 알맞은 말을 쓰시오.

01 Last weekend, I went to a local park _____ an event called Help Our Park with my brother.

지난 주말, 나는 남동생과 함께 '우리 공원 돕기'라는 행사에 참여하기 위해 지역 공원에 다녀왔다.

02 _____, we painted old playground equipment.

행사 중에, 우리는 놀이터의 낡은 기구들을 칠했다.

03 After that, we _____ around the pond in the park.

그 이후에, 우리는 공원 내 연못 주변에 꽃을 심었다.

04 I felt proud that I _____ my community.

나는 내가 우리 지역 공동체에 기여했다는 것에 자부심을 느꼈다.

05 I think events like this _____.

나는 이런 행사들이 우리 동네를 더 나은 공간으로 만든다고 생각한다.

01 (A), (B), (C)의 각 네모 안에서 문맥에 맞는 낱말로 가장 적절한 것은?

We need to improve our school's facilities for people with disabilities. This is important so that everyone can reach all the areas in our school. So, what can we do? First, we need to install an elevator for people with (A) mental / physical disabilities. This will make all areas of our school easier to access. Second, all signs should be (B) improved / removed for blind people. Signs with voice guidance would be especially helpful. Lastly, we should (C) place / replace all blackboards with greenboards. They make words easier to see, especially for people with low vision. Let's work together to make these changes.

	(A)		(B)		(C)
①	mental	⋯	improved	⋯	place
②	mental	⋯	removed	⋯	place
③	physical	⋯	improved	⋯	place
④	physical	⋯	removed	⋯	replace
⑤	physical	⋯	improved	⋯	replace

02 밑줄 친 부분 중, 문맥상 낱말의 쓰임이 적절하지 않은 것은?

What Is Crowdfunding?

Crowdfunding is a way of ① raising money for a product, company, or ② charity. These days, people can use crowdfunding websites to ③ collect money. Crowdfunding is especially advantageous for individuals or ④ large companies that can't attract big investors. If the campaign is successful, the investors receive ⑤ direct rewards for their contribution.

①   ②   ③   ④   ⑤

03 (A), (B), (C)의 각 네모 안에서 문맥에 맞는 낱말로 가장 적절한 것은?

My grandparents were (A) thrilled / threatened when I told them my idea. With the help of investors, we could build a large greenhouse and grow a lot more strawberries. (B) Moreover / Therefore, we could reward the investors for their help by sending them jars of organic jam! With this plan in mind, the next step was to (C) figure / find out the details.

	(A)		(B)		(C)
①	thrilled	⋯	Moreover	⋯	figure
②	thrilled	⋯	Therefore	⋯	figure
③	thrilled	⋯	Moreover	⋯	find
④	threatened	⋯	Therefore	⋯	find
⑤	threatened	⋯	Moreover	⋯	find

04 밑줄 친 부분 중, 문맥상 낱말의 쓰임이 적절하지 않은 것은?

Campaign Details

① Before beginning your campaign, be sure to plan all the production details. How many ② products will you make? How long will it take to make the product? This planning is important because your ③ potential investors will want to see a clear schedule. Once your plan is ④ complete, remember to set your funding goal. It should be enough to complete the project and fulfill the rewards for the investors. Consider all the necessary ⑤ incomes before deciding on the amount.

①   ②   ③   ④   ⑤

05 (A), (B), (C)의 각 네모 안에서 문맥에 맞는 낱말로 가장 적절한 것은?

After doing some calculations, we decided on an 8-by-12-foot greenhouse. We thought it would cost (A) appropriately / approximately $4,000. Once it was built, we could fill it with strawberry plants and expect a harvest within about four months. Then it would take a few weeks to turn the strawberries into delicious jam. We decided to set our funding goal at $5,000 to (B) cover / pay all the costs. Also, we planned to run the campaign for three months. I was really excited when I filled out the form to launch the campaign. In less than a week, our application was (C) accepted / rejected and funding began!

	(A)		(B)		(C)
①	appropriately	…	cover	…	accepted
②	appropriately	…	pay	…	accepted
③	approximately	…	cover	…	accepted
④	approximately	…	pay	…	rejected
⑤	approximately	…	cover	…	rejected

06 밑줄 친 부분 중, 문맥상 낱말의 쓰임이 적절하지 <u>않은</u> 것은?

Campaign Promotion and Communication

For a successful crowdfunding campaign, promoting it is necessary. You should consider making a video. This ① allows investors to get to know you and learn about your product. In the video, ② describe your situation clearly and show your product. You also need to express how ③ important the product is to you. Don't forget to include a direct request for ④ support at the end. During a campaign, it is important to send investors updates every week. Through the update, the investors will be able to track the ⑤ result of the campaign.

①   ②   ③   ④   ⑤

07 밑줄 친 부분 중, 문맥상 낱말의 쓰임이 적절하지 <u>않은</u> 것은?

After our application was accepted, I was eager to make a good first ① expression with our investors. To achieve this, I made a video about my grandparents and their jam. In the video, I ② highlighted how the strawberries were grown without using chemicals. I also ③ included clips of my grandparents. In the clips, they were making the jam with all-natural ingredients. Finally, I explained ④ where I wanted to put the new greenhouse and asked for support. After some editing, I posted the video on many social media sites. It didn't take long for word of our campaign to ⑤ spread.

①   ②   ③   ④   ⑤

08 (A), (B), (C)의 각 네모 안에서 문맥에 맞는 낱말로 가장 적절한 것은?

Last weekend, I went to a local park to participate (A) at / in an event called Help Our Park with my brother. During the event, we painted old playground equipment. After that, we (B) planted / picked some flowers around the pond in the park. I felt proud that I had (C) attributed / contributed to my community. I think events like this make our town a better place.

	(A)		(B)		(C)
①	at	…	planted	…	attributed
②	at	…	picked	…	attributed
③	in	…	planted	…	attributed
④	in	…	picked	…	contributed
⑤	in	…	planted	…	contributed

01 다음 글의 밑줄 친 부분 중, 어법상 틀린 것은?

My grandparents sell their delicious organic jam at the local market every weekend. I went to help them last weekend. However, they ① have already sold all of their jam! They didn't have enough strawberries ② to make any more jam. That evening, I sat by the window and ③ stared out at the empty field behind their house. Suddenly, I got an idea. The field ④ would be the perfect place for a larger greenhouse. Then they could grow more strawberries! I immediately ⑤ started searching for a way, and I found the perfect solution. I would start a crowdfunding campaign!

①   ②   ③   ④   ⑤

02 (A), (B), (C)의 각 네모 안에서 어법에 맞는 표현으로 가장 적절한 것은?

My grandparents (A) thrilled / were thrilled when I told them my idea. With the help of investors, we could build a large greenhouse and (B) grow / grew a lot more strawberries. Moreover, we could reward the investors for their help by sending them jars of organic jam! With this plan in mind, the next step was (C) figured / to figure out the details.

	(A)		(B)		(C)
①	thrilled	…	grow	…	figured
②	thrilled	…	grew	…	figured
③	were thrilled	…	grow	…	figured
④	were thrilled	…	grew	…	to figure
⑤	were thrilled	…	grow	…	to figure

03 (A), (B), (C)의 각 네모 안에서 어법에 맞는 표현으로 가장 적절한 것은?

Before beginning your campaign, be sure to plan all the production details. How many products will you make? How long will (A) it / that take to make the product? This planning is important because your potential investors will want to see a clear schedule. Once your plan is complete, remember (B) setting / to set your funding goal. It should be enough to complete the project and fulfill the rewards for the investors. Consider all the necessary costs before (C) deciding / to decide on the amount.

	(A)		(B)		(C)
①	it	…	setting	…	deciding
②	it	…	to set	…	deciding
③	it	…	setting	…	to decide
④	that	…	to set	…	to decide
⑤	that	…	setting	…	to decide

04 다음 글의 밑줄 친 부분 중, 어법상 틀린 것은?

After doing some calculations, we decided on an 8-by-12-foot greenhouse. We thought ① it would cost approximately $4,000. ② Once it was built, we could fill it with strawberry plants and expect a harvest within about four months. Then it would ③ take a few weeks to turn the strawberries into delicious jam. We decided to set our funding goal at $5,000 to cover all the costs. Also, we ④ planned to run the campaign for three months. I was really excited when I filled out the form to launch the campaign. In less than a week, our application ⑤ accepted and funding began!

①   ②   ③   ④   ⑤

05 다음 글의 밑줄 친 부분 중, 어법상 틀린 것은?

For a successful crowdfunding campaign, promoting it is necessary. You should consider making a video. This allows investors ① to get to know you and learn about your product. In the video, describe your situation clearly and show your product. You also need to express ② how important is the product to you. Don't forget ③ to include a direct request for support at the end. During a campaign, ④ it is important to send investors updates every week. Through the update, the investors ⑤ will be able to track the progress of the campaign.

①   ②   ③   ④   ⑤

06 (A), (B), (C)의 각 네모 안에서 어법에 맞는 표현으로 가장 적절한 것은?

In the video, I highlighted how the strawberries were grown without (A) using / to use chemicals. I also included clips of my grandparents. In the clips, they were making the jam with all-natural ingredients. Finally, I explained where I (B) want / wanted to put the new greenhouse and asked for support. After some editing, I posted the video on many social media sites. It didn't take long (C) for / of word of our campaign to spread.

	(A)	(B)	(C)
①	using	want	for
②	using	wanted	for
③	using	want	of
④	to use	wanted	of
⑤	to use	want	of

07 (A), (B), (C)의 각 네모 안에서 어법에 맞는 표현으로 가장 적절한 것은?

Last weekend, I went to a local park to participate in an event (A) calling / called Help Our Park with my brother. During the event, we painted old playground equipment. After that, we (B) plant / planted some flowers around the pond in the park. I felt proud (C) of / that I had contributed to my community. I think events like this make our town a better place.

	(A)	(B)	(C)
①	calling	plant	of
②	calling	planted	of
③	calling	plant	that
④	called	planted	that
⑤	called	plant	that

08 다음 글의 밑줄 친 부분 중, 어법상 틀린 것은?

We need to improve our school's facilities for people with disabilities. This is important ① so that everyone can reach all the areas in our school. So, what can we do? First, we need to install an elevator for people ② with physical disabilities. This will make all areas of our school easier to access. Second, all signs ③ should be improved for blind people. Signs with voice guidance would be especially helpful. Lastly, we should replace all blackboards with greenboards. They make words ④ easily to see, especially for people with low vision. Let's work together ⑤ to make these changes.

①   ②   ③   ④   ⑤

01 다음 대화의 빈칸에 들어갈 말로 가장 적절한 것은?

M Excuse me. Do you need help?
W I think I lost my cell phone.
M You can use mine to call your phone.
W Thank you. ... Nobody is answering it.
M I think _____.
W I agree with you. Can you tell me where it is?
M It is near the information center.
W Oh, is it between the roller coaster and the gift shop?
M Yes. That's right.

① you lost your cell phone
② you called the wrong number
③ you'd better buy a new phone
④ you should check with lost and found
⑤ you should go to the place you had put it

02 글의 흐름으로 보아, 주어진 문장이 들어가기에 가장 적절한 곳은?

(A) Last weekend, I went to a local park to participate in an event called Help Our Park with my brother. (B) During the event, we painted old playground equipment. (C) I felt proud that I had contributed to my community. (D) I think events like this make our town a better place. (E)

After that, we planted some flowers around the pond in the park.

① (A) ② (B) ③ (C) ④ (D) ⑤ (E)

[03~04] 다음 글을 읽고, 물음에 답하시오.

Good morning, students of Happyville High School! My name is Lucy, and I'm in grade 11. Today, I want to tell everyone an important message. We need to improve our school's facilities for people with disabilities. This is important so that everyone can reach all the areas in our school. So, what can we do? First, we need to install an elevator for people with physical disabilities. This will make all areas of our school easier to access. Second, all signs should be improved for blind people. Signs with voice guidance would be especially helpful. Lastly, we should replace all blackboards with greenboards. They make words easier to see, especially for people with low vision. Let's work together to make these changes. With your help, Happyville High School can become a welcoming place for everyone!

03 윗글의 요지로 가장 적절한 것은?

① Everybody in the school tries their best to make a more welcoming environment.
② Old elevators, signs, and blackboards must be changed for safety reasons.
③ The school should improve its facilities to make it easier for everyone to access.
④ Students must be able to access anywhere to enhance teacher-student relationship.
⑤ The school must open special classes for the students with physical disabilities.

04 윗글의 밑줄 친 these changes로 Lucy가 열거한 세 가지를 찾아 쓰시오.

(1) _____

(2) _____

(3) _____

[05~06] 다음 글을 읽고, 물음에 답하시오.

My grandparents sell their delicious organic jam at the local market every weekend. I went to help them last weekend. However, they had already sold all of their jam! They didn't have enough strawberries to make any more jam. That evening, I sat by the window and stared out at the empty field behind their house. Suddenly, I got an idea. The field would be the perfect place for a larger greenhouse. Then _____ _____! I immediately started searching for a way, and I found the perfect solution. I would start a crowdfunding campaign!

05 윗글의 빈칸에 들어갈 말로 가장 적절한 것은?

① I could invest in agriculture
② they could run a fruit jam factory
③ they could grow more strawberries
④ I could help them to sell their jam
⑤ we could attract generous investors

06 윗글에 드러난 I의 심경 변화로 가장 적절한 것은?

① worried → relieved
② disappointed → hopeful
③ excited → frustrated
④ upset → amazed
⑤ proud → ashamed

[07~08] 다음 글을 읽고, 물음에 답하시오.

My grandparents were thrilled when I told them my idea. With the help of investors, we could build a large greenhouse and grow a lot more strawberries. _____(A)_____, we could reward the investors for their help by sending them jars of organic jam! With this plan in mind, the next step was to figure out the details.

Campaign Details

Before beginning your campaign, be sure to plan all the production details. How many products will you make? How long will it take to make the product? This planning is important because your potential investors will want to see a clear schedule. _____(B)_____ your plan is complete, remember to set your funding goal. It should be enough to complete the project and fulfill the rewards for the investors. Consider all the necessary costs before deciding on the amount.

07 윗글의 빈칸 (A)와 (B)에 들어갈 말이 바르게 짝지어진 것은?

	(A)		(B)
①	Moreover	⋯	Once
②	Hence	⋯	Before
③	Therefore	⋯	Because
④	Consequently	⋯	As
⑤	Though	⋯	Unless

08 윗글의 밑줄 친 sending과 쓰임이 다른 것은?

① Making decisions is often very hard.
② We watched Jaden dancing alone.
③ Everybody enjoyed talking with my grandma.
④ You can improve any skill by practicing every day.
⑤ Without knocking on the door, he entered the room.

[09~10] 다음 글을 읽고, 물음에 답하시오.

After doing some calculations, we decided on an 8-by-12-foot ⓐ greenhouse. We thought it would cost approximately $4,000. Once ⓑ it was built, we could fill ⓒ it with strawberry plants and expect a harvest within about four months. Then ⓓ it would take a few weeks to turn the strawberries in ⓔ the greenhouse into delicious jam. We decided to set our funding goal at $5,000 to cover all the costs. Also, we planned to run the campaign for three months. I was really excited when I filled out the form to launch the campaign. In less than a week, our application was accepted and funding began!

09 윗글의 내용과 일치하지 <u>않는</u> 것은?

① The size of the greenhouse would be 8-by-12 feet.
② It would take about four months to grow strawberries in the greenhouse.
③ The production of the strawberry jam would take a few weeks.
④ The duration of the campaign would be three months.
⑤ Crowdfunding began one month after the application was submitted.

10 윗글의 밑줄 친 부분 중 가리키는 대상이 나머지 넷과 <u>다른</u> 것은?

① ⓐ   ② ⓑ   ③ ⓒ   ④ ⓓ   ⑤ ⓔ

[11~12] 다음 글을 읽고, 물음에 답하시오.

For a successful crowdfunding campaign, promoting it is necessary. You should consider making a video. This allows investors (A) get / to get to know you and learn about your product. In the video, describe your situation clearly and show your product. You also need to express how important the product is to you. Don't forget (B) including / to include a direct request for support at the end. During a campaign, it is important (C) sending / to send investors updates every week. Through the update, the investors will be able to track the progress of the campaign.

11 윗글의 내용을 요약할 때, 빈칸 (A), (B)에 들어갈 말로 가장 적절한 것은?

To succeed in crowdfunding, effective ____(A)____ is essential. Create a video introducing yourself and your product. Also, regularly ____(B)____ investors on progress to maintain their support.

	(A)	(B)
①	planning	invest
②	planning	invite
③	calculation	upload
④	promotion	update
⑤	promotion	invest

12 (A), (B), (C)의 각 네모 안에서 어법에 맞는 표현으로 가장 적절한 것은?

	(A)	(B)	(C)
①	get	including	sending
②	get	to include	sending
③	get	including	to send
④	to get	to include	to send
⑤	to get	including	to send

After our application was accepted, I was eager to make a good first impression with our investors. To (A) achieve / receive this, I made a video about my grandparents and their jam. In the video, I highlighted how the strawberries were grown (B) with / without using chemicals. I also included clips of my grandparents. In the clips, they were making the jam with all-natural ingredients. Finally, I explained where I wanted to put the new greenhouse and asked for support. After some editing, I posted the video on many social media sites. 우리 캠페인에 대한 소식이 퍼지는 데는 오래 걸리지 않았다.

Funding for our campaign started slowly. When the first investor committed to supporting us, _____. Now, after six weeks, we have (C) raised / risen almost $2,500. It seems like we might make our funding goal!

13 (A), (B), (C)의 각 네모 안에서 문맥에 맞는 낱말로 가장 적절한 것은?

	(A)		(B)		(C)
①	achieve	⋯	with	⋯	raised
②	achieve	⋯	without	⋯	raised
③	achieve	⋯	with	⋯	risen
④	receive	⋯	without	⋯	risen
⑤	receive	⋯	with	⋯	risen

14 윗글의 밑줄 친 우리말과 일치하도록 주어진 조건에 맞게 문장을 완성하시오.

> **조건**
> 1. It을 사용하여 문장을 시작할 것
> 2. 다음 표현을 활용할 것: word of our campaign, spread

> 우리 캠페인에 대한 소식이 퍼지는 데는 오래 걸리지 않았다.

→ _____
_____

15 윗글의 빈칸에 들어갈 말로 가장 적절한 것은?

① I started another crowdfunding campaign
② we were disappointed at the result
③ we sent him our delicious jam
④ we hurried to make jam
⑤ I almost jumped for joy

[01~02] 다음 대화를 읽고, 물음에 답하시오.

G Hey, Michael! The community center is looking for volunteers ① to teach children.
B Teaching children ② sounds fun.
G How about ③ volunteering with me? It would be a great opportunity.
B Okay. What do you want to teach?
G Painting, of course. You know I love to paint.
B Hmm... I don't know ④ what can I teach, though.
G You can teach basketball to the children. You're ⑤ good at it.
B You're right! I'll do that.

01 위 대화의 내용과 일치하는 것은?

① 두 사람은 주민센터에서 자원봉사를 하고 있다.
② 두 사람의 장래 희망은 모두 교사가 되는 것이다.
③ 여학생은 아이들에게 그림을 가르치고 싶어 한다.
④ 남학생은 아이들에게 농구를 가르치고 싶어 한다.
⑤ 남학생은 여학생의 조언이 적절하지 않다고 생각한다.

02 윗글의 밑줄 친 부분 중 어법상 틀린 것은?

①   ②   ③   ④   ⑤

[03~04] 다음 글을 읽고, 물음에 답하시오.

My grandparents sell their delicious organic jam at the local market every weekend. I went to help them last weekend. However, ⓐ they already sold all of their jam! They didn't have enough strawberries to make any more jam. That evening, I sat by the window and stared out at the empty field behind their house. Suddenly, I got an idea. The field would be the perfect place for a larger greenhouse. Then they could grow more strawberries! I immediately started searching for a way, and I found ⓑ the perfect solution. I would start a crowdfunding campaign!

03 윗글의 밑줄 친 ⓐ에서 어법상 어색한 부분을 찾아 바르게 고쳐 쓰시오.

However, they already sold all of their jam!

→ However, _____!

04 윗글의 밑줄 친 ⓑ the perfect solution이 가리키는 내용으로 가장 적절한 것은?

① delicious organic jam
② the empty field
③ a large green house
④ more strawberries
⑤ a crowdfunding campaign

05 다음 글의 ①~⑤ 중 전체 흐름과 관계 없는 문장은?

① Crowdfunding is a way of raising money for a product, company, or charity. ② These days, people can use crowdfunding websites to collect money. ③ For a successful crowdfunding campaign, promoting it is necessary. ④ Crowdfunding is especially advantageous for individuals or small companies that can't attract big investors. ⑤ If the campaign is successful, the investors receive direct rewards for their contribution.

①   ②   ③   ④   ⑤

06 다음 글 뒤에 이어질 내용으로 가장 적절한 것은?

My grandparents were thrilled when I told them my idea. With the help of investors, we could build a large greenhouse and grow a lot more strawberries. Moreover, we could reward the investors for their help by sending them jars of organic jam! With this plan in mind, the next step was to figure out the details.

① the size of the greenhouse
② a special recipe for the organic jam
③ ways to reward the investors
④ personal information about the investors
⑤ specific plans for drawing in investment

[07~08] 다음 글을 읽고, 물음에 답하시오.

Before ⓐ begin your campaign, be sure to plan all the production details.

(A) Once your plan is complete, remember to set your funding goal.
(B) How many products will you make? How long will it take to make the product?
(C) This planning is important because your potential investors will want to see a clear schedule.
(D) It should be enough to complete the project and fulfill the rewards for the investors. Consider all the necessary costs before ⓑ decide on the amount.

07 주어진 글 다음에 이어질 글의 순서로 가장 적절한 것은?

① (A) – (C) – (B) – (D)
② (B) – (C) – (A) – (D)
③ (B) – (D) – (C) – (A)
④ (C) – (A) – (B) – (D)
⑤ (C) – (D) – (A) – (B)

08 윗글의 밑줄 친 ⓐ와 ⓑ를 알맞은 형태로 바꿔 쓰시오. (한 단어)
ⓐ begin → _____
ⓑ decide → _____

[09~10] 다음 글을 읽고, 물음에 답하시오.

After doing some calculations, we decided on an 8-by-12-foot greenhouse. We thought it would cost approximately $4,000. Once it was built, we could fill it with strawberry plants and expect a harvest within about four months. Then it would take a few weeks to turn the strawberries into delicious jam. We decided to set our funding goal at $5,000 to cover all the costs. Also, we planned to run the campaign for three months. I was really excited when I filled out the form to launch the campaign. 일주일이 채 안 되어, our application was accepted and funding began!

09 윗글을 읽고 답을 찾을 수 있는 질문이 <u>아닌</u> 것은?

① What is the size of the greenhouse?
② What is the estimated cost of building the greenhouse?
③ How long does it take to grow strawberries?
④ What is the price of the organic strawberry jam?
⑤ What is the duration of the fundraising campaign?

10 윗글의 밑줄 친 우리말을 영어로 바르게 옮긴 것은?

① For a week
② A week ago
③ A week later
④ In less than a week
⑤ As late as a week ago

[11~12] 다음 글을 읽고, 물음에 답하시오.

For a successful crowdfunding campaign, promoting it is necessary. You should consider making a video. This allows investors to get to know you and learn about your (A) product / production . In the video, describe your situation clearly and show your product. You also need to express how important the product is to you. Don't forget to (B) exclude / include a direct request for support at the end. During a campaign, it is important to send investors updates every week. Through the update, the investors will be able to (C) track / trick the progress of the campaign.

11 윗글의 주제로 가장 적절한 것은?

① what crowdfunding is
② the planning process of crowdfunding
③ why crowdfunding campaigns are important
④ how to calculate the amount for funding
⑤ how to promote a funding campaign

12 (A), (B), (C)의 각 네모 안에서 문맥에 맞는 낱말로 가장 적절한 것은?

	(A)	(B)	(C)
①	product	exclude	track
②	product	include	track
③	product	exclude	trick
④	production	include	trick
⑤	production	exclude	trick

[13~14] 다음 글을 읽고, 물음에 답하시오.

After our application was accepted, I was eager to make a good first impression with our investors. (A) To achieve this, I made a video about my grandparents and their jam. (B) In the video, I highlighted how the strawberries were grown without using chemicals. (C) I also included clips of my grandparents. (D) Finally, I explained where I wanted to put the new greenhouse and asked for support. (E) After some editing, I posted the video on many social media sites. It didn't take long for word of our campaign to spread.

13 글의 흐름으로 보아, 주어진 문장이 들어가기에 가장 적절한 곳은?

In the clips, they were making the jam with all-natural ingredients.

① (A)   ② (B)   ③ (C)   ④ (D)   ⑤ (E)

14 다음 영어 뜻풀이에 해당하는 단어를 윗글에서 찾아 쓰시오.

to emphasize something or make people notice something

→ _____

15 다음 글의 밑줄 친 부분 중 어법상 틀린 것을 모두 고른 것은?

Good morning, students of Happyville High School! My name is Lucy, and I'm in grade 11. Today, I want to ⓐ tell to everyone an important message. We need to improve our school's facilities ⓑ for people with disabilities. This is important ⓒ so that everyone can reach all the areas in our school. So, what can we do? First, we need to install an elevator for people with physical disabilities. This will make all areas of our school ⓓ easier to access. Second, all signs ⓔ should improve for blind people. Signs with voice guidance would be especially helpful. Lastly, we should replace all blackboards with greenboards. They make words easier to see, especially for people with low vision. Let's work together ⓕ to make these changes. With your help, Happyville High School can become a welcoming place for everyone!

① ⓐ, ⓔ   ② ⓑ, ⓓ
③ ⓐ, ⓒ, ⓓ   ④ ⓑ, ⓔ, ⓕ
⑤ ⓐ, ⓓ, ⓕ

[01~02] 다음 대화를 읽고, 물음에 답하시오.

G Brian, is everything okay?

B Well, I'm a little upset. I just can't believe this news story from the local animal shelter.

G What is it?

B According to the shelter, many pets are abandoned by their owners when they go on vacation.

G (A) That's terrible.

B I don't understand those people. Pets are not toys.

G I agree with you. (B) Didn't you adopt your dog from the shelter?

B I did. (C) After that, several of my friends also adopted pets.

G (D) You're already making a difference.

B You're right. (E) Maybe everyone's small actions can help solve the problem someday.

01 대화의 흐름으로 보아, 주어진 말이 들어가기에 가장 적절한 곳은?

Look on the bright side.

① (A) ② (B) ③ (C) ④ (D) ⑤ (E)

02 Brian에 관해 위 대화의 내용과 일치하는 것은?

① He is angry about pet policies.
② He volunteered at an animal shelter.
③ He persuaded his friends to volunteer.
④ He adopted his dog from an animal shelter.
⑤ He participated in animal protection activities.

[03~04] 다음 글을 읽고, 물음에 답하시오.

My grandparents sell their ⓐ delicious organic jam at the local market every weekend. I went to help them last weekend. However, they had already sold all of their jam! They didn't have enough strawberries to make any more jam. That evening, I sat by the window and stared out at the empty field behind their house. Suddenly, I got an idea. The field would be the perfect place for a larger greenhouse. Then they could grow more strawberries! I immediately started searching for a way, and I found the perfect ⓑ solution. I would start a crowdfunding campaign!

What Is Crowdfunding?

Crowdfunding is a way of ⓒ raising money for a product, company, or charity. These days, people can use crowdfunding websites to collect money. Crowdfunding is especially ⓓ advantageous for individuals or small companies that can't attract big investors. If the campaign is successful, the investors receive direct ⓔ rewards for their contribution.

03 윗글을 읽고 답할 수 있는 질문이 아닌 것은?

① What do the writer's grandparents sell at the local market?
② Where can a greenhouse for strawberries be built?
③ How much does it cost to build a large greenhouse?
④ How would the writer attract investors to grow more strawberries?
⑤ For whom is the crowdfunding campaign advantageous?

04 윗글의 밑줄 친 부분과 바꿔 쓸 수 있는 말이 아닌 것은?

① ⓐ tasty
② ⓑ answer
③ ⓒ saving
④ ⓓ beneficial
⑤ ⓔ benefits

05 다음 글의 밑줄 친 우리말과 일치하도록 주어진 조건 에 맞게 문장을 완성하시오.

My grandparents were thrilled when I told them my idea to draw investment and build a greenhouse. With the help of investors, we could build a large greenhouse and grow a lot more strawberries. Moreover, we could reward the investors for their help by sending them jars of organic jam! 이 계획을 마음에 품고서, the next step was to figure out the details.

조건

1. With를 사용하여 문장을 시작할 것
2. 다음 표현을 활용할 것: plan, mind

→ _____ ,

the next step was to figure out the details.

06 다음 글의 빈칸에 들어갈 말로 가장 적절한 것은?

Last weekend, I went to a local park to participate in an event called Help Our Park with my brother. During the event, we painted old playground equipment. After that, we planted some flowers around the pond in the park. I felt _____ that I had contributed to my community. I think events like this make our town a better place.

① proud　　　　② upset
③ bored　　　　④ frustrated
⑤ nervous

[07~08] 다음 글을 읽고, 물음에 답하시오.

Before beginning your campaign, be sure to plan all the production details. How many products will you make? How long will it (A) make / take to make the product? This planning is important because your (B) potent / potential investors will want to see a clear schedule. Once your plan is complete, remember to set your funding goal. It should be enough to complete the project and fulfill the (C) loss / rewards for the investors. Consider all the necessary costs before deciding on the amount.

07 윗글의 제목으로 가장 적절한 것은?

① Setting a Production Schedule
② Who Will Be Your Future Investors?
③ What Is the Purpose of the Campaign?
④ What to Consider Before Starting a Campaign
⑤ Estimating the Exact Amount of Your Product

08 (A), (B), (C)의 각 네모 안에서 문맥에 맞는 낱말로 가장 적절한 것은?

	(A)	(B)	(C)
①	make	potent	loss
②	make	potential	loss
③	take	potent	loss
④	take	potential	rewards
⑤	take	potent	rewards

[09~10] 다음 글을 읽고, 물음에 답하시오.

After doing some calculations, we decided on an 8-by-12-foot greenhouse. We thought it would cost approximately $4,000. Once it was built, we could fill it with strawberry plants and expect a harvest within about four months. Then it would take a few weeks to turn the strawberries into delicious jam. We decided to set our funding goal at $5,000 to cover all the costs. Also, we planned to run the campaign for three months. I was really excited when I filled out the form to launch the campaign. In less than a week, our application was accepted and funding began!

09 윗글의 밑줄 친 calculation의 영어 뜻풀이로 알맞은 것은?

① an action that helps the achievement of something
② the process of using numbers to determine an amount
③ the time when the crops are gathered
④ activities done in order to increase the sales of a product
⑤ a substance used to make plants grow well

10 윗글의 내용과 일치하도록 다음 질문에 대한 답을 쓰시오.

What was the target amount for the funding?

→ _____

[11~12] 다음 글을 읽고, 물음에 답하시오.

____(A)____ a successful crowdfunding campaign, promoting it is necessary. You should consider making a video. This allows investors to get to know you and learn about your product. In the video, describe your situation clearly and show your product. You also need to express how important the product is to you. Don't forget to include a direct request for support at the end. During a campaign, it is important to send investors updates every week. ____(B)____ the update, the investors will be able to track the progress of the campaign.

11 윗글의 내용과 일치하지 않는 것은?

① Making a video is one way to promote the campaign.
② You can introduce yourself and your product in the video.
③ Avoid making a direct request for support.
④ Regularly let the investors know how the campaign is going.
⑤ Send the investors updates at least once a week.

12 윗글의 빈칸 (A)와 (B)에 들어갈 말이 바르게 짝지어진 것은?

	(A)		(B)
①	In	…	During
②	For	…	Through
③	To	…	For
④	By	…	With
⑤	About	…	To

[13~14] 다음 글을 읽고, 물음에 답하시오.

After our application was accepted, I was ① eager to make a good first impression with our investors. To achieve this, I made a video about my grandparents and their jam. In ⓐ the video, I highlighted how the strawberries were grown ② without using chemicals. I also included clips of my grandparents. In the clips, they were making the jam with all-natural ingredients. Finally, I explained ③ where did I want to put the new greenhouse and asked for support. After some editing, I posted the video on many social media sites. It didn't take long ④ for word of our campaign to spread.

Funding for our campaign started slowly. When the first investor committed ⑤ to supporting us, I almost jumped for joy. Now, after six weeks, we have raised almost $2,500. It seems like we might make our funding goal!

13 윗글의 밑줄 친 ⓐ the video에 관한 설명으로 글의 내용과 일치하지 <u>않는</u> 것은?

① 투자자들에게 좋은 인상을 주기 위해 만들었다.
② 조부모님과 그들이 만드는 잼에 관해 소개했다.
③ 딸기가 유기농으로 재배되는 모습을 강조했다.
④ 새로 만든 온실을 소개하는 영상을 포함했다.
⑤ 여러 소셜 미디어에 영상을 게시했다.

14 윗글의 밑줄 친 부분 중 어법상 <u>틀린</u> 것은?

①   ②   ③   ④   ⑤

15 다음 글의 (A)~(E) 중 주어진 문장이 들어가기에 가장 적절한 곳을 쓰시오.

Good morning, students of Happyville High School! My name is Lucy, and I'm in grade 11. Today, I want to tell everyone an important message. (A) We need to improve our school's facilities for people with disabilities. This is important so that everyone can reach all the areas in our school. (B) So, what can we do? First, we need to install an elevator for people with physical disabilities. (C) Second, all signs should be improved for blind people. (D) Lastly, we should replace all blackboards with greenboards. (E) Let's work together to make these changes. With your help, Happyville High School can become a welcoming place for everyone!

(1) Signs with voice guidance would be especially helpful. (   )
(2) This will make all areas of our school easier to access. (   )
(3) They make words easier to see, especially for people with low vision. (   )

01 다음 글의 어조로 가장 적절한 것은?

My grandparents sell their organic jam at the local market every weekend. Last weekend, I went to help them, but they'd sold out! They didn't have enough strawberries to make more. That night, I had an idea. The empty field behind their house would be a great spot for a larger greenhouse. They could grow more strawberries! I started looking for a way to do it and decided to start a crowdfunding campaign.

① hopeful
② relieved
③ gloomy
④ irritated
⑤ sympathetic

02 다음 글의 빈칸에 들어갈 말로 어색한 것은?

Crowdfunding is a method of collecting money for a business or cause. Nowadays, people can use online platforms to raise funds. It's particularly helpful for individuals or small businesses _____. If the campaign is successful, the contributors receive direct rewards for their support.

① that can't attract big investors
② who struggle to invite large investment
③ as they have difficulty meeting big investors
④ that have a lot of experience in drawing investments
⑤ who don't have big capital to start something

[03~04] 다음 글을 읽고, 물음에 답하시오.

My idea was to build a larger greenhouse through a crowdfunding. ① When I shared the idea, my grandparents were excited. ② With the help of investors, we could build a bigger greenhouse. ③ Then, we could grow more strawberries and make more jam. ④ Various kinds of organic jam are sold at the farmer's market. ⑤ We could also thank the investors by sending them jars of our organic jam! Next, we needed to work out the details of our plan.

03 윗글의 ①~⑤ 중 전체 흐름과 관계 없는 문장은?

①   ②   ③   ④   ⑤

04 윗글 다음에 이어질 내용으로 가장 적절한 것은?

① recipes for organic jam
② details of the crowdfunding plan
③ marketing strategies for jam sales
④ research on possible investors
⑤ communication with my grandparents

[05~06] 다음 글을 읽고, 물음에 답하시오.

Before starting your crowdfunding campaign, carefully plan the production details. (A) Decide on the number of products you'll make and the time it will take to produce them. (B) This planning is crucial because potential investors will want to see a clear timeline. (C) Once your plan is ready, set a funding goal. (D) You should also consider all necessary expenses before determining the amount. (E)

05 글의 흐름으로 보아, 주어진 문장이 들어가기에 가장 적절한 곳은?

It should be sufficient to complete the project and fulfill the rewards for investors.

① (A)   ② (B)   ③ (C)   ④ (D)   ⑤ (E)

06 윗글의 요지로 가장 적절한 것은?

① 적은 자본으로 프로젝트를 시작할 때 크라우드펀딩은 좋은 투자 방법이다.
② 제품의 생산량과 생산 시기를 명확히 파악하는 것은 쉽지 않다.
③ 크라우드펀딩을 시작하기 전 상세한 생산 계획과 적절한 펀딩 목표액을 정해야 한다.
④ 크라우드펀딩의 목표액을 정확히 산출하기 위해 고려할 요소가 많다.
⑤ 잠재적 투자자를 모으기 위해서는 합리적 의사소통이 중요하다.

[07~08] 다음 글을 읽고, 물음에 답하시오.

After calculating the costs, we decided on an 8-by-12-foot greenhouse, which we ① estimated would cost around 4,000 dollars. Once it was built, we could plant strawberries and expect a harvest in about four months. It would then take ② few weeks to make the strawberries into jam. We set our funding goal at 5,000 dollars to ③ cover all expenses and planned to run the campaign for three months. I was really excited when I ④ submitted the form to start the campaign. In less than a week, our application was ⑤ approved, and we began receiving funding!

07 윗글의 내용과 일치하지 않는 것은?

① 온실의 크기는 8×12 피트이다.
② 딸기를 심어 수확하기까지는 4개월 정도 걸린다.
③ 딸기로 잼을 만드는 데에는 몇 주가 소요된다.
④ 캠페인의 운영 기간은 3개월이다.
⑤ 기금 조성 목표액은 4,000달러이다.

08 윗글의 밑줄 친 부분 중 문맥상 낱말의 쓰임이 적절하지 않은 것은?

①   ②   ③   ④   ⑤

[09~10] 다음 글을 읽고, 물음에 답하시오.

To have a successful crowdfunding campaign, promoting ⓐ it is essential. Creating a video is a good idea. ⓑ This allows investors to get to know you and learn about your product. In the video, explain your situation clearly and showcase your product. Also, emphasize how important the product is to you. Don't forget to directly ask for support at the end. During a campaign, it is important to send weekly updates to your investors. This way, investors can follow the progress of the campaign.

09 윗글의 제목으로 가장 적절한 것은?

① Video Marketing and Investor Communication
② The Importance of Regular Updates
③ Constant Support from Investors
④ An Impressive Showcase of Your Product
⑤ Popular Crowdfunding Websites

10 윗글의 밑줄 친 ⓐ와 ⓑ가 가리키는 말이 바르게 짝지어진 것은?

① a video ⋯ asking for support
② your product ⋯ creating a video
③ your product ⋯ promoting a campaign
④ a crowdfunding campaign ⋯ creating a video
⑤ a crowdfunding campaign ⋯ asking for support

[11~12] 다음 글을 읽고, 물음에 답하시오.

After our application was approved, I wanted to make a good first impression on our investors. To do this, I created a video about my grandparents and their jam. In the video, I emphasized how ① the strawberries were grown organically. I also included clips of my grandparents ② make the jam with natural ingredients. Finally, I explained where ③ I wanted to build the new greenhouse and asked for support. After editing the video, I shared it on various social media platforms. News of our campaign ④ spread quickly.

Funding for our campaign started slowly. When the first investor pledged their support, I was overjoyed. Now, after six weeks, we've raised almost 2,500 dollars. It looks like we ⑤ might reach our funding goal!

11 윗글의 내용과 일치하지 <u>않는</u> 것은?

① 필자는 좋은 첫인상을 주기 위해 영상을 만들었다.
② 딸기를 재배하고 잼을 만드는 모습을 영상에 담았다.
③ 제작한 영상을 여러 소셜 미디어로 공유했다.
④ 펀딩을 시작한 후 6주 정도 경과했다.
⑤ 펀딩 목표액인 2,500달러를 달성했다.

12 윗글의 밑줄 친 부분 중 어법상 <u>틀린</u> 것은?

①   ②   ③   ④   ⑤

[13~14] 다음 글을 읽고, 물음에 답하시오.

Good morning, students of Happyville High School! I'm Lucy, and I'm a junior here. Today, I want to share an important message. We need to (A) approve / improve our school's facilities for people with _____ . This is important so everyone can access all parts of our school. So, what can we do? First, we need to install an elevator for people with physical _____ . This will make all areas of our school more accessible. Second, all signs should be improved for (B) blind / deaf people. Signs with voice guidance would be very helpful. Lastly, we should replace all blackboards with greenboards. They make words easier to see, especially for people with (C) high / low vision. Let's work together to make these changes. With your help, Happyville High School can become a welcoming place for everyone!

13 윗글의 빈칸에 공통으로 들어갈 말로 가장 적절한 것은?

① abilities   ② advantages
③ disabilities   ④ similarities
⑤ accessibility

14 (A), (B), (C)의 각 네모 안에서 문맥에 맞는 낱말로 가장 적절한 것은?

	(A)		(B)		(C)
①	approve	···	blind	···	high
②	approve	···	deaf	···	high
③	improve	···	blind	···	high
④	improve	···	deaf	···	low
⑤	improve	···	blind	···	low

15 (A), (B), (C)의 각 네모 안에서 어법에 맞는 표현으로 가장 적절한 것은?

Last weekend, my brother and I went to a park in my neighborhood for a community event (A) called / calling Help Our Park. We made the park look nicer by painting old playground equipment and (B) plant / planting flowers near the pond. It was great to give back to our community, and I think events like this really (C) improve / improves our town.

	(A)		(B)		(C)
①	called	···	plant	···	improve
②	called	···	planting	···	improve
③	called	···	plant	···	improves
④	calling	···	planting	···	improves
⑤	calling	···	plant	···	improves

[01~02] 다음 글을 읽고, 물음에 답하시오.

Good morning, students of Happyville High School! My name is Lucy, and I'm in grade 11. Today, I want to tell everyone an important message. We need to improve our school's facilities for people with disabilities. This is important so that everyone can reach all the areas in our school. So, what can we do? First, we need to install an elevator for people with physical disabilities. ⓐ This will make all areas of our school easier to access. Second, all signs should be improved for blind people. Signs with voice guidance would be especially helpful. Lastly, we should replace all blackboards with greenboards. ⓑ They make words easier to see, especially for people with low vision. Let's work together to make these changes. With your help, Happyville High School can become a welcoming place for everyone!

01 윗글의 밑줄 친 ⓐ와 ⓑ가 가리키는 것을 글에서 찾아 쓰시오.

ⓐ This → _____

ⓑ They → _____

02 윗글의 내용을 요약할 때 빈칸에 알맞은 말을 글에서 찾아 쓰시오.

Facilities like a(n) (1) _____, signs with (2) _____ guidance, and greenboards would make Happyville High School a more (3) _____ place for everyone.

[03~05] 다음 글을 읽고, 물음에 답하시오.

My grandparents sell their delicious organic jam at the local market every weekend. I went to help them last weekend. ⓐ However, they already sold all of their jam! They didn't have enough strawberries to make any more jam. That evening, I sat by the window and stared out at the empty field behind their house. Suddenly, I got ⓑ an idea. The field would be the perfect place for a larger greenhouse. Then they could grow more strawberries! I immediately started searching for a way, and I found the perfect solution. I would start a crowdfunding campaign!

Crowdfunding is a way of raising money for a product, company, or ____(A)____. These days, people can use crowdfunding websites to collect money. Crowdfunding is especially ____(B)____ for individuals or small companies that can't attract big investors. If the campaign is successful, the investors receive direct rewards for their contribution.

03 윗글의 밑줄 친 ⓐ에서 어법상 어색한 부분을 찾아 바르게 고쳐 쓰시오.

However, they already sold all of their jam!

→ However, _____!

04 윗글의 밑줄 친 ⓑ an idea가 의미하는 것을 완성하여 쓰시오.

We could (1) _____ a greenhouse in an empty field to grow more (2) _____.

05 윗글의 빈칸 (A)와 (B)에 들어갈 말을 다음 영어 뜻풀이를 참고하여 주어진 철자로 시작하여 쓰시오.

(A) an official organization for helping those in need

(B) helping to make you more successful

(A) c_____

(B) a_____

[06~07] 다음 글을 읽고, 물음에 답하시오.

My grandparents were thrilled when I told them my idea. With the help of investors, we could build a large greenhouse and grow a lot more strawberries. Moreover, we could reward the investors for their help by ⓐ send them jars of organic jam! With this plan in mind, the next step was to figure out the details.

Campaign Details

Before beginning your campaign, be sure to plan all the ⓑ production details. How many products will you make? How long will it take to make the product? This planning is important because your potential investors will want to see a clear schedule. Once your plan is complete, remember ⓒ set your funding goal. It should be enough to complete the project and fulfill the rewards for the investors. Consider all the necessary costs before deciding on the amount.

06 윗글의 밑줄 친 ⓐ와 ⓒ를 알맞은 형태로 바꿔 쓰시오. (필요하면 단어를 추가할 것)

ⓐ send → _____

ⓒ set   → _____

07 윗글의 밑줄 친 ⓑ production details의 예시 한 가지를 글에서 찾아 쓰시오.

→ _____

[08~09] 다음 글을 읽고, 물음에 답하시오.

After doing some calculations, 우리는 가로 8피트에 세로 12피트 크기의 온실로 결정했다. We thought it would cost approximately $4,000. Once it was built, we could fill it with strawberry plants and expect a harvest within about four months. Then it would take a few weeks to turn the strawberries into delicious jam. We decided to set our funding goal at $5,000 to cover all the costs. Also, we planned to run the campaign for three months. I was really excited when I filled out the form to launch the campaign. In less than a week, our application was accepted and funding began!

08 윗글의 내용과 일치하도록 주어진 질문에 대한 답을 완성하여 쓰시오.

(1) How long would it take to grow strawberry plants to a harvest?

→ _____

(2) How much would it cost to build a greenhouse?

→ _____

(3) How long would they run the campaign?

→ _____

09 윗글의 밑줄 친 우리말과 일치하도록 주어진 조건에 맞게 영작하시오.

> **조건**
> 1. by와 숫자를 사용하여 크기를 표현할 것
> 2. 다음 표현을 활용할 것: decide, foot

→ After doing some calculations, _____
_____.

10 다음 글의 밑줄 친 우리말과 일치하도록 보기의 표현을 활용하여 영작하시오.

> For a successful crowdfunding campaign, promoting it is necessary. You should consider making a video. 이것은 투자자들이 당신을 알게 하고 당신의 제품에 대해 배울 수 있게 한다. In the video, describe your situation clearly and show your product. You also need to express how important the product is to you. Don't forget to include a direct request for support at the end. During a campaign, it is important to send investors updates every week. Through the update, the investors will be able to track the progress of the campaign.

보기
allow, investors, get to, product

→ _____

_____

11 다음 글의 내용과 일치하도록 표의 빈칸에 알맞은 말을 글에서 찾아 완성하시오.

> Last weekend, I went to a local park to participate in an event called Help Our Park with my brother. During the event, we painted old playground equipment. After that, we planted some flowers around the pond in the park. I felt proud that I had contributed to my community. I think events like this make our town a better place.

When	last weekend
Where	(1) _____
With whom	my brother
What	painted old playground equipment
	(2) _____

[12~13] 다음 글을 읽고, 물음에 답하시오.

> After our application was accepted, I was eager to make a good first impression with our investors. To achieve this, I made a video about my grandparents and their jam. In the video, I highlighted ⓐ 어떻게 딸기가 화학 약품을 사용하지 않고 재배되는지. I also included clips of my grandparents. In the clips, they were making the jam with all-natural ingredients. Finally, I explained where I wanted to put the new greenhouse and asked for support. After some editing, I posted the video on many social media sites. ⓑ It didn't take long for word of our campaign to spread.
>
> Funding for our campaign started slowly. When the first investor committed to supporting us, I almost jumped for joy. Now, after six weeks, we have raised almost $2,500. It seems like we might make our funding goal!

12 윗글의 밑줄 친 ⓐ의 우리말과 일치하도록 조건에 맞게 영작하시오.

조건
1. how로 시작할 것
2. 전치사 without을 사용할 것
3. 다음 표현을 활용할 것: grow, use, chemicals

→ In the video, I highlighted _____

_____.

13 윗글의 밑줄 친 ⓑ를 우리말로 바르게 해석하시오.

→ _____

01

—

The True Treasure

The Golden Windows
금으로 된 창문

01 After working hard <u>all day long</u>, a boy <u>would</u> go up to the top of a hill and <u>look</u> across at another hill.
온종일   ~하곤 했다 (과거의 습관)   (would)

온종일 열심히 일을 하고 나서, 소년은 언덕의 꼭대기에 올라 다른 언덕을 건너다보곤 했다.

02 → 부사구를 강조하기 위한 주어–동사 도치
[On this far hill] <u>stood</u> <u>a house</u> (with windows of gold and diamond).
부사구   동사   주어 ↑   전치사구

이 먼 언덕에는 금과 다이아몬드로 만들어진 창문이 있는 집이 서 있었다.

03 → windows of gold and diamond
<u>They</u> shone at sunset, but <u>after a while</u>, the fascinating light disappeared.
잠시 후

창문은 일몰에 반짝였지만 얼마 후에 그 매혹적인 빛이 사라졌다.

04 → 명사절 (supposed의 목적어)
The boy supposed [that <u>the people</u> (in the house) closed the shutters because it was dinnertime].
↑   전치사구

소년은 저녁 식사 시간이므로 집 안의 사람들이 덧문을 닫았다고 추측했다.

05 One day, the boy's father <u>called him over</u> and said, "You <u>have been</u> a good boy and <u>have earned</u> a holiday.
call over: ~을 부르다   현재완료 (계속)   현재완료 (완료)

어느 날 소년의 아버지가 소년을 불러 "네가 착하게 굴어서 휴일을 얻었단다.

06 <u>Take the day off</u>, but try to learn <u>something important</u>."
take a day off: 하루 휴가를 얻다   ↑   형용사가 뒤에서 수식

쉬는 날을 가지되 중요한 것을 배우려고 노력하렴."이라고 말했다.

07 The boy thanked his father and kissed his mother; then he took a piece of bread, and left <u>to find</u> to부정사의 부사적 용법 (목적)
the house (with the golden windows).
↑   전치사구

소년은 아버지에게 감사를 표하고 어머니에게 키스했다. 그리고 나서 그는 빵 한 조각을 챙겨 금으로 된 창문이 있는 집을 찾으러 떠났다.

08 His journey was enjoyable.

그의 여정은 즐거웠다.

09   His <u>bare feet</u> made marks in the white sand.
맨발

그의 맨발은 흰 모래 위에 자국을 남겼다.

10   병렬 연결

When he looked back, the footprints <u>seemed to be following</u> him and <u>keeping him company</u>.
seem to-V: ～인 것 같다   keep ... company: ～의 곁에 있어 주다

그가 뒤를 돌아보았을 때 그의 발자국은 그를 뒤따르면서 그의 길동무가 된 것 같았다.

11   His shadow, too, stayed <u>beside</u> him and would dance or run with him <u>as</u> he pleased.
～ 옆에   접속사 (～할 때)

그의 그림자 역시 그의 옆에 머물면서 그가 기뻐할 때 그와 함께 춤을 추거나 달리곤 했다.

12   (+to)

<u>Before long</u>, he felt hungry, so he sat down <u>by</u> a stream [<u>to eat his bread and drink the clear water</u>].
오래지 않아   ～ 옆에   to부정사의 부사적 용법 (목적)

오래지 않아 그는 배가 고파서 빵을 먹고 깨끗한 물을 마시기 위해 개울가에 앉았다.

13   He <u>scattered</u> the remaining pieces of bread for the birds, <u>as</u> his mother <u>had taught him to do</u>, and
접속사 (～대로)   teach + 목적어 + to-V: ～가 … 하도록 가르치다

<u>went on his way</u>. 병렬 연결

그는 어머니가 가르친 대로, 남아 있는 빵 조각들을 새들을 위해 흩뿌리고 길을 떠났다.

14   <u>After a long time</u>, he came to a high green hill, and the house was at the top.
전치사구

오랜 시간 후에 그는 높고 푸른 언덕에 왔고 그 집은 꼭대기에 있었다.

15   <u>It seemed that</u> the shutters <u>were closed</u>, <u>for</u> he could not see the golden windows.
～인 것 같았다   수동태   접속사 (왜냐하면)

덧문이 닫힌 것처럼 보였는데, 왜냐하면 그가 금으로 된 창문을 볼 수 없었기 때문이었다.

16   병렬 연결   명사절 (find의 목적어)

He <u>came</u> up to the house and <u>was disappointed to find</u> [that the windows <u>were made of</u> clear glass,
to부정사의 부사적 용법 (감정의 원인)   be made of: ～으로 만들어지다

(like any others), and there was no gold anywhere around them].
삽입구   (that)

그는 그 집으로 가서 창문들이 다른 것들과 마찬가지로 투명한 유리로 만들어졌으며 그 창문들 주변 어디에도 금은 없다는 것을 알고 실망했다.

17   간접목적어   직접목적어 (간접의문문)

A woman <u>came</u> to the door, <u>looked</u> kindly at the boy, and <u>asked</u> him [what he wanted].
동사 1   동사 2   동사 3

한 여자가 문으로 와서 소년을 친절하게 바라보았고 그에게 무엇을 원하는지 물었다.

18 "I saw the golden windows from the top of our hill," he said, "and I came to see them, but now

= the golden windows

to부정사의 부사적 용법 (목적)

they are only glass."

"저는 저희 쪽 언덕 꼭대기에서 금으로 된 창문을 봤어요. 그리고 그것들을 보러 왔지만 이제 보니 그저 유리일 뿐이에요."라고 그가 말했다.

19 The woman shook her head and laughed.

병렬 연결

그 여성은 고개를 흔들고 웃었다.

20 "We are poor farming people," she said, "and are not likely to have windows (made of gold); but

(we)

be likely to-V: ~할 것 같다

과거분사구

glass is better to see through."

to부정사의 부사적 용법 (형용사 수식)

"우리는 가난한 농부들이고 우리가 금으로 만들어진 창문을 가졌을 것 같지 않구나. 하지만 유리는 들여다보기에 더 좋지."라고 그녀가 말했다.

21 She told the boy to sit down on the step (in front of the door), brought him a snack, and called

동사 1

tell + 목적어 + to-V: ~에게 …하라고 말하다

전치사구

동사 2

간접목적어 직접목적어

동사 3

her daughter, a girl of his own age.

동격 관계

그녀는 소년에게 문 앞의 계단에 앉으라고 말하고 그에게 간식을 가져다준 뒤 그와 비슷한 나이의 소녀인 그녀의 딸을 불렀다.

22 Then she smiled at the two and went back to her work.

= the boy and the girl

그리고 그녀는 두 사람에게 미소를 지은 뒤 일을 하러 돌아갔다.

23 Although the girl's clothes were modest, her hair was golden like the windows [he had seen], and

(which[that])

접속사 (비록 ~지만)

목적격 관계대명사절

her eyes were blue like the sky.

비록 소녀의 옷은 수수했지만 그녀의 머리카락은 그가 봤던 창문처럼 금빛이었고, 그녀의 눈은 하늘처럼 파란색이었다.

24 She led the boy around the farm and showed him her black calf, [which had a white star on its

병렬 연결

간접목적어 직접목적어

= and it

계속적 용법의 주격 관계대명사절

forehead].

그녀는 소년을 농장으로 데리고 가서 그녀의 검은 송아지를 보여 주었는데, 그 송아지는 이마에 흰색 별이 있었다.

25 The boy told her about his own calf (at home), [which was red like a chestnut and had white feet].

전치사구

계속적 용법의 주격 관계대명사절

소년은 그녀에게 집에 있는 자신의 송아지에 대해 이야기했는데, 그 송아지는 밤처럼 붉은색이었고 흰색 발을 갖고 있었다.

26 [Feeling as if they were now friends], the boy asked her about the golden windows.
분사구문   마치 ~인 것처럼

이제 마치 그들이 친구인 것처럼 느껴져서 소년은 그녀에게 금으로 된 창문에 대해 물었다.

27 The girl said (that) she knew all about them, only he had mistaken [which house had them].
접속사 (다만)   과거완료 (대과거)   mistaken의 목적어 (간접의문문)

소녀는 그것에 대해 모두 알고 있다고 했고, 다만 어떤 집이 그것들을 가지고 있는지를 그가 착각한 거라고 말했다.

28 "You have come the wrong way!" she said.
현재완료 (완료)

"네가 잘못 왔어!"라고 그녀가 말했다.

29 "Come with me. I will show you the house (with the golden windows), and then you will see for yourself."
간접목적어 직접목적어   전치사구   for oneself: 직접, 스스로

"나와 함께 가자. 내가 금으로 된 창문이 있는 집을 보여 주면 네가 직접 보게 될 거야."

30 The girl told him [that the golden windows could only be seen at sunset].
간접목적어 직접목적어 (명사절)   조동사가 있는 수동태

소녀는 그에게 금으로 된 창문은 일몰에만 볼 수 있다고 말했다.

31 "Yes, I know that!" said the boy. They went to a high place and saw a house (with windows of gold and diamond) (on a hill far away), just as the boy had seen before.
병렬 연결   전치사구 1   전치사구 2   꼭 ~처럼   과거완료 (대과거)

"맞아, 나도 알아!"라고 소년이 말했다. 그들은 높은 장소로 가서 소년이 전에 봤던 것처럼 금과 다이아몬드로 된 창문이 있는 멀리 있는 언덕 위의 집을 보았다.

32 And when they looked again, the boy recognized [that it was his own home].
명사절 (recognized의 목적어)

그리고 그들이 다시 보았을 때, 소년은 그것이 자신의 집이라는 것을 알아보았다.

33 Then he told the girl [that he must go]; and he gave her his best pebble, a white one (with a red stripe) [that he had carried with him for a year]; and she gave him three horse-chestnuts, one red, one spotted, and one white.
간접목적어 직접목적어 (명사절)   간접목적어 직접목적어   동격   전치사구   (that was)   목적격 관계대명사절   과거완료 (대과거)   간접목적어 직접목적어 (마로니에 열매)   (that was)   (that was)

그리고 나서 그는 소녀에게 가야 한다고 말하고 그의 최고의 조약돌인, 그가 일 년 동안 갖고 다녔던 빨간색 줄무늬가 있는 흰색 조약돌을 그녀에게 주었고, 그녀는 그에게 하나는 빨간색, 하나는 점무늬, 하나는 흰색인 마로니에 열매 세 개를 주었다.

34 He promised to come again, but he did not tell her [what he had learned].
과거완료 (대과거)
promise to-V: ~하기로 약속하다   간접목적어 직접목적어 (관계대명사절)

그는 다시 오겠다고 약속했지만 그가 깨달았던 것을 그녀에게 말하지 않았다.

35 The girl stood (in the light of the sunset) and watched him go.
전치사구   지각동사 + 목적어 + 동사원형

소녀는 해 질 녘 빛 속에 서서 그가 가는 것을 보았다.

36 It was dark when the boy finally returned home, but the windows (of his home) were shining with
비인칭 주어 (명암)   주어   동사 (과거진행형)
전치사구

the light of lamps just like he had seen from the top of the hill.
접속사 (~처럼)   과거완료 (대과거)

소년이 마침내 집에 돌아왔을 때 (밖은) 어두웠지만 그의 집 창문은 그가 언덕 꼭대기에서 봤던 것처럼 전등 불빛으로 빛나고 있었다.

37 His family welcomed him warmly.

그의 가족은 그를 따뜻하게 맞이했다.

38 "Have you had a good day?" asked his mother.
현재완료

"좋은 하루를 보냈니?"라고 그의 어머니가 물었다.

39 Yes, the boy had had a very good day.
과거완료 (완료)

맞다, 소년은 정말 좋은 하루를 보냈다.

40 "And have you learned anything?" asked his father.

"그리고 무언가를 배웠니?"라고 그의 아버지가 물었다.

41 "Yes!" said the boy. "I have learned [that our house has windows (of gold and diamond)]."
현재완료 (완료)   명사절 (have learned의 목적어)   전치사구

"네!"라고 소년이 말했다. "저는 금과 다이아몬드로 된 창문이 우리 집에 있다는 것을 배웠어요."

교과서 본문 익히기 ❶ 빈칸 완성하기

♣ 다음 빈칸에 알맞은 말을 쓰시오.

01 After working hard all day long, a boy _____ and look across at another hill.

온종일 열심히 일을 하고 나서, 소년은 언덕의 꼭대기에 올라 다른 언덕을 건너다보곤 했다.

02 On this far hill _____ with windows of gold and diamond.

이 먼 언덕에는 금과 다이아몬드로 만들어진 창문이 있는 집이 서 있었다.

03 _____, but after a while, the fascinating light disappeared.

창문은 일몰에 반짝였지만 얼마 후에 그 매혹적인 빛이 사라졌다.

04 The boy _____ the people in the house closed the shutters because it was dinnertime.

소년은 저녁 식사 시간이므로 집 안의 사람들이 덧문을 닫았다고 추측했다.

05 One day, the boy's father called him over and said, "You have been a good boy and

_____.

어느 날 소년의 아버지가 소년을 불러 "네가 착하게 굴어서 휴일을 얻었단다.

06 Take the day off, but try to _____."

쉬는 날을 가지되 중요한 것을 배우려고 노력하렴."이라고 말했다.

07 The boy _____ and kissed his mother; then he took a piece of bread, and left to find _____.

소년은 아버지에게 감사를 표하고 어머니에게 키스했다. 그러고 나서 그는 빵 한 조각을 챙겨 금으로 된 창문이 있는 집을 찾으러 떠났다.

08 _____ made marks in the white sand.

그의 맨발은 흰 모래 위에 자국을 남겼다.

09 When he looked back, the footprints _____ and keeping him company.

그가 뒤를 돌아보았을 때 그의 발자국은 그를 뒤따르면서 그의 길동무가 된 것 같았다.

10 His shadow, too, _____ and would dance or run with him as he pleased.

그의 그림자 역시 그의 옆에 머물면서 그가 기뻐할 때 그와 함께 춤을 추거나 달리곤 했다.

11 _____, he felt hungry, so he sat down by a stream to eat his bread and

_____.

오래지 않아 그는 배가 고파서 빵을 먹고 깨끗한 물을 마시기 위해 개울가에 앉았다.

12 He scattered the remaining pieces of bread for the birds, _____, and went on his way.

그는 어머니가 가르친 대로, 남아 있는 빵 조각들을 새들을 위해 흩뿌리고 길을 떠났다.

13 After a long time, he came _____, and the house was at the top.

오랜 시간 후에 그는 높고 푸른 언덕에 왔고 그 집은 꼭대기에 있었다.

14 It seemed that the shutters were closed, _____ the golden windows.

덧문이 닫힌 것처럼 보였는데, 왜냐하면 그가 금으로 된 창문을 볼 수 없었기 때문이었다.

15 He came up to the house and _____ that the windows were made of clear glass, like any others, and _____ anywhere around them.

그는 그 집으로 가서 창문들이 다른 것들과 마찬가지로 투명한 유리로 만들어졌으며 그 창문들 주변 어디에도 금은 없다는 것을 알고 실망했다.

16 A woman came to the door, looked kindly at the boy, and _____.

한 여자가 문으로 와서 소년을 친절하게 바라보았고 그에게 무엇을 원하는지 물었다.

17 "I saw the golden windows from the top of our hill," he said, "and I came to see them, but now _____."

"저는 저희 쪽 언덕 꼭대기에서 금으로 된 창문을 봤어요. 그리고 그것들을 보러 왔지만 이제 보니 그저 유리일 뿐이에요."라고 그가 말했다.

18 "We are poor farming people," she said, "and _____ windows made of gold; but glass is _____."

"우리는 가난한 농부들이고 우리가 금으로 만들어진 창문을 가졌을 것 같지 않구나. 하지만 유리는 들여다보기에 더 좋지."라고 그녀가 말했다.

19 She told the boy _____ in front of the door, _____, and called her daughter, a girl of his own age.

그녀는 소년에게 문 앞의 계단에 앉으라고 말하고 그에게 간식을 가져다준 뒤 그와 비슷한 나이의 소녀인 그녀의 딸을 불렀다.

20 Although the girl's clothes were modest, her hair was golden like the windows he had seen, and _____.

비록 소녀의 옷은 수수했지만 그녀의 머리카락은 그가 봤던 창문처럼 금빛이었고, 그녀의 눈은 하늘처럼 파란색이었다.

21 She led the boy around the farm and showed him her black calf, _____ on its forehead.

그녀는 소년을 농장으로 데리고 가서 그녀의 검은 송아지를 보여 주었는데, 그 송아지는 이마에 흰색 별이 있었다.

22 The boy told her _____, which was red like a chestnut and had white feet.

소년은 그녀에게 집에 있는 자신의 송아지에 대해 이야기했는데, 그 송아지는 밤처럼 붉은색이었고 흰색 발을 갖고 있었다.

23 Feeling _____, the boy asked her about the golden windows.

이제 마치 그들이 친구인 것처럼 느껴져서 소년은 그녀에게 금으로 된 창문에 대해 물었다.

24 The girl said she knew all about them, only _____ which house had them.

소녀는 그것에 대해 모두 알고 있다고 했고, 다만 어떤 집이 그것들을 가지고 있는지를 그가 착각한 거라고 말했다.

25 "You have come _____!" she said.

"네가 잘못 왔어!"라고 그녀가 말했다.

26 "Come with me. I will show you the house with the golden windows, and then you will see
_____."

"나와 함께 가자. 내가 금으로 된 창문이 있는 집을 보여 주면 네가 직접 보게 될 거야."

27 The girl told him that the golden windows _____.

소녀는 그에게 금으로 된 창문은 일몰에만 볼 수 있다고 말했다.

28 They went to a high place and saw a house with windows of gold and diamond on a hill far away,
_____.

그들은 높은 장소로 가서 소년이 전에 봤던 것처럼 금과 다이아몬드로 된 창문이 있는 멀리 있는 언덕 위의 집을 보았다.

29 And when they looked again, the boy _____ his own home.

그리고 그들이 다시 보았을 때, 소년은 그것이 자신의 집이라는 것을 알아보았다.

30 Then he told the girl that he must go; and he _____, a white one with a red
stripe _____ for a year; and she gave him three horse-chestnuts, one red, one
spotted, and one white.

그러고 나서 그는 소녀에게 가야 한다고 말하고 그의 최고의 조약돌인, 그가 일 년 동안 갖고 다녔던 빨간색 줄무늬가 있는 흰색 조약돌을 그녀에게 주었고, 그녀는 그에게 하나는 빨간색, 하나는 점무늬, 하나는 흰색인 마로니에 열매 세 개를 주었다.

31 He _____, but he did not tell her what he had learned.

그는 다시 오겠다고 약속했지만 그가 깨달았던 것을 그녀에게 말하지 않았다.

32 The girl stood _____ and watched him go.

소녀는 해 질 녘 빛 속에 서서 그가 가는 것을 보았다.

33 _____ when the boy finally returned home, but the windows of his home were
shining with the light of lamps _____ from the top of the hill.

소년이 마침내 집에 돌아왔을 때 (밖은) 어두웠지만 그의 집 창문은 그가 언덕 꼭대기에서 봤던 것처럼 전등 불빛으로 빛나고 있었다.

34 His family _____.

그의 가족은 그를 따뜻하게 맞이했다.

35 Yes, the boy _____.

맞다, 소년은 정말 좋은 하루를 보냈다.

36 "And have you _____?" asked his father.

"그리고 무언가를 배웠니?"라고 그의 아버지가 물었다.

37 "Yes!" said the boy. "I have learned that our house has _____."

"네!"라고 소년이 말했다. "저는 금과 다이아몬드로 된 창문이 우리 집에 있다는 것을 배웠어요."

♣ 다음 네모 안에서 옳은 것을 고르시오.

01 After working hard / hardly all day long, a boy would go up to the top of a hill and look / looked across at another hill.

02 On this far hill stood a house of / with windows of gold and diamond.

03 They shone at sunset, but after a while, the fascinating light appeared / disappeared .

04 The boy supposed that the people in the house closed the shutters because / though it was dinnertime.

05 " Make / Take the day off, but try to learn something important."

06 His bare / bear feet made marks in the white sand.

07 When he looked back, the footprints seemed to be following him and kept / keeping him company.

08 His shadow, too, stayed beside / besides him and would dance or run with him as he pleased.

09 Before long, he felt hungry, so he sat down by a stream to eat his bread and drink / drank the clear water.

10 It seemed that the shutters were closed / open , for he could not see the golden windows.

11 He came up to the house and was disappointing / disappointed to find that the windows were made of clear glass, like any others, and there was no gold anywhere around them.

12 A woman came to the door, looked kindly at the boy, and asked him what / whether he wanted.

13 "We are poor farming people," she said, "and are not like / likely to have windows made of gold; but glass is better to see through."

14 She told the boy to sit down on the step in front of the door, brought him / to him a snack, and called her daughter, a girl of / with his own age.

15 Although the girl's clothes were modern / modest , her hair was golden like the windows he saw / had seen , and her eyes were blue like the sky.

16 She led the boy around the farm and showed him her black calf, that / which had a white star on its forehead.

17 The boy told her about his own calf at home, which was red like a chestnut and have / had white feet.

18 Feeling as if they are / were now friends, the boy asked her about the golden windows.

19 The girl said she knew all about them, only he had mistook / mistaken which house had them.

20 "You have come the right / wrong way!" she said.

21 "Come with me. I will show you the house with the golden windows, and then you will see for / of yourself."

22 The girl told him that the golden windows could only be seen at sunrise / sunset.

23 They went to a high place and saw a house with windows of gold and diamond on a hill far away, just as the boy seen / had seen before.

24 And when they looked again, the boy recognized / wondered that it was his own home.

25 Then he told the girl that he must go; and he gave her his best pebble, a white one with a red stripe / striped that he had carried with him for a year; and she gave him three horse-chestnuts, one red, one spotted, and one white.

26 He promised coming / to come again, but he did not tell her what he had learned.

27 The girl stood in the light of the sunset and watched him go / to go.

28 It was bright / dark when the boy finally returned home, but the windows of his home were shining with the light of lamps just like he had seen from the top of the hill.

29 "Have you been / had a good day?" asked his mother.

♣ 다음 밑줄 친 부분을 바르게 고쳐 쓰시오.

01   After working hard all day long, a boy would go up to the top of a hill and <u>looked</u> across at another hill.

02   On this far hill <u>did a house stand</u> with windows of gold and diamond.

03   The boy supposed that the people in the house closed the shutters because it <u>is</u> dinnertime.

04   Take the day off, but try to learn <u>important something</u>."

05   The boy thanked his father and kissed his mother; then he took a piece of bread, and <u>leave</u> to find the house with the golden windows.

06   His bare <u>foots</u> made marks in the white sand.

07   When he looked back, the footprints <u>seemed following</u> him and keeping him company.

08   Before long, he felt hungry, so he sat down by a stream to eat his bread and <u>drank</u> the clear water.

09   He scattered the remaining pieces of bread for the birds, as his mother had taught <u>to him doing</u>, and went on his way.

10   It seemed that the shutters <u>closed</u>, for he could not see the golden windows.

11   A woman came to the door, looked kindly at the boy, and asked him what <u>did he want</u>.

12   "I saw the golden windows from the top of our hill," he said, "and I came to see them, but now <u>it is</u> only glass."

13   "We are poor farming people," she said, "and are not likely to have windows made of gold; but glass is better <u>seeing</u> through."

14   She told the boy to sit down on the step in front of the door, <u>bring</u> him a snack, and called her daughter, a girl of his own age.

15 <u>Since</u> the girl's clothes were modest, her hair was golden like the windows he had seen, and her eyes were blue like the sky.

16 She led the boy around the farm and showed him her black calf, <u>and</u> had a white star on its forehead.

17 The boy told her about his own calf at home, which was red <u>as</u> a chestnut and had white feet.

18 Feeling <u>as that</u> they were now friends, the boy asked her about the golden windows.

19 The girl said she knew all about them, only he had mistaken which house <u>have it</u>.

20 "Come with me. I will show you the house with the golden windows, and then you will see for <u>you</u>."

21 The girl told him that the golden windows could only <u>see</u> at sunset.

22 And when they looked again, the boy recognized <u>if</u> it was his own home.

23 Then he told the girl that he must go; and he gave her his best pebble, a white one with a red stripe that he <u>carried</u> with him for a year; and she gave him three horse-chestnuts, one red, <u>other</u> spotted, and one white.

24 He promised to come again, but he did not tell her <u>that</u> he had learned.

25 The girl stood in the light of the sunset and watched him <u>to go</u>.

26 <u>That</u> was dark when the boy finally returned home, but the windows of his home were shining with the light of lamps just like he had seen from the top of the hill.

[01~02] 다음 글을 읽고, 물음에 답하시오.

After working hard all day long, a boy would go up to the top of a hill and look across at another hill. A house with windows of gold and diamond stood on this far hill. They shone at sunset, but after a while, the fascinating light disappeared. The boy supposed that the people in the house closed the shutters because it was dinnertime.

One day, the boy's father called him over and said, "You have been a good boy and have earned a holiday. Take the day off, but try to learn something important." The boy thanked his father and kissed his mother; then he took a piece of bread, and left to find the house with the golden windows.

01 윗글 바로 뒤에 이어질 내용으로 가장 적절한 것은?

① what the boy's parents are worried about
② the relationship between the boy and his parents
③ the lesson the boy should learn during his day off
④ the secret of the house with the golden windows
⑤ the boy's journey to the house with the golden windows

02 윗글의 밑줄 친 문장을 주어진 조건 에 맞게 바꿔 쓰시오.

조건
1. on this far hill이 강조되도록 문장 맨앞에 쓸 것
2. 문장의 표현과 의미를 그대로 살릴 것

_____

_____

[03~04] 다음 글을 읽고, 물음에 답하시오.

His journey was enjoyable. His bare feet made marks in the white sand. When he looked back, the footprints seemed to be following him and keeping him company. His shadow, too, stayed beside him and would dance or run with him as he pleased. Before long, he felt hungry, so he sat down by a stream to eat his bread and drink the clear water. He scattered the remaining pieces of bread for the birds, as his mother had taught him to do, and went on his way.

03 윗글의 분위기로 가장 적절한 것은?

① sad   ② festive
③ peaceful   ④ humorous
⑤ frightening

04 윗글의 요약문을 완성할 때 빈칸 (A)와 (B)에 들어갈 말이 바르게 짝지어진 것은?

The boy enjoyed his walk on the beach. He left ____(A)____ in the sand and was accompanied by his shadow. After eating bread, he fed the birds and continued his ____(B)____ .

	(A)		(B)
①	bread	···	trip
②	company	···	footprints
③	shadow	···	bread
④	journey	···	company
⑤	footprints	···	journey

[05~06] 다음 글을 읽고, 물음에 답하시오.

A woman came to the door, looked kindly at the boy, and asked him (A) if / what he wanted. "I saw the golden windows from the top of our hill," he said, "and I came to see them, but now they are only glass." The woman shook her head and laughed. "We are poor farming people," she said, "and are not likely to have windows made of gold; but glass is better (B) seeing / to see through."

She told the boy to sit down on the step in front of the door, brought him a snack, and (C) calls / called her daughter, a girl of his own age. Then she smiled at the two and went back to her work.

05 윗글의 밑줄 친 부분에서 알 수 있는 소년의 심경으로 가장 적절한 것은?

① pleased   ② surprised

③ furious   ④ proud

⑤ disappointed

06 (A), (B), (C)의 각 네모 안에서 어법에 맞는 표현으로 가장 적절한 것은?

	(A)		(B)		(C)
①	if	…	seeing	…	calls
②	if	…	to see	…	calls
③	what	…	seeing	…	calls
④	what	…	to see	…	called
⑤	what	…	seeing	…	called

[07~08] 다음 글을 읽고, 물음에 답하시오.

Although the girl's clothes were modest, her hair was golden like the windows he ① had seen, and her eyes were blue like the sky. She led the boy around the farm and showed ② him her black calf, which had a white star on its forehead. The boy told her about his own calf at home, ③ which was red like a chestnut and had white feet. Feeling ④ as if they were now friends, the boy asked her about the golden windows. The girl said she knew all about them, only he had mistaken ⑤ that house had them.

07 윗글의 내용과 일치하는 것은?

① The girl had blonde hair and brown eyes.

② The girl's calf was red and had a star shape on its forehead.

③ The boy had a calf with a white head at his home.

④ The boy and girl become friends.

⑤ The girl was curious about the golden windows.

08 윗글의 밑줄 친 부분 중 어법상 틀린 것은?

①   ②   ③   ④   ⑤

[09~10] 다음 글을 읽고, 물음에 답하시오.

"You have come the wrong way!" she said. "Come with ⓐ me. I will show you the house with the golden windows, and then ⓑ you will see for yourself." The girl told ⓒ him that the golden windows could only be seen at sunset. "Yes, ⓓ I know that!" said the boy. They went to a high place and saw a house with windows of gold and diamond on a hill far away, just as the boy had seen before. And when they looked again, the boy recognized that it was ⓔ his own home.

09 윗글의 내용과 일치하지 <u>않는</u> 것은?

① 소녀는 소년이 길을 잘못 찾았다고 알려주었다.

② 황금 창문은 해가 질 때에만 볼 수 있다.

③ 두 사람은 높은 곳에 올라 멀리 떨어진 언덕 위의 황금 창문이 있는 집을 바라보았다.

④ 두 사람이 본 황금 창문의 집은 소년이 전에 보았던 것과는 다른 모습이었다.

⑤ 소년은 두 사람이 보고 있는 황금 창문의 집이 사실은 자신의 집이라는 것을 깨달았다.

10 윗글의 밑줄 친 부분 중 가리키는 대상이 나머지 넷과 <u>다른</u> 것은?

 ① ⓐ　　② ⓑ　　③ ⓒ　　④ ⓓ　　⑤ ⓔ

[11~12] 다음 글을 읽고, 물음에 답하시오.

Then he told the girl that he must go; and he gave her his best pebble, a white one with a red stripe that he had carried with him for a year; and she gave him three horse-chestnuts, one red, one spotted, and one white. He promised to come again, but he did not tell her what he had learned. <u>소녀는 해 질 녘 빛 속에 서서 그가 가는 것을 지켜보았다.</u>

It was dark when the boy finally returned home, but the windows of his home were shining with the light of lamps just like he had seen from the top of the hill. His family welcomed him warmly. "Have you had a good day?" asked his mother. Yes, the boy had had a very good day. "And have you learned anything?" asked his father. "Yes!" said the boy. "I have learned that _____."

11 윗글의 밑줄 친 우리말과 일치하도록 주어진 말을 활용하여 문장을 완성하시오.

소녀는 해 질 녘 빛 속에 서서 그가 가는 것을 지켜보았다.
(stand, light, sunset, watch)

→ The girl _____
_____.

12 윗글의 빈칸에 들어갈 말로 <u>어색한</u> 것은?

① our house is the most precious place in the world

② my family has much more money than others

③ our house has windows of gold and diamond

④ there was no house with golden windows

⑤ important things are not far away

[01~02] 다음 글을 읽고, 물음에 답하시오.

I've been an inspirational speaker for many years. I've learned that teenagers often compare themselves to others and are ashamed of their flaws. Do you have the same problems? If so, you need to practice self-love. Self-love means loving yourself just like you love your friends or family. It also means that you put your happiness first. Here's how to love yourself more. First, think about your skills and talents. Write down whatever comes to mind. For example, you might be good at playing sports. You'll probably be surprised at how long the list is. Next, celebrate yourself for your achievements. They can even be small ones, like _____.
This will increase your self-confidence and inspire you to try new things. So, love yourself as you are right now.

01 윗글의 요지로 가장 적절한 것은?

① 십 대들이 자신을 사랑하고 자신의 행복을 최우선으로 하는 자기애를 키울 필요가 있다.
② 십 대들이 타인과 자신을 비교하며 자기 비하를 하는 것은 좋지 않다.
③ 자신과 타인의 행복을 모두 존중하려는 자세를 가져야 한다.
④ 십 대 때에는 자신만의 고유한 기술과 재능을 갖추는 것이 중요하다.
⑤ 아침에 일찍 일어나는 것과 같은 사소한 습관이 성공으로 이끄는 지름길이다.

02 윗글의 빈칸에 들어갈 말로 어색한 것은?

① not being late for school this morning
② winning the national swimming championship
③ giving a speech in English class
④ scoring a goal during P.E.
⑤ learning how to bake cookies

[03~04] 다음 글을 읽고, 물음에 답하시오.

Do you ever find yourself suddenly feeling angry? One moment you're fine, and the next moment you're slamming doors or rolling your eyes at your parents. Some people may think you just have a bad attitude or are getting too upset about a small problem. However, these feelings don't simply come from stress about everyday life.

As a teen, you may feel like an adult, but your brain is still growing. In your brain, there is a part that is responsible for solving problems and controlling your emotions. In your teen years, this part is still in development. The changes in your brain lead you toward independence, social engagement, and creativity. At the same time, however, you may feel confused about who you are. You may also be more sensitive to unfairness. Furthermore, your body is flowing with hormones. This significantly affects your mood. The combination of these factors intensifies your strong emotions.

03 윗글의 밑줄 친 that과 쓰임이 같은 것은?

① It is strange that he didn't come to the show.
② We all think that Ms. Han is a great teacher.
③ He was so disappointed that he burst into tears.
④ They built a house that has seven windows.
⑤ It was yesterday that we had an argument.

04 십 대의 특징에 관해 윗글의 내용과 일치하지 않는 것은?

① 자신이 다 자란 성인이라고 생각한다.
② 집단에 소속되며 집단의 결정에 의존한다.
③ 자신의 정체성에 대한 혼란이 생긴다.
④ 공정하지 못한 일에 민감하게 반응한다.
⑤ 호르몬 분비가 많아 감정 기복이 심하다.

[05~06] 다음 글을 읽고, 물음에 답하시오.

To feel angry from time to time is natural; it doesn't mean there is something wrong with you. Anger can sometimes be a useful tool. For example, an angry but open conversation can resolve a conflict between friends. ① The important thing is to manage your anger so that it does not turn into aggressive or violent behavior. ② This does not mean that you should stop yourself from feeling angry. ③ When some physical signs show up, take action to reduce your anger. ④ Rather, you should express your anger in a productive way. ⑤ Ask yourself some questions about your angry feelings. This can help you to better understand your anger.

05 윗글의 ①~⑤ 중 전체 흐름과 관계 없는 문장은?

① ② ③ ④ ⑤

06 윗글의 밑줄 친 문장을 조건에 맞게 바꿔 쓰시오.

조건
1. 가주어 it을 사용하여 문장을 시작할 것
2. 문장의 의미가 변하지 않도록 할 것

To feel angry from time to time is natural.

→ _____

[07~09] 다음 글을 읽고, 물음에 답하시오.

Questions to Ask Yourself
✓ How often do I feel angry?
✓ What situations make me feel the most intense anger?
✓ Is my anger directed at anyone or anything in particular?
✓ Do I focus on the causes of my anger instead of solutions?
✓ Can I control my emotions when I get angry?
✓ How do I react and behave when I get angry?

You need to learn how to deal with anger in a socially appropriate way. Remember: anger is a feeling, but behavior is a choice. The first step is recognizing the physical signs of anger. It is possible to recognize those signs in advance. They include an increased heart rate, a flushed face, and the clenching of your fists. When these things happen, _____. For example, you could try taking a break to organize your thoughts or ending a conversation before it gets too intense.

07 윗글의 목적으로 가장 적절한 것은?

① 분노의 양상을 파악하고 적절한 대응 방법을 안내하기 위해
② 분노와 관련된 사람들의 반응을 조사하기 위해
③ 분노가 건강에 미치는 영향을 알려주기 위해
④ 분노를 조절하는 명상 센터를 홍보하기 위해
⑤ 사회적으로 적절한 행동의 범위를 설명하기 위해

08 윗글의 밑줄 친 Questions to Ask Yourself에 대한 응답으로 어색한 것은?

① About twice a week.
② When people don't listen to me.
③ Yes, I'm usually angry with my parents.
④ No, I can't control my anger.
⑤ My friend Tony is usually angry with me.

09 윗글의 빈칸에 들어갈 말로 가장 적절한 것은?

① go and see a doctor
② it means that you are angry
③ take action to reduce your anger
④ recognize the physical signs of anger
⑤ they may have a serious impact

In some cases, the strategies mentioned above may not be enough, so you may need to find proper coping skills for your personal situation. Without the right coping skills, you may find yourself becoming verbally or even physically aggressive. Explore various strategies to discover (A) that / what is best for you, such as taking a walk, drawing a picture, or writing down things that come to your mind. You can also try to find possible solutions to a problem and then compare the advantages and disadvantages of each one. By developing problem-solving skills, you will learn that there are many ways to solve a problem without getting angry.

Anger is an emotion (B) that / who we all experience. By managing your anger properly, you can be the boss of your feelings, not the other way around. This is an important step in finding your true self and (C) take / taking control of your life.

10 윗글의 앞에 언급되었을 내용으로 가장 적절한 것은?

① positive aspect of feeling angry
② why teens easily get angry
③ physical signs that accompany angry emotions
④ actions that help to calm yourself down
⑤ why controlling your emotions is important

11 (A), (B), (C)의 각 네모 안에서 어법에 맞는 표현으로 가장 적절한 것은?

	(A)	(B)	(C)
①	that	that	take
②	that	who	take
③	what	that	take
④	what	who	taking
⑤	what	that	taking

Good morning, students of Happyville High School! My name is Lucy, and I'm in grade 11. Today, I want to tell everyone an important message. We need to improve our school's facilities for people with disabilities. This is important so that everyone can reach all the areas in our school. (A) So, what can we do? First, we need to install an elevator for people with physical disabilities. (B) Second, all signs should be improved for blind people. (C) Signs with voice guidance would be especially helpful. (D) Lastly, we should replace all blackboards with greenboards. (E) They make words easier to see, especially for people with low vision. Let's work together to make these changes. With your help, Happyville High School can become a welcoming place for everyone!

12 윗글에 드러난 필자의 어조로 가장 적절한 것은?

① humorous   ② critical
③ informative   ④ regretful
⑤ persuasive

13 글의 흐름으로 보아, 주어진 문장이 들어갈 위치로 가장 적절한 곳은?

This will make all areas of our school easier to access.

① (A)   ② (B)   ③ (C)   ④ (D)   ⑤ (E)

[14~15] 다음 글을 읽고, 물음에 답하시오.

My grandparents sell their delicious organic jam at the local market every weekend. I went to help them last weekend. However, they already sold all of their jam! They didn't have enough strawberries to make any more jam. That evening, I sat by the window and stared out at the empty field behind their house. Suddenly, I got an idea. The field would be the perfect place for a larger greenhouse. Then they could grow more strawberries! I immediately started searching for a way, and I found the perfect solution. I would start a crowdfunding campaign!

Crowdfunding is a way of raising money for a product, company, or charity. These days, people can use crowdfunding websites to collect money. Crowdfunding is especially advantageous for individuals or small companies that can't attract big investors. If the campaign is successful, the investors receive direct rewards for their contribution.

14 윗글의 내용과 일치하는 것은?

① 필자는 시장에서 조부모님이 딸기잼 파는 일을 도와드렸다.
② 필자의 조부모님은 딸기잼을 만들기에 충분한 딸기를 재배하신다.
③ 조부모님의 집 뒤에는 큰 딸기 밭이 있다.
④ 필자는 대형 온실을 세우기 위해 크라우드펀딩을 계획한다.
⑤ 크라우드펀딩은 대형 기업이 투자자를 유치하는 데 도움이 된다.

15 다음 영어 뜻풀이에 해당하는 단어를 윗글에서 찾아 주어진 철자로 시작하여 쓰시오.

ⓐ an official organization for helping those in need
ⓑ helping to make you more successful

ⓐ → c_____
ⓑ → a_____

16 다음 글의 캠페인 세부 계획과 일치하지 <u>않는</u> 것은?

After doing some calculations, we decided on an 8-by-12-foot greenhouse. We thought it would cost approximately $4,000. Once it was built, we could fill it with strawberry plants and expect a harvest within about four months. Then it would take a few weeks to turn the strawberries into delicious jam. We decided to set our funding goal at $5,000 to cover all the costs. Also, we planned to run the campaign for three months. I was really excited when I filled out the form to launch the campaign. In less than a week, our application was accepted and funding began!

① 온실의 크기: 8×12미터
② 온실을 세우는 데 드는 비용: 4000달러
③ 딸기 재배 기간: 4개월 이내
④ 펀딩 목표액: 5000달러
⑤ 캠페인 운영 기간: 3개월

17 다음 글의 밑줄 친 우리말과 일치하도록 조건 에 맞게 영작하시오.

For a successful crowdfunding campaign, promoting it is necessary. You should consider making a video. <u>이것은 투자자들이 당신에 대해 알게 하고 당신의 제품에 대해 배울 수 있게 한다.</u> In the video, describe your situation clearly and show your product. You also need to express how important the product is to you. Don't forget to include a direct request for support at the end. During a campaign, it is important to send investors updates every week. Through the update, the investors will be able to track the progress of the campaign.

조건
1. 동사 allow를 사용할 것
2. 다음 표현을 사용할 것: investor, get to

→ This _____

about your product.

After our application was accepted, I was eager to make a good first impression with our investors. To achieve this, I made a video about my grandparents and their jam. In the video, I highlighted how the strawberries were grown without using chemicals. I also (A) excluded / included clips of my grandparents. In the clips, they were making the jam with all-natural ingredients. Finally, I explained where I wanted to put the new greenhouse and asked for support. After some editing, I (B) posed / posted the video on many social media sites. It didn't take long for word of our campaign to spread.

Funding for our campaign started slowly. When the first investor committed to supporting us, I almost jumped for joy. Now, after six weeks, we have (C) raised / risen almost $2,500. It seems like we might make our funding goal!

18 윗글의 내용과 일치하지 <u>않는</u> 것은?

① 필자는 투자자들을 위해 영상을 제작했다.
② 영상에서는 유기농으로 딸기를 재배하고 잼을 만든다는 사실을 강조했다.
③ 제작한 영상을 여러 소셜 미디어에 게시했다.
④ 영상은 업로드와 동시에 투자를 유치했다.
⑤ 펀딩 목표액을 달성할 수 있을 것으로 예상된다.

19 (A), (B), (C)의 각 네모 안에서 문맥에 맞는 낱말로 가장 적절한 것은?

	(A)		(B)		(C)
①	excluded	⋯	posed	⋯	raised
②	excluded	⋯	posed	⋯	risen
③	included	⋯	posed	⋯	raised
④	included	⋯	posted	⋯	risen
⑤	included	⋯	posted	⋯	raised

After working hard all day long, a boy would go up to the top of a hill and look across at another hill. A house with windows of gold and diamond stood on this far hill. They shone at sunset, but after a while, the fascinating light disappeared. The boy supposed that the people in the house closed the shutters because it was dinnertime.

One day, the boy's father called him over and said, "You have been a good boy and have earned a holiday. Take the day off, but try to learn something important." The boy thanked his father and kissed his mother; then he took a piece of bread, and left to find the house with the golden windows.

20 윗글의 내용과 일치하는 것은?

① The boy was working with his father on top of the hill.
② The house on the opposite hill shone brightly through the night.
③ The boy's father granted him a day off.
④ The boy left his home to find the gold.
⑤ The boy's mother shed tears when he left home.

21 윗글의 밑줄 친 문장을 주어진 말로 시작하여 바꿔 쓰시오.

A house with windows of gold and diamond stood on this far hill.

→ On this far hill _____

_____ .

[22~23] 다음 글을 읽고, 물음에 답하시오.

A woman came to the door, looked kindly at the boy, and asked him what he wanted. "I saw the golden windows from the top of our hill," he said, "and I came to see them, but now they are only glass." The woman shook her head and laughed. "We are poor farming people," she said, "and are not likely to have windows made of gold; but glass is better to see through."

She told the boy to sit down on the step in front of the door, brought him a snack, and called ⓐ her daughter, a girl of his own age. Then she smiled at the two and went back to ⓑ her work.

Although the girl's clothes were modest, ⓒ her hair was golden like the windows he had seen, and her eyes were blue like the sky. She led the boy around the farm and showed him her black calf, which had a white star on its forehead. The boy told ⓓ her about his own calf at home, which was red like a chestnut and had white feet. Feeling as if they were now friends, the boy asked her about the golden windows. The girl said ⓔ she knew all about them, only he had mistaken which house had them.

22 윗글의 밑줄 친 부분 중 가리키는 대상이 나머지 넷과 다른 것은?

① ⓐ   ② ⓑ   ③ ⓒ   ④ ⓓ   ⑤ ⓔ

23 윗글에서 소녀에 관해 소년이 답할 수 있는 질문이 아닌 것은?

① How old is she?
② What color is her hair?
③ What does her calf look like?
④ How old is her calf?
⑤ Does she know about the house with golden windows?

[24~25] 다음 글을 읽고, 물음에 답하시오.

Then he told the girl that he must go; and he gave her his best pebble, a white one with a red stripe that he had carried with him for a year; and she gave him three horse-chestnuts, one red, one spotted, and one white. He promised to come again, but he did not tell her what he had learned. The girl stood in the light of the sunset and watched him go.

It was dark when the boy finally returned home, but the windows of his home were shining with the light of lamps just like he had seen from the top of the hill. His family welcomed him warmly. "Have you had a good day?" asked his mother. Yes, the boy had had a very good day. "And have you learned anything?" asked his father. "Yes!" said the boy. "I have learned that our house has windows of gold and diamond."

24 윗글의 인물들이 말했을 대사로 어색한 것은?

① Boy: I have to go home now.
② Boy: I want to give you my favorite pebble.
③ Girl: I'll wait for you until you come back.
④ Boy's mother: How was your day?
⑤ Boy's father: What lesson did you learn on your trip?

25 윗글의 밑줄 친 what he had learned에 해당하는 내용을 글에서 찾아 완전한 문장으로 쓰시오.

→ _____

03

How Our Body Works

Functions

▶ 궁금증 표현하기
I'm curious about how vaccines help prevent some diseases.

▶ 알거나 모름 표현하기
Are you aware of the recommended daily amount of caffeine?

Grammar

▶ Doctors **recommend that** people **eat** food containing carbohydrates.

▶ Can you explain **how long we should wait** after eating?

교과서 어휘

Words

☐ prevent	⑧ 막다, 예방하다
☐ fascinating	⑱ 매력적인, 흥미로운 (fascinate ⑧ 마음을 사로잡다)
☐ recommend	⑧ 추천하다 (recommendation ⑲ 추천)
☐ dizzy	⑱ 어지러운
☐ contain	⑧ ~이 함유되어 있다
☐ realize	⑧ 깨닫다
☐ muscle	⑲ 근육
☐ long-lasting	⑱ 오래 지속되는
☐ despite	㉮ ~에도 불구하고 (=in spite of)
☐ automatically	⑨ 자동적으로
☐ professional	⑱ 직업의, 전문적인
☐ diet	⑲ 식단
☐ sugary	⑱ 설탕이 든
☐ release	⑧ 방출하다
☐ digestive	⑱ 소화의 (digestion ⑲ 소화)
☐ absorb	⑧ 흡수하다
☐ nutrient	⑲ 영양소
☐ supply	⑧ 공급하다
☐ oxygen	⑲ 산소
☐ pause	⑧ 잠시 멈추다
☐ harmful	⑱ 해로운 (harm ⑲ 해, ⑧ 해를 끼치다)
☐ fuel	⑲ 연료

☐ provide	⑧ 제공하다 (=supply)
☐ carbohydrate	⑲ 탄수화물
☐ liver	⑲ 간
☐ completely	⑨ 완전히, 전적으로
☐ unusually	⑨ 대단히, 비정상적으로 (↔ usually)
☐ store	⑧ 저장하다
☐ outcome	⑲ 결과
☐ nausea	⑲ 메스꺼움
☐ faint	⑧ 실신하다
☐ replace	⑧ 대신하다, 대체하다
☐ basically	⑨ 기본적으로
☐ weigh	⑧ 무게가 나가다 (weight ⑲ 무게)
☐ consume	⑧ 먹다, 마시다
☐ discomfort	⑲ 불편함 (↔ comfort)
☐ vary	⑧ 서로 다르다
☐ matter	⑧ 중요하다
☐ extremely	⑨ 극히, 극도로 (extreme ⑱ 극심한)
☐ active	⑱ 활동적인
☐ moderate	⑱ 중간의, 보통의
☐ casual	⑱ 일상적인
☐ relieve	⑧ 완화하다
☐ grateful	⑱ 감사하는
☐ overwhelm	⑧ (감정이) 압도하다

Phrases

☐ immune system	면역체계
☐ be aware of	~을 알다, 알아채다
☐ cut down on	~을 줄이다
☐ musical instrument	악기
☐ get used to	~에 익숙해지다
☐ work out	운동하다

☐ break down	분해하다
☐ supply A with B	A에게 B를 공급하다
☐ as a result	그 결과
☐ suffer from	~으로 고통받다
☐ equal to	~과 동일한
☐ use up	다 써 버리다

132

work out 운동하다 = exercise	I try to **work out** at the gym three times a week to stay fit. 나는 건강을 유지하기 위해 일주일에 세 번 체육관에서 운동하려고 노력한다.
contain 포함하다 = include	The news report should **contain** all the relevant facts. 뉴스 보도는 모든 관련된 사실을 포함해야 한다.
store 저장하다 = save	Many countries use traditional methods to **store** food. 많은 나라들은 음식을 저장하기 위해 전통적인 방식을 사용한다.

Useful Expressions

break down 분해하다	The digestive system **breaks down** food into various nutrients. 소화 기관은 음식을 다양한 영양소로 분해한다.
suffer from ~으로 고통받다	Some people **suffer from** excessive stress before job interviews. 어떤 사람들은 구직 면접 전에 과도한 스트레스로 고통받는다.
use up 소진하다, 다 써버리다	They **used up** all the paper in the printer and had to reload it. 그들은 프린터의 모든 종이를 소진해서 다시 채워 놓아야 했다.

Word Mates

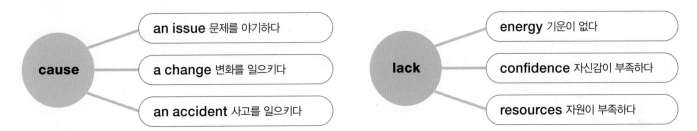

cause
- an issue 문제를 야기하다
- a change 변화를 일으키다
- an accident 사고를 일으키다

lack
- energy 기운이 없다
- confidence 자신감이 부족하다
- resources 자원이 부족하다

English-English Dictionary

- ☐ **absorb** 흡수하다 — to take in a liquid or gas from the surface or the space around
- ☐ **nutrient** 영양소 — a substance that is needed to keep a living thing alive and healthy
- ☐ **pause** 잠시 멈추다 — to stop doing something for a short time
- ☐ **completely** 완전히, 전적으로 — in every way or as much as possible
- ☐ **outcome** 결과 — the result or effect of an action or event
- ☐ **nausea** 메스꺼움 — the unpleasant feeling of wanting to vomit
- ☐ **faint** 실신하다 — to become unconscious when not enough blood is going to your brain
- ☐ **replace** 대신하다, 대체하다 — to start using another thing instead of the one that you are using now
- ☐ **consume** 먹다, 마시다 — to eat or drink something
- ☐ **vary** 서로 다르다 — to be different from each other
- ☐ **moderate** 중간의, 보통의 — average in size or amount and not too much
- ☐ **diet** 식단 — the type of food that you usually eat

교과서 어휘 익히기

✤ 다음 영어는 우리말로, 우리말은 영어로 쓰시오.

01 absorb 동 _____

02 outcome 명 _____

03 carbohydrate 명 _____

04 get used to _____

05 replace 동 _____

06 nausea 명 _____

07 supply A with B _____

08 completely 부 _____

09 harmful 형 _____

10 basically 부 _____

11 work out _____

12 contain 동 _____

13 moderate 형 _____

14 consume 동 _____

15 use up _____

16 matter 동 _____

17 prevent 동 _____

18 provide 동 _____

19 grateful 형 _____

20 fascinating 형 _____

21 casual 형 _____

22 fuel 명 _____

23 vary 동 _____

24 unusually 부 _____

25 형 소화의 _____

26 동 잠시 멈추다 _____

27 분해하다 _____

28 명 영양소 _____

29 동 무게가 나가다 _____

30 면역 체계 _____

31 명 산소 _____

32 동 실신하다 _____

33 형 활동적인 _____

34 ~으로 고통받다 _____

35 형 오래 지속되는 _____

36 동 추천하다 _____

37 부 자동적으로 _____

38 ~을 줄이다 _____

39 형 어지러운 _____

40 명 간 _____

41 명 식단 _____

42 부 극히, 극도로 _____

43 명 근육 _____

44 전 ~에도 불구하고 _____

45 형 설탕이 든 _____

46 동 저장하다 _____

47 동 공급하다 _____

48 명 불편함 _____

A 다음 밑줄 친 부분과 바꿔 쓸 수 있는 것을 보기 에서 골라 기호를 쓰시오.

보기 ⓐ exercise   ⓑ replace   ⓒ save

01 Squirrels <u>store</u> nuts for the winter. (   )

02 She started to <u>work out</u> every day to run a marathon next year. (   )

B 빈칸에 들어갈 말로 알맞은 것을 고르시오.

01 We break _____ food first in our mouth.

ⓐ down   ⓑ in   ⓒ out

02 Jessie should not have _____ all her savings on bags and shoes.

ⓐ saved by   ⓑ set by   ⓒ used up

03 If you _____ from a lack of sleep, you must not drink coffee after six.

ⓐ suffer   ⓑ trouble   ⓒ deprive

C 네모 안에서 알맞은 말을 골라 문장을 완성하시오.

01 What caused / led the accident is unknown until now.

02 It is natural to lack / make confidence when speaking in front of many people.

D 다음 밑줄 친 부분의 영어 뜻풀이로 알맞은 것을 보기 에서 골라 기호를 쓰시오.

보기 ⓐ to stop doing something for a short time
      ⓑ to take in a liquid or gas from the surface or the space around
      ⓒ to become unconscious when not enough blood is going to your brain

01 When you eat, blood rushes to the digestive system to help break down the food and <u>absorb</u> its nutrients. (   )

02 As a result, the digestion process is <u>paused</u> until the blood returns. (   )

03 Some people end up suffering from nausea and headaches, and others even <u>faint</u>. (   )

교과서 핵심 대화문

G Mr. Bruce, today's class about viruses was interesting.

M Oh, I'm glad that you enjoyed it.
　　　　　　　　　= today's class about viruses

G But I want to know more about the topic.

M What do you want to know about?
　　　　　　　　　→ 간접의문문 (about의 목적어)

G **I'm curious about** [how vaccines help prevent some diseases].
　　　　　　　　　help + (to)동사원형: ～하는 것을 돕다

M Well, vaccines are weak versions of viruses. They allow our bodies to
　　　　　　　　　allow + 목적어 + to부정사: ～가 …하게 하다

　　practice [fighting against those viruses].
　　동명사구 (practice의 목적어)

G How interesting! Our immune system is fascinating.

M If you would like to learn more, you can watch some videos about the
　　would like to-V: ～하고 싶다

　　topic.

G Could you recommend some to me?

M Sure. I will let you know a good website.
　　let(사역동사) + 목적어 + 동사원형: ～가 …하게 해주다

≪ G: Bruce 선생님, 바이러스에 관한 오늘 강의가 흥미로웠어요.

M: 오, 즐겁게 들어주어서 기쁘구나.

G: 그런데 그 주제에 관해 저는 좀 더 알고 싶어요.

M: 무엇에 관해 알고 싶니?

G: 저는 백신이 어떻게 질병을 예방하는 데 도움이 되는지 궁금해요.

M: 음, 백신은 바이러스의 약한 버전이란다. 백신은 우리 몸이 바이러스에 맞서 싸우는 연습을 할 수 있게 해줘.

G: 정말 흥미로워요! 우리의 면역체계는 환상적이에요.

M: 좀 더 배우고 싶다면 이 주제에 관한 영상을 볼 수 있어.

G: 제게 몇 가지 영상을 추천해주실 수 있나요?

M: 당연하지. 내가 좋은 웹사이트를 알려줄게.

Study Point ☁

I'm curious about ～은 '나는 ～가 궁금하다'라는 뜻으로, 궁금증을 나타내는 표현이다.

More Expressions ☁

궁금증을 나타내는 표현

- **I wonder** if we can finish the project by the due date.
  나는 우리가 프로젝트를 기일까지 끝낼 수 있을지 궁금하다.

- **Please tell me about** your skills and experience.
  당신의 기술과 경력에 관해 얘기해 주세요.

- **I'd be very interested to know** when your next album will be released.
  당신의 다음 앨범이 언제 발매될지 무척 궁금합니다.

Check-up ☁

다음 대화의 밑줄 친 부분과 바꿔 쓸 수 있는 표현은?

A I'm curious about the side effects of this medicine.

B It can sometimes cause stomachaches.

ⓐ I heard about　　　　　ⓑ Please tell me about　　　　　ⓒ I'm looking forward to

Function 2 알거나 모름 표현하기

B I can't sleep these days, and sometimes I feel dizzy.

G Maybe you drink too many energy drinks. **Are you aware of** the recommended daily amount of caffeine?
과거분사

B No, I'm not. But I only drink two per day.
~당, ~마다

G Well, just 2.5 mg of caffeine [per kilogram of body weight] is enough for you.
주어 · 전치사구 · 동사

B I didn't know that. In that case, I should only have about 150 mg of caffeine per day.

G But each [of those energy drinks] contains 120 mg.
주어 · 전치사구 · 동사

B Oh my goodness! I never realized [that I was drinking so much caffeine]!
명사절 (realized의 목적어)

G I think you should cut down on energy drinks.
~을 줄이다

B You're right. Starting tomorrow, I will only drink one per day.
분사구문

B: 나는 요즘 잠을 못 자겠어. 그리고 가끔 어지럽기도 해.

G: 아마도 네가 에너지 음료를 너무 많이 마셔서 그럴 거야. 너는 카페인의 일일 권장량을 알고 있니?

B: 아니. 하지만 나는 하루에 두 병만 마셔.

G: 음, 체중 1kg당 카페인 2.5mg이 충분한 양이야.

B: 그건 몰랐어. 그렇다면 나는 하루에 150mg의 카페인만 섭취해야 하네.

G: 그런데 그 에너지 음료 한 병에는 120mg이 들어 있어.

B: 세상에! 내가 그렇게 많은 카페인을 마시고 있었다는 걸 전혀 깨닫지 못했어.

G: 내 생각에 너는 에너지 음료를 줄여야 해.

B: 네 말이 맞아. 내일부터 시작해서 나는 하루에 한 병만 마시겠어.

Study Point ❦

Are you aware of ~?는 '~을 알고 있니?'라는 의미로, 상대방이 어떤 사실을 알고 있는지 물을 때 쓰는 표현이다.

More Expressions ❦

알고 있는지 묻는 표현

- **Do you know about** Nelson Mandela? He was South Africa's first black president.
  당신은 Nelson Mandela에 관해 알고 있는가? 그는 남아프리카공화국의 첫 흑인 대통령이었다.

- **Have you heard about** Songkran? It is one of the most important festivals in Thailand.
  당신은 '송크란'에 대해 들어본 적이 있는가? 그것은 태국의 가장 중요한 축제 중 하나이다.

Check-up ❦

다음 대화의 빈칸에 들어갈 말로 가장 적절한 것은?

> **A** Are you aware of the risks of the expedition?
>
> **B** _____

ⓐ Yes. I've always dreamed of the expedition.

ⓑ The expedition was delayed due to the bad weather.

ⓒ Of course. We'll try our best to stay safe.

교과서 기타 대화문

Watch and Communicate   A. Watch

M ❶Once someone learns ❷how to ride a bike, the person will never forget how to do it. ❸The same goes with other skills like ❹eating with chopsticks or ❹playing musical instruments. Once you learn the skill and ❺get used to it, you can perform it ❻without thinking about the necessary muscle movements. This long-lasting memory for certain skills is called muscle memory. ❼Despite its name, it doesn't mean that our muscles remember the skills. Interestingly, muscle memory mostly develops in the brain. Different parts of the brain are used ❽to perform a skill. When we practice a skill, these parts become strongly connected. This makes the skill easier ❾to perform automatically. ❿That's why professional musicians seem to play Mozart's songs so easily! ⓫Without muscle memory, this would be much harder.

M: 일단 자전거 타는 법을 배우면, 그 사람은 자전거를 어떻게 타는지 절대 잊지 않을 것입니다. 젓가락으로 식사를 하거나 악기를 연주하는 것과 같은 다른 기술들도 마찬가지입니다. 일단 당신이 기술을 배우고 그 기술에 익숙해지면, 당신은 필요한 근육의 움직임을 생각하지 않고도 그 기술을 수행할 수 있습니다. 특정 기술에 대해 이렇듯 오랜 시간 지속되는 기억을 근육 기억이라고 합니다. 그 이름에도 불구하고, 그것은 우리의 근육이 그 기술들을 기억한다는 것을 의미하지는 않습니다. 흥미롭게도, 근육 기억은 대부분 뇌에서 발달합니다. 한 가지의 기술을 수행하는 데에는 뇌의 여러 부분들이 사용됩니다. 우리가 기술을 연마할 때, 뇌의 이 부분들은 강력하게 연결됩니다. 이것은 그 기술을 자동적으로 수행하기 더 쉽게 만듭니다. 그래서 전문적인 연주자들이 모차르트의 곡을 아주 쉽게 연주하는 것처럼 보이는 것입니다! 근육 기억이 없다면 이것은 훨씬 더 어려울 것입니다.

❶ once: 접속사 (일단 ~하면) ❷ how+to부정사: ~하는 방법 ❸ The same goes with: ~도 마찬가지이다 ❹ 전치사 like의 목적어 역할을 하는 동명사 eating과 playing이 병렬 연결되어 있다. ❺ get used to: ~에 익숙해지다 ❻ without: 전치사 (~ 없이) ❼ despite = in spite of ❽ to perform: 부사적 용법의 to부정사 (목적) ❾ to perform: 부사적 용법의 to부정사 (easier 수식) ❿ That's why: 그것(앞문장)이 ~인 이유이다 ⓫ = If it were not for muscle memory

Q1 When we learn a skill, our muscles remember the skill. (T / F)

Lesson Review   A

B Hello, Jane. You look ❶much healthier these days.
G Thanks.
B I'm curious about ❷what you did.
G Well, I actually changed my diet.
B Really? How did you change ❸it?
G I eat more vegetables and less sugary food now.
B I see. I should consider ❹changing my diet, too.

B: 안녕, Jane. 너 요즘 훨씬 건강해 보인다.
G: 고마워.
B: 네가 무엇을 했는지 궁금하구나.
G: 음, 나는 사실 식단을 바꾸었어.
B: 정말? 그것을 어떻게 바꿨는데?
G: 이제 나는 채소를 더 많이 먹고 단 음식을 덜 먹어.
B: 알겠어. 나도 내 식단 바꾸는 걸 고려해봐야겠어.

❶ much: 비교급 앞에 쓰여 비교급을 강조 (훨씬) ❷ about의 목적어로 쓰인 간접의문문 ❸ =your diet ❹ consider의 목적어로 쓰인 동명사구

Q2 After changing her (diet / exercise), Jane got much healthier.

교과서 핵심 대화문 익히기

01 자연스러운 대화가 되도록 문장을 순서대로 배열하시오.

> G Mr. Bruce, today's class about viruses was interesting.
> M Oh, I'm glad that you enjoyed it.
>
> (　　　　) What do you want to know about?
> (　　　　) But I want to know more about the topic.
> (　　　　) How interesting! Our immune system is fascinating.
> (　　　　) I'm curious about how vaccines help prevent some diseases.
> (　　　　) Well, vaccines are weak versions of viruses. They allow our bodies to practice fighting against those viruses.
>
> M If you would like to learn more, you can watch some videos about the topic.
> G Could you recommend some to me?
> M Sure. I will let you know a good website.

02 다음 대화에서 밑줄 친 부분의 정확한 수치를 찾아 쓰시오.

> B I can't sleep these days, and sometimes I feel dizzy.
> G Maybe you drink too many energy drinks. Are you aware of <u>the recommended daily amount of caffeine?</u>
> B No, I'm not. But I only drink two per day.
> G Well, just 2.5 mg of caffeine per kilogram of body weight is enough for you.
> B I didn't know that. In that case, I should only have about 150 mg of caffeine per day.
> G But each of those energy drinks contains 120 mg.
> B Oh my goodness! I never realized that I was drinking so much caffeine!
> G I think you should cut down on energy drinks.
> B You're right. Starting tomorrow, I will only drink one per day.

→ _____

03 다음 대화에서 밑줄 친 부분의 의도로 알맞은 것을 고르시오.

> B Hello, Jane. You look much healthier these days.
> G Thanks.
> B <u>I'm curious about what you did.</u>
> G Well, I actually changed my diet.
> B Really? How did you change it?
> G I eat more vegetables and less sugary food now.
> B I see. I should consider changing my diet, too.

① 안부 묻기　　　　② 권유하기　　　　③ 정보 수정 요청하기
④ 알고 있는 것 표현하기　　　⑤ 궁금증 표현하기

교과서 핵심 문법 ─────────

(POINT 1) 목적어 역할을 하는 that절의 「(should)+동사원형」

예제	(should) The police **demanded that** she show her driver's license. 동사＋that＋주어＋동사원형 경찰은 그녀에게 운전면허증을 제시하라고 요구했다.
교과서	Doctors **recommend that** people eat food containing carbohydrates within thirty minutes after working out. (should) 의사들은 사람들에게 운동 후 30분 이내에 탄수화물을 함유한 음식을 먹을 것을 권장한다.

▶ 요구, 주장, 제안 등을 나타내는 동사의 목적어로 쓰이는 that절은 「that＋주어＋should＋동사원형」의 형태가 되며, 이때 should는 흔히 생략된다.

Study Point ♉

1 that+주어+(should)+동사원형

의향이나 당위를 나타내는 동사 뒤에 that이 이끄는 명사절이 목적어로 쓰일 때, that절에는 조동사 should가 쓰여 「that＋주어(＋should)＋동사원형」의 형태가 된다. 이때 should는 흔히 생략된다.

> 의향이나 당위를 나타내는 동사
> demand(요구하다), suggest(제안하다), require(요구하다), insist(주장하다), recommend(권하다), propose(제안하다) 등

- I **suggested that** she **leave** home earlier because of the traffic jam.
  나는 교통 체증 때문에 그녀가 집에서 일찍 출발해야 한다고 제안했다.
- The school soccer team **requires that** the players **participate** in practice every day.
  학교 축구팀은 선수들이 매일 훈련에 참가해야 한다고 요구한다.
- He **insisted that** we **have** more face-to-face communication.
  그는 우리가 좀 더 많은 대면 의사소통을 해야 한다고 주장했다.
- The coach **demanded that** the athletes **eat** a healthier diet.
  코치는 운동선수들이 좀 더 건강한 음식을 먹어야 한다고 요구했다.

Q 다음 네모 안에서 어법상 알맞은 것을 고르시오.

1 We believe that Brian | have / has | excellent skills for the job.

2 Ted proposed that the restaurant | provide / provided | free meal once a month.

3 They recommend that the child | see / sees | a doctor right away.

Check-up ☕

01 다음 문장에서 밑줄 친 should를 생략할 수 있으면 ○, 없으면 × 표시를 하시오.

(1) You look tired. I think you <u>should</u> take a few days off. (　　)

(2) She insisted that her daughter <u>should</u> read a book every day. (　　)

(3) The driver knows that he <u>should</u> have fastened his seat belt. (　　)

(4) We demanded we <u>should</u> have breakfast every morning. (　　)

(5) Mom says I <u>should</u> work out at least twice a week. (　　)

02 주어진 말을 바르게 배열하여 문장을 완성하시오.

(1) The customer ＿＿＿＿＿＿＿＿＿＿＿＿＿＿ for the damaged phone.
(get / that / she / a refund / insisted)

(2) The doctor ＿＿＿＿＿＿＿＿＿＿＿＿ to stay healthy.
(recommended / you / less meat / that / eat)

(3) The director of the movie ＿＿＿＿＿＿＿＿＿＿ for the role.
(the actor / that / suggested / his hair / grow out)

(4) Ms. Han ＿＿＿＿＿＿＿＿＿＿＿＿.
(required / take care of / the school / that / every kid)

(5) I propose that ＿＿＿＿＿＿＿＿＿＿.
(check out / before / we / decisions / every detail / making)

03 다음 문장에서 어법상 어색한 부분을 찾아 바르게 고쳐 쓰시오.

(1) The student council proposed that the students wore school uniforms.
→ The student council ＿＿＿＿＿＿＿＿.

(2) We suggest Brian publishes his amazing story.
→ We ＿＿＿＿＿＿＿＿.

(3) His dad recommended that he practiced piano every day.
→ His dad ＿＿＿＿＿＿＿＿.

(4) The meditation class requires that she turns off her cell phone.
→ The meditation class ＿＿＿＿＿＿＿＿.

(POINT 2) 간접의문문

예제	We want to know **why the flight is delayed**.
	간접의문문: know의 목적어
	우리는 왜 비행이 지연되는지 알고 싶다.
교과서	Can you explain **How long we should wait** after eating?
	간접의문문: explain의 목적어
	우리가 식사 후에 얼마나 오래 기다려야 하는지 설명해 주시겠어요?

▶ 동사의 목적어 역할을 하는 간접의문문은 「의문사＋주어＋동사」의 어순으로 쓴다.

Study Point ❧

1 간접의문문: 의문사가 있는 경우

의문문이 문장의 일부가 되어 주어, 목적어, 보어와 같은 역할을 할 수 있는데, 이를 간접의문문이라 한다.
의문사가 있는 의문문을 간접의문문으로 만들 때에는 의문사가 절을 이어주는 접속사의 역할을 한다.
이때 간접의문문의 어순은 평서문과 같은 「의문사＋주어＋동사」가 되어야 한다. ※ 의문사가 주어인 경우 「의문사 + 동사」의 어순으로 쓰인다.

- I don't know **when his birthday is**. 나는 그의 생일이 언제인지 모른다.
  ← I don't know. + When is his birthday?
- Tell me **who the next speaker is**. 다음 연사가 누구인지 내게 말해줘.
  ← Tell me. + Who is the next speaker?
- **Who won the scholarship** is unknown to the applicants.
  주어
  누가 장학금을 탔는지는 지원자들에게 알려져 있지 않다.
- We talked about **why the musician retired so early**.
  전치사의 목적어
  우리는 왜 그 음악가가 그렇게 일찍 은퇴했는지에 관해 이야기 나눴다.

2 간접의문문: 의문사가 없는 경우

의문사가 없는 의문문이 간접의문문으로 쓰일 때에는 접속사 if나 whether를 써서 연결하며, 이때에도 「주어＋동사」의 어순이 된다.

- I wondered **if she was a vegetarian**. 나는 그녀가 채식주의자인지 궁금했다.
  ← I wondered. + Is she a vegetarian?

Q 다음 네모 안에서 어법상 알맞은 것을 고르시오.

1 Please tell me | who broke / who did break | my glasses.

2 The police officer asked me | if / that | I knew the woman's name.

3 Let's talk about | how can we / how we can | support the organization.

Check-up ☙

01 다음 보기에서 알맞은 말을 골라 문장을 완성하시오.

> 보기   why   what   when   how often

(1) Let me know _____ I should buy at the market.

(2) We talked about _____ we worked out.

(3) My grandparents wondered _____ my train arrived.

(4) Can you explain _____ eco-friendly products are important?

02 주어진 문장을 연결하여 하나의 문장으로 완성하시오.

(1) We want to know. + Where is his house?

→ _____

(2) I'd like to find out. + Who entered the room at that time?

→ _____

(3) They can't be sure. + Is the dog abandoned?

→ _____

(4) Let's discuss. + How can we deal with this problem?

→ _____

(5) Tell me. + Do you believe the news?

→ _____

03 다음 문장에서 어법상 어색한 부분을 찾아 바르게 고쳐 쓰시오.

(1) I will ask the staff what time does the concert start.

→ I will ask the staff _____.

(2) Nobody knows why was the soccer match canceled.

→ Nobody knows _____.

(3) My parents wondered that I passed the exam.

→ My parents wondered _____.

(4) The reporter explained what did cause the accident.

→ The reporter explained _____.

Timing Is Everything
시기 선택이 모든 것이다

Host

01 Welcome back to *Today's Health*.

〈오늘의 건강〉에 돌아오신 것을 환영합니다.

02 Today we're going to be talking about exercise.

be going to-V: ~할 예정이다

오늘 우리는 운동에 대해 이야기하겠습니다.

03 Dr. Victoria Hill is here, and she is going to share some useful tips.

Victoria Hill 박사님이 여기 나와 계시며 유용한 조언을 공유해 주실 예정입니다.

04 So, Dr. Hill, let's start with a question [about my experience last month].

전치사구 지난달

자, Hill 박사님, 지난달 제 경험에 관한 질문으로 시작하겠습니다.

05 I worked out right after dinner and got a stomachache.

~ 직후에

저는 저녁을 먹은 후에 바로 운동을 했고, 복통을 느꼈습니다.

06 Why did that happen?

앞 문장의 내용

왜 그런 일이 일어났을까요?

Dr. Hill

07 Well, the problem is [that you exercised too soon after eating].

명사절 (보어)

음, 문제는 당신이 식사 후 너무 빨리 운동을 했다는 겁니다.

08 This can cause various stomach issues.

=exercising too soon after eating

이는 다양한 위장 문제를 일으킬 수 있습니다.

09 When you eat, blood rushes to the digestive system [to help break down the food and absorb
its nutrients].
= the food's

병렬 연결
to부정사의 부사적 용법 (목적), help (to)-V: ∼하는 것을 돕다

당신이 식사를 할 때 혈액은 음식을 분해하고 음식의 영양분을 흡수하는 것을 돕기 위해 소화 기관으로 급히 움직입니다.

10 But when you start to exercise, blood moves from the digestive system to your muscles.
= start exercising
from A to B: A에서 B로

그러나 당신이 운동을 시작하면 혈액은 소화 기관에서 당신의 근육으로 이동합니다.

11 앞문장의 내용 (혈액이 소화 기관에서 근육으로 이동하는 것)
which[that]
This happens in order to supply your muscles with the oxygen and nutrients [they require].
in order to-V: ∼하기 위해
supply A with B: A에게 B를 공급하다
목적격 관계대명사절

이는 당신의 근육에 그것이 필요로 하는 산소와 영양분을 공급하기 위해 일어납니다.

12 As a result, the digestion process is paused until the blood returns.
그 결과
수동태
접속사 (∼까지)

그 결과, 소화 과정은 혈액이 돌아올 때까지 중단됩니다.

13 (you're)
So, whether you're lifting weights or going for a jog, you shouldn't do it with a stomach full of
whether A or B: A이든 B이든
with + 목적어 + 형용사구: ∼가 …한 채로
food.

따라서 당신이 역기를 들든 조깅을 하러 가든, 당신은 위장에 음식이 가득한 채로 하면 안 됩니다.

Host

14 I see. That makes sense.
말이 되다

그렇군요. 말이 되네요.

15 (that)
So, does that mean [I should exercise on an empty stomach]?
명사절 (mean의 목적어)

그렇다면 그것은 제가 빈속에 운동을 해야 한다는 것을 의미하나요?

Dr. Hill

16 No, it doesn't. That can also be harmful and unpleasant.
= exercising on an empty stomach

아니요, 그렇지 않습니다. 그것 또한 해롭고 불쾌할 수 있습니다.

17

This is because the body needs energy to exercise.

_{+o부정사의 부사적 용법 (목적)}

이는 신체가 운동하기 위해서는 에너지가 필요하기 때문입니다.

18

The fuel [that provides this energy] is glycogen.

_{주격 관계대명사절}

이 에너지를 제공하는 연료는 글리코겐입니다.

19

which[that]

Carbohydrates [in the food (we eat)] are broken down into a kind of sugar [called glucose].

_{주어}　_{전치사구}　_{동사 (수동태)}　_{과거분사구}

우리가 먹는 음식의 탄수화물은 글루코스(포도당)라고 불리는 일종의 당분으로 분해됩니다.

20

근육과 간에 저장된 포도당 ←

When this glucose is stored in parts of the body, (such as the muscles and the liver,) it is called glycogen.

_{수동태}　_{삽입구}　_{수동태}

이 글루코스(포도당)가 근육과 간과 같은 신체 일부에 저장되면 그것은 글리코겐이라 불립니다.

21

동명사구　　　　　　삽입구

This is why [exercising on a completely empty stomach]—[such as when you first wake up in the morning]—can be such a challenge.

_{명사절 (전치사의 목적어)}

이것이 당신이 아침에 처음 일어났을 때와 같이 완전히 빈속에 운동하는 것이 그렇게나 힘들 수 있는 이유입니다.

22

Your blood sugar levels are low, and you don't have enough glycogen [stored in your body].

_{혈당 수치}　_{과거분사구}

당신의 혈당 수치는 낮고, 당신은 신체에 저장된 글리코겐을 충분히 갖고 있지 않습니다.

23

아마, 필시

If you exercise on an empty stomach, you will most likely lack energy and feel unusually tired.

_{부사절 (조건): 현재시제가 미래시제 대신}　_{병렬 연결}
_(will 뒤의 동사원형)

만일 당신이 빈속에 운동한다면, 당신은 아마 에너지가 부족하고 유난히 피곤하게 느낄 것입니다.

24

There can also be more serious outcomes.

_{비교급}

또한 더 심각한 결과가 있을 수 있습니다.

25

some ~, others ....: 어떤 사람들은 ~하고, 또 어떤 사람들은 … 하다

Some people end up suffering from nausea and headaches, and others even faint.

end up V-ing: 결국 ~하다, suffer from: ~으로 고통받다

어떤 사람들은 결국 구역감과 두통을 겪고, 다른 사람들은 실신하기도 합니다.

26

소진하다

This is because intense exercise uses up all the glycogen [in your muscles].

전치사구

이는 강한 운동이 당신의 근육에 있는 모든 글리코겐을 다 써 버리기 때문입니다.

Host

27

It ~ that 강조 구문의 의문문

So, is it the loss of glycogen that causes us to have low levels of energy?

cause + 목적어 + to부정사: ~가 … 하게 야기하다

그렇다면, 우리가 낮은 수준의 에너지를 갖도록 만드는 것이 바로 글리코겐의 손실인가요?

Dr. Hill

28

명사절 (recommend의 목적어)

That's correct. For this reason, doctors recommend [that people eat food (containing carbohydrates)

(should)   현재분사구

within thirty minutes after working out].

동명사구 (after의 목적어)

맞습니다. 이러한 이유로 의사들은 사람들에게 운동 후 30분 이내에 탄수화물을 함유한 음식을 먹을 것을 권장합니다.

29

(that)

This replaces the muscle glycogen [you have lost].

목적격 관계대명사절

이것이 당신이 잃어버린 근육 글리코겐을 대체합니다.

30

Basically, you need between (one) and (one and a half) grams of carbohydrates for every kilogram

between A and B: A(one)와 B(one and a half) 사이

you weigh.

기본적으로 당신의 체중 1kg당 1에서 1.5g 사이의 탄수화물이 필요합니다.

31

Let's do the math.

산수를 해봅시다.

32

접속사 (~하면)

If you weigh 60 kilograms, you should try to consume between 60 and 90 grams of carbohydrates

try + to부정사: ~하려고 노력하다

after you exercise.

접속사 (~한 후)

만일 당신이 60kg이라면 당신은 운동한 후에 60에서 90g 사이의 탄수화물을 섭취하려고 노력해야 합니다.

33

This is equal to about one bowl of white rice or three bananas.

~과 동일한

이는 대략 흰 쌀밥 한 그릇 또는 바나나 세 개와 동일합니다.

Host

34

접속사 (~하기 전에)

That's very interesting. But what about [eating before we exercise]?

동명사구 (about의 목적어)

정말 흥미롭네요. 그런데 운동하기 전에 식사하는 것은 어떤가요?

35

전치사 (~ 후에)

Can you explain [how long we should wait after eating]?

간접의문문 (explain의 목적어)

우리가 식사 후에 얼마나 오래 기다려야 하는지 설명해 주시겠어요?

Dr. Hill

36

접속사 (~한대로)

Well, as I said before, [exercising right after you eat] will cause feelings of discomfort.

동명사구 (주어)   동사

음, 제가 앞에서 말했던 것처럼, 식사 직후에 운동하는 것은 불편한 느낌을 유발할 것입니다.

37

But, if you wait too long to exercise after eating, you'll suffer from a lack of energy.

to부정사의 부사적 용법 (~하기 위해)

그러나 식사 후 운동하기 위해 너무 오래 기다린다면 당신은 에너지 부족을 겪을 것입니다.

38

The best time [to eat (before you exercise)] varies from one to three hours.

주어   to부정사의 형용사적 용법   동사

운동 전에 식사할 가장 좋은 시간은 1시간에서 3시간으로 다릅니다.

39

~에 의해 결정되다

Basically, it depends on several factors [such as the type and amount of food as well as body size,

전치사구   B as well as A: A뿐만 아니라 B도

age, and gender].

기본적으로 그것은 체구, 나이, 성별뿐만 아니라 음식의 종류와 양과 같은 여러 요소에 의해 결정됩니다.

40　The type of exercise also matters.
　　　　　　　　　　　　　　　　중요하다

운동의 종류 또한 중요합니다.

41　For extremely active exercise [like cycling], I suggest [that you wait between (one and a half) and
　　　　　　　　　　　　　　　　　　　　　　　　　　　　　　　　　　　(should)
　　　　　　　　　　　　　　　　　　　　　　　　　　　　　　　명사절 (suggest의 목적어)
(three) hours after eating a moderate-sized meal].
　　　　　　전치사

사이클링과 같은 매우 활동적인 운동의 경우, 저는 적정량의 식사를 한 후 1시간 30분에서 3시간 사이를 기다릴 것을 권장합니다.

42　But for something more casual, such as golfing, [waiting for one hour after a meal] should be
　　　　　　　　　　　　　↑　　　　　　　　　　　　　　　　　　　동명사구 (주어)　　　　　　　　　　　동사
enough.　비교급의 형용사구가 뒤에서 수식

그러나 골프 치기와 같이 좀 더 일상적인 운동의 경우, 식사 후 1시간을 기다리는 것으로 충분합니다.

43　Clearly, you can wait less after eating a snack.
　　　　　　　　　　　　　　　　　　동명사구 (after의 목적어)

분명히, 간식을 먹은 후에는 덜 기다려도 됩니다.

Host

44　Thank you very much for this fascinating information, Dr. Hill.
　thank + 목적어 + for: ~에게 …에 대해 감사하다

Hill 박사님, 대단히 흥미로운 이 정보에 정말 감사드립니다.

　　　　　　　(that) → = this fascinating information
45　I'm sure [it will be very helpful for all of our viewers].
　be sure (that): ~라고 확신하다

저는 그것이 모든 시청자들에게 매우 도움이 될 거라고 확신합니다.

♣ 다음 빈칸에 알맞은 말을 쓰시오.

01 Welcome _____ *Today's Health.*
〈오늘의 건강〉에 돌아오신 것을 환영합니다.

02 Today we're _____ talking about exercise.
오늘 우리는 운동에 대해 이야기하겠습니다.

03 Dr. Victoria Hill is here, and she is going to share _____.
Victoria Hill 박사님이 여기 나와 계시며 유용한 조언을 공유해 주실 예정입니다.

04 So, Dr. Hill, let's _____ about my experience last month.
자, Hill 박사님, 지난달 제 경험에 관한 질문으로 시작하겠습니다.

05 I worked out _____ and got a stomachache.
저는 저녁을 먹은 후에 바로 운동을 했고, 복통을 느꼈습니다.

06 _____ that happen?
왜 그런 일이 일어났을까요?

07 Well, the problem is _____ too soon after eating.
음, 문제는 당신이 식사 후 너무 빨리 운동을 했다는 겁니다.

08 _____ various stomach issues.
이는 다양한 위장 문제를 일으킬 수 있습니다.

09 _____, blood rushes to the digestive system _____
the food and absorb its nutrients.
당신이 식사를 할 때 혈액은 음식을 분해하고 음식의 영양분을 흡수하는 것을 돕기 위해 소화 기관으로 급히 움직입니다.

10 But when you start to exercise, blood moves _____ to your muscles.
그러나 당신이 운동을 시작하면 혈액은 소화 기관에서 당신의 근육으로 이동합니다.

11 This happens in order to supply your muscles with the _____.
이는 당신의 근육에 그것이 필요로 하는 산소와 영양분을 공급하기 위해 일어납니다.

12 _____, the digestion process is paused until the blood returns.
그 결과, 소화 과정은 혈액이 돌아올 때까지 중단됩니다.

13 So, whether you're lifting weights or going for a jog, you shouldn't do it _____.
따라서 당신이 역기를 들든 조깅을 하러 가든, 당신은 위장에 음식이 가득한 채로 하면 안 됩니다.

14 I see. _____.
그렇군요. 말이 되네요.

15 So, _____ I should exercise on an empty stomach?
그렇다면 그것은 제가 빈속에 운동을 해야 한다는 것을 의미하나요?

16   No, it doesn't. That can also be _____.
아니요, 그렇지 않습니다. 그것 또한 해롭고 불쾌할 수 있습니다.

17   _____ the body needs energy to exercise.
이는 신체가 운동하기 위해서는 에너지가 필요하기 때문입니다.

18   The fuel _____ is glycogen.
이 에너지를 제공하는 연료는 글리코겐입니다.

19   Carbohydrates in the food we eat _____ into a kind of sugar
_____.
우리가 먹는 음식의 탄수화물은 글루코스(포도당)라고 불리는 일종의 당분으로 분해됩니다.

20   When this glucose is stored in parts of the body, _____, it is called glycogen.
이 글루코스(포도당)가 근육과 간과 같은 신체 일부에 저장되면 그것은 글리코겐이라 불립니다.

21   _____ exercising on a completely empty stomach—such as when you first
wake up in the morning—_____.
이것이 당신이 아침에 처음 일어났을 때와 같이 완전히 빈속에 운동하는 것이 그렇게나 힘들 수 있는 이유입니다.

22   Your blood sugar levels are low, and you don't have enough glycogen _____.
당신의 혈당 수치는 낮고, 당신은 신체에 저장된 글리코겐을 충분히 갖고 있지 않습니다.

23   If you exercise on an empty stomach, _____ energy and feel unusually tired.
만일 당신이 빈속에 운동한다면, 당신은 아마 에너지가 부족하고 유난히 피곤하게 느낄 것입니다.

24   There can also be _____.
또한 더 심각한 결과가 있을 수 있습니다.

25   Some people _____ nausea and headaches, and others even faint.
어떤 사람들은 결국 구역감과 두통을 겪고, 다른 사람들은 실신하기도 합니다.

26   This is because _____ all the glycogen in your muscles.
이는 강한 운동이 당신의 근육에 있는 모든 글리코겐을 다 써 버리기 때문입니다.

27   So, is it the loss of glycogen _____ low levels of energy?
그렇다면, 우리가 낮은 수준의 에너지를 갖도록 만드는 것이 바로 글리코겐의 손실인가요?

28   That's correct. For this reason, doctors recommend _____ containing
carbohydrates _____ after working out.
맞습니다. 이러한 이유로 의사들은 사람들에게 운동 후 30분 이내에 탄수화물을 함유한 음식을 먹을 것을 권장합니다.

29   This _____ you have lost.
이것이 당신이 잃어버린 근육 글리코겐을 대체합니다.

30   Basically, you need _____ grams of carbohydrates for every kilogram you weigh.
기본적으로 당신의 체중 1kg당 1에서 1.5g 사이의 탄수화물이 필요합니다.

31 Let's _____.
산수를 해봅시다.

32 _____, you should try to consume between 60 and 90 grams of carbohydrates _____.
만일 당신이 60kg이라면 당신은 운동한 후에 60에서 90g 사이의 탄수화물을 섭취하려고 노력해야 합니다.

33 This is _____ about one bowl of white rice or three bananas.
이는 대략 흰 쌀밥 한 그릇 또는 바나나 세 개와 동일합니다.

34 That's very interesting. But _____ before we exercise?
정말 흥미롭네요. 그런데 운동하기 전에 식사하는 것은 어떤가요?

35 Can you explain _____ after eating?
우리가 식사 후에 얼마나 오래 기다려야 하는지 설명해 주시겠어요?

36 Well, as I said before, exercising right after you eat _____.
음, 제가 앞에서 말했던 것처럼, 식사 직후에 운동하는 것은 불편한 느낌을 유발할 것입니다.

37 But, if you _____ after eating, you'll suffer from a lack of energy.
그러나 식사 후 운동하기 위해 너무 오래 기다린다면 당신은 에너지 부족을 겪을 것입니다.

38 _____ before you exercise varies from one to three hours.
운동 전에 식사할 가장 좋은 시간은 1시간에서 3시간으로 다릅니다.

39 Basically, it _____ such as the type and amount of food _____ body size, age, and gender.
기본적으로 그것은 체구, 나이, 성별뿐만 아니라 음식의 종류와 양과 같은 여러 요소에 의해 결정됩니다.

40 The type of exercise _____.
운동의 종류 또한 중요합니다.

41 For extremely active exercise like cycling, _____ between one and a half and three hours after eating _____.
사이클링과 같은 매우 활동적인 운동의 경우, 저는 적정량의 식사를 한 후 1시간 30분에서 3시간 사이를 기다릴 것을 권장합니다.

42 But for something more casual, such as golfing, _____ should be enough.
그러나 골프 치기와 같이 좀 더 일상적인 운동의 경우, 식사 후 1시간을 기다리는 것으로 충분합니다.

43 Clearly, you _____ after eating a snack.
분명히, 간식을 먹은 후에는 덜 기다려도 됩니다.

44 Thank you very much _____, Dr. Hill.
Hill 박사님, 대단히 흥미로운 이 정보에 정말 감사드립니다.

45 _____ it will be very helpful for all of our viewers.
저는 그것이 모든 시청자들에게 매우 도움이 될 거라고 확신합니다.

교과서 본문 익히기 ② 옳은 어법·어휘 고르기

♣ 다음 네모 안에서 옳은 것을 고르시오.

01 Today we're going to be talking / telling about exercise.

02 So, Dr. Hill, let's start with a question about my experience last / the last month.

03 I worked out only / right after dinner and got a stomachache.

04 Well, the problem is that / what you exercised too soon after eating.

05 This can cause / take various stomach issues.

06 When you eat, blood rushes to the digestive / immune system to help break down the food and absorb / absorbs its nutrients.

07 But when you start to exercise, blood moves from the digestive system to your stomach / muscles .

08 This happens in order to apply / supply your muscles with the oxygen and nutrients it / they require.

09 As a result, the digestion process is posed / paused until the blood returns.

10 So, whether you're lifting weights or go / going for a jog, you shouldn't do it with a stomach full / filled of food.

11 I see. That makes sense / sensitive .

12 So, does that mean I should / should I exercise on an empty stomach?

13 No, it doesn't. That can also be harmful and pleasant / unpleasant .

14 This is because / why the body needs energy to exercise.

15 Carbohydrates in the food we eat is / are broken down into a kind of sugar called / calling glucose.

16 When this glucose stores / is stored in parts of the body, such as the muscles and the liver, it is called glycogen.

17 This is how / why exercising on a completely empty stomach—so that / such as when you first wake up in the morning—can be such a challenge.

18 Your blood sugar levels are high / low, and you don't have enough glycogen stored in your body.

19 If you exercise / will exercise on an empty stomach, you will most likely lack energy and feel unusually tired.

20 There can also be more / most serious outcomes.

21 Some people end up suffer / suffering from nausea and headaches, and other / others even faint.

22 This is because inner / intense exercise uses up all the glycogen in your muscles.

23 So, is it / that the loss of glycogen that causes us have / to have low levels of energy?

24 That's correct. For this reason, doctors recommend that people eat / eating food containing carbohydrates before / within thirty minutes after working out.

25 This replaces the muscle glycogen you have gained / lost.

26 Basically, you need about / between one and one and a half grams of carbohydrates for every kilogram you weigh / weight.

27 If you weigh 60 kilograms, you should try to assume / consume between 60 and 90 grams of carbohydrates after you exercise.

28   This is equal / equally to about one bowl of white rice or three bananas.

29   That's very interesting. But what about / if eating before we exercise?

30   Can you explain how long we should / should we wait after eating?

31   Well, as / like I said before, exercising right after you eat will cause feelings of discomfort / uncomfort .

32   But, if you wait too long to exercise after eating, you'll suffer from / by a lack of energy.

33   The best time to eat before you exercise vary / varies from one to three hours.

34   Basically, it depends on several factors for example / such as the type and amount of food as well as body size, age, and gender.

35   For extremely active / actual exercise like cycling, I suggest that you wait between one and a half and / or three hours after eating a moderate-sized meal.

36   But for something more casual, such as golfing, wait / waiting for one hour after a meal should be enough.

37   Thank you very much for this fascinating / fascinated information, Dr. Hill.

38   I'm sure / surely it will be very helpful for all of our viewers.

♣ 다음 밑줄 친 부분을 바르게 고쳐 쓰시오.

01   Today we're going <u>talking</u> about exercise.

02   Dr. Victoria Hill is here, and she is going to <u>share with</u> some useful tips.

03   So, Dr. Hill, <u>let</u> start with a question about my experience last month.

04   I worked out right after dinner and <u>get</u> a stomachache.

05   Well, the problem is that you exercised too soon after <u>to eat</u>.

06   This can <u>be caused</u> various stomach issues.

07   When you eat, blood rushes to the digestive system to help break down the food and <u>absorbs</u> its nutrients.

08   But when you start to exercise, blood <u>moves the digestive system</u> to your muscles.

09   This happens in order to supply your muscles <u>for</u> the oxygen and nutrients <u>it requires</u>.

10   As a result, the digestion process is paused until the blood <u>will return</u>.

11   So, <u>if</u> you're lifting weights or going for a jog, you shouldn't do it with a stomach full <u>with</u> food.

12   I see. That makes <u>to sense</u>.

13   So, <u>is</u> that mean I should exercise on an empty stomach?

14   No, it doesn't. That can also be harmful and <u>pleasant</u>.

15   This is because the body needs energy <u>exercising</u>.

16   The fuel that <u>provide</u> this energy is glycogen.

17   Carbohydrates in the food we eat <u>break down</u> into a kind of sugar <u>calling</u> glucose.

18   When this glucose is stored in parts of the body, such as the muscles and the liver, <u>they are</u> called glycogen.

19   This is why exercising on a <u>complete</u> empty stomach—such as when you first wake up in the morning—can be <u>so</u> a challenge.

20   Your blood sugar levels are low, and you don't have enough glycogen <u>storing</u> in your body.

21   If you exercise on an empty stomach, you will most <u>like</u> lack energy and feel unusually tired.

22   There can also be <u>seriouser</u> outcomes.

23   Some people end up <u>suffer</u> from nausea and headaches, and <u>other</u> even faint.

24   This is <u>why</u> intense exercise uses up all the glycogen in your muscles.

25   So, is it the loss of glycogen that <u>causes us have</u> low levels of energy?

26   For this reason, doctors recommend that people eat food <u>contained</u> carbohydrates within thirty minutes after working out.

27   This replaces the muscle glycogen you <u>lose</u>.

28   Basically, you need <u>from</u> one and one and a half grams of carbohydrates for every <u>kilograms</u> you weigh.

29   If you <u>weight</u> 60 kilograms, you should try to consume between 60 <u>to</u> 90 grams of carbohydrates after you exercise.

30   This is equal <u>with</u> about one bowl of white rice or three bananas.

31   Can you explain how long <u>should we</u> wait after eating?

32   Well, as I said before, <u>exercise</u> right after you eat will cause feelings of discomfort.

33   But, if you wait too long to exercise after eating, you'll suffer <u>of</u> a lack of energy.

34   The best time to eat before you exercise <u>vary</u> from one to three hours.

35   Basically, it depends on several factors such as the type and amount of food <u>as much as</u> body size, age, and gender.

36   The type of exercise also <u>matter</u>.

37   For extremely active exercise like cycling, I suggest that you wait between one and a half and three hours after eating a <u>moderate-size</u> meal.

38   But for something more casual, such as golfing, <u>wait</u> for one hour after a meal should be enough.

39   Clearly, you can wait <u>few</u> after eating a snack.

40   I'm sure <u>of it</u> will be very helpful for all of our viewers.

교과서 본문 외 지문 분석

Think and Write 🏅 (교과서 73쪽)

Tips on Maintaining Your Mental Health

Do you often get stressed because you have too many things ❶to do? If so, then here are some useful tips ❷to help you relieve your stress. The first tip is ❸to think of your favorite person or place. This will ❹help you to feel ❺much better than before. The second tip is to write down ❻what you're grateful for. You will ❼be able to focus more on the positive things in your life. Always ❽remember to ask your friends or family for help when you're overwhelmed with stress.

당신의 정신 건강을 유지하는 방법

당신은 할 일이 너무 많아 자주 스트레스를 받곤 하는가? 만일 그렇다면, 여기 당신의 스트레스를 완화하는 데 도움을 줄 유용한 방법이 몇 가지 있다. 첫 번째 팁은 당신이 좋아하는 사람이나 공간을 떠올리는 것이다. 이것은 당신이 전보다 훨씬 더 기분이 나아지도록 도와줄 것이다. 두 번째 팁은 당신이 감사하는 것에 대해 써 보는 것이다. 당신은 삶에서 긍정적인 것들에 더욱 초점을 맞출 수 있을 것이다. 당신이 스트레스에 휩싸여 있을 때 친구들이나 가족에게 도움을 요청할 것을 항상 기억하라.

❶ to do: 앞에 쓰인 명사 things를 수식하는 형용사적 용법의 to부정사 ❷ to help: tips를 수식하는 형용사적 용법의 to부정사, help(준사역동사)+목적어+목적격 보어(동사원형) ❸ to think: is의 보어 역할을 하는 to부정사 ❹ help(준사역동사)+목적어+목적격 보어(to부정사) ❺ much: 비교급 better를 강조 ❻ what: 선행사를 포함하는 관계대명사 (=things that you're grateful for) ❼ be able to-V: ~할 수 있다 ❽ to ask: remember의 목적어로 to부정사가 쓰이면 '~할 것을 기억하다'라는 의미, ask ~ for help: ~에게 도움을 요청하다

Q One of the ways to relieve stress is to write down things that you are grateful for. (T / F)

Check-up 🏅

다음 빈칸에 알맞은 말을 쓰시오.

01 Do you often get stressed because you have _____?
당신은 할 일이 너무 많아 자주 스트레스를 받곤 하는가?

02 If so, then here are some useful tips _____ your stress.
만일 그렇다면, 여기 당신의 스트레스를 완화하는 데 도움을 줄 유용한 방법이 몇 가지 있다.

03 The first tip is _____ your favorite person or place.
첫 번째 팁은 당신이 좋아하는 사람이나 공간을 떠올리는 것이다.

04 This will help you to feel _____.
이것은 당신이 전보다 훨씬 더 기분이 나아지도록 도와줄 것이다.

05 The second tip is to write down _____.
두 번째 팁은 당신이 감사하는 것에 대해 써 보는 것이다.

06 You _____ more on the positive things in your life.
당신은 삶에서 긍정적인 것들에 더욱 초점을 맞출 수 있을 것이다.

07 Always _____ your friends or family for help when you're overwhelmed with stress.
당신이 스트레스에 휩싸여 있을 때 친구들이나 가족에게 도움을 요청할 것을 항상 기억하라.

01 밑줄 친 부분 중, 문맥상 낱말의 쓰임이 적절하지 <u>않은</u> 것은?

Once someone learns how to ride a bike, the person will never ① <u>forget</u> how to do it. Once you learn the skill and get used to it, you can perform it without thinking about the ② <u>necessary</u> muscle movements. This long-lasting memory for certain skills is called muscle memory. ③ <u>Despite</u> its name, it doesn't mean that our muscles remember the skills. Interestingly, muscle memory mostly develops in the brain. ④ <u>Different</u> parts of the brain are used to perform a skill. When we practice a skill, these parts become strongly connected. This makes the skill ⑤ <u>harder</u> to perform automatically.

①   ②   ③   ④   ⑤

02 밑줄 친 부분 중, 문맥상 낱말의 쓰임이 적절하지 <u>않은</u> 것은?

Host   Welcome back to *Today's Health*. Today we're going to be talking ① <u>about</u> exercise. Dr. Victoria Hill is here, and she is going to share some useful tips. So, Dr. Hill, let's start ② <u>with</u> a question about my experience ③ <u>last</u> month. I worked ④ <u>out</u> right after dinner and got a stomachache. Why did that happen?

Dr. Hill   Well, the problem is that you exercised too ⑤ <u>late</u> after eating. This can cause various stomach issues.

①   ②   ③   ④   ⑤

03 (A), (B), (C)의 각 네모 안에서 문맥에 맞는 낱말로 가장 적절한 것은?

When you eat, blood rushes to the digestive system to help break down the food and (A) absorb / observe its nutrients. But when you start to exercise, blood moves from the digestive system to your muscles. This happens in order to supply your muscles with the oxygen and nutrients they require. As a result, the digestion process is (B) paused / posed until the blood returns. So, whether you're lifting weights or going for a jog, you shouldn't do it with a stomach (C) filled / full of food.

(A)	(B)	(C)
① absorb	⋯ paused	⋯ filled
② absorb	⋯ posed	⋯ filled
③ absorb	⋯ paused	⋯ full
④ observe	⋯ posed	⋯ full
⑤ observe	⋯ paused	⋯ full

04 밑줄 친 부분 중, 문맥상 낱말의 쓰임이 적절하지 <u>않은</u> 것은?

Host   I see. That ① <u>makes</u> sense. So, does that mean I should exercise on an empty stomach?

Dr. Hill   No, it doesn't. That can also be ② <u>harmful</u> and unpleasant. This is because the body needs energy to exercise. The fuel that ③ <u>consumes</u> this energy is glycogen. Carbohydrates in the food we eat are broken ④ <u>down</u> into a kind of sugar called glucose. When this glucose is ⑤ <u>stored</u> in parts of the body, such as the muscles and the liver, it is called glycogen. This is why exercising on a completely empty stomach can be such a challenge.

①   ②   ③   ④   ⑤

05 (A), (B), (C)의 각 네모 안에서 문맥에 맞는 낱말로 가장 적절한 것은?

Exercising on a completely (A) empty / full stomach—such as when you first wake up in the morning—can be a challenge. Your blood sugar levels are low, and you don't have enough glycogen stored in your body. If you exercise on an empty stomach, you will most likely lack energy and feel (B) usually / unusually tired. There can also be more serious outcomes. Some people end up suffering from nausea and headaches, and others even faint. This is (C) because / why intense exercise uses up all the glycogen in your muscles.

	(A)	(B)	(C)
①	empty	⋯ usually	⋯ because
②	empty	⋯ unusually	⋯ because
③	empty	⋯ usually	⋯ why
④	full	⋯ unusually	⋯ why
⑤	full	⋯ usually	⋯ why

06 (A), (B), (C)의 각 네모 안에서 문맥에 맞는 낱말로 가장 적절한 것은?

Doctors recommend that people eat food containing carbohydrates within thirty minutes after working out. This (A) places / replaces the muscle glycogen you have lost. Basically, you need between one and one and a half grams of carbohydrates for every kilogram you (B) weigh / weight. Let's do the math. If you weigh 60 kilograms, you should try to consume between 60 and 90 grams of carbohydrates after you exercise. This is (C) equal / same to about one bowl of white rice or three bananas.

	(A)	(B)	(C)
①	places	⋯ weigh	⋯ equal
②	replaces	⋯ weigh	⋯ equal
③	places	⋯ weigh	⋯ same
④	replaces	⋯ weight	⋯ same
⑤	places	⋯ weight	⋯ same

07 밑줄 친 부분 중, 문맥상 낱말의 쓰임이 적절하지 <u>않은</u> 것은?

The best time to eat before you exercise ① <u>varies</u> from one to three hours. Basically, it depends on ② <u>several</u> factors such as the type and amount of food as well as body size, age, and gender. The type of exercise also matters. For extremely ③ <u>light</u> exercise like cycling, I suggest that you wait between one and a half and three hours after eating a moderate-sized meal. But for something more ④ <u>casual</u>, such as golfing, waiting for one hour after a meal should be ⑤ <u>enough</u>. Clearly, you can wait less after eating a snack.

①   ②   ③   ④   ⑤

08 (A), (B), (C)의 각 네모 안에서 문맥에 맞는 낱말로 가장 적절한 것은?

Do you often get stressed because you have too many things to do? If so, then here are some useful tips to help you (A) release / relieve your stress. The first tip is to think of your favorite person or place. This will help you to feel much better than before. The second tip is to write down what you're (B) grateful / regretful for. You will be able to focus more on the positive things in your life. Always remember to ask your friends or family for help when you're (C) overjoyed / overwhelmed with stress.

	(A)	(B)	(C)
①	release	⋯ grateful	⋯ overjoyed
②	release	⋯ regretful	⋯ overjoyed
③	relieve	⋯ grateful	⋯ overjoyed
④	relieve	⋯ regretful	⋯ overwhelmed
⑤	relieve	⋯ grateful	⋯ overwhelmed

01 다음 글의 밑줄 친 부분 중, 어법상 틀린 것은?

Once someone learns how to ride a bike, the person will never forget ① how to do it. The same goes with other skills like eating with chopsticks or ② playing musical instruments. Once you learn the skill and get used to it, you can perform it without thinking about the necessary muscle movements. This long-lasting memory for certain skills ③ are called muscle memory. Despite its name, it doesn't mean that our muscles remember the skills. Interestingly, muscle memory mostly develops in the brain. Different parts of the brain ④ are used to perform a skill. When we practice a skill, these parts become strongly connected. This ⑤ makes the skill easier to perform automatically.

①   ②   ③   ④   ⑤

02 (A), (B), (C)의 각 네모 안에서 어법에 맞는 표현으로 가장 적절한 것은?

Host   Welcome back to *Today's Health*. Today we're going to be talking about exercise. Dr. Victoria Hill is here, and she is going to share some useful tips. So, Dr. Hill, let's (A) start / to start with a question about my experience last month. I worked out right after dinner and (B) get / got a stomachache. Why did that happen?

Dr. Hill   Well, the problem is (C) that / what you exercised too soon after eating. This can cause various stomach issues.

	(A)		(B)		(C)
①	start	…	get	…	that
②	start	…	got	…	that
③	start	…	get	…	what
④	to start	…	got	…	what
⑤	to start	…	get	…	what

03 (A), (B), (C)의 각 네모 안에서 어법에 맞는 표현으로 가장 적절한 것은?

When you eat, blood rushes to the digestive system to help break down the food and (A) absorb / absorbs its nutrients. But when you start to exercise, blood moves from the digestive system to your muscles. This happens In order to supply your muscles with the oxygen and nutrients (B) it / they require. As a result, the digestion process is paused until the blood returns. So, (C) where / whether you're lifting weights or going for a jog, you shouldn't do it with a stomach full of food.

	(A)		(B)		(C)
①	absorb	…	it	…	where
②	absorbs	…	it	…	where
③	absorb	…	it	…	whether
④	absorbs	…	they	…	whether
⑤	absorb	…	they	…	whether

04 (A), (B), (C)의 각 네모 안에서 어법에 맞는 표현으로 가장 적절한 것은?

Host   I see. That makes sense. So, does that mean I should exercise on an empty stomach?

Dr. Hill   No, it doesn't. That can also be harmful and unpleasant. This is because the body needs energy to exercise. The fuel (A) that / what provides this energy is glycogen. Carbohydrates in the food we eat (B) is / are broken down into a kind of sugar (C) called / calling glucose.

	(A)		(B)		(C)
①	that	…	is	…	called
②	that	…	are	…	called
③	that	…	is	…	calling
④	what	…	are	…	calling
⑤	what	…	is	…	calling

05 (A), (B), (C)의 각 네모 안에서 어법에 맞는 표현으로 가장 적절한 것은?

When this glucose is stored in parts of the body, such as the muscles and the liver, it (A) calls / is called glycogen. This is why exercising on a completely empty stomach — such as when you first wake up in the morning — can be such a challenge. Your blood sugar levels are low, and you don't have enough glycogen (B) stored / storing in your body. If you exercise on an empty stomach, you will most likely lack energy and feel unusually tired. There can also be more serious outcomes. Some people end up (C) suffer / suffering from nausea and headaches, and others even faint. This is because intense exercise uses up all the glycogen in your muscles.

	(A)	(B)	(C)
①	calls	stored	suffer
②	calls	storing	suffer
③	is called	stored	suffer
④	is called	storing	suffering
⑤	is called	stored	suffering

06 다음 글의 밑줄 친 부분 중, 어법상 틀린 것은?

Host So, is it the loss of glycogen that causes us ① have low levels of energy?

Dr. Hill That's correct. For this reason, doctors recommend ② that people eat food containing carbohydrates within thirty minutes after working out. This replaces the muscle glycogen ③ you have lost. Basically, you need between one and one and a half grams of carbohydrates for every kilogram ④ you weigh. Let's do the math. If you weigh 60 kilograms, you should try ⑤ to consume between 60 and 90 grams of carbohydrates after you exercise. This is equal to about one bowl of white rice or three bananas.

① ② ③ ④ ⑤

07 다음 글의 밑줄 친 부분 중, 어법상 틀린 것은?

Host That's very interesting. But what about eating before we exercise? Can you explain how long ① should we wait after eating?

Dr. Hill Well, as I said before, exercising right after you eat will cause feelings of discomfort. But, if you wait too long ② to exercise after eating, you'll suffer from a lack of energy. The best time to eat before you exercise ③ varies from one to three hours. Basically, it depends on several factors such as the type and amount of food as well as body size, age, and gender. The type of exercise ④ also matters. For extremely active exercise like cycling, I suggest ⑤ that you wait between one and a half and three hours after eating a moderate-sized meal.

① ② ③ ④ ⑤

08 (A), (B), (C)의 각 네모 안에서 어법에 맞는 표현으로 가장 적절한 것은?

Do you often get stressed because you have too many things to do? If so, then here are some useful tips to help you relieve your stress. The first tip is to think of your favorite person or place. This will help you to feel (A) much / very better than before. The second tip is to write down (B) that / what you're grateful for. You will be able to focus more on the positive things in your life. Always remember (C) asking / to ask your friends or family for help when you're overwhelmed with stress.

	(A)	(B)	(C)
①	much	that	asking
②	very	that	asking
③	much	what	asking
④	very	what	to ask
⑤	much	what	to ask

[01~02] 다음 대화를 읽고, 물음에 답하시오.

G Mr. Bruce, today's class about viruses was interesting.

M Oh, I'm glad that you enjoyed it.

G But I want to know more about the topic.

M What do you want to know about?

G I'm curious about (A) how / what vaccines help prevent some diseases.

M Well, vaccines are weak versions of viruses. They allow our bodies (B) practice / to practice fighting against those viruses.

G How interesting! Our immune system is fascinating.

M If you would like to learn more, you can watch some videos about the topic.

G Could you recommend some to me?

M Sure. I will let you (C) know / to know a good website.

01 위 대화의 내용과 일치하지 않는 것은?

① 여학생은 Bruce 선생님의 수업을 흥미롭게 들었다.

② 오늘 수업의 주제는 바이러스에 관한 것이었다.

③ 여학생은 백신이 질병을 예방하는 방식에 관심이 있다.

④ 백신은 우리 몸이 질병과 싸우도록 훈련시키는 역할을 한다.

⑤ Bruce 선생님은 면역 체계와 관련된 영상을 촬영했다.

02 (A), (B), (C)의 각 네모 안에서 어법에 맞는 표현으로 가장 적절한 것은?

	(A)		(B)		(C)
①	how	…	practice	…	know
②	how	…	to practice	…	know
③	how	…	practice	…	to know
④	what	…	to practice	…	to know
⑤	what	…	practice	…	to know

[03~04] 다음 글을 읽고, 물음에 답하시오.

Once someone learns how to ride a bike, the person will never forget how to do it. The same goes with other skills like eating with chopsticks or playing musical instruments. (A) Once you learn the skill and get used to it, you can perform it without thinking about the necessary muscle movements. (B) This long-lasting memory for certain skills is called muscle memory. (C) Despite its name, it doesn't mean that our muscles remember the skills. Interestingly, muscle memory mostly develops in the brain. (D) Different parts of the brain are used to perform a skill. (E) This makes the skill easier to perform automatically. That's why professional musicians seem to _____! Without muscle memory, this would be much harder.

03 글의 흐름으로 보아, 주어진 문장이 들어가기에 가장 적절한 곳은?

When we practice a skill, these parts become strongly connected.

① (A) ② (B) ③ (C) ④ (D) ⑤ (E)

04 윗글의 빈칸에 들어갈 말로 가장 적절한 것은?

① play Mozart's songs so easily

② compose a symphony as a child

③ always practice musical instruments

④ have difficulty learning songs

⑤ strengthen their muscles

[05~06] 다음 글을 읽고, 물음에 답하시오.

Host	Welcome back to *Today's Health*. Today we're going to be talking about exercise. Dr. Victoria Hill is here, and she is going to share some useful tips. So, Dr. Hill, let's start with a question about my experience last month. I worked out right after dinner and got a stomachache. Why did that happen?
Dr. Hill	Well, the problem is that you exercised too soon after eating. This can cause various stomach issues. When you eat, blood rushes to the digestive system to help break down the food and absorb its nutrients. ____(A)____ when you start to exercise, blood moves from the digestive system to your muscles. This happens in order to supply your muscles with the oxygen and nutrients they require. ____(B)____, the digestion process is paused until the blood returns. So, whether you're lifting weights or going for a jog, you shouldn't do it with a stomach full of food.

05 윗글의 주제로 가장 적절한 것은?

① the differences between working out before and after a meal
② the nutrients that muscles need to work properly
③ the best times to go out to exercise
④ the way blood helps the digestive system function
⑤ the reason it is uncomfortable to exercise after a meal

06 윗글의 빈칸 (A)와 (B)에 들어갈 말이 바르게 짝지어진 것은?

	(A)		(B)
①	So	⋯	For example
②	And	⋯	In other words
③	Though	⋯	In addition
④	But	⋯	As a result
⑤	For	⋯	On the other hand

[07~08] 다음 글을 읽고, 물음에 답하시오.

Host	I see. That makes sense. So, does that mean I should exercise on an empty stomach?

Dr. Hill

(A) The fuel that provides this energy is glycogen. Carbohydrates in the food we eat are broken down into a kind of sugar called glucose.

(B) This is why exercising on a completely _____ stomach—such as when you first wake up in the morning—can be such a challenge.

(C) No, it doesn't. That can also be harmful and unpleasant. This is because the body needs energy to exercise.

(D) When this glucose is stored in parts of the body, such as the muscles and the liver, it is called glycogen.

07 주어진 질문 뒤에 이어질 Dr. Hill의 답변 순서로 가장 적절한 것은?

① (A) – (B) – (D) – (C)
② (B) – (C) – (D) – (A)
③ (C) – (A) – (D) – (B)
④ (D) – (B) – (C) – (A)
⑤ (D) – (C) – (A) – (B)

08 윗글의 빈칸에 알맞은 말을 찾아 한 단어로 쓰시오.

→ _____

[09~10] 다음 글을 읽고, 물음에 답하시오.

When this glucose is stored in parts of the body, such as the muscles and the liver, it is called glycogen. This is why exercising on a completely empty stomach—such as when you first wake up in the morning—can be such a challenge. Your blood sugar levels are low, and you don't have enough glycogen stored in your body. If you exercise on an empty stomach, you will most likely lack energy and feel unusually tired. There can also be more serious outcomes. Some people end up suffering from nausea and headaches, and others even faint. This is because intense exercise uses up all the glycogen in your muscles.

09 윗글의 내용과 일치하지 <u>않는</u> 것은?

① Glycogen is stored in the liver and muscles.
② When the stomach is empty, your blood sugar levels are low.
③ Exercising on an empty stomach may lead to tiredness.
④ People with nausea and headaches must exercise early in the morning.
⑤ While exercising, you use up energy in your muscles.

10 다음 영어 뜻풀이에 해당하는 단어를 윗글에서 찾아 쓰시오.

the result or effect of an action or event

→ _____

[11~12] 다음 글을 읽고, 물음에 답하시오.

Host So, is it the loss of glycogen <u>that</u> causes us to have low levels of energy?

Dr. Hill That's correct. For this reason, doctors recommend that people eat food containing carbohydrates within thirty minutes after working out. This replaces the muscle glycogen you have lost. Basically, you need between one and one and a half grams of carbohydrates for every kilogram you weigh. Let's do the math. If you weigh 60 kilograms, you should try to consume between 60 and 90 grams of carbohydrates after you exercise. This is equal to about one bowl of white rice or three bananas.

11 윗글의 밑줄 친 that과 쓰임이 같은 것은?

① Is it true <u>that</u> Jessie has a twin brother?
② He was so disappointed <u>that</u> he said nothing.
③ Doctors recommend <u>that</u> people eat a balanced diet.
④ It was at this restaurant <u>that</u> we first ate spaghetti.
⑤ The news <u>that</u> she won the Nobel Prize made us feel proud.

12 윗글의 내용과 일치하도록 빈칸에 알맞은 말을 완성하여 쓰시오.

Sojin weighs 50 kilograms. She is recommended to consume between _____ and _____ grams of carbohydrates after working out.

Exercising right after you eat will cause feelings of discomfort. But, if you wait too long to exercise after eating, you'll suffer from a lack of energy. The best time to eat before you exercise ① varies from one to three hours. Basically, it depends on several factors such as the type and amount of food as well as body size, age, and gender. The type of exercise also ② matters. For extremely active exercise like cycling, I suggest ③ that you wait between one and a half and three hours after eating a moderate-sized meal. But for something ④ more casual, such as golfing, ⑤ wait for one hour after a meal should be enough. Clearly, you can wait less after eating a snack.

13 다음 질문에 대한 답으로 윗글에서 언급되지 <u>않은</u> 것은?

What determines the proper time to eat before exercising?

① how old you are
② how much you weigh
③ what kind of food you ate
④ what your blood sugar level is
⑤ what kind of exercise you will do

14 윗글의 밑줄 친 부분 중, 어법상 틀린 것은?

①   ②   ③   ④   ⑤

15 다음 글의 내용을 요약할 때, 빈칸 (A), (B)에 들어갈 말로 가장 적절한 것은?

Do you often get stressed because you have too many things to do? If so, then here are some useful tips to help you relieve your stress. The first tip is to think of your favorite person or place. This will help you to feel much better than before. The second tip is to write down what you're grateful for. You will be able to focus more on the positive things in your life. Always remember to ask your friends or family for help when you're overwhelmed with stress.

There are two useful tips for managing stress. They are thinking about a ____(A)____ person or place to improve your mood and writing down things to be ____(B)____ for to focus on the positive. Seeking help from friends or family is also important.

(A)		(B)
① popular	⋯	regretful
② funny	⋯	thankful
③ interesting	⋯	sorry
④ famous	⋯	forgetful
⑤ favorite	⋯	grateful

[01~02] 다음 대화를 읽고, 물음에 답하시오.

B I can't sleep these days, and sometimes I feel dizzy.

G Maybe you drink too many energy drinks. Are you aware of the recommended daily amount of caffeine?

B No, I'm not. But I only drink two per day.

G Well, just 2.5 mg of caffeine per kilogram of body weight is enough for you.

B I didn't know that. In that case, I should only have about 150 mg of caffeine per day.

G But each of those energy drinks contains 120 mg.

B Oh my goodness! I never realized that I was drinking so much caffeine!

G _____

B You're right. Starting tomorrow, I will only drink one per day.

01 위 대화를 읽고 유추할 수 있는 내용이 <u>아닌</u> 것은?

① 남학생의 수면 부족은 과도한 에너지 음료 섭취 때문이다.
② 카페인의 일일 섭취 권장량은 체중1kg당 2.5mg이다.
③ 남학생의 현재 체중은 60kg이다.
④ 남학생은 매일 150mg의 카페인을 섭취하고 있다.
⑤ 남학생은 당장 에너지 음료 섭취를 줄일 것이다.

02 위 대화의 빈칸에 들어갈 말로 가장 적절한 것은?

① The recommended daily amount of caffeine is too high.
② If you want to sleep well, you should work out regularly.
③ You should eat more vegetables to stay healthy.
④ You drink two bottles of energy drinks every day.
⑤ I think you should cut down on energy drinks.

[03~04] 다음 글을 읽고, 물음에 답하시오.

Once someone learns how to ride a bike, the person will never forget how to do it. The same goes with other skills like eating with chopsticks or playing musical instruments.

(A) Different parts of the brain are used to perform a skill. When we practice a skill, these parts become strongly connected. This makes the skill easier to perform automatically.

(B) Despite its name, it doesn't mean that our muscles remember the skills. Interestingly, muscle memory mostly develops in the brain.

(C) Once you learn the skill and get used to it, you can perform it without thinking about the necessary muscle movements. This long-lasting memory for certain skills is called muscle memory.

(D) That's why professional musicians seem to play Mozart's songs so easily! Without muscle memory, this would be much harder.

03 주어진 글 다음에 이어질 글의 순서로 가장 적절한 것은?

① (A) – (B) – (D) – (C)
② (A) – (C) – (D) – (B)
③ (B) – (C) – (A) – (D)
④ (C) – (B) – (A) – (D)
⑤ (C) – (A) – (D) – (B)

04 윗글의 내용을 요약할 때, 빈칸에 공통으로 알맞은 말을 찾아 쓰시오.

Muscle memory is a long-lasting memory for certain skills like riding a bike. It's primarily a(n) _____ function, not a muscular one. When we practice a skill, different parts of our _____ build strong connections, making it easier to perform automatically.

[05~06] 다음 글을 읽고, 물음에 답하시오.

> **Host** I worked out _____.
> Why did that happen?
>
> **Dr. Hill** Well, the problem is that you exercised too soon after eating. This can cause various stomach issues. When you eat, blood rushes to the digestive system to help break down the food and absorb its <u>nutrients</u>. But when you start to exercise, blood moves from the digestive system to your muscles. This happens in order to supply your muscles with the oxygen and nutrients they require. As a result, the digestion process is paused until the blood returns. So, whether you're lifting weights or going for a jog, you shouldn't do it with a stomach full of food.

05 윗글의 빈칸에 들어갈 말로 가장 적절한 것은?

① right after dinner and got a stomachache
② with an empty stomach and I felt discomfort
③ two hours after I had a meal and felt energized
④ with my close friends and had an argument
⑤ at the gym in my school and broke my leg

06 윗글의 밑줄 친 nutrient의 영어 뜻풀이로 가장 적절한 것은?

① the type of food that you usually eat
② the result or effect of an action or event
③ the unpleasant feeling of wanting to vomit
④ average in size or amount and not too much
⑤ a substance needed to keep a living thing alive

[07~08] 다음 글을 읽고, 물음에 답하시오.

> **Host** I see. That makes sense. So, does that mean I should exercise on an empty stomach?
>
> **Dr. Hill** No, it doesn't. That can also be harmful and unpleasant. This is ____(A)____ the body needs energy to exercise. The fuel that provides this energy is glycogen. Carbohydrates in the food we eat are broken down into a kind of sugar called glucose. When this glucose is stored in parts of the body, such as the muscles and the liver, it is called glycogen. This is ____(B)____ exercising on a completely empty stomach—such as when you first wake up in the morning—can be such a challenge.

07 윗글의 내용과 일치하지 <u>않는</u> 것은?

① 신체는 운동하기 위해 에너지를 필요로 한다.
② 글리코겐은 신체에 에너지를 공급하는 연료이다.
③ 음식물로 섭취하는 탄수화물은 글루코스라는 당으로 분해된다.
④ 간이나 근육 같은 신체 조직에 저장되는 당을 글루코스라고 부른다.
⑤ 기상 직후 공복 상태에서 운동하는 것은 힘든 일이다.

08 윗글의 빈칸 (A)와 (B)에 들어갈 말이 바르게 짝지어진 것은?

	(A)		(B)
①	why	⋯	when
②	what	⋯	because
③	because	⋯	why
④	the reason	⋯	how
⑤	the cause	⋯	what

[09~10] 다음 글을 읽고, 물음에 답하시오.

When this glucose (A) stores / is stored in parts of the body, such as the muscles and the liver, it is called glycogen. This is why exercising on a completely empty stomach—such as when you first wake up in the morning—can be such a (B) challenge / challenging . Your blood sugar levels are low, and you don't have enough glycogen stored in your body. If you exercise on an empty stomach, you will most likely _____. There can also be more serious outcomes. Some people end up suffering from nausea and headaches, and (C) other / others even faint. This is because intense exercise uses up all the glycogen in your muscles.

09 윗글의 빈칸에 들어갈 말로 가장 적절한 것은?

① store glycogen in the muscles and the liver
② feel full and don't want to have something
③ feel energetic and exercise vigorously
④ lack energy and feel unusually tired
⑤ produce more energy in your body

10 (A), (B), (C)의 각 네모 안에서 어법에 맞는 표현으로 가장 적절한 것은?

	(A)		(B)		(C)
①	stores	⋯	challenge	⋯	other
②	stores	⋯	challenging	⋯	other
③	is stored	⋯	challenge	⋯	other
④	is stored	⋯	challenging	⋯	others
⑤	is stored	⋯	challenge	⋯	others

[11~12] 다음 글을 읽고, 물음에 답하시오.

Host So, is it the loss of glycogen that causes us to have low levels of energy?

Dr. Hill That's correct. For this reason, 의사들은 사람들이 음식을 먹으라고 권장한다 containing carbohydrates within thirty minutes after working out. This replaces the muscle glycogen you have lost. Basically, you need between one and one and a half grams of carbohydrates for every kilogram you weigh. Let's do the math. If you weigh 60 kilograms, you should try to consume between 60 and 90 grams of carbohydrates after you exercise. This is equal to about one bowl of white rice or three bananas.

11 윗글의 내용과 일치하지 <u>않는</u> 것은?

① Loss of glycogen may lead to lack of energy.
② Eating food containing carbohydrates is needed to restore muscle glycogen.
③ After working out, eating some food within 30 minutes is necessary.
④ We should have about one gram of carbohydrates per kilogram of body weight.
⑤ A person weighing 60 kg can eat a bowl of rice and three bananas after exercising.

12 윗글의 밑줄 친 우리말과 일치하도록 주어진 조건에 맞게 문장을 완성하시오.

조건
1. 동사 recommend를 사용할 것
2. 접속사 that을 사용할 것

의사들은 사람들이 음식을 먹으라고 권장한다

→ _____

Host That's very interesting. But what about eating before we exercise? <u>Can you explain how long should we wait after eating?</u>

Dr. Hill Well, as I said before, exercising right after you eat will cause feelings of discomfort. (A) But, if you wait too long to exercise after eating, you'll suffer from a lack of energy. (B) Basically, it depends on several factors such as the type and amount of food as well as body size, age, and gender. (C) The type of exercise also matters. (D) For extremely active exercise like cycling, I suggest that you wait between one and a half and three hours after eating a moderate-sized meal. (E) But for something more casual, such as golfing, waiting for one hour after a meal should be enough. Clearly, you can wait less after eating a snack.

Host Thank you very much for this fascinating information, Dr. Hill. I'm sure it will be very helpful for all of our viewers.

13 글의 흐름으로 보아, 주어진 문장이 들어가기에 가장 적절한 곳은?

> The best time to eat before you exercise varies from one to three hours.

① (A) ② (B) ③ (C) ④ (D) ⑤ (E)

14 Kevin이 운동하기 전 식사 시간을 결정할 사항으로 윗글에서 언급되지 <u>않은</u> 것은?

① Kevin is a male aged 17.
② Kevin weighs 70 kilograms.
③ Kevin lives in urban area.
④ Kevin ate two hamburgers.
⑤ Kevin swims for an hour at the pool.

15 윗글의 밑줄 친 문장에서 틀린 곳을 찾아 바르게 고쳐 쓰시오.

> Can you explain how long should we wait after eating?

→ _____

_____

[01~02] 다음 대화를 읽고, 물음에 답하시오.

B I can't sleep these days, and sometimes I feel dizzy.

G Maybe you drink too many energy drinks. Are you aware of the (A) recommended / recommending daily amount of caffeine?

B No, I'm not. But I only drink two per day.

G Well, just 2.5 mg of caffeine per kilogram of body weight is enough for you.

B I didn't know that. In that case, I should only have about 150 mg of caffeine per day.

G But each of those energy drinks (B) contain / contains 120 mg.

B Oh my goodness! I never realized that _____!

G I think you should cut down on energy drinks.

B You're right. (C) Starting / To start tomorrow, I will only drink one per day.

01 위 대화의 빈칸에 들어갈 말로 어색한 것은?

① I was drinking so much caffeine
② I have been consuming large amounts of caffeine
③ I couldn't sleep because of energy drinks
④ I drank two energy drinks a day
⑤ an energy drink contains 120 mg of caffeine

02 (A), (B), (C)의 각 네모 안에서 어법에 맞는 표현으로 가장 적절한 것은?

	(A)	(B)	(C)
①	recommended	… contain	… Starting
②	recommended	… contains	… Starting
③	recommended	… contain	… To start
④	recommending	… contains	… To start
⑤	recommending	… contain	… To start

[03~04] 다음 글을 읽고, 물음에 답하시오.

Once someone learns how to ride a bike, the person will never forget how to do it. Once you learn the skill and get used to it, you can perform it without thinking about the necessary muscle movements. This long-lasting memory for certain skills is called muscle memory. _____(A)_____ its name, it doesn't mean that our muscles remember the skills. Interestingly, muscle memory mostly develops in the brain. Different parts of the brain are used to perform a skill. When we practice a skill, these parts become strongly connected. This makes the skill easier to perform automatically. That's why professional musicians seem to play Mozart's songs so easily! _____(B)_____ muscle memory, this would be much harder.

03 윗글의 주제로 가장 적절한 것은?

① what muscle memory is
② how to strengthen your muscles
③ special skills that musicians have
④ people with extraordinary skills
⑤ parts of the brain that control movement

04 윗글의 빈칸 (A)와 (B)에 들어갈 말이 바르게 짝지어진 것은?

	(A)	(B)
①	Despite	… With
②	Through	… Without
③	But for	… By
④	Despite	… Without
⑤	Through	… By

[05~06] 다음 글을 읽고, 물음에 답하시오.

Host	Dr. Hill, let's start with a question about my experience last month. I worked out right after dinner and got a stomachache. Why did that happen?
Dr. Hill	Well, the problem is that you exercised too soon after eating. This can cause various stomach issues. When you eat, blood rushes to the digestive system to help break down the food and absorb ⓐ its nutrients. But when you start to exercise, blood moves from the digestive system to your muscles. This happens in order to supply your muscles with the oxygen and nutrients ⓑ they require. As a result, the digestion process is paused until the blood returns. So, whether you're lifting weights or going for a jog, you shouldn't do it with a stomach full of food.

05 윗글의 내용과 일치하지 <u>않는</u> 것은?

① Exercising too soon after eating can cause some digestive problems.
② Blood moves to the digestive system when we have meals.
③ Blood moves to the muscles when you start to exercise.
④ A pause in the digestive system helps break down food.
⑤ Exercising on a full stomach is not recommended.

06 윗글의 밑줄 친 ⓐ its와 ⓑ they가 가리키는 것이 바르게 짝지어진 것은?

① the blood's ··· your muscles
② the blood's ··· nutrients
③ the food's ··· your muscles
④ the food's ··· nutrients
⑤ the digestive system's ··· nutrients

[07~08] 다음 글을 읽고, 물음에 답하시오.

Host	I see. That makes sense. So, does that mean I should exercise on an empty stomach?
Dr. Hill	No, it doesn't. That can also be harmful and unpleasant. This is because the body needs energy to exercise. The fuel that ⓐ provide this energy is glycogen. Carbohydrates in the food we eat are ⓑ break down into a kind of sugar ⓒ call glucose. When this glucose is stored in parts of the body, such as the muscles and the liver, it is called glycogen. This is why ⓓ exercise on a completely empty stomach—such as when you first ⓔ waking up in the morning—can be such a challenge.

07 윗글에서 Dr. Hill이 주장하는 바를 바르게 이해하지 <u>않은</u> 두 사람은?

① Jiho: Glycogen is vital chemical for our body.
② Fred: Food we eat is broken down into a kind of sugar called glucose.
③ Cathy: Glycogen levels are high when we first wake up in the morning.
④ Bora: The more carbohydrates we eat, the better our muscles work.
⑤ Susie: Exercising on an empty stomach is not the best option since the muscles need energy.

08 윗글에서 밑줄 친 ⓐ~ⓔ를 바르게 고쳐 쓰지 <u>않은</u> 것은?

① ⓐ provide → provides
② ⓑ break → broken
③ ⓒ call → calling
④ ⓓ exercise → exercising
⑤ ⓔ waking → wake

[09~10] 다음 글을 읽고, 물음에 답하시오.

Exercising on a completely empty stomach—such as when you first wake up in the morning—can be such a challenge. ① Your blood sugar levels are low, and you don't have enough glycogen stored in your body. ② If you exercise on an empty stomach, you will most likely lack energy and feel unusually tired. ③ Basically, you need between one and one and a half grams of carbohydrates for every kilogram you weigh. ④ There can also be more serious outcomes. ⑤ Some people end up suffering from nausea and headaches, and others even faint. This is because intense exercise uses up all the glycogen in your muscles.

09 윗글의 ①~⑤ 중 전체 흐름과 관계 없는 문장은?

①   ②   ③   ④   ⑤

10 윗글의 내용을 요약할 때, 빈칸 (A), (B), (C)에 들어갈 말로 가장 적절한 것은?

Exercising on a(n) _____(A)_____ stomach can be challenging due to low blood sugar and insufficient _____(B)_____ stores. This can lead to fatigue, nausea, headaches, or even _____(C)_____.

	(A)	(B)	(C)
①	empty	glycogen	fainting
②	full	glycogen	fainting
③	empty	muscle	fainting
④	full	muscle	discomfort
⑤	empty	muscle	discomfort

11 다음 글의 밑줄 친 부분 중, 문맥상 어구의 쓰임이 적절하지 않은 것은?

Host So, is it the loss of glycogen that ① causes us to have low levels of energy?

Dr. Hill That's correct. For this reason, doctors recommend that people eat food ② containing carbohydrates within thirty minutes after working out. This replaces the muscle glycogen you have lost. Basically, you need ③ between one and one and a half grams of carbohydrates for every kilogram you weigh. Let's do the math. If you weigh 60 kilograms, you should try to ④ use up between 60 and 90 grams of carbohydrates after you exercise. This is ⑤ equal to about one bowl of white rice or three bananas.

①   ②   ③   ④   ⑤

12 다음 대화의 밑줄 친 ⓐ~ⓔ 중 어법상 틀린 것을 찾아 바르게 고쳐 쓰시오.

B Hello, Jane. You look ⓐ much healthier these days.

G Thanks.

B I'm curious about ⓑ what did you do.

G Well, I actually changed my diet.

B Really? ⓒ How did you change it?

G I eat more vegetables and ⓓ less sugary food now.

B I see. I should consider ⓔ changing my diet, too.

_____ → _____

[13~14] 다음 글을 읽고, 물음에 답하시오.

Host That's very interesting. But what about eating before we exercise? Can you explain how long we should wait after eating?

Dr. Hill Well, as I said before, exercising right after you eat will cause feelings of discomfort. But, if you wait too long to exercise after eating, you'll suffer from a lack of energy. The best time to eat before you exercise ⓐ <u>vary</u> from one to three hours. Basically, it depends on several factors such as the type and amount of food as well as body size, age, and gender. The type of exercise also matters. For extremely active exercise like cycling, I suggest that you ⓑ <u>wait</u> between one and a half and three hours after eating a moderate-sized meal. But for something more casual, such as golfing, waiting for one hour after a meal should be enough. Clearly, you can wait less after eating a snack.

13 윗글의 요지로 가장 적절한 것은?

① Choose the type of exercise that suits you best.
② Some time between meals and exercising is needed.
③ Exercising on an empty stomach causes discomfort.
④ Before you exercise, eat a snack instead of a heavy meal.
⑤ Exercising at least four hours after a meal is recommended.

14 윗글의 밑줄 친 ⓐ vary와 ⓑ wait을 문맥상 알맞은 형태로 바꿔 쓰시오.

ⓐ vary → _____

ⓑ wait → _____

15 다음 글의 빈칸에 들어갈 말로 가장 적절한 것은?

Do you often get stressed because you have too many things to do? If so, then here are some useful tips to help you relieve your stress. The first tip is to think of your favorite person or place. This will help you to feel much better than before. The second tip is to write down what you're grateful for. You will be able to focus more on the _____ in your life. Always remember to ask your friends or family for help when you're overwhelmed with stress.

① positive things
② negative aspects
③ possible reasons
④ great challenges
⑤ potential dangers

[01~02] 다음 글을 읽고, 물음에 답하시오.

Host	Welcome back to *Today's Health*. Today we're discussing exercise. Dr. Victoria Hill is here to share some helpful tips. So, Dr. Hill, let's start with a question about something that happened to me last month. I worked out right after dinner and got a stomachache. Why did ⓐ that happen?
Dr. Hill	The problem could be that you exercised too soon after eating. ⓑ This can lead to various stomach problems. When you eat, blood flows to your digestive system to help break down food and absorb nutrients. But when you start exercising, blood shifts from the digestive system to your muscles to supply ⓒ them with oxygen and nutrients. ⓓ This pauses the digestion process until the blood returns. So, whether you're lifting weights or going for a run, ⓔ it's best to avoid exercising on a full stomach.

01 윗글에서 Dr. Hill이 이야기하는 요지로 가장 적절한 것은?

① Blood delivers oxygen as it circulates through your body.
② Lifting weights and running are the best exercises for teenagers.
③ Exercise is the cause of many stomach problems.
④ The digestive system needs blood to break down the nutrients.
⑤ Working out right after a meal may cause discomfort.

02 윗글의 밑줄 친 ⓐ~ⓔ가 가리키는 것이 바르게 연결되지 <u>않은</u> 것은?

① ⓐ that: getting a stomachache
② ⓑ This: exercising too soon after eating
③ ⓒ them: your muscles
④ ⓓ This: blood shifting from the digestive system to the muscles
⑤ ⓔ it: going for a run

[03~04] 다음 글을 읽고, 물음에 답하시오.

The body needs energy to exercise, and the fuel for this energy is glycogen. (A) When this glucose is stored in parts of the body, like the muscles and liver, it's called glycogen. (B) This is why exercising on a completely empty stomach, like first thing in the morning, can be so difficult. (C) Your blood sugar levels are low, and you don't have a lot of glycogen stored in your body. (D) If you exercise on an empty stomach, you're likely to lack energy and feel unusually tired. (E)

03 글의 흐름으로 보아, 주어진 문장이 들어가기에 가장 적절한 곳은?

Carbohydrates in the food we eat are broken down into a type of sugar called glucose.

① (A)　② (B)　③ (C)　④ (D)　⑤ (E)

04 윗글의 내용과 일치하지 <u>않는</u> 것은?

① Your body needs energy to work out.
② Glycogen works as the fuel for your body.
③ Glycogen is stored in the muscles and liver.
④ Before breakfast, your body doesn't have a lot of glycogen.
⑤ Exercise helps store glycogen in your body.

[05~06] 다음 글을 읽고, 물음에 답하시오.

Host So, is it the loss of glycogen ① what causes us to have low energy levels?

Dr. Hill That's right. For this reason, doctors recommend ② eating food containing carbohydrates within thirty minutes ③ after working out. This replaces the muscle glycogen ④ you've lost. Basically, you need around one to one and a half grams of carbohydrates for every kilogram ⑤ you weigh. Let's calculate. If you weigh 50 kilograms, you should aim to consume _____ after exercise. This is equivalent to about one bowl of white rice or three bananas.

05 윗글의 밑줄 친 부분 중 어법상 틀린 것은?

①   ②   ③   ④   ⑤

06 윗글의 빈칸에 들어갈 말로 가장 적절한 것은?

① around 90 grams of carbohydrates
② about two apples and one orange
③ as much carbohydrates as possible
④ between 50 and 75 grams of carbohydrates
⑤ from 60 to 90 grams of carbohydrates

[07~08] 다음 글을 읽고, 물음에 답하시오.

Host That's very interesting. But what about eating before we exercise? Can you explain how long we should wait after eating?

Dr. Hill Well, as I mentioned earlier, exercising immediately after eating can cause discomfort. However, waiting too long to exercise after a meal (A) lead / leads to a lack of energy. The optimal time to eat before exercising varies from one to three hours. It depends on several factors like the type and amount of food, body size, age, and gender. The type of exercise also matters. For intense exercise like cycling, I recommend (B) wait / waiting between one and a half and three hours after a moderate-sized meal. But for something less intense, like golfing, waiting for one hour after a meal should be sufficient. Of course, you can wait less after (C) eat / eating a snack.

Host Thank you very much for this valuable information, Dr. Hill. I'm sure it will be very helpful for all of our viewers.

07 윗글의 내용과 일치하지 <u>않는</u> 것은?

① 식사 후 오래 지나 운동을 하면 에너지 부족 현상이 있다.
② 운동 전 적정 식사 시간은 1~3시간이다.
③ 운동 전 적정 식사 시간은 식사량, 신체 조건, 운동의 종류 등에 따라 달라진다.
④ 격렬한 운동을 할 때는 1.5~3시간 전에 식사하는 것이 좋다.
⑤ 가벼운 운동은 식후 3시간 정도에 하는 것이 좋다.

08 (A), (B), (C)의 각 네모 안에서 어법에 맞는 표현으로 가장 적절한 것은?

	(A)		(B)		(C)
①	lead	…	wait	…	eat
②	lead	…	waiting	…	eat
③	leads	…	wait	…	eat
④	leads	…	waiting	…	eating
⑤	leads	…	wait	…	eating

[09~10] 다음 글을 읽고, 물음에 답하시오.

Do you often feel overwhelmed by having too much to do? If so, here are some helpful tips to reduce your stress. ① First, think about your favorite person or place. ② This can help you feel much better. ③ Second, write down what you're grateful for. ④ Writers often use metaphors to create images that are easier for readers to understand. ⑤ You'll be able to focus more on the positive aspects of your life. Always remember to ask your friends or family for help when you're feeling stressed.

09 윗글의 ①~⑤ 중 전체 흐름과 관계 <u>없는</u> 문장은?

①   ②   ③   ④   ⑤

10 윗글의 제목으로 가장 적절한 것은?

① How to Maintain Your Mental Health
② Stress Harms Your Body and Soul
③ Always Be Grateful for Others
④ What Is Your Favorite Place?
⑤ Tips on Positive Thinking

[11~12] 다음 글을 읽고, 물음에 답하시오.

B I can't sleep these days, and sometimes I feel ① <u>alert</u> during the day.
G Maybe you drink too many energy drinks. Are you ② <u>aware</u> of the recommended daily amount of caffeine?
B No, I'm not. But I only drink two a day.
G Well, just 2.5 mg of caffeine per kilogram of body weight is ③ <u>sufficient</u> for you.
B I didn't know that. In that case, I should only have about 150 mg of caffeine per day.
G But each of those energy drinks ④ <u>contains</u> 120 mg.
B Oh my goodness! I never realized that I was drinking so much caffeine!
G I think you should cut down on energy drinks.
B You're right. ⑤ <u>Starting</u> tomorrow, I will only drink one per day.

11 위 대화의 내용과 일치하지 <u>않는</u> 것은?

① The boy has difficulty sleeping.
② The boy drinks two energy drinks a day.
③ The boy weighs 60 kilograms.
④ An energy drink contains 150 mg of caffeine.
⑤ The girl recommends that the boy drink fewer energy drinks.

12 윗글의 밑줄 친 부분 중, 문맥상 낱말의 쓰임이 적절하지 <u>않은</u> 것은?

①   ②   ③   ④   ⑤

[13~15] 다음 글을 읽고, 물음에 답하시오.

Once someone learns to ride a bike, they never forget how to do it. The same is true for other skills like using chopsticks or playing instruments. After learning and practicing a skill, you can do it without (A) automatically / consciously thinking about the muscle movements. This long-lasting memory for certain skills is called muscle memory. _____, it's not our muscles that remember the skills. Muscle memory actually develops in the brain. Different parts of the brain are involved in performing a skill. When we practice a skill, these parts become strongly (B) connected / divided, making it easier to do automatically. That's why professional musicians can play Mozart's pieces so effortlessly! Without muscle memory, this would be much more (C) difficult / efficient.

13 Muscle memory에 관해 윗글의 내용과 일치하지 <u>않는</u> 것은?

① It involves learning to ride a bike or to play instrument.
② Thanks to it, we can easily do skills without consciously thinking about the movement.
③ Muscles play the most important role in obtaining it.
④ Practice is needed to develop it.
⑤ Musicians' ability to play Mozart's music effortlessly is an example.

14 윗글의 빈칸에 들어갈 말로 가장 적절한 것은?

① Because of the skills
② In spite of the name
③ Thanks to the long-lasting memory
④ As you can assume from the name
⑤ Since muscle movements are concerned

15 (A), (B), (C)의 각 네모 안에서 문맥에 맞는 낱말로 가장 적절한 것은?

	(A)	(B)	(C)
①	automatically	connected	difficult
②	automatically	divided	difficult
③	consciously	connected	difficult
④	consciously	divided	efficient
⑤	consciously	connected	efficient

내신 1등급
서술형

[01~02] 다음 글을 읽고, 물음에 답하시오.

Once someone learns how to ride a bike, the person will never forget how to do it. The same goes with other skills like eating with chopsticks or ⓐ play musical instruments. Once you learn the skill and get used to it, you can perform it without ⓑ think about the necessary muscle movements. This long-lasting memory for certain skills is called muscle memory. Despite its name, it doesn't mean that our muscles remember the skills. Interestingly, muscle memory mostly develops in the brain. Different parts of the brain ⓒ use to perform a skill. When we practice a skill, these parts become strongly connected. This makes the skill easier to perform automatically. That's why professional musicians seem to play Mozart's songs so easily! Without muscle memory, this would be much harder.

01 주어진 질문에 대한 답을 윗글에서 찾아 완성하시오.

(1) What is muscle memory?
  → It _____.
(2) Where does muscle memory develop?
  → It _____.

02 윗글의 밑줄 친 ⓐ~ⓒ를 알맞은 형태로 바꿔 쓰시오. (필요하면 단어를 추가할 것)

ⓐ play → _____
ⓑ think → _____
ⓒ use → _____

[03~04] 다음 글을 읽고, 물음에 답하시오.

Host Welcome back to *Today's Health*. Today we're going to be talking about exercise. Dr. Victoria Hill is here, and she is going to share some useful tips. So, Dr. Hill, let's start with a question about my experience last month. I worked out right after dinner and got a stomachache. Why did that happen?

Dr. Hill Well, the problem is that you exercised too soon after eating. This can cause various stomach issues. When you eat, blood rushes to the digestive system to help break down the food and absorb its nutrients. But when you start to exercise, blood moves from the digestive system to your muscles. This happens in order to supply your muscles _____ the oxygen and nutrients they require. As a result, the digestion process is paused until the blood returns. So, whether you're lifting weights or going for a jog, you shouldn't do it _____ a stomach full of food.

03 윗글의 밑줄 친 worked out과 바꿔 쓸 수 있는 말을 글에서 찾아 쓰시오.

→ _____

04 윗글의 빈칸에 공통으로 알맞은 말을 쓰시오.

→ _____

[05~07] 다음 글을 읽고, 물음에 답하시오.

> **Host** I see. That makes sense. So, does that mean I should exercise on an empty stomach?
>
> **Dr. Hill** No, it doesn't. That can also be harmful and unpleasant. ⓐ <u>This is why the body needs energy to exercise.</u> The fuel that provides this energy is glycogen. Carbohydrates in the food we eat are broken down into a kind of sugar called glucose. When this glucose is stored in parts of the body, such as the muscles and the liver, it is called glycogen. This is why exercising on a completely empty stomach — such as when you first wake up in the morning — can be such a challenge. Your blood sugar levels are low, and you don't have enough glycogen stored in your body. ⓑ <u>If you exercise on an empty stomach, you will most likely possess energy and feel unusually tired.</u> There can also be more serious outcomes. Some people end up suffering from nausea and headaches, and others even faint. This is because intense exercise uses up all the glycogen in your muscles.

05 윗글의 내용과 일치하도록 주어진 문장의 빈칸에 알맞은 말을 글에서 찾아 쓰시오.

> When we eat food, we absorb carbohydrates in the food. Carbohydrates are (1) _____ into glucose. Glucose stored in the muscles and the liver is called (2) _____.

06 윗글의 밑줄 친 문장 ⓐ와 ⓑ에서 문맥상 <u>어색한</u> 단어를 한 개씩 찾아 바르게 고쳐 쓰시오.

ⓐ _____ → _____

ⓑ _____ → _____

07 다음 영어 뜻풀이에 해당하는 단어를 윗글에서 찾아 쓰시오.

> to become unconscious when not enough blood is going to your brain

→ _____

[08~09] 다음 글을 읽고, 물음에 답하시오.

> **Host** So, <u>the loss of glycogen causes us to have low levels of energy?</u>
>
> **Dr. Hill** That's correct. For this reason, doctors recommend that people eat food containing carbohydrates within thirty minutes after working out. This replaces the muscle glycogen you have lost. Basically, you need between one and one and a half grams of carbohydrates for every kilogram you weigh. Let's do the math. If you weigh 60 kilograms, you should try to consume between _____ grams of carbohydrates after you exercise. This is equal to about one bowl of white rice or three bananas.

08 윗글의 밑줄 친 문장을 **조건**에 맞게 바꿔 쓰시오.

> **조건**
> 1. it과 that을 사용하여 the loss of glycogen을 강조하여 쓸 것
> 2. 의문문으로 쓸 것

→ So _____

_____?

09 윗글의 빈칸에 알맞은 말을 쓰시오. (3단어)

→ between _____ grams

[10~12] 다음 글을 읽고, 물음에 답하시오.

> **Host**   That's very interesting. But what about eating before we exercise? ⓐ <u>Can you explain how long should we wait after eat?</u>
>
> **Dr. Hill**   Well, as I said before, exercising right after you eat will cause feelings of discomfort. But, if you wait too long to exercise after eating, you'll suffer from a lack of energy. The best time to eat before you exercise varies from one to three hours. Basically, it depends on ⓑ <u>several factors</u> such as the type and amount of food as well as body size, age, and gender. The type of exercise also matters. For extremely active exercise like cycling, ⓒ <u>나는 여러분이 1시간 30분에서 3시간 사이를 기다릴 것을 권장합니다</u> after eating a moderate-sized meal. But for something more casual, such as golfing, waiting for one hour after a meal should be enough. Clearly, you can wait less after eating a snack.

10 윗글의 밑줄 친 문장 ⓐ에서 어법상 틀린 부분을 찾아 바르게 고쳐 쓰시오. (두 군데)

> Can you explain how long should we wait after eat?

→ _____

11 윗글의 밑줄 친 ⓑ several factors에 해당하는 것을 글에서 찾아 세 가지 이상 쓰시오.

(1) _____

(2) _____

(3) _____

12 윗글의 밑줄 친 ⓒ의 우리말과 일치하도록 조건에 맞게 영작하시오.

> **조건**
>
> 1. 동사 suggest와 접속사 that을 사용할 것
> 2. 다음 표현을 사용할 것: between, half

→ _____

_____

13 다음 글의 빈칸에 알맞은 문장을 보기의 말을 바르게 배열하여 완성하시오.

> Do you often get stressed because you have too many things to do? If so, then here are some useful tips to help you relieve your stress. The first tip is to think of your favorite person or place. This will help you to feel much better than before. The second tip is to write down what you're grateful for. You will be able to focus more on the positive things in your life. Always remember _____.

> **보기**
>
> your friends or family / overwhelmed / to ask / when / stress / you're / with / for help

→ Always remember _____

_____.

04

—

The Future Ahead of Us

Functions

▶ 기대 표현하기
I'm looking forward to asking the general about the Battle of Noryang.

▶ 설명 요청하기
Could you explain how it works?

Grammar

▶ AI may lead to changes **not only** in the art world **but also** in the music industry.

▶ There are *concerns* **that** AI may imitate the styles of human artists without their consent.

교과서 어휘

Words

□ install	동 설치하다	□ blend	동 조합하다, 섞다
□ application	명 애플리케이션	□ complex	형 복잡한
□ general	명 장군	□ industry	명 산업
□ battle	명 전투, 투쟁	□ compose	동 작곡하다
□ drill	명 훈련	□ option	명 선택, 옵션
□ average	형 보통의, 일반적인	□ virtual	형 가상의
□ originally	부 원래, 본래	□ influencer	명 인플루언서, 영향력을 행사하는 사람
□ commercial	형 상업의	□ realistic	형 사실적인, 실제 그대로의
□ portrait	명 초상화	□ release	동 발표하다, 발매하다
□ category	명 범주	□ spark	동 촉발하다
□ controversy	명 논란 (controversial 형 논쟁적인)	□ impact	명 영향 (=influence)
□ complain	동 불평하다 (complaint 명 불평)	□ imitate	동 모방하다 (imitation 명 모방)
□ instruction	명 지시, 설명 (instruct 동 지시하다)	□ consent	명 동의
□ fair	형 공정한 (↔ unfair 불공정한)	□ exceed	동 넘어서다
□ rest	명 (어떤 것의) 나머지	□ imagination	명 상상력, 창의력 (imagine 동 상상하다)
□ numerous	형 많은	□ assistance	명 도움 (assist 동 돕다)
□ generator	명 발생기	□ limitation	명 한계 (limit 동 제한하다, 한정하다)
□ ability	명 능력 (able 형 능력 있는)	□ diversity	명 다양성
□ analyze	동 분석하다 (analysis 명 분석)	□ eventually	부 결국에, 결과적으로 (=finally)
□ corresponding	형 해당하는	□ output	명 생산(량), 결과(물)
□ description	명 서술, 묘사 (describe 동 묘사하다)	□ boundary	명 경계, 한계
□ landscape	명 풍경	□ ethically	부 윤리적으로 (ethical 형 윤리적인)
□ existing	형 기존의, 현존하는	□ collaborate	동 협력하다 (collaboration 명 협력)
□ overall	형 종합적인, 전체의		

Phrases

□ historical figure	역사적 인물	□ lead to	~으로 이어지다
□ virtual reality	가상 현실	□ be dependent on	~에 의존하다
□ fire extinguisher	소화기	□ be based on	~을 기반으로 하다
□ freeze drying	동결 건조	□ figure out	생각해 내다
□ artificial intelligence	인공 지능	□ take over	인계하다, 장악하다

Word Focus

compose	구성하다	The school council is currently **composed** of only four students. 학교 운영 위원회는 현재 단 4명의 학생으로 구성되어 있다.
	(마음을) 가다듬다, 가라앉히다	I tried to **compose** myself by listening to soft music. 나는 부드러운 음악을 들음으로써 스스로 마음을 가라앉히려 애썼다.
	작곡하다	Beethoven **composed** Symphony No. 9 after he completely lost his hearing. 베토벤은 그의 청력을 완전히 잃은 후에 교향곡 제9번을 작곡했다.

Useful Expressions

lead to ~으로 이어지다	Being kind to others can **lead to** a more enjoyable and positive life. 타인에게 친절을 베푸는 것은 더욱 즐겁고 긍정적인 삶으로 이어질 수 있다.
be dependent on ~에 의존하다	The economy of the country **is dependent on** the tourism industry. 그 국가의 경제는 관광 산업에 의존한다.
be based on ~을 기반으로 하다	Our restaurant's menu **is based on** recipes that were passed down for generations. 우리 식당의 메뉴는 여러 세대에 걸쳐 전해 내려온 조리법을 기반으로 한다.

Word Mates

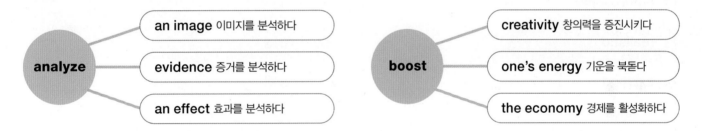

- **analyze**
  - an image 이미지를 분석하다
  - evidence 증거를 분석하다
  - an effect 효과를 분석하다
- **boost**
  - creativity 창의력을 증진시키다
  - one's energy 기운을 북돋다
  - the economy 경제를 활성화하다

English-English Dictionary

- ☐ **controversy** 논란 — public disagreement about something
- ☐ **numerous** 많은 — many in number
- ☐ **blend** 조합하다, 섞다 — to mix or combine two things together
- ☐ **compose** 작곡하다 — to write a piece of music
- ☐ **virtual** 가상의 — created and existing on a computer software or network
- ☐ **imitate** 모방하다 — to copy the way something looks, sounds, or behaves
- ☐ **exceed** 넘어서다 — to be greater than something in number or amount
- ☐ **diversity** 다양성 — the state having different things or people together in a group
- ☐ **boundary** 경계, 한계 — a line that signals the end or limit of something
- ☐ **ethically** 윤리적으로 — in a way that follows moral beliefs
- ☐ **collaborate** 협력하다 — to work together in order to achieve something

✤ 다음 영어는 우리말로, 우리말은 영어로 쓰시오.

01	spark	동 _____	25	인공 지능	_____
02	virtual	형 _____	26	명 상상력, 창의력	_____
03	instruction	명 _____	27	명 산업	_____
04	collaborate	동 _____	28	소화기	_____
05	eventually	부 _____	29	형 종합적인, 전체의	_____
06	historical figure	_____	30	동 모방하다	_____
07	lead to	_____	31	명 생산(량), 결과(물)	_____
08	exceed	동 _____	32	명 풍경	_____
09	blend	동 _____	33	부 윤리적으로	_____
10	impact	명 _____	34	명 서술, 묘사	_____
11	virtual reality	_____	35	동 작곡하다	_____
12	controversy	명 _____	36	명 (어떤 것의) 나머지	_____
13	realistic	형 _____	37	명 다양성	_____
14	existing	형 _____	38	형 복잡한	_____
15	portrait	명 _____	39	명 도움	_____
16	battle	명 _____	40	부 원래, 본래	_____
17	numerous	형 _____	41	명 동의	_____
18	boundary	명 _____	42	동 분석하다	_____
19	application	명 _____	43	동 불평하다	_____
20	limitation	명 _____	44	형 공정한	_____
21	average	형 _____	45	명 능력	_____
22	generator	명 _____	46	형 상업의	_____
23	install	동 _____	47	인계하다, 장악하다	_____
24	figure out	_____	48	명 범주	_____

A 다음 밑줄 친 부분과 바꿔 쓸 수 있는 것을 보기에서 골라 기호를 쓰시오.

> 보기 ⓐ calmed   ⓑ written   ⓒ made up

01 The writer's newest release is <u>composed</u> of seven books. (   )

02 The singer has <u>composed</u> more than 100 songs so far. (   )

B 빈칸에 들어갈 말로 알맞은 것을 고르시오.

01 Reading can _____ to increased knowledge and a wider vocabulary.

    ⓐ guide   ⓑ lead   ⓒ end

02 Young children are dependent _____ their parents for most things.

    ⓐ against   ⓑ by   ⓒ on

03 Many people couldn't believe that the shocking movie was _____ on a true story.

    ⓐ based   ⓑ derived   ⓒ created

C 네모 안에서 알맞은 말을 골라 문장을 완성하시오.

01 Scientists are ⏥ analyzing / struggling ⏥ the effects of the new medicine on patients.

02 The government hopes to ⏥ boost / raise ⏥ the economy by increasing the employment rates.

D 다음 밑줄 친 부분의 영어 뜻풀이로 알맞은 것을 보기에서 골라 기호를 쓰시오.

> 보기 ⓐ to work together in order to achieve something
> ⓑ to be greater than something in number or amount
> ⓒ created and existing on a computer software or network

01 <u>Virtual</u> influencers with extremely realistic faces, bodies, and voices have already released several songs. (   )

02 Others think that AI cannot <u>exceed</u> human imagination and that it is still dependent on human assistance. (   )

03 What we need to do is figure out how to use AI tools ethically and think about how humans and AI can <u>collaborate</u>. (   )

교과서 핵심 대화문

기대 표현하기

B Hi, Emma. What are you doing on your phone?

G Oh hi, Mark. I'm chatting with General Yi Sunsin.

B General Yi Sunsin? How is <u>that</u> possible?
= chatting with General Yi Sunsin

G I installed a chatbot application. I can talk to any historical figure with <u>it</u>.
= the chatbot application

B That sounds amazing!

G Yes, it is amazing! **I'm looking forward to** asking the general about the
look forward to + (동)명사: ~을 고대하다
Battle of Noryang.

B What are you going to ask?

G I want to know [how he felt during the battle].
간접의문문 (know의 목적어)

B I want to try <u>that</u>, too. I would love to talk to Marie Curie about her work.
= talking to a historical figure with the chatbot application

B: 안녕, Emma. 전화기로 뭐 하고 있니?

G: 오, 안녕, Mark. 이순신 장군과 채팅하고 있어.

B: 이순신 장군이라고? 어떻게 그게 가능하니?

G: 나는 챗봇 앱을 설치했어. 이 앱으로 역사적 인물 누구하고든 대화할 수 있어.

B: 그거 놀랍다!

G: 맞아, 놀랍지. 나는 장군님에게 노량해전에 관해 물어보길 고대하고 있어.

B: 무엇을 물어보려고 하니?

G: 나는 전쟁을 치르는 동안 장군님이 어떤 심경이었을지 알고 싶어.

B: 나도 그거 해보고 싶어. 나는 퀴리 부인에게 그녀의 업적에 관해 얘기하고 싶어.

Study Point 🎗

I'm looking forward to ~는 '~하기를 고대하고 있다'라는 뜻으로, 바람이나 기대를 나타낼 때 쓰는 표현이다. 이때 to는 전치사이므로 뒤에 명사나 동명사를 쓴다.

More Expressions 🎗

기대를 나타내는 표현

• **A** The Major League Baseball season begins next month.
  메이저 리그 야구 시즌이 다음 달에 시작돼.

  B Yeah, **I can't wait to** go see the games. I'll go to the ballpark every weekend.
  맞아, 난 경기 보는 게 너무 기대돼. 나는 주말마다 야구장에 갈 거야.

• **A** You didn't forget about our camping trip this weekend, did you?
  너는 이번 주말 우리 캠핑 여행 잊지 않았지?

  B Of course not. **I really want to** spend the weekend fishing and stargazing.
  물론 기억하지. 나는 정말로 낚시와 별 관측을 하며 주말을 보내고 싶어.

Check-up 🎗

다음 대화의 빈칸에 들어갈 말로 알맞은 것은?

> **A** AI technology can convert low-quality paintings to high-quality paintings.
> **B** How interesting. I'm looking forward to _____.

ⓐ painting pictures　　　　ⓑ talking with the AI chatbot　　　　ⓒ trying that function

Function 2 설명 요청하기

B Hey, Grace, I heard [there is going to be a fire drill today].
    (that) 명사절 (heard의 목적어)

G That's right. But I'm a bit worried. I hurt my leg during our last fire drill.
    다리를 다쳤다   지난

B Oh, don't worry! This time, we are going to have a VR fire drill.

G A VR fire drill? What's that?

B We will be trained using virtual reality technology.
    미래시제의 수동태

G Oh! **Could you explain** [how it works]?
    간접의문문 (explain의 목적어)

B Sure. Everyone will use VR equipment and experience [what a fire is really
                                                          간접의문문 (experience의 목적어)
    like].

G That sounds interesting.

B It will be. We will also learn how to use a fire extinguisher without real
                               how to-V: ~하는 방법
    danger.

G I'm glad we can safely practice what to do.
                                    = what we should do

B: 안녕, Grace, 나는 오늘 소방 훈련이 있을 거라고 들었어.

G: 맞아. 그런데 나는 조금 걱정이 돼. 지난 소방 훈련 때 나는 다리를 다쳤거든.

B: 오, 걱정하지 않아도 돼! 이번에는 VR 소방 훈련이 이루어질 거야.

G: VR 소방 훈련? 그게 뭐야?

B: 가상 현실 기술을 이용해서 우리가 훈련을 받을 거야.

G: 오! 그게 어떻게 이뤄지는지 설명해 줄 수 있니?

B: 물론이지. 모든 사람이 VR 장비를 이용해서 실제 화재가 어떤지를 경험하는 거야.

G: 흥미롭겠다.

B: 그럴 거야. 우리는 또 실제 위험 없이 소화기를 사용하는 방법도 배울 거야.

G: 우리가 무엇을 해야 하는지를 안전히 훈련할 수 있어서 기뻐.

Study Point ☙

Could you explain ~?은 '~을 설명해줄 수 있니?'라는 의미로, 상대방에게 설명을 요청할 때 쓰는 표현이다.

More Expressions ☙

설명을 요청하는 표현

• A **What is** an axis? 축이 뭐지?

  B It is a real or imaginary straight line that goes through the center of a spinning object.
  그것은 회전하는 물체의 중심을 관통하는 실제의 또는 가상의 선이야.

• A **What do you mean by** "a hot potato"? '뜨거운 감자'가 무슨 뜻이니?

  B It is a difficult or controversial issue that no one wants to deal with.
  그것은 아무도 다루고 싶어 하지 않는 어렵고 논쟁적인 이슈를 말해.

Check-up ☙

자연스러운 대화가 되도록 괄호 안에 주어진 말을 바르게 배열하시오.

A _____ a smart speaker system can keep us safe?
    (explain, you, could, how)

B It reminds seniors to take their medicine on schedule.

교과서 기타 대화문

Watch and Communicate A. Watch

W Space technology may not seem useful to the average person. But did you know that many of the items ❶ <u>we use every day</u> come from space technology? For example, the image sensors in modern cameras were originally developed ❷ <u>to be used</u> in space. However, they were easy ❸ <u>to produce</u> and didn't require much power, so companies started using them in commercial products. These days, an updated version of this technology can be found in many devices, including smartphones and video cameras. Freeze drying is another technology ❹ <u>that was originally developed</u> for use in space. Freeze-dried foods are long-lasting and easy to prepare. Now, however, freeze-dried foods such as soups and fruit can be found in your local market! These are just two examples of ❺ <u>how space technology has benefited everyone</u>. Look around you. What other common items ❻ <u>do you think</u> come from space technology?

W: 우주 기술은 일반적인 사람에게 유용하지 않아 보일지도 모른다. 하지만 당신은 우리가 매일 사용하는 많은 물건이 우주 기술로부터 왔다는 것을 알고 있는가? 예를 들어, 현대 카메라에 있는 이미지 센서는 원래 우주에서 사용되도록 개발된 것이다. 하지만 그것은 생산이 쉽고 전력이 많이 필요하지 않아 기업들이 상업적인 제품에 사용하기 시작했다. 오늘날 이 기술의 업데이트된 버전은 스마트폰이나 비디오 카메라를 포함한 많은 기기에서 찾아볼 수 있다. 동결 건조는 원래 우주에서 사용하기 위해 개발되었던 또 다른 기술이다. 동결 건조된 음식들은 오래 지속되고 준비하기 쉽다. 하지만 이제 동결 건조된 수프나 과일을 동네 상점에서 찾아볼 수 있다! 이것들은 우주 기술이 어떻게 모든 사람들에게 혜택을 주었는지를 보여 주는 두 가지의 예시일 뿐이다. 당신 주위를 둘러보라. 다른 어떤 흔한 물건들이 우주 기술로부터 왔다고 생각하는가?

❶ 선행사 the items를 수식하는 목적격 관계대명사절 ❷ 수동태로 된 to부정사의 부사적 용법 (목적) ❸ to부정사의 부사적 용법 (앞에 있는 easy 를 수식) ❹ 선행사 technology를 수식하는 주격 관계대명사절 ❺ 간접의문문 (전치사 of의 목적어) ❻ Do you think?의 목적어로 의문문 What other common items come from space technology?가 쓰인 구조로서, 의문사(What other common items)가 문장 맨 앞에 위치하고 있다.

Q1 Image sensors and freeze drying are two examples of daily items that come from space technology. (T / F)

Lesson Review A

B Miju, is this a portrait of you?
G Yes, it is!
B I didn't know you ❶ <u>were good at</u> painting.
G Well, actually, an AI program painted this.
B AI did this? How is that possible?
G I just ❷ <u>shared</u> my picture <u>with</u> this website.
B And then the AI program ❸ <u>changed</u> it <u>into</u> a painting?
G That's right. ❹ <u>I'm looking forward to</u> trying other photos tonight.
B Sounds fun. I want to try that website too!

B: 미주야, 이것은 네 초상화니?
G: 응, 맞아!
B: 네가 그림을 잘 그리는지 몰랐어.
G: 음, 사실 인공지능 프로그램이 이걸 그렸어.
B: 인공지능이 이걸 그렸다고? 어떻게 그게 가능하지?
G: 나는 이 웹사이트에 내 사진을 공유하기만 했어.
B: 그리고 다음에 인공지능이 그걸 그림으로 바꾸었다고?
G: 맞아. 나는 오늘 밤 다른 사진들로 해보기를 기대하고 있어.
B: 재미있겠다. 나도 그 웹사이트에서 해봐야겠어!

❶ be good at: ~을 잘하다 ❷ share A with B: A를 B와 공유하다 ❸ change A into B: A를 B로 바꾸다, it: my picture ❹ I'm looking forward to V-ing: ~하기를 고대하다

Q2 Miju used a(n) (AI program / special paintbrush) to paint her self-portrait.

교과서 핵심 대화문 익히기

01 다음 대화의 밑줄 친 우리말과 일치하도록 주어진 말을 활용하여 문장을 완성하시오.

> **B** Hi, Emma. What are you doing on your phone?
> **G** Oh hi, Mark. I'm chatting with General Yi Sunsin.
> **B** General Yi Sunsin? How is that possible?
> **G** I installed a chatbot application. I can talk to any historical figure with it.
> **B** That sounds amazing!
> **G** Yes, it is amazing! <u>나는 장군님에게 노량해전에 관해 물어보길 고대하고 있어.</u> (look forward, general)
> **B** What are you going to ask?
> **G** I want to know how he felt during the battle.

→ _____ about the Battle of Noryang.

02 자연스러운 대화가 되도록 다음 문장을 순서대로 배열하시오.

> **B** Hey, Grace, I heard there is going to be a fire drill today.
> **G** That's right. But I'm a bit worried. I hurt my leg during our last fire drill.
> **B** Oh, don't worry! This time, we are going to have a VR fire drill.
>
> (   ) A VR fire drill? What's that?
> (   ) Oh! Could you explain how it works?
> (   ) We will be trained using virtual reality technology.
> (   ) Sure. Everyone will use VR equipment and experience what a fire is really like.
>
> **G** That sounds interesting.

03 다음 대화의 내용과 일치하도록 빈칸에 알맞은 말을 쓰시오.

> **B** Miju, is this a portrait of you?
> **G** Yes, it is!
> **B** I didn't know you were good at painting.
> **G** Well, actually, an AI program painted this.
> **B** AI did this? How is that possible?
> **G** I just shared my picture with this website.
> **B** And then the AI program changed it into a painting?
> **G** That's right. I'm looking forward to trying other photos tonight.
> **B** Sounds fun. I want to try that website too.

→ Miju painted her _____ using a(n) _____ program on a website.

교과서 핵심 문법

POINT 1 not only A but also B

예제	The tomato soup is **not only** tasty **but also** good for your health.
	not only A(형용사) but also B(형용사구)
	그 토마토 수프는 맛있을 뿐 아니라 건강에도 좋다.
교과서	AI may lead to changes **not only** in the art world **but also** in the music industry.
	not only A(전치사구) but also B(전치사구)
	인공 지능 프로그램은 미술 세계뿐만 아니라 음악 산업에서의 변화로도 이어질 수 있다.

▶ not only A but also B는 'A뿐만 아니라 B도'라는 의미로, A와 B의 자리에는 어법상 대등한 성격의 말이 와야 한다.

Study Point ✿

1 not only A but also B

not only A but also B는 문법적으로 대등한 성격의 단어나 구를 연결하는 상관접속사이다. 이때 A와 B에는 명사(구), 동사(구), 형용사(구), 부사(구) 등이 올 수 있다. also는 종종 생략되기도 한다.

- Josh gave out **not only** *pencils* **but also** *books*. 〔명사〕
  Josh는 연필뿐 아니라 책도 나눠주었다.
- A true leader has to be **not only** *strong* **but also** *decisive*. 〔형용사〕
  진정한 리더는 강인할 뿐 아니라 결단력도 있어야 한다.
- The bakery **not only** *sells* bread **but also** *serves* nice coffee. 〔동사〕
  그 빵집은 빵을 팔 뿐만 아니라 멋진 커피도 제공한다.
- Dorothy is good at **not only** *playing the guitar* **but also** *playing soccer*. 〔동명사구〕
  Dorothy는 기타를 잘 칠 뿐 아니라 축구도 잘한다.

2 상관접속사

- The TV program is informative **as well as** entertaining. B as well as A: A뿐 아니라 B도
  그 TV 프로그램은 흥미로울 뿐 아니라 유익한 정보가 많다.
- **Both** Kevin **and** his brother should be blamed for the accident. both A and B: A와 B 둘 다
  Kevin과 그의 남동생 모두 그 사고에 대해 비난 받아야 한다.
- Tony has **neither** the time **nor** the money to go on a trip. neither A nor B: A도 아니고 B도 아닌
  Tony는 여행을 갈 시간도 돈도 없다.
- I didn't have the cake **not** because I didn't like it **but** because I was full. not A but B: A가 아니고 B인
  나는 케이크를 좋아하지 않아서가 아니라 배가 불러서 먹지 않았다.

Q 다음 네모 안에서 어법상 알맞은 것을 고르시오.

1 Thank you for not only helping me but also standing / to stand by me.

2 Neither the restaurant or / nor its neighboring cafe opens today.

3 Both April and her sister need / needs to save money for their mom's birthday.

Check-up ☂

01 괄호 안에 주어진 말을 알맞은 형태로 바꿔 빈칸에 넣으시오.

(1) Her lecture was not only interesting but also _____. (education)

(2) Sarah not only wrote some storybooks but also _____ a movie. (direct)

(3) She enjoys painting as well as _____ in her free time. (read)

(4) My leg injury affected me not only _____ but also mentally. (phisical)

02 우리말과 일치하도록 괄호 안에 주어진 말을 이용하여 문장을 완성하시오.

(1) 그 가수는 노래를 잘할 뿐만 아니라 춤도 잘 춘다. (as well as)

→ The singer is good at _____.

(2) 그녀의 삼촌은 그녀에게 도움이 되는 조언과 재정적 지원을 제공했다. (both, and)

→ Her uncle provided her with _____ financial

support.

(3) 전시장에서는 사진을 찍을 수도, 통화를 할 수도 없다. (neither, nor)

→ In the exhibition hall, you can _____ talk on the

phone.

(4) 우리 고양이는 주로 침대 밑이나 소파 뒤에 숨는다. (either, or)

→ My cat usually hides _____ behind the sofa.

03 다음 문장에서 어법상 <u>어색한</u> 부분을 찾아 바르게 고쳐 쓰시오.

(1) Both the boy and his mother seems shocked about the news.

→ _____ about the news.

(2) The news article was neither correct or trustworthy.

→ The news article _____.

(3) You can choose either taking the exam or to submit the report.

→ You can choose _____ the report.

(4) The woman not only rescued the cat also brought it to the shelter.

→ The woman _____ to the shelter.

POINT 2) 동격의 접속사 that

예제	We support *the idea* **that** seniors should have access to technology.
	명사 = 동격의 명사절
	우리는 노령층도 기술에 접근할 수 있어야 한다는 의견을 지지한다.
교과서	There are *concerns* **that** AI may imitate the styles of human artists without their consent.
	명사 = 동격의 명사절
	AI가 인간 예술가의 동의 없이 그들의 화풍을 모방할지도 모른다는 염려가 있다.

▶ 접속사 that이 이끄는 절이 명사 뒤에 쓰여 동격의 관계로 그 명사를 부연 설명한다.

Study Point ♨

1 동격의 명사절을 이끄는 접속사 that

접속사 that이 이끄는 절이 일부 명사 뒤에 쓰여 그 명사를 부연 설명하는 기능이 있다. 이때 이 명사와 that이 이끄는 명사절은 동격 관계에 있다.

> 동격절을 이끄는 대표적인 명사
> idea(생각), fact(사실), concern(염려), news(뉴스), opinion(의견), belief(믿음), thought(생각), doubt(의심), suggestion(제안), conclusion(결론) 등

· Many people agree with *your opinion* **that** we should invest more in the project.
　　　　　　　　　　　　　　　your opinion = that we should invest more in the project
많은 사람들은 우리가 그 사업에 더 투자해야 한다는 당신의 의견에 동의한다.

· We were all surprised at *the fact* **that** Jamie and Susie were not sisters.
우리 모두는 Jamie와 Susie가 자매가 아니라는 사실에 놀랐다.

· Ancient people had *the belief* **that** the earth was the center of the universe.
고대인들은 지구가 우주의 중심이라는 믿음을 가지고 있었다.

2 동격의 that vs. 관계대명사 that

동격의 that이 이끄는 절은 완전한 문장이다. 이에 반해 관계대명사 that이 이끄는 문장은 앞에 쓰인 선행사가 주어나 목적어 역할을 하기 때문에 불완전한 문장이다.

· The news **that** the singer canceled her concert surprised her fans.
　　　　　　뉴스 = 가수가 공연을 취소했다 〈완전한 문장〉
그 가수가 공연을 취소했다는 소식은 그녀의 팬들을 놀라게 했다.

· The news **that** was broadcasted last night surprised her fans.
　　　　뉴스 ↑_____ 지난 밤 방송된 〈불완전한 문장〉

지난 밤 방송된 소식은 그녀의 팬들을 놀라게 했다.

Q 다음 네모 안에서 어법상 알맞은 것을 고르시오.

1 Emily thought if / that she could win the championship.

2 Everyone liked the idea who / that was proposed during the meeting.

3 We came to the conclusion that / which the man was telling truth.

Check-up 🍅

01 다음 문장의 알맞은 위치에 that을 넣어 문장을 고쳐 쓰시오.

(1) They came to the conclusion they should take the bus to the airport.

→ They came to _____ to the airport.

(2) It is believed Judy published the book under her pen name.

→ It is believed _____ under her pen name.

(3) The museum holds a special exhibition of van Gogh is crowded with people.

→ The museum _____ of van Gogh is crowded with people.

02 우리말과 일치하도록 주어진 말을 바르게 배열하여 문장을 완성하시오.

(1) 나는 그 베스트셀러 작가가 옆집에 살고 있다는 사실이 놀랍다.

→ I am surprised at _____ next door.

(lives / the fact / the best-seller writer / that)

(2) 우리는 그의 판단이 공정하지 않다는 결론에 이르렀다.

→ We reached _____ .

(was / the conclusion / his judgment / that / unfair)

(3) 우리 모두는 우리가 결국 경주에서 이길 거라는 믿음이 있다.

→ We all have _____ in the end.

(a belief / we / that / win / the race / will)

03 다음 문장에서 밑줄 친 that의 쓰임이 같은 것끼리 바르게 짝지어진 것은?

ⓐ Mr. Bush has a strong belief that getting up early is important.
ⓑ The picture that you're looking at was created by an AI program.
ⓒ Do you believe that technology will improve our lives?
ⓓ My parents have a concern that I don't get along well with my classmates.
ⓔ The students know that their homeroom teacher is a good person.
ⓕ We don't support the opinion that was expressed by the chairman.

① ⓐ, ⓑ   ② ⓐ, ⓓ   ③ ⓑ, ⓓ   ④ ⓑ, ⓔ   ⑤ ⓒ, ⓕ

교과서 본문 분석

AI: Opportunity or Threat?

인공 지능: 기회인가 위협인가?

01 Recently, an artist used an artificial intelligence (AI) system [to create the image above (for an art contest)].

to부정사의 부사적 용법 (목적)

최근 한 화가가 미술 대회를 위한 위의 그림을 만들기 위해 인공 지능 시스템을 사용했다.

02 The image won first place in the digital arts category.

우승하다

그 그림은 디지털 예술 부문에서 1등을 했다.

03 This led to a controversy in the art community.

lead to: ~으로 이어지다

이는 미술계에서 논란으로 이어졌다.

04 Some people complained [that the artist simply provided the system with basic instructions and let it do all the work].

명사절 (complained의 목적어) 병렬 연결
provide A with B: A에게 B를 제공하다 let + 목적어 + 동사원형: ~가 … 하게 하다
= the system

어떤 사람들은 그 화가가 단순히 시스템에 기본적인 지시 사항을 제공했으며 그것(시스템)이 모든 작업을 하게 했다고 불평했다.

05 They felt [this wasn't fair to the rest of the artists (in the contest)].

(that)
명사절 (felt의 목적어) 전치사구

그들은 이것이 대회의 나머지 화가들에게 공평하지 않다고 느꼈다.

06 However, there were also people [who were excited by the potential of AI].

주격 관계대명사절

그러나, 인공 지능의 잠재력에 들뜬 사람들도 있었다.

07 Today, there are numerous AI programs [that can create various forms of art including images, songs, and novels].

전치사 (~을 포함하여)
주격 관계대명사절

오늘날 그림, 노래, 소설을 포함하여 다양한 형태의 예술을 창조해 낼 수 있는 많은 인공 지능 프로그램들이 있다.

Example 1. Making Digital Images with AI

예시 1: 인공 지능으로 디지털 그림 만들기

08 AI image generators create images <u>based on</u> our text requests.
~에 기반하여

인공 지능 그림 생성기들은 우리의 텍스트 요청에 기반하여 그림을 생성한다.

09 They <u>do this</u> by [copying other <u>images</u> (that were created by humans)].
= create images
동명사구
주격 관계대명사절

그것들은 인간에 의해 만들어진 다른 그림들을 모방함으로써 그림을 만든다.

10 The generators have <u>the ability</u> [to analyze <u>millions of images</u> and <u>their corresponding descriptions</u>].
analyze의 목적어 1
analyze의 목적어 2
to부정사의 형용사적 용법

그 생성기들은 수백만 개의 그림과 그에 상응하는 설명을 분석할 능력을 갖고 있다.

11 This <u>allows them to create</u> works of art in a short time based on the <u>provided instructions</u>.
allow + 목적어 + to부정사: ~가 …하게 하다
과거분사

이는 그것들이 주어진 설명에 기반하여 짧은 시간 안에 예술 작품을 만들어 낼 수 있게 한다.

12 Moreover, AI programs can mix the styles of <u>existing</u> images <u>upon request</u>.
현존하는
요청에 따라

게다가, 인공 지능 프로그램들은 요청에 따라 현존하는 그림들의 화풍을 혼합할 수 있다.

13 For example, you can <u>blend</u> a photograph of a cat <u>with</u> Johannes Vermeer's *Girl with a Pearl Earring*.
blend A with B: A와 B를 섞다

예를 들어, 당신은 고양이의 사진을 요하네스 페르메이르의 〈진주 귀걸이를 한 소녀〉와 혼합할 수 있다.

14 These two images have <u>a few</u> differences.
a few + 셀 수 있는 명사: 약간의 ~

이 두 개의 그림은 몇 가지 차이가 있다.

15 However, the overall design, the eyes, and the scarf (around the head) are clearly based on
주어 1   주어 2   주어 3 ↑└──────┘ 전치사구   동사
Vermeer's painting.

그러나 전체적인 디자인, 눈, 머리 주위의 스카프는 확실히 페르메이르의 그림에 기반하고 있다.

16 A simple request was enough to create this complex and detailed image.
enough to-V: ~하기에 충분하다   └────┘ ↑

간단한 요청이면 이러한 복잡하고 상세한 그림을 만들어 내기에 충분했다.

Example 2. Making Music with AI
예시 2: 인공 지능으로 음악 만들기

not only A but also B: A뿐만 아니라 B도

17 AI programs may lead to changes not only [in the art world] but also [in the music industry].
조동사 (약한 추측)   └──────── 병렬 연결 (전치사구) ────────┘

인공 지능 프로그램은 미술 세계뿐만 아니라 음악 산업에서의 변화로도 이어질 수 있다.

간접목적어 ←   → 직접목적어

18 These programs are already able to compose songs, and they give you many options.
be able to-V: ~할 수 있다

이러한 프로그램들은 이미 노래를 작곡할 수 있으며 당신에게 여러 선택 사항을 준다.

19 For example, you can choose the style and key, such as C major or A minor.
~같은 (예시)

예를 들어, 당신은 장르와 다장조나 가단조와 같은 조성을 선택할 수 있다.

20 You can also set [how long the song will be].
간접의문문 (set의 목적어)

당신은 또한 노래가 얼마나 길어질지도 설정할 수 있다.

접속사 (일단 ~하면)

21 Once you've entered the information, the program will produce a song [that you can edit or use
                                                              ↑└────┘ 목적격 관계대명사절
as it is].
있는 그대로

일단 당신이 정보를 입력하고 나면, 프로그램은 당신이 편집하거나 그대로 사용할 수 있는 노래를 제작할 것이다.

22

게다가 (앞문장을 부연 설명하는 연결어)

Furthermore, computer-generated imagery (commonly known as CGI) has opened up new

~라고 알려진   현재완료 (완료)

possibilities [in the music industry].

전치사구 (부사구)

게다가, (흔히 CGI라고 알려진) 컴퓨터 생성 이미지는 음악 산업에서 새로운 가능성을 열었다.

23

주어   동사 (현재완료)

Virtual influencers [with extremely realistic faces, bodies, and voices] have already released several

전치사구 (~을 가진)

songs.

대단히 사실적인 얼굴, 신체, 목소리를 가진 가상의 인플루언서들이 이미 여러 노래를 발매했다.

24

Some of them have many followers on social media, just like human singers.

= the virtual influencers   꼭 ~처럼

그들 중 일부는 인간 가수와 마찬가지로 소셜 미디어에 많은 팔로워를 보유하고 있다.

25

노래를 발매하고 많은 팔로워를 가진

These types of virtual musicians are able to speak and move realistically with the help of their

~의 도움으로

human creators.

이러한 유형의 가상 음악가들은 인간 창작자들의 도움으로 사실적으로 말하고 움직일 수 있다.

The Debate on Using AI

인공 지능 사용을 둘러싼 논쟁

26

(that)   명사절 (means의 목적어)

Many AI programs are open to the public, which means [they can be used freely and conveniently].

계속적 용법의 주격 관계대명사 (앞의 절이 선행사)

많은 인공 지능 프로그램들은 대중에 공개되어 있는데, 그것은 그것들이 자유롭고 편리하게 이용될 수 있다는 것을 의미한다.

27

~에 관한

However, these programs have sparked a debate [over their impact on humans].

현재완료   전치사구

그러나 이러한 프로그램들은 인간에게 미치는 그들의 영향력에 관해 논쟁을 불러일으켰다.

28 Since AI has the potential [to learn skills and perform them better than humans], some people
접속사 (이유)   to부정사의 형용사적 용법
(to)

view it as a threat.
view A as B: A를 B로 여기다

인공 지능이 인간보다 기술을 더 잘 배우고 수행할 잠재력이 있기 때문에 어떤 사람들은 그것을 위협으로 본다.

29 They worry [that AI will replace humans in more and more areas].
명사절 (worry의 목적어)   점점 더 많은

그들은 인공 지능이 점점 더 많은 분야에서 인간을 대체할 것이라 걱정한다.

30 There are also concerns [that AI may imitate the styles of human artists (without their consent)].
concerns와 동격의 명사절

인간 예술가의 동의 없이 그들의 화풍을 모방할지도 모른다는 염려도 있다.

31 반면에 (역접 관계를 나타내는 연결어)   병렬 연결
On the other hand, others think [that AI cannot exceed human imagination] and [that it is still
명사절 1 (think의 목적어)   명사절 2 (think의 목적어)

dependent on human assistance].
~에 의존하는

반면에, 다른 사람들은 인공 지능이 인간의 상상력을 뛰어넘을 수 없으며 여전히 인간의 도움에 의존하고 있다고 생각한다.

32 This is because the data [that AI uses] can have flaws or limitations.
목적격 관계대명사절

이는 인공 지능이 사용하는 정보에는 결함이나 한계가 있을 수 있기 때문이다.

33 주어   동사
A dependence [on imperfect data (with little diversity)] eventually limits the output of AI
전치사구   전치사구

programs.

다양성이 거의 없는 불완전한 정보에 의존하는 것은 결국 인공 지능 프로그램의 결과물을 제한한다.

34 Human imagination, on the other hand, has no limits or boundaries.
주어   동사

반면, 인간의 상상력은 한계나 경계가 없다.

35

주절 →

What kind of future (do you think) lies ahead of us?

간접의문문 (think의 목적어 역할), 주절의 동사가 think일 때 의문사가 앞으로 나간 형태

어떠한 종류의 미래가 우리 앞에 놓여 있다고 생각하는가?

36

Will more people use AI programs [to boost their creativity and productivity]?

to부정사의 부사적 용법 (목적)

더 많은 사람들이 그들의 창의력과 생산성을 증진하기 위해 인공 지능 프로그램을 사용할 것인가?

37

Or will people grow tired of the limitations of AI tools?

grow + 형용사: ~하게 되다

아니면 사람들이 인공 지능 도구의 한계에 지치게 될 것인가?

38

AI provides many benefits and new opportunities.

인공 지능은 많은 이점과 새로운 기회를 제공한다.

39

관계대명사절 (주어) →   동사 ←   (to)   의문사 + to부정사구 (figure out의 목적어)   (to)   간접의문문 (about의 목적어) →

[What we need to do] is figure out [how to use AI tools ethically] and think about [how humans and AI can collaborate].

병렬 연결
(is의 보어)

우리가 해야 할 것은 인공 지능 도구를 윤리적으로 사용하는 방법을 알아내고 인간과 인공 지능이 어떻게 협력할 수 있을지에 관해 생각하는 것이다.

✤ 다음 빈칸에 알맞은 말을 쓰시오.

01 Recently, _____ an artificial intelligence (AI) system to create the image above _____.

최근 한 화가가 미술 대회를 위한 위의 그림을 만들기 위해 인공 지능 시스템을 사용했다.

02 The image _____ in the digital arts category.

그 그림은 디지털 예술 부문에서 1등을 했다.

03 This _____ in the art community.

이는 미술계에서 논란으로 이어졌다.

04 Some people _____ the artist simply provided the system with basic instructions and _____.

어떤 사람들은 그 화가가 단순히 시스템에 기본적인 지시 사항을 제공했으며 그것(시스템)이 모든 작업을 하게 했다고 불평했다.

05 They felt _____ to the rest of the artists in the contest.

그들은 이것이 대회의 나머지 화가들에게 공평하지 않다고 느꼈다.

06 However, there were also people who were excited _____.

그러나, 인공 지능의 잠재력에 들뜬 사람들도 있었다.

07 Today, there are numerous AI programs _____ various forms of art _____, and novels.

오늘날 그림, 노래, 소설을 포함하여 다양한 형태의 예술을 창조해 낼 수 있는 많은 인공 지능 프로그램들이 있다.

08 AI image generators create images _____.

인공 지능 그림 생성기들은 우리의 텍스트 요청에 기반하여 그림을 생성한다.

09 They do this _____ that were created by humans.

그것들은 인간에 의해 만들어진 다른 그림들을 모방함으로써 그림을 만든다.

10 The generators _____ to analyze millions of images and their _____.

그 생성기들은 수백만 개의 그림과 그에 상응하는 설명을 분석할 능력을 갖고 있다.

11 This allows them to create works of art _____ based on the provided instructions.

이는 그것들이 주어진 설명에 기반하여 짧은 시간 안에 예술 작품을 만들어 낼 수 있게 한다.

12 Moreover, AI programs can mix _____ upon request.

게다가, 인공 지능 프로그램들은 요청에 따라 현존하는 그림들의 화풍을 혼합할 수 있다.

13 For example, you can _____ with Johannes Vermeer's *Girl with a Pearl Earring*.

예를 들어, 당신은 고양이의 사진을 요하네스 페르메이르의 〈진주 귀걸이를 한 소녀〉와 혼합할 수 있다.

14   These two images have _____ .

이 두 개의 그림은 몇 가지 차이가 있다.

15   However, the overall design, the eyes, and the scarf around the head _____

Vermeer's painting.

그러나 전체적인 디자인, 눈, 머리 주위의 스카프는 확실히 페르메이르의 그림에 기반하고 있다.

16   A simple request was _____ this complex and detailed image.

간단한 요청이면 이러한 복잡하고 상세한 그림을 만들어 내기에 충분했다.

17   AI programs may lead to changes _____ but also in the music industry.

인공 지능 프로그램은 미술 세계뿐만 아니라 음악 산업에서의 변화로도 이어질 수 있다.

18   These programs are already _____ , and they give you many options.

이러한 프로그램들은 이미 노래를 작곡할 수 있으며 당신에게 여러 선택 사항을 준다.

19   _____ , you can choose the style and key, such as C major or A minor.

예를 들어, 당신은 장르와 다장조나 가단조와 같은 조성을 선택할 수 있다.

20   You can _____ the song will be.

당신은 또한 노래가 얼마나 길어질지도 설정할 수 있다.

21   _____ the information, the program will produce a song

_____ as it is.

일단 당신이 정보를 입력하고 나면, 프로그램은 당신이 편집하거나 그대로 사용할 수 있는 노래를 제작할 것이다.

22   Furthermore, computer-generated imagery (commonly known as CGI) _____

in the music industry.

게다가, (흔히 CGI라고 알려진) 컴퓨터 생성 이미지는 음악 산업에서 새로운 가능성을 열었다.

23   Virtual influencers with extremely realistic faces, bodies, and voices _____

several songs.

대단히 사실적인 얼굴, 신체, 목소리를 가진 가상의 인플루언서들이 이미 여러 노래를 발매했다.

24   Some of them have many followers on social media, _____ .

그들 중 일부는 인간 가수와 마찬가지로 소셜 미디어에 많은 팔로워를 보유하고 있다.

25   These types of _____ are able to speak and move realistically with the help of

_____ .

이러한 유형의 가상 음악가들은 인간 창작자들의 도움으로 사실적으로 말하고 움직일 수 있다.

26   Many AI programs _____ , which means they can be used freely and

conveniently.

많은 인공 지능 프로그램들은 대중에 공개되어 있는데, 그것은 그것들이 자유롭고 편리하게 이용될 수 있다는 것을 의미한다.

27   However, these programs have sparked a debate _____ .

그러나 이러한 프로그램들은 인간에게 미치는 그들의 영향력에 관해 논쟁을 불러일으켰다.

28 Since AI has _____ and perform them better than humans, some people

_____ .

인공 지능이 인간보다 기술을 더 잘 배우고 수행할 잠재력이 있기 때문에 어떤 사람들은 그것을 위협으로 본다.

29 They worry that _____ in more and more areas.

그들은 인공 지능이 점점 더 많은 분야에서 인간을 대체할 것이라 걱정한다.

30 There are also concerns that AI may _____ of human artists without their

consent.

인간 예술가의 동의 없이 그들의 화풍을 모방할지도 모른다는 염려도 있다.

31 _____ , others think that AI cannot exceed human imagination and that

_____ human assistance.

반면에, 다른 사람들은 인공 지능이 인간의 상상력을 뛰어넘을 수 없으며 여전히 인간의 도움에 의존하고 있다고 생각한다.

32 This is because the data _____ can have flaws or limitations.

이는 인공 지능이 사용하는 정보에는 결함이나 한계가 있을 수 있기 때문이다.

33 A dependence on _____ eventually limits the output of AI programs.

다양성이 거의 없는 불완전한 정보에 의존하는 것은 결국 인공 지능 프로그램의 결과물을 제한한다.

34 Human imagination, on the other hand, _____ .

반면, 인간의 상상력은 한계나 경계가 없다.

35 What kind of future do you think _____ ?

어떠한 종류의 미래가 우리 앞에 놓여 있다고 생각하는가?

36 Will more people use AI programs _____ and productivity?

더 많은 사람들이 그들의 창의력과 생산성을 증진하기 위해 인공 지능 프로그램을 사용할 것인가?

37 Or will people _____ the limitations of AI tools?

아니면 사람들이 인공 지능 도구의 한계에 지치게 될 것인가?

38 AI provides many benefits and _____ .

인공 지능은 많은 이점과 새로운 기회를 제공한다.

39 What we need to do is figure out _____ and think about how humans and AI

can collaborate.

우리가 해야 할 것은 인공 지능 도구를 윤리적으로 사용하는 방법을 알아내고 인간과 인공 지능이 어떻게 협력할 수 있을지에 관해
생각하는 것이다.

교과서 본문 익히기 ② 옳은 어법·어휘 고르기

♣ 다음 네모 안에서 옳은 것을 고르시오.

01 Recently, an artist used an artificial intelligence / intelligent (AI) system to create the image above for an art contest.

02 Some people complained that the artist simply provided the system with basic instructions and let it do / to do all the work.

03 They felt this wasn't fair to the most / rest of the artists in the contest.

04 However, there were also people who were exciting / excited by the potential of AI.

05 Today, there are numerous AI programs that can create various forms of art including / included images, songs, and novels.

06 AI image generators create images based in / on our text requests.

07 They do this by copying other images that were created by humans / computers .

08 The generators have the ability to analyze millions of images and their responding / corresponding descriptions.

09 This allows them create / to create works of art in a short time based on the provided instructions.

10 Eventually / Moreover , AI programs can mix the styles of existing images upon / with request.

11 These two images have a few / little differences.

12 However, the complete / overall design, the eyes, and the scarf around the head is / are clearly based on Vermeer's painting.

13   A simple request was enough / lack to create this complex and detailed image.

14   AI programs may lead to changes as well / not only in the art world but also in the music industry.

15   These programs are already able to compose / make songs, and they give you / to you many options.

16   For example, you can choose the style and beat / key , such as C major or A minor.

17   You can also set how long / short the song will be.

18   Once / Upon you've entered the information, the program will produce a song that you can edit or use as / that it is.

19   Furthermore, computer-generating / computer-generated imagery (commonly known as CGI) has opened up new possibilities in the music industry.

20   Real / Virtual influencers with extremely realistic faces, bodies, and voices have already published / released several songs.

21   Some of them have many followers on social media, just like cyber / human singers.

22   These types of virtual musicians are able to speak and move realistically with the help of their human creaters / creators .

23   Many AI programs are open to the public, that / which means they can be used freely and conveniently.

24   However / Moreover , these programs have sparked a debate over / with their impact on humans.

25   Since AI has the potential to learn skills and perform / performs them better than humans, some people see / view it as a threat.

26   They worry that AI will place / replace humans in more and more areas.

27   There are also concerns that / which AI may imitate the styles of human artists with / without their consent.

28   On the other hand / hands, others think that AI cannot exceed human imagination and that it is still depend / dependent on human assistance.

29   This is because the data that AI uses can have flows / flaws or limitations.

30   A dependence on imperfect data with little / a little diversity eventually limits the output of AI programs.

31   Human imagination, on the other hand, have / has no limits or boundaries.

32   What kind of future do you think lays / lies ahead of us?

33   Will more people use AI programs to boast / boost their creativity and productivity?

34   Or will people grow / raise tired of the limitations of AI tools?

35   What we need to do is figure of / out how to use AI tools ethically and think about how / what humans and AI can collaborate.

♣ 다음 밑줄 친 부분을 바르게 고쳐 쓰시오.

01   Recently, an artist used an artificial intelligence (AI) system to <u>be created</u> the image above for an art contest.

02   The image <u>was</u> first place in the digital arts category.

03   This <u>led</u> a controversy in the art community.

04   Some people complained that the artist simply provided the system <u>basic instructions</u> and let it do all the work.

05   They felt this <u>was</u> fair to the rest of the artists in the contest.

06   However, there were also people who <u>excited</u> by the potential of AI.

07   Today, <u>there is</u> numerous AI programs that can create various forms of art including images, songs, and novels.

08   They do this by copying other images that <u>created</u> by humans.

09   The generators have the ability to analyze <u>million of</u> images and their corresponding descriptions.

10   This allows them <u>create</u> works of art in a short time based on the provided instructions.

11   Moreover, AI programs can mix the styles of existing images <u>by request</u>.

12   For example, you can blend a photograph of a cat <u>to</u> Johannes Vermeer's *Girl with a Pearl Earring*.

13   These two images have a few <u>difference</u>.

14   However, the overall design, the eyes, and the scarf around the head <u>is clearly basing</u> on Vermeer's painting.

15   A simple request was enough <u>for creating</u> this complex and detailed image.

16   AI programs may lead to changes not only in the art world but also <u>the music industry</u>.

17   These programs are already able to compose songs, and <u>it gives</u> you many options.

18   For example, you can choose the style and key, <u>so as</u> C major or A minor.

19   You can also set how long <u>will the song be</u>.

20   Once you've entered the information, the program will produce a song that <u>can edit</u> or use as it is.

21   Furthermore, computer-generated imagery (<u>commonly know</u> as CGI) has opened up new possibilities in the music industry.

22   Virtual influencers with extremely realistic faces, bodies, and voices <u>had already released</u> several songs.

23   Some of them have many followers on social media, <u>just as</u> human singers.

24   These types of virtual musicians are able to speak and <u>moving</u> realistically with the help of their human creators.

25   Many AI programs are open to the public, which means they can be used <u>free and convenient</u>.

26   However, these programs have sparked a debate over <u>its impact</u> on humans.

27   Since AI has the potential to learn skills and perform them better than humans, some people view it
      <u>a threat</u>.

28   They worry that AI will replace humans in <u>many and many</u> areas.

29   There are also concerns <u>which</u> AI may imitate the styles of human artists <u>with</u> their consent.

30   On the other hand, <u>other thinks</u> that AI cannot exceed human imagination and <u>what</u> it is still dependent on
      human assistance.

31   This is <u>why</u> the data that AI uses can have flaws or limitations.

32   A dependence on imperfect data with little diversity eventually <u>limit</u> the output of AI programs.

33   Human imagination, on the other hand, has <u>not</u> limits or boundaries.

34   What kind of future <u>you think</u> lies ahead of us?

35   Or will people <u>grow tire of</u> the limitations of AI tools?

36   What we need to do is figure out how to use AI tools ethically and think about how <u>can humans and AI</u>
      collaborate.

Think and Write ❦ 교과서 93쪽

> **Will Robots Replace Humans?**
>
> ❶As AI technology advances, will robots ❷take over human work? I think ❸robots can replace humans in many roles. ❹There are two reasons for my opinion. First, robots can work ❺more productively than humans. This means ❻that they can produce more in a shorter amount of time. Second, robots can work in dangerous places ❼that humans cannot reach. Therefore, they can reduce the risk of accidents. For these reasons, I think ❽that robots will replace human workers in the future.

로봇이 인간을 대체할 것인가?

　AI 기술이 진화하면서, 로봇이 인간의 업무를 인계할 것인가? 나는 로봇이 인간의 많은 역할을 대체할 수 있을 것으로 생각한다. 나의 의견에는 두 가지 이유가 있다. 첫 번째, 로봇은 인간보다 더욱 생산적으로 일할 수 있다. 이것은 로봇이 더 짧은 시간 동안 더 많은 것을 생산할 수 있다는 것을 의미한다. 두 번째, 로봇은 인간이 닿을 수 없는 위험한 곳에서 일할 수 있다. 그러므로, 로봇은 사고의 위험을 줄일 수 있다. 이러한 이유로, 나는 로봇이 미래에 인간 노동자를 대체할 것이라고 생각한다.

❶ as: '~함에 따라'라는 의미의 접속사 ❷ take over: 인계하다 ❸ robots 앞에 목적어 역할을 하는 명사절을 이끄는 접속사 that이 생략 ❹ There are+복수명사: ~이 있다 ❺ more productively: 부사의 비교급 ❻ that: means의 목적어가 되는 명사절을 이끄는 접속사 ❼ 선행사 places를 설명하는 목적격 관계대명사절 ❽ that: think의 목적어 역할을 하는 명사절을 이끄는 접속사

Q The writer thinks robots will replace human work in the future. (T / F)

Check-up ❦

다음 빈칸에 알맞은 말을 쓰시오.

01　As AI technology advances, will robots _____?
　　　AI 기술이 진화하면서, 로봇이 인간의 업무를 인계할 것인가?

02　I think robots can replace humans _____.
　　　나는 로봇이 인간의 많은 역할을 대체할 수 있을 것으로 생각한다.

03　_____ for my opinion.
　　　나의 의견에는 두 가지 이유가 있다.

04　First, robots can work _____ humans.
　　　첫 번째, 로봇은 인간보다 더욱 생산적으로 일할 수 있다.

05　This means that they can produce more _____.
　　　이것은 로봇이 더 짧은 시간 동안 더 많은 것을 생산할 수 있다는 것을 의미한다.

06　Second, robots can work in dangerous places _____.
　　　두 번째, 로봇은 인간이 닿을 수 없는 위험한 곳에서 일할 수 있다.

07　Therefore, they _____ of accidents.
　　　그러므로, 로봇은 사고의 위험을 줄일 수 있다.

08　_____, I think that robots will replace human workers in the future.
　　　이러한 이유로, 나는 로봇이 미래에 인간 노동자를 대체할 것이라고 생각한다.

01 (A), (B), (C)의 각 네모 안에서 문맥에 맞는 낱말로 가장 적절한 것은?

Space technology may not seem (A) useful / useless to the average person. But did you know that many of the items we use every day come from space technology? For example, the image sensors in modern cameras were originally developed to be used in space. However, they were (B) easy / hard to produce and didn't require much power, so companies started using them in commercial products. These days, an (C) outdated / updated version of this technology can be found in many devices, including smartphones and video cameras.

	(A)		(B)		(C)
①	useful	⋯	easy	⋯	outdated
②	useful	⋯	hard	⋯	outdated
③	useful	⋯	easy	⋯	updated
④	useless	⋯	hard	⋯	updated
⑤	useless	⋯	easy	⋯	updated

02 밑줄 친 부분 중, 문맥상 낱말의 쓰임이 적절하지 <u>않은</u> 것은?

Recently, an artist used an artificial intelligence (AI) system to create the image above for an art contest. The image won ① <u>first</u> place in the digital arts category. This led to a controversy in the art community. Some people ② <u>complained</u> that the artist simply provided the system with basic instructions and let it do all the work. They felt this wasn't ③ <u>fair</u> to the rest of the artists in the contest. However, there were also people who were excited by the ④ <u>potential</u> of AI. Today, there are numerous AI programs that can create various forms of art ⑤ <u>except</u> images, songs, and novels.

①   ②   ③   ④   ⑤

03 (A), (B), (C)의 각 네모 안에서 문맥에 맞는 낱말로 가장 적절한 것은?

Making Digital Images with AI

AI image generators create images based on our text requests. They do this by (A) coping / copying other images that were created by humans. The generators have the ability to analyze (B) million / millions of images and their corresponding descriptions. This allows them to create works of art in a short time based on the provided (C) constructions / instructions.

	(A)		(B)		(C)
①	coping	⋯	million	⋯	constructions
②	coping	⋯	millions	⋯	constructions
③	copying	⋯	million	⋯	constructions
④	copying	⋯	millions	⋯	instructions
⑤	copying	⋯	million	⋯	instructions

04 밑줄 친 부분 중, 문맥상 낱말의 쓰임이 적절하지 <u>않은</u> 것은?

Moreover, AI programs can mix the styles of existing images ① <u>at</u> request. ② <u>For</u> example, you can blend a photograph of a cat ③ <u>with</u> Johannes Vermeer's *Girl with a Pearl Earring*. These two images have a few differences. However, the overall design, the eyes, and the scarf ④ <u>around</u> the head are clearly based ⑤ <u>on</u> Vermeer's painting. A simple request was enough to create this complex and detailed image.

①   ②   ③   ④   ⑤

05 밑줄 친 부분 중, 문맥상 어구의 쓰임이 적절하지 <u>않은</u> 것은?

AI programs may ① <u>lead to</u> changes not only in the art world but also in the music industry. These programs are already able to compose songs, and they give you many options. For example, you can ② <u>choose</u> the style and key, such as C major or A minor. You can also set ③ <u>how long</u> the song will be. Once you've entered the information, the program will produce a song that you can ④ <u>edit</u> or use as it is. Furthermore, computer-generated imagery (commonly known as CGI) has opened up new possibilities in the music industry. Virtual influencers with extremely ⑤ <u>artificial</u> faces, bodies, and voices have already released several songs.

①   ②   ③   ④   ⑤

06 밑줄 친 부분 중, 문맥상 낱말의 쓰임이 적절하지 <u>않은</u> 것은?

Many AI programs are open to the public, which means they can be used ① <u>freely</u> and conveniently. However, these programs have sparked a debate over their ② <u>impact</u> on humans. Since AI has the potential to learn skills and perform them better than humans, some people view it as a threat. They worry that AI will replace humans in more and more areas. There are also ③ <u>concerns</u> that AI may imitate the styles of human artists without their ④ <u>content</u>. On the other hand, others think that AI cannot exceed human imagination and that it is still dependent on human assistance. This is because the data that AI uses can have ⑤ <u>flaws</u> or limitations. A dependence on imperfect data with little diversity eventually limits the output of AI programs. Human imagination, on the other hand, has no limits or boundaries.

①   ②   ③   ④   ⑤

07 (A), (B), (C)의 각 네모 안에서 문맥에 맞는 낱말로 가장 적절한 것은?

What kind of future do you think (A) [lays / lies] ahead of us? Will more people use AI programs to boost their creativity and (B) [production / productivity]? Or will people grow tired of the limitations of AI tools? AI provides many benefits and new opportunities. What we need to do is (C) [consider / figure] out how to use AI tools ethically and think about how humans and AI can collaborate.

	(A)	(B)	(C)
①	lays	⋯ production	⋯ consider
②	lays	⋯ productivity	⋯ consider
③	lays	⋯ production	⋯ figure
④	lies	⋯ productivity	⋯ figure
⑤	lies	⋯ production	⋯ figure

08 (A), (B), (C)의 각 네모 안에서 문맥에 맞는 낱말로 가장 적절한 것은?

As AI technology advances, will robots take (A) [over / up] human work? I think robots can replace humans in many roles. There are two reasons for my opinion. First, robots can work more productively than humans. This means that they can produce more in a (B) [fewer / shorter] amount of time. Second, robots can work in dangerous places that humans cannot reach. Therefore, they can reduce the (C) [chance / risk] of accidents. For these reasons, I think that robots will replace human workers in the future.

	(A)	(B)	(C)
①	over	⋯ fewer	⋯ chance
②	up	⋯ fewer	⋯ chance
③	up	⋯ shorter	⋯ chance
④	up	⋯ shorter	⋯ risk
⑤	over	⋯ shorter	⋯ risk

01 다음 글의 밑줄 친 부분 중, 어법상 틀린 것은?

Recently, an artist used an artificial intelligence (AI) system ① to create the image above for an art contest. The image won first place in the digital arts category. This led to a controversy in the art community. Some people complained ② that the artist simply provided the system with basic instructions and let it ③ to do all the work. They felt this wasn't fair to the rest of the artists in the contest. However, there were also people who ④ were excited by the potential of AI. Today, there are numerous AI programs ⑤ that can create various forms of art including images, songs, and novels.

①   ②   ③   ④   ⑤

02 (A), (B), (C)의 각 네모 안에서 어법에 맞는 표현으로 가장 적절한 것은?

AI image generators create images based on our text requests. They do this by (A) copy / copying other images that (B) created / were created by humans. The generators have the ability to analyze millions of images and their corresponding descriptions. This allows them (C) create / to create works of art in a short time based on the provided instructions.

	(A)		(B)		(C)
①	copy	…	created	…	create
②	copy	…	were created	…	create
③	copying	…	created	…	create
④	copying	…	were created	…	to create
⑤	copying	…	created	…	to create

03 (A), (B), (C)의 각 네모 안에서 어법에 맞는 표현으로 가장 적절한 것은?

Moreover, AI programs can mix the styles of (A) existed / existing images upon request. For example, you can blend a photograph of a cat with Johannes Vermeer's *Girl with a Pearl Earring*. These two images have (B) few / a few differences. However, the overall design, the eyes, and the scarf around the head are clearly based on Vermeer's painting. A simple request was enough (C) creating / to create this complex and detailed image.

	(A)		(B)		(C)
①	existed	…	few	…	creating
②	existed	…	a few	…	creating
③	existing	…	few	…	creating
④	existing	…	a few	…	to create
⑤	existing	…	few	…	to create

04 다음 글의 밑줄 친 부분 중, 어법상 틀린 것은?

AI programs may lead to changes not only in the art world but also ① the music industry. These programs are already able to compose songs, and they give ② you many options. For example, you can choose the style and key, such as C major or A minor. You can also set how long ③ the song will be. Once you've entered the information, the program will produce a song that you can edit or use ④ as it is. Furthermore, computer-generated imagery (commonly known as CGI) has opened up new possibilities in the music industry. Virtual influencers with extremely realistic faces, bodies, and voices ⑤ have already released several songs. Some of them have many followers on social media, just like human singers.

①   ②   ③   ④   ⑤

05 다음 글의 밑줄 친 부분 중, 어법상 **틀린** 것은?

Many AI programs are open to the public, ① which means they can be used freely and conveniently. However, these programs have sparked a debate over their impact on humans. Since AI has the potential ② to learn skills and perform them better than humans, some people view it ③ as a threat. They worry that AI will replace humans in more and more areas. There are also ④ concerns which AI may imitate the styles of human artists without their consent. On the other hand, others think that AI cannot exceed human imagination ⑤ and that it is still dependent on human assistance. This is because the data that AI uses can have flaws or limitations. A dependence on imperfect data with little diversity eventually limits the output of AI programs. Human imagination, on the other hand, has no limits or boundaries.

①   ②   ③   ④   ⑤

06 (A), (B), (C)의 각 네모 안에서 어법에 맞는 표현으로 가장 적절한 것은?

What kind of future do you think lies ahead of us? Will more people use AI programs to boost (A) its / their creativity and productivity? Or will people grow tired of the limitations of AI tools? AI provides many benefits and new opportunities. (B) That / What we need to do is figure out how to use AI tools ethically and (C) think / thinking about how humans and AI can collaborate.

	(A)		(B)		(C)
①	its	⋯	That	⋯	think
②	their	⋯	That	⋯	thinking
③	their	⋯	What	⋯	think
④	their	⋯	What	⋯	thinking
⑤	its	⋯	What	⋯	think

07 (A), (B), (C)의 각 네모 안에서 어법에 맞는 표현으로 가장 적절한 것은?

As AI technology advances, will robots take over human work? I think robots can replace humans in many roles. There (A) is / are two reasons for my opinion. First, robots can work more productively than humans. This means that they can produce more in a shorter amount of time. Second, robots can work in dangerous places (B) that / where humans cannot reach. Therefore, they can reduce the risk of accidents. For these reasons, I think that robots (C) replace / will replace human workers in the future.

	(A)		(B)		(C)
①	is	⋯	that	⋯	replace
②	is	⋯	where	⋯	replace
③	are	⋯	that	⋯	replace
④	are	⋯	where	⋯	will replace
⑤	are	⋯	that	⋯	will replace

08 다음 글의 밑줄 친 부분 중, 어법상 **틀린** 것은?

Space technology may not ① seem useful to the average person. But did you know that many of the items we use every day come from space technology? For example, the image sensors in modern cameras were originally developed ② to use in space. However, they were easy to produce and didn't require much power, so companies started ③ using them in commercial products. These days, an updated version of this technology can be found in many devices, including smartphones and video cameras. ④ Freeze drying is another technology that was originally developed for use in space. These are just two examples of how space technology has benefited everyone. Look around you. What other common items do you think ⑤ come from space technology?

①   ②   ③   ④   ⑤

[01~02] 다음 대화를 읽고, 물음에 답하시오.

> B Hi, Emma. What are you doing on your phone?
> G Oh hi, Mark. I'm chatting with General Yi Sunsin.
> B General Yi Sunsin? How is that possible?
> G I installed a chatbot application. I can talk to any historical figure with it.
> B That sounds amazing!
> G Yes, it is amazing! _____ the general about the Battle of Noryang.
> B What are you going to ask?
> G I want to know how he felt during the battle.
> B I want to try that, too. I would love to talk to Marie Curie about her work.

01 위 대화의 내용과 일치하지 <u>않는</u> 것은?

① The girl is chatting with a historical figure.
② The girl wants to know about World War Ⅱ.
③ The girl is going to ask the figure about his feelings during the battle.
④ The boy is going to install the app the girl is using.
⑤ The boy wants to talk to Marie Curie.

02 위 대화의 빈칸에 들어갈 말로 가장 적절한 것은?

① I look forward asking
② I look forward to ask
③ I'll look forward to ask
④ I'm looking forward to ask
⑤ I'm looking forward to asking

[03~04] 다음 글을 읽고, 물음에 답하시오.

> Space technology may not seem useful to the average person. (A) But did you know that many of the items we use every day come from space technology? (B) For example, the image sensors in modern cameras were originally developed to be used in space. (C) These days, an updated version of this technology can be found in many devices, including smartphones and video cameras. (D) Freeze drying is another technology that was originally developed for use in space. (E) Freeze-dried foods are long-lasting and easy to prepare. Now, however, freeze-dried foods such as soups and fruit can be found in your local market! These are just two examples of how space technology has benefited everyone. Look around you. What other common items do you think come from space technology?

03 윗글의 주제로 가장 적절한 것은?

① kinds of freeze-dried food
② the most current space technologies
③ space technology used in everyday life
④ an international competition in space technology
⑤ commercial products with built-in image sensors

04 글의 흐름으로 보아, 주어진 문장이 들어가기에 가장 적절한 곳은?

> However, they were easy to produce and didn't require much power, so companies started using them in commercial products.

① (A) ② (B) ③ (C) ④ (D) ⑤ (E)

[05~06] 다음 글을 읽고, 물음에 답하시오.

Recently, an artist used an artificial intelligence (AI) system to create the image above for an art contest. The image won first place in the digital arts category. This led to a controversy in the art community. Some people complained that the artist simply provided the system with basic instructions and (A) allowed / let it do all the work. They felt this wasn't fair to the rest of the artists in the contest. However, there (B) was / were also people who were excited by the potential of AI. Today, there are numerous AI programs that can create various forms of art (C) included / including images, songs, and novels.

05 윗글의 밑줄 친 this의 내용으로 가장 적절한 것은?

① A lot of AI programs are creating songs and novels.
② Most of the artists create their work using AI.
③ The image created by an AI won an art contest.
④ Some people welcomed the use of AI.
⑤ The artist gave an instruction to an AI.

06 (A), (B), (C)의 각 네모 안에서 어법에 맞는 표현으로 가장 적절한 것은?

	(A)	(B)	(C)
①	allowed	was	included
②	allowed	were	included
③	allowed	was	including
④	let	were	including
⑤	let	was	including

[07~08] 다음 글을 읽고, 물음에 답하시오.

AI image generators create images based on our text requests. They do this by copying other images that were created by humans. The generators have the ability to analyze millions of images and their corresponding descriptions. This allows them to create works of art in a short time based on the provided instructions.

_____(A)_____, AI programs can mix the styles of existing images upon request. For example, you can blend a photograph of a cat with Johannes Vermeer's *Girl with a Pearl Earring*. These two images have a few differences. _____(B)_____, the overall design, the eyes, and the scarf around the head are clearly based on Vermeer's painting. A simple request was enough to create this complex and detailed image.

07 윗글의 제목으로 가장 적절한 것은?

① A Collaboration of AI and Human Artists
② The Future of Art: AI's Creative Genius
③ The Limitations of AI in the Digital Era
④ The Ethical Implications of AI Art
⑤ Making Digital Images with the Help of AI

08 윗글의 빈칸 (A)와 (B)에 들어갈 말이 바르게 짝지어진 것은?

	(A)	(B)
①	Therefore	In short
②	However	Accordingly
③	Consequently	On the other hand
④	Moreover	However
⑤	In fact	Consequently

[09~10] 다음 글을 읽고, 물음에 답하시오.

AI programs may lead to <u>changes</u> not only in the art world but also in the music industry. These programs are already able to compose songs, and they give ① <u>you many options</u>. For example, you can choose the style and key, such as C major or A minor. You can also set how long ② <u>will be the song</u>. Once you've entered the information, the program will produce a song that you can edit or use as it is. Furthermore, computer-generated imagery (commonly ③ <u>known as</u> CGI) has opened up new possibilities in the music industry. Virtual influencers with ④ <u>extremely realistic</u> faces, bodies, and voices have already released several songs. Some of them have many followers on social media, just like human singers. These types of virtual musicians are ⑤ <u>able to speak</u> and move realistically with the help of their human creators.

09 윗글의 밑줄 친 changes에 해당하지 <u>않는</u> 것은?

① 음악의 조성을 다양하게 선택할 수 있다.
② 노래 길이를 쉽게 설정할 수 있다.
③ 가상 음악가가 등장하고 있다.
④ 인간 가수의 팔로워가 점점 많아진다.
⑤ 가상 음악가의 소셜 미디어에서 팬덤이 형성된다.

10 윗글의 밑줄 친 부분 중, 어법상 틀린 것은?

①   ②   ③   ④   ⑤

[11~13] 다음 글을 읽고, 물음에 답하시오.

Many AI programs are open to the public, which means they can be used freely and conveniently. However, these programs have sparked a debate over their ⓐ <u>impact</u> on humans. Since AI has the potential to learn skills and perform them better than humans, some people ⓑ <u>view</u> it as a threat. They worry that AI will replace humans in more and more areas. There are also ⓒ <u>concerns</u> that AI may imitate the styles of human artists without their ⓓ <u>consent</u>. On the other hand, others think that AI cannot exceed human imagination and that it is still dependent on human ⓔ <u>assistance</u>. This is because the data that AI uses can have flaws or limitations. A dependence on imperfect data with little diversity eventually limits the output of AI programs. Human imagination, on the other hand, _____.

11 윗글의 밑줄 친 부분과 바꿔 쓸 수 있는 말이 <u>아닌</u> 것은?

① ⓐ influence   ② ⓑ consider
③ ⓒ worries   ④ ⓓ agreement
⑤ ⓔ direction

12 윗글의 빈칸에 들어갈 말로 가장 적절한 것은?

① has no limits or boundaries
② needs instruction and correction
③ is imperfect and risky to depend on
④ will finally imitate the output of AI
⑤ requires cooperation with AI

13 윗글의 내용을 요약할 때, 빈칸 (A), (B)에 들어갈 말로 가장 적절한 것은?

> AI programs are accessible to the public but raise concerns about their impact on humans. Some worry that AI will _____(A)_____ humans in various fields, while others believe AI is limited by its dependence on _____(B)_____ data.

	(A)		(B)
①	assist	⋯	false
②	assist	⋯	imperfect
③	threaten	⋯	perfect
④	replace	⋯	imperfect
⑤	replace	⋯	perfect

14 다음 글의 어조로 가장 적절한 것은?

> What kind of future do you think lies ahead of us? Will more people use AI programs to boost their creativity and productivity? Or will people grow tired of the limitations of AI tools? AI provides many benefits and new opportunities. What we need to do is figure out how to use AI tools ethically and think about how humans and AI can collaborate.

① persuasive ② pessimistic
③ humorous ④ affirmative
⑤ skeptical

15 다음 글의 밑줄 친 these reasons에 해당하는 이유로 적절한 것은?

> As AI technology advances, will robots take over human work? I think robots can replace humans in many roles. There are two reasons for my opinion. First, robots can work more productively than humans. This means that they can produce more in a shorter amount of time. Second, robots can work in dangerous places that humans cannot reach. Therefore, they can reduce the risk of accidents. For these reasons, I think that robots will replace human workers in the future.

① Robots can work in risky conditions.
② Robots have flaws and limited imagination.
③ Robots can cooperate with human workers.
④ Robots are more intelligent than humans.
⑤ Robots work under human instruction.

[01~02] 다음 대화를 읽고, 물음에 답하시오.

> B Hey, Grace, I heard there is going to be a fire drill today.
> G That's right. But I'm a bit worried. I (A) | hurt / hurted | my leg during our last fire drill.
> B Oh, don't worry! This time, we are going to have a VR fire drill.
> G A VR fire drill? What's that?
> B We will be trained using virtual reality technology.
> G Oh! Could you explain (B) | how/ what | it works?
> B Sure. Everyone will use VR equipment and experience what (C) | a fire is / is a fire | really like.
> G That sounds interesting.
> B It will be. We will also learn how to use a fire extinguisher without real danger.
> G I'm glad we can safely practice what to do.

01 위 대화의 내용을 요약할 때 빈칸에 알맞은 말을 대화에서 찾아 쓰시오.

> There is a fire drill at school today. Using (1) _____ equipment, the students will experience a real fire situation and learn how to use a fire (2) _____.

02 (A), (B), (C)의 각 네모 안에서 어법에 맞는 표현으로 가장 적절한 것은?

	(A)		(B)		(C)
①	hurt	⋯	how	⋯	a fire is
②	hurt	⋯	what	⋯	a fire is
③	hurt	⋯	how	⋯	is a fire
④	hurted	⋯	what	⋯	is a fire
⑤	hurted	⋯	how	⋯	is a fire

03 다음 글 앞에 언급되었을 내용으로 가장 적절한 것은?

> Freeze drying is another technology that was originally developed for use in space. Freeze-dried foods are long-lasting and easy to prepare. Now, however, freeze-dried foods such as soups and fruit can be found in your local market! These are just two examples of how space technology has benefited everyone. Look around you. What other common items do you think come from space technology?

① the impact of freeze-dried products on food industry
② an everyday item that came from space technology
③ the reason for developing space technology
④ the advancement in space technology
⑤ freeze drying and living in space

04 다음 글의 빈칸에 들어갈 말로 가장 적절한 것은?

> Space technology may not seem useful to the average person. But did you know that many of the items we use every day come from space technology? _____, the image sensors in modern cameras were originally developed to be used in space. However, they were easy to produce and didn't require much power, so companies started using them in commercial products. These days, an updated version of this technology can be found in many devices, including smartphones and video cameras.

① Similarly ② In short
③ In addition ④ For example
⑤ That is to say

[05~06] 다음 글을 읽고, 물음에 답하시오.

Recently, an artist used an artificial intelligence (AI) system to create the image above for an art contest. The image won first place in the digital arts category. (A) This led to a controversy in the art community. (B) Some people complained that the artist simply provided the system with basic instructions and let it do all the work. (C) They felt this wasn't fair to the rest of the artists in the contest. (D) Today, there are numerous AI programs that can create various forms of art including images, songs, and novels. (E)

05 글의 흐름으로 보아, 주어진 문장이 들어가기에 가장 적절한 곳은?

However, there were also people who were excited by the potential of AI.

① (A)　　② (B)　　③ (C)　　④ (D)　　⑤ (E)

06 다음 영어 뜻풀이에 해당하는 단어를 윗글에서 찾아 쓰시오.

public disagreement about something

→ _____

[07~08] 다음 글을 읽고, 물음에 답하시오.

AI image generators create images based ① on our text requests. They do this ② by copying other images that were created by humans. The generators have the ability to analyze millions of images and their corresponding descriptions. This allows them to create works of art ③ in a short time based on the provided instructions.

Moreover, AI programs can mix the styles of existing images ④ at request. For example, you can blend a photograph of a cat ⑤ with Johannes Vermeer's *Girl with a Pearl Earring*. These two images have a few differences. However, the overall design, the eyes, and the scarf around the head are clearly based on Vermeer's painting. A simple request was enough to create this complex and detailed image.

07 밑줄 친 AI image generators에 관한 설명으로 윗글의 내용과 일치하지 <u>않는</u> 것은?

① 텍스트로 된 요청에 따라 이미지를 생성한다.
② 사람이 그린 이미지를 모방한다.
③ 이미지와 이미지에 관한 설명을 분석한다.
④ 기존의 이미지를 요청에 맞게 혼합하기도 한다.
⑤ 특정 이미지를 명작과 혼합하는 데에는 정교한 요청이 필요하다.

08 윗글의 밑줄 친 부분 중 문맥상 낱말의 쓰임이 적절하지 <u>않은</u> 것은?

①　　　②　　　③　　　④　　　⑤

[09~10] 다음 글을 읽고, 물음에 답하시오.

AI programs may lead to changes ⓐ not only in the art world but also in the music industry. These programs are already able to compose songs, and they give you many options. For example, you can choose the style and key, such as C major or A minor. You can also set how long the song will be. Once you've entered the information, the program will produce a song that you can edit or use as it is. Furthermore, computer-generated imagery (commonly known as CGI) has opened up new possibilities in the music industry. Virtual influencers with extremely realistic faces, bodies, and voices have already released several songs. Some of ⓑ them have many followers on social media, just like human singers. These types of virtual musicians are able to speak and move realistically with the help of their human creators.

09 윗글의 밑줄 친 ⓐ를 주어진 조건에 맞게 바꿔 쓰시오.

조건
1. as well as를 사용할 것
2. 문장의 의미가 변하지 않도록 바꿀 것

not only in the art world but also in the music industry

→ AI programs may lead to changes _____ _____ .

10 윗글의 밑줄 친 ⓑ them이 가리키는 내용으로 적절한 것은?

① human singers
② virtual influencers
③ followers on social media
④ AI image-making programs
⑤ new possibilites in the music industry

[11~12] 다음 글을 읽고, 물음에 답하시오.

Many AI programs are open to the public, which means they can be used freely and conveniently. However, these programs have sparked a debate over their impact on humans. Since AI has the potential to learn skills and perform them better than humans, some people view it as a threat. They worry ① that AI will replace humans in more and more areas. There are also concerns ② that AI may imitate the styles of human artists without their consent. On the other hand, others think ③ that AI cannot exceed human imagination and ④ that it is still dependent on human assistance. This is because the data ⑤ that AI uses can have flaws or limitations. A dependence on imperfect data with little diversity eventually limits the output of AI programs. Human imagination, on the other hand, has no limits or boundaries.

11 윗글의 내용과 일치하지 <u>않는</u> 것은?

① 자유롭고 편리하게 쓸 수 있는 다양한 AI 프로그램이 등장하고 있다.
② AI가 인간에게 미치는 영향에 관한 논쟁이 있다.
③ 일부 사람들은 AI가 많은 영역에서 인간을 대체할 거라고 생각한다.
④ 예술가의 동의 없이 AI가 창조적 작품을 모방할지도 모른다는 우려가 있다.
⑤ AI를 환영하는 사람들은 결국 AI가 인간의 상상력을 넘어설 거라고 믿는다.

12 윗글의 밑줄 친 부분 중 주어진 문장의 밑줄 친 that과 쓰임이 같은 것은?

We all had a strong belief <u>that</u> the lost child would return safely.

① ② ③ ④ ⑤

13 다음 글의 빈칸에 들어갈 말로 <u>어색한</u> 것은?

What kind of future do you think lies ahead of us? Will more people use AI programs to boost their creativity and productivity? Or will people grow tired of the limitations of AI tools? AI provides many benefits and new opportunities. What we need to do is figure out how to use AI tools ethically and think about _____ _____.

① the social impact of AI
② the role of humans in the era of AI
③ how humans and AI can collaborate
④ the future of work in an AI-driven world
⑤ ways to protect the world from the threat of AI

[14~15] 다음 글을 읽고, 물음에 답하시오.

Will Robots Replace Humans?

As AI technology ① advances, will robots take over human work? I think robots can replace humans in many ② roles. There are two reasons for my opinion. First, robots can work more ③ creatively than humans. This means that they can produce more in a shorter amount of time. Second, robots can work in dangerous places that humans cannot ④ reach. Therefore, they can ⑤ reduce the risk of accidents. For these reasons, I think that robots will replace human workers in the future.

14 윗글의 필자가 가진 입장과 가장 가까운 주장을 가진 사람은?

① Molly: More and more people will lose their jobs because of robots.
② Jin: In the field of art and education, robots can't replace humans.
③ Ted: Robots work better in difficult and dangerous situations.
④ Cindy: It is more costly to use robots in the workplace.
⑤ Ken: Robots do a good job assisting humans in their work.

15 윗글의 밑줄 친 부분 중, 문맥상 낱말의 쓰임이 적절하지 <u>않은</u> 것은?

①   ②   ③   ④   ⑤

[01~02] 다음 대화를 읽고, 물음에 답하시오.

> B Miju, is ⓐ this a portrait of you?
> G Yes, ⓑ it is!
> B I didn't know you were good at painting.
> G Well, actually, an AI program painted ⓒ this.
> B AI did ⓓ this? How is that possible?
> G I just shared my picture with this website.
> B And then the AI program changed ⓔ it into a painting?
> G That's right. I'm looking forward to trying other photos tonight.
> B Sounds fun. I want to try that website too.

01 위 대화의 주제로 가장 적절한 것은?

① a popular website about artists and their art
② an AI program that creates images
③ skills needed to paint portraits
④ taking pictures with friends
⑤ paining portraits of friends

02 위 대화의 밑줄 친 부분 중 가리키는 대상이 나머지 넷과 다른 것은?

① ⓐ   ② ⓑ   ③ ⓒ   ④ ⓓ   ⑤ ⓔ

[03~04] 다음 글을 읽고, 물음에 답하시오.

> Space technology may not seem useful to the average person. But did you know that many of the items we use every day ① comes from space technology? For example, the image sensors in modern cameras were originally developed ② to be used in space. However, they were easy to produce and didn't require much power, so companies ③ started using them in commercial products. These days, an updated version of this technology can be found in many devices, including smartphones and video cameras.
>
> Freeze drying is another technology that was _____. Freeze-dried foods are long-lasting and ④ easy to prepare. Now, however, freeze-dried foods such as soups and fruit can be found in your local market! These are just two examples of how space technology ⑤ has benefited everyone. Look around you. What other common items do you think come from space technology?

03 윗글의 빈칸에 들어갈 말로 가장 적절한 것은?

① originally developed for use in space
② easy to produce within a short time
③ revolutionary in the food industry
④ easily cooked and prepared
⑤ useful in our everyday lives

04 윗글의 밑줄 친 부분 중, 어법상 틀린 것은?

①   ②   ③   ④   ⑤

[05~06] 다음 글을 읽고, 물음에 답하시오.

Recently, an artist used an artificial intelligence (AI) system to create the image above for an art contest. The image won first place in the digital arts category.

(A) However, there ⓐ be also people who were excited by the potential of AI.

(B) Some people complained that the artist simply provided the system with basic instructions and let it ⓑ do all the work.

(C) They felt this wasn't fair to the rest of the artists in the contest.

(D) This led to a controversy in the art community.

05 주어진 문장 뒤에 이어질 글의 순서로 가장 적절한 것은?

① (A) – (B) – (D) – (C)
② (B) – (C) – (D) – (A)
③ (B) – (A) – (C) – (D)
④ (C) – (A) – (B) – (D)
⑤ (D) – (B) – (C) – (A)

06 윗글의 밑줄 친 동사 ⓐ와 ⓑ를 알맞은 형태로 쓰시오.

ⓐ be → _____

ⓑ do → _____

[07~08] 다음 글을 읽고, 물음에 답하시오.

AI image generators create images based on our text requests. They do this by copying other images that were created by humans. The generators have the ability to analyze millions of images and their (A) corresponding / responding descriptions. This allows them to create works of art in a short time based on the provided instructions.

Moreover, AI programs can (B) fix / mix the styles of existing images upon request. For example, you can blend a photograph of a cat with Johannes Vermeer's *Girl with a Pearl Earring*. These two images have a few differences. However, the (C) overall / partial design, the eyes, and the scarf around the head are clearly based on Vermeer's painting. A simple request was enough to create this complex and detailed image.

07 윗글의 밑줄 친 These two images에 관해 유추할 수 있는 내용이 아닌 것은?

① They are a painting by Johannes Vermeer and an image by an AI program.
② Photograghs of a cat are used to make one of them.
③ The two images have a lot of similarities.
④ The girl in the painting is wearing a scarf.
⑤ Johannes Vermeer used the AI program to generate the image.

08 (A), (B), (C)의 각 네모 안에서 문맥에 맞는 낱말로 가장 적절한 것은?

	(A)		(B)		(C)
①	corresponding	…	fix	…	overall
②	corresponding	…	mix	…	overall
③	corresponding	…	fix	…	partial
④	responding	…	mix	…	partial
⑤	responding	…	fix	…	partial

[09~10] 다음 글을 읽고, 물음에 답하시오.

AI programs may lead to changes not only in the art world but also in the music industry. These programs are already able to compose songs, and they give you many options. For example, you can choose the style and key, such as C major or A minor. You can also set how long the song will be. _____(A)_____ you've entered the information, the program will produce a song that you can edit or use as it is. _____(B)_____, computer-generated imagery (commonly known as CGI) has opened up new possibilities in the music industry. Virtual influencers with extremely realistic faces, bodies, and voices have already released several songs. Some of them have many followers on social media, just like human singers. These types of virtual musicians are able to speak and move realistically with the help of their human creators.

09 윗글을 읽고 알 수 있는 내용이 **아닌** 것은?

① AI 프로그램이 곡을 만들 때 제공하는 옵션
② AI 프로그램으로 작곡을 하는 방법
③ CGI가 음악 산업에 미친 영향
④ 음악 산업에서 가상 인플루언서의 활동
⑤ 인간 음악가와 가상 음악가의 차이

10 윗글의 빈칸 (A)와 (B)에 들어갈 말이 바르게 짝지어진 것은?

	(A)		(B)
①	As	⋯	However
②	While	⋯	Moreover
③	Once	⋯	Furthermore
④	Since	⋯	Whereas
⑤	For	⋯	In short

[11~12] 다음 글을 읽고, 물음에 답하시오.

Many AI programs are open to the public, (A) that / which means they can be used freely and conveniently. However, these programs have sparked a debate over their impact on humans. Since AI has the potential to learn skills and (B) perform / performing them better than humans, some people view it as a threat. They worry that AI will replace humans in more and more areas. There are also concerns (C) that / what AI may imitate the styles of human artists without their consent. On the other hand, others think that AI cannot exceed human imagination and that it is still dependent on human assistance. This is because the data that AI uses can have flaws or limitations. A dependence on imperfect data with little diversity eventually limits the output of AI programs. Human imagination, on the other hand, has no limits or boundaries.

11 윗글의 주제로 가장 적절한 것은?

① the future of AI in the art and music industry
② the debate over the impact of AI on humans
③ the ethical problems in the era of AI
④ AI and the future of jobs
⑤ AI and human creativity

12 (A), (B), (C)의 네모 안에서 어법에 맞는 표현으로 가장 적절한 것은?

	(A)		(B)		(C)
①	that	⋯	perform	⋯	that
②	that	⋯	performing	⋯	that
③	which	⋯	perform	⋯	that
④	which	⋯	performing	⋯	what
⑤	which	⋯	perform	⋯	what

[13~14] 다음 글을 읽고, 물음에 답하시오.

What kind of future do you think lies ahead of us? ① Will more people use AI programs to boost their creativity and productivity? ② Or will people grow tired of the limitations of AI tools? ③ AI programs can mix the styles of existing images upon request. ④ AI provides many benefits and new opportunities. ⑤ What we need to do is figure out how to use AI tools ethically and think about how humans and AI can collaborate.

13 윗글의 ①~⑤ 중 전체 흐름과 관계 <u>없는</u> 문장은?

①   ②   ③   ④   ⑤

14 윗글의 낱말 중 다음 영어 뜻풀이에 해당하는 것은?

to work together in order to achieve something

① lie   ② boost
③ request   ④ provide
⑤ collaborate

15 다음 글의 내용을 요약할 때 빈칸에 알맞은 말을 글에서 찾아 쓰시오.

As AI technology advances, will robots take over human work? I think robots can replace humans in many roles. There are two reasons for my opinion. First, robots can work more productively than humans. This means that they can produce more in a shorter amount of time. Second, robots can work in dangerous places that humans cannot reach. Therefore, they can reduce the risk of accidents. For these reasons, I think that robots will replace human workers in the future.

Robots will likely (1) _____ human workers in the future due to their superior productivity and ability to work in (2) _____ conditions.

[01~02] 다음 글을 읽고, 물음에 답하시오.

The image above was recently created by an artist for an art contest using artificial intelligence (AI) technology. In the digital arts category, the picture took first place. The art community became divided about the result. Some people expressed dissatisfaction, claiming that the artist only (A) gave / provided the system basic instructions and let it handle everything. They believed (B) that / what this was unfair to the other contestants. Some, on the other hand, were thrilled about AI's promise. Many AI programs available today (C) is / are capable of producing novels, songs, and photographs, among other types of art.

01 윗글의 주제로 가장 적절한 것은?

① the appearance of AI in the field of art
② the threat we face in the digital era
③ the judging process of an art contest
④ pros and cons on digital privacy
⑤ issues concerning AI programs

02 (A), (B), (C)의 각 네모 안에서 어법에 맞는 표현으로 가장 적절한 것은?

	(A)		(B)		(C)
①	gave	…	that	…	is
②	gave	…	what	…	is
③	gave	…	that	…	are
④	provided	…	what	…	are
⑤	provided	…	that	…	are

[03~04] 다음 글을 읽고, 물음에 답하시오.

AI image generators use our text commands to produce images. They accomplish this by copying other human-made images. The generators can examine millions of photos and the captions that go with ⓐ them. This enables ⓑ them to quickly produce artwork in accordance with the given guidelines.

Additionally, AI systems can blend the styles of existing photos upon request. For instance, you can combine Johannes Vermeer's *Girl with a Pearl Earring* with a picture of a cat. There are some differences between these two pictures. Nevertheless, it is evident that Vermeer's painting served as the inspiration for the overall pattern, the eyes, and the scarf around the head. All that it took to produce this detailed and beautiful artwork was a straightforward request.

03 윗글의 내용과 일치하지 않는 것은?

① AI 이미지 생성기는 텍스트 명령으로 작동한다.
② 수많은 사진과 사진 설명을 분석하기 위해 AI 이미지 생성에는 오랜 시간이 소요된다.
③ AI는 현존하는 예술 작품을 활용하여 그림을 만들기도 한다.
④ '진주 귀걸이를 한 소녀'와 AI가 고양이를 합성한 그림은 유사점이 많다.
⑤ AI로 정교한 예술 작품을 만드는 데에는 간단한 명령만으로 충분하다.

04 윗글의 밑줄 친 ⓐ와 ⓑ가 가리키는 내용이 바르게 짝지어진 것은?

① the photos … the photos
② the photos … the generators
③ the generators … the photos
④ the captions … the generators
⑤ the captions … the photos

[05~06] 다음 글을 읽고, 물음에 답하시오.

AI programs have the potential to transform the music industry ① as well as the art world. There are a lot of options that can already compose tunes. _____(A)_____, you can select the key and style of the song you want to create. You can also specify the song's duration. ② After you input the data, the application will create a song that you can ③ either edit nor just use as is. _____(B)_____, computer-generated imagery (CGI) has also created new opportunities in the music industry. There are already ④ a number of songs made by virtual influencers with incredibly realistic voices. Some of them, like human singers, ⑤ have a large social media following. These virtual musicians, with the assistance of their human designers, can move and speak in a realistic manner.

05 윗글의 빈칸 (A)와 (B)에 들어갈 말이 바르게 연결된 것은?

	(A)		(B)
①	In addition	…	Nevertheless
②	In short	…	Furthermore
③	For example	…	Therefore
④	For instance	…	Moreover
⑤	On the other hand	…	However

06 윗글의 밑줄 친 부분 중 어법상 틀린 것은?

①   ②   ③   ④   ⑤

[07~08] 다음 글을 읽고, 물음에 답하시오.

Many ⓐ AI tools are publicly available, making ⓑ them easily accessible. (A) However, ⓒ their growing capabilities have raised concerns about ⓓ their impact on humans. (B) Some worry that AI could surpass human abilities in various tasks, leading to job displacement. (C) Others argue that AI is limited by its reliance on human-generated data, which can be flawed or biased. (D) ⓔ They believe that human imagination is superior and unrestricted. (E)

07 윗글의 흐름으로 보아, 주어진 문장이 들어가기에 가장 적절한 곳은?

There are also concerns about AI copying the styles of human artists without permission.

① (A)   ② (B)   ③ (C)   ④ (D)   ⑤ (E)

08 윗글의 밑줄 친 부분 중 가리키는 대상이 나머지 넷과 다른 것은?

① ⓐ   ② ⓑ   ③ ⓒ   ④ ⓓ   ⑤ ⓔ

[09~10] 다음 글을 읽고, 물음에 답하시오.

> What kind of future do you think (A) lie / lies ahead of us? ① Will AI become a common tool for enhancing creativity and efficiency? ② AI-generated art is becoming increasingly popular. ③ Or will people grow (B) tired / tiring of the shortcomings of AI tools? ④ AI offers numerous advantages. ⑤ However, it's crucial to consider its ethical implications and explore ways (C) for / of humans and AI to work together effectively.

09 윗글의 ①~⑤ 중 전체 흐름과 관계 없는 문장은?

①   ②   ③   ④   ⑤

10 (A), (B), (C)의 각 네모 안에서 어법에 맞는 표현으로 가장 적절한 것은?

	(A)		(B)		(C)
①	lie	…	tired	…	for
②	lies	…	tired	…	for
③	lie	…	tired	…	of
④	lies	…	tiring	…	of
⑤	lie	…	tiring	…	of

[11~12] 다음 글을 읽고, 물음에 답하시오.

> As AI technology ① improves, will robots replace human workers?

> (A) They can ② handle hazardous tasks that humans cannot.
> (B) For these reasons, I think robots will become ③ increasingly prevalent in the workforce.
> (C) Robots can also work more ④ safely than humans.
> (D) I believe so because of two reasons. First, robots can work more efficiently producing ⑤ less in less time.

11 주어진 글 다음에 이어질 글의 순서로 가장 적절한 것은?

① (A) – (C) – (B) – (D)
② (B) – (C) – (D) – (A)
③ (C) – (A) – (D) – (B)
④ (C) – (B) – (D) – (A)
⑤ (D) – (C) – (A) – (B)

12 윗글의 밑줄 친 부분 중 문맥상 낱말의 쓰임이 적절하지 않은 것은?

①   ②   ③   ④   ⑤

For the typical person, space technology might not appear practical. However, did you know that a large number of the things we use on a daily basis were _____ ? Image sensors in modern cameras, for instance, were first created with space travel in (A) action / mind . However, businesses began utilizing them in commercial products because they were simple to make and required (B) few / little power. These days, many gadgets, such as cell phones and video cameras, use an upgraded version of this technology. Another technology that was (C) consequently / initially created for use in space is freeze-drying. This technology helped astronauts have food that is easy to prepare and long-lasting. However, your local shop now sells freeze-dried items like fruit and soups! Here are only two instances of how space technology has benefited everyone.

13 윗글의 요지로 가장 적절한 것은?

① More and more countries are joining in the space race.
② Products in grocery stores were originally developed for space travel.
③ Space technology has had a significant impact on everyday life.
④ Space technology should be used responsibly for the benefit of everyone.
⑤ Image sensors are widely used for modern cameras and cell phones.

14 윗글의 빈칸에 들어갈 말로 어색한 것은?

① products of space technology
② on the shelves of local grocery stores
③ initially intended to be used in space
④ created for the purpose of space travel
⑤ items originating from space technology

15 (A), (B), (C)의 각 네모 안에서 문맥에 맞는 낱말로 가장 적절한 것은?

	(A)	(B)	(C)
①	action	few	consequently
②	action	little	consequently
③	action	few	initially
④	mind	little	initially
⑤	mind	few	initially

내신 1 등급

서술형

[01~03] 다음 글을 읽고, 물음에 답하시오.

Space technology may not seem useful to the average person. But did you know that many of the items we use every day come from space technology? For example, the image sensors in modern cameras were originally developed ⓐ to use in space. However, they were easy to produce and didn't require much power, so companies started ⓑ use them in commercial products. These days, an updated version of this technology can be found in many devices, including smartphones and video cameras. Freeze drying is another technology that was originally developed for use in space. Freeze-dried foods are long-lasting and easy to prepare. Now, however, freeze-dried foods such as soups and fruit can be found in your local market! ⓒ These are just two examples of how space technology has benefited everyone. Look around you. What other common items do you think come from space technology?

01 윗글의 밑줄 친 ⓐ와 ⓑ를 어법에 맞게 고쳐 쓰시오.

ⓐ to use → _____

ⓑ use → _____

02 윗글의 밑줄 친 ⓒ These가 가리키는 것을 찾아 쓰시오.

ⓒ These → _____

03 주어진 질문에 대한 답을 윗글에서 찾아 쓰시오.

(1) What made the image sensors commercially available?

→ _____

_____

(2) What kind of freeze-dried food can be found at the local market?

→ _____

_____

04 다음 글의 빈칸 (A)와 (B)에 들어갈 말을 다음 영어 뜻풀이를 참고하여 주어진 철자로 시작하여 쓰시오.

Recently, an artist used an artificial intelligence (AI) system to create the image above for an art contest. The image won first place in the digital arts category. This led to a ____(A)____ in the art community. Some people complained that the artist simply provided the system with basic instructions and let it do all the work. They felt this wasn't fair to the rest of the artists in the contest. However, there were also people who were excited by the potential of AI. Today, there are ____(B)____ AI programs that can create various forms of art including images, songs, and novels.

(A) piblic disagreement about something
(B) many in number

(A) c_____
(B) n_____

[05~06] 다음 글을 읽고, 물음에 답하시오.

AI image generators create images based on our text requests. They do this by copying other images that were created by humans. The generators have the ability to analyze millions of images and their corresponding descriptions. This allows them create works of art in a short time based on the providing instructions.

Moreover, AI programs can mix the styles of existing images upon request. For example, you can blend a photograph of a cat ___(A)___ Johannes Vermeer's *Girl with a Pearl Earring*. These two images have a few differences. However, the overall design, the eyes, and the scarf around the head are clearly based ___(B)___ Vermeer's painting. A simple request was enough to create this complex and detailed image.

05 윗글의 밑줄 친 문장에서 어법상 틀린 부분을 찾아 바르게 고쳐 쓰시오. (두 군데)

This allows them create works of art in a short time based on the providing instructions.

→ _____

_____

06 윗글의 빈칸 (A)와 (B)에 알맞은 말을 쓰시오.

(A) _____

(B) _____

[07~08] 다음 글을 읽고, 물음에 답하시오.

ⓐ 인공 지능 프로그램은 미술 세계에서뿐만 아니라 음악 산업에서의 변화로도 이어질 수 있다. These programs are already able to compose songs, and they give you many options. For example, you can choose the style and key, such as C major or A minor. You can also set how long the song will be. Once you've entered the information, the program will produce a song that you can edit or use as it is. Furthermore, computer-generated imagery (commonly known as CGI) has opened up new possibilities in the music industry. ⓑ Virtual influencers with extremely artificial faces, bodies, and voices have already released several songs. Some of them have many followers on social media, just like human singers. These types of virtual musicians are able to speak and move realistically with the help of their human creators.

07 윗글의 밑줄 친 ⓐ의 우리말과 일치하도록 〈조건〉에 맞게 영작하시오.

〈조건〉
1. not only ~ but also를 사용할 것
2. 다음 표현을 활용할 것: change, art world, music industry

→ AI programs may lead to _____

_____ .

08 윗글의 밑줄 친 문장 ⓑ에서 문맥상 어색한 낱말을 찾아 바르게 고쳐 쓰시오.

_____ → _____

[09~10] 다음 글을 읽고, 물음에 답하시오.

Many AI programs are open to the public, which means they can be used freely and conveniently. However, these programs have sparked a debate over their impact on humans. Since AI has the potential to learn skills and perform them better than humans, some people view it as a threat. They worry that AI will replace humans in more and more areas. ⓐ There are also concerns which AI may imitate the styles of human artists without their consent. On the other hand, ⓑ others think that AI cannot exceed human imagination and that it is still dependent on human assistance. This is because the data that AI uses can have flaws or limitations. A dependence on imperfect data with little diversity eventually limits the output of AI programs. Human imagination, on the other hand, has no limits or boundaries.

09 윗글의 밑줄 친 문장 ⓐ에서 어법상 어색한 부분을 찾아 바르게 고쳐 쓰시오.

→ _____

_____

10 윗글의 밑줄 친 ⓑ others가 주장하는 내용을 요약할 때 빈칸에 알맞은 말을 글에서 찾아 쓰시오.

They believe AI is limited by (1) _____ data and cannot surpass human (2) _____ .

11 다음 글의 빈칸에 알맞은 말을 보기에 주어진 표현을 바르게 배열하여 쓰시오.

What kind of future do you think lies ahead of us? Will more people use AI programs to boost their creativity and productivity? Or will people grow tired of the limitations of AI tools? AI provides many benefits and new opportunities. What we need to do is figure out how to use AI tools ethically and _____ .

보기

AI / think about / collaborate / and / how / can / humans

→ _____

_____

12 다음 글의 밑줄 친 two reasons가 무엇인지 빈칸에 알맞은 말을 찾아 쓰시오.

As AI technology advances, will robots take over human work? I think robots can replace humans in many roles. There are two reasons for my opinion. First, robots can work more productively than humans. This means that they can produce more in a shorter amount of time. Second, robots can work in dangerous places that humans cannot reach. Therefore, they can reduce the risk of accidents. For these reasons, I think that robots will replace human workers in the future

↓

Robots can work more (1) _____ than humans. They can also work in (2) _____ places.

02

–

Ready to Be Wicked

A Journey into a Magical World
마법 세계로의 여정

01 I had been wanting to see the musical *Wicked* for a long time.
과거완료진행 ／ 오랫동안

나는 오랫동안 뮤지컬 〈위키드〉를 보고 싶었다.

02 It opened in 2003 on Broadway and got great reviews.
병렬 연결

그것은 2003년에 브로드웨이에서 시작되었고 훌륭한 평가를 받았다.

03 Everyone recommends it. I finally got to see it last weekend.

모든 사람들이 그것을 추천한다. 나는 마침내 지난 주말에 그것을 보게 되었다.

04 The musical is based on an imaginative story [of two characters (from the book *The Wizard of*
~을 기반으로 하다 ／ 전치사구 ／ 전치사구
Oz): Elphaba, the wicked witch, and Glinda, the good witch].
동격 ／ 동격

그 뮤지컬은 책 〈오즈의 마법사〉에 나오는 두 명의 등장인물인 사악한 마녀 Elphaba와 착한 마녀 Glinda에 관한 창작 이야기를 기반으로 한다.

05 It tells their background story and explains [how they became known as wicked and good].
병렬 연결 ／ 간접의문문 (explains의 목적어)

그것은 그들의 배경 이야기를 말해 주고 그들이 어떻게 사악하고 착한 것으로 알려지게 되었는지를 설명한다.

06 [What impressed me the most] was the theme of the musical.
주어 (선행사를 포함한 관계대명사절) ／ 동사

나에게 가장 감명을 준 것은 뮤지컬의 주제였다.

07 = the theme of the musical
It is about forming friendships, getting to know oneself, and accepting differences.
동명사구 1 (about의 목적어) ／ 동명사구 2 ／ 동명사구 3

그것은 우정을 형성하는 것, 스스로를 알아가는 것, 그리고 차이를 받아들이는 것에 대한 것이다.

A Fascinating Storyline
매력적인 줄거리

08 The story begins in a magical place, the Land of Oz.
동격

이야기는 마법의 장소인 오즈의 나라에서 시작한다.

09 In the musical, Elphaba and Glinda first meet at university.

뮤지컬에서 Elphaba와 Glinda는 대학에서 처음 만난다.

10 Elphaba was born with green skin and usually stays away from others.
~으로부터 거리를 두다

Elphaba는 초록색 피부를 갖고 태어났으며 대체로 다른 이들로부터 거리를 둔다.

11 Because of her unusual appearance and cold personality, she has very few friends.
전치사구 (~ 때문에)　　　　　　　　　　　　　　　　　　　　　few + 복수 명사: 거의 없는 ~들

그녀의 특이한 외모와 냉정한 성격 때문에 그녀에게는 친구가 거의 없다.

12 Meanwhile, Glinda has a very kind personality, which makes her quite popular.
한편　　　　　　　　　　　　　　　　　　　계속적 용법의 주격 관계대명사: 앞 문장을 부연 설명

한편 Glinda는 친절한 성격을 갖고 있는데, 이것은 그녀를 꽤나 인기 있게 만든다.

13 At first, Elphaba and Glinda do not get along.
잘 지내다

처음에 Elphaba와 Glinda는 잘 지내지 않는다.

14 However, as they get to know and learn about each other, they become close friends.
접속사 (~함에 따라)　　　　(to)　　　서로

그러나 그들이 서로를 알아가고 배워가면서 그들은 친한 친구가 된다.

15 Elphaba has exceptional magical powers, and some other characters try to take advantage of this.
~을 이용하다

Elphaba에게는 특별한 마력이 있어서 몇몇 다른 등장인물들이 이것을 이용하려고 한다.

16 Glinda and Elphaba's friendship is continuously challenged in the story.
수동태

Glinda와 Elphaba의 우정은 이야기 속에서 계속해서 도전을 받는다.

17 Nevertheless, in the end, their friendship wins.
그럼에도 불구하고　　　결국

그럼에도 불구하고 결국에는 그들의 우정이 승리한다.

18 Every relationship has its ups and downs, so I could easily relate to the main characters.
기복　　　　　　　　　　　　~에 공감하다

모든 관계에는 우여곡절이 있으므로 나는 쉽게 주요 등장인물들에게 공감할 수 있었다.

The Unforgettable Songs
잊을 수 없는 노래들

19 Of course, I cannot review a musical without [talking about the songs].
cannot ~ without ...: …하지 않고 ~할 수 없다　　동명사구 (without의 목적어)

물론 노래에 관해 이야기하지 않고는 뮤지컬을 평가할 수 없다.

20 *Wicked* has many great songs, but there are two [that I especially like].
목적격 관계대명사절

〈위키드〉에는 많은 훌륭한 노래들이 있지만 내가 특히 좋아하는 두 곡의 노래가 있다.

21 "Defying Gravity" is the most famous song in the musical.
최상급

'Defying Gravity(중력을 거슬러)'는 그 뮤지컬에서 가장 유명한 노래이다.

22 It comes at a key turning point in the story.
전환점

그것은 이야기의 주요 전환점에 나온다.

used to-V: ~하곤 했다, (과거 한때는) ~했다

23 Elphaba used to admire a wizard, but one day she finds out [that he has an evil plan and can't be trusted anymore].
명사절 (finds out의 목적어)   not ~ anymore: 더 이상 ~아닌   (he)

Elphaba는 한 마법사를 존경했지만, 어느 날 그에게 사악한 계획이 있으며 그가 더 이상 신뢰받을 수 없다는 것을 깨닫는다.

24 She sings about her determination to fight against him.
to부정사의 형용사적 용법

그녀는 그에게 맞서 싸우려는 그녀의 결심에 관해 노래한다.

25 She shows her true powers and rises into the air on her broom while singing this song.
병렬 연결   접속사가 생략되지 않은 분사구문

그녀는 이 노래를 부르면서 자신의 진정한 힘을 보여 주고 빗자루를 타고 공중으로 올라간다.

26 She sings [that she will not let people bring her down anymore.
명사절 (sings의 목적어)   let(사역동사) + 목적어 + 동사원형: ~가 …하게 하다

그녀는 사람들이 더 이상 그녀를 끌어내리지 못하게 할 것이라고 노래한다.

27 Her powerful voice fascinated me.

그녀의 강력한 목소리는 나를 매료시켰다.

28 When the song ended, the entire audience clapped enthusiastically.

노래가 끝났을 때, 전체 관중이 열광적으로 박수를 쳤다.

29 The second song [that had a great impact on me] was "For Good."
주어   주격 관계대명사절   동사

나에게 큰 영향을 준 두 번째 노래는 'For Good(영원히)'이었다.

30 At the end of the musical, the two friends have to choose different paths and say goodbye to each
~해야 한다 ⎿━━━ 병렬 연결 ━━━⎤ 서로

other.

뮤지컬의 마지막에, 두 친구는 다른 길을 선택해야 하고 서로에게 작별 인사를 해야 한다.

31 ⎡━━━━━ 병렬 연결 ━━━━━⎤
Elphaba decides to leave her home and asks Glinda to protect the people of Oz.
to부정사 (decides의 목적어)   ask + 목적어 + to-V: ~에게 …하도록 부탁하다

Elphaba는 그녀의 고향을 떠나기로 결정하고 Glinda에게 오즈의 사람들을 보호해 달라고 부탁한다.

32 At this moment, they start to sing to each other.
바로 이때   = start singing

바로 이때, 그들은 서로에게 노래를 부르기 시작한다.

33 명사절 (explain의 목적어)
The song moved me because Glinda and Elphaba explain [that meeting each other has changed
동명사구 (명사절의 주어)   명사절의 동사 (현재완료)

them for the better].
더 나은 쪽으로

그 노래는 나를 감동시켰는데, Glinda와 Elphaba가 서로를 만난 것이 그들을 더 나은 쪽으로 바꿨다고 설명하기 때문이다.

34 It is a truly touching moment [that shows their strong friendship].
⎿━━━━━━━━━⎤ 주격 관계대명사절

그것은 그들의 강한 우정을 보여 주는 진정으로 감동적인 순간이다.

눈을 사로잡는
The Eye-Catching Visuals
눈을 사로잡는 시각 정보들

35 The exciting story and beautiful songs of *Wicked* are accompanied by beautiful visuals.
be accompanied by: ~을 동반하다

〈위키드〉의 흥미로운 이야기와 아름다운 노래는 아름다운 시각 정보와 동반된다.

36 First, the costumes were incredible. In one scene, we see the people of Oz wearing unique clothes.
see(지각동사) + 목적어 + 현재분사: ~가 …하고 있는 것을 보다

첫째로 의상이 훌륭했다. 한 장면에서 우리는 오즈의 사람들이 독특한 옷을 입고 있는 것을 본다.

37 I couldn't believe the detail and beauty [of the masks, wigs, and dresses].
↑_____⎤ 전치사구

나는 가면, 가발, 옷의 정교함과 아름다움을 믿을 수 없었다.

38 Furthermore, all kinds of tricks invited me into the magical world.
게다가

게다가, 모든 기교들이 나를 마법의 세계로 초대했다.

39 I really enjoyed [noticing the symbols used in the performance].

동명사구 (enjoyed의 목적어)

과거분사구

나는 공연에 사용된 상징들을 알아채는 것을 정말 즐겼다.

40 For example, a huge dragon-shaped device was hanging above the stage.

용 모양의

과거진행

예를 들어 거대한 용 모양의 장치가 무대 위에 걸려 있었다.

41 It seemed to move [whenever Elphaba or Glinda made a choice].

복합관계부사 (~할 때마다)

seem to-V: ~인 것 같다

make a choice: 선택하다

그것은 Elphaba나 Glinda가 선택을 내릴 때마다 움직이는 것처럼 보였다.

42 I think [using these visual effects made the musical more exciting].

(that) 명사절 (think의 목적어)

make + 목적어 + 목적격 보어(형용사): ~을 …하게 만들다

나는 이러한 시각적 효과들을 사용하는 것이 뮤지컬을 더 흥미롭게 만들었다고 생각한다.

43 In my opinion, the musical *Wicked* is an incredible work.

내 생각에는

내 생각에 뮤지컬 〈위키드〉는 훌륭한 작품이다.

44 It has great music and is visually impressive.

병렬 연결

그것은 멋진 음악을 갖고 있으며 시각적으로 인상적이다.

45 It also has a strong plot [that kept me engaged from beginning to end].

keep + 목적어 + 과거분사: ~가 계속 …되게 하다

주격 관계대명사절

from A to B: A부터 B까지

그것은 또한 시작부터 끝까지 나를 사로잡았던 탄탄한 줄거리 구성을 갖고 있다.

46 I highly recommend this show to anyone interested in musicals.

과거분사구

나는 뮤지컬에 관심이 있는 누구에게나 이 공연을 적극 추천한다.

47 You will be able to explore the themes of friendship and personal change in a magical setting.

be able to-V: ~할 수 있다

동격 (~라는)

당신은 황홀한 무대 배경에서 우정과 개인의 변화라는 주제를 탐험할 수 있을 것이다.

교과서 본문 익히기 ① 빈칸 완성하기

♣ 다음 빈칸에 알맞은 말을 쓰시오.

01 I had been _____ the musical *Wicked* for a long time.
나는 오랫동안 뮤지컬 〈위키드〉를 보고 싶었다.

02 It opened in 2003 on Broadway and _____.
그것은 2003년에 브로드웨이에서 시작되었고 훌륭한 평가를 받았다.

03 _____ it. I finally got to see it _____.
모든 사람들이 그것을 추천한다. 나는 마침내 지난 주말에 그것을 보게 되었다.

04 The musical _____ an imaginative story of two characters from the book *The Wizard of Oz*: Elphaba, _____, and Glinda, the good witch.
그 뮤지컬은 책 〈오즈의 마법사〉에 나오는 두 명의 등장인물인 사악한 마녀 Elphaba와 착한 마녀 Glinda에 관한 창작 이야기를 기반으로 한다.

05 It tells their background story and explains how they became _____.
그것은 그들의 배경 이야기를 말해 주고 그들이 어떻게 사악하고 착한 것으로 알려지게 되었는지를 설명한다.

06 _____ was the theme of the musical.
나에게 가장 감명을 준 것은 뮤지컬의 주제였다.

07 It is about forming friendships, _____, and accepting differences.
그것은 우정을 형성하는 것, 스스로를 알아가는 것, 그리고 차이를 받아들이는 것에 대한 것이다.

08 The story begins _____, the Land of Oz.
이야기는 마법의 장소인 오즈의 나라에서 시작한다.

09 Elphaba was _____ and usually stays away from others.
Elphaba는 초록색 피부를 갖고 태어났으며 대체로 다른 이들로부터 거리를 둔다.

10 Because of her unusual appearance and cold personality, _____.
그녀의 특이한 외모와 냉정한 성격 때문에 그녀에게는 친구가 거의 없다.

11 Meanwhile, Glinda has a very kind personality, _____.
한편 Glinda는 친절한 성격을 갖고 있는데, 이것은 그녀를 꽤나 인기 있게 만든다.

12 However, _____ and learn about each other, they become close friends.
그러나 그들이 서로를 알아가고 배워가면서 그들은 친한 친구가 된다.

13 Elphaba has exceptional magical powers, and some other characters try to _____ this.
Elphaba에게는 특별한 마력이 있어서 몇몇 다른 등장인물들이 이것을 이용하려고 한다.

14 Glinda and Elphaba's friendship _____ in the story.
Glinda와 Elphaba의 우정은 이야기 속에서 계속해서 도전을 받는다.

15 Nevertheless, _____, their friendship wins.

그럼에도 불구하고 결국에는 그들의 우정이 승리한다.

16 Every relationship has its _____, so I could easily relate to the main characters.

모든 관계에는 우여곡절이 있으므로 나는 쉽게 주요 등장인물들에게 공감할 수 있었다.

17 Of course, I cannot review a musical _____ the songs.

물론 노래에 관해 이야기하지 않고는 뮤지컬을 평가할 수 없다.

18 *Wicked* has many great songs, but there are two _____.

〈위키드〉에는 많은 훌륭한 노래들이 있지만 내가 특히 좋아하는 두 곡의 노래가 있다.

19 "Defying Gravity" is _____ in the musical.

'Defying Gravity(중력을 거슬러)'는 그 뮤지컬에서 가장 유명한 노래이다.

20 It comes _____ in the story.

그것은 이야기의 주요 전환점에 나온다.

21 Elphaba _____ a wizard, but one day she finds out that he has an evil plan and _____.

Elphaba는 한 마법사를 존경했지만, 어느 날 그에게 사악한 계획이 있으며 그가 더 이상 신뢰받을 수 없다는 것을 깨닫는다.

22 She sings about her determination _____.

그녀는 그에게 맞서 싸우려는 그녀의 결심에 관해 노래한다.

23 She shows her true powers and _____ on her broom while singing this song.

그녀는 이 노래를 부르면서 자신의 진정한 힘을 보여 주고 빗자루를 타고 공중으로 올라간다.

24 She sings that she will not _____.

그녀는 사람들이 더 이상 그녀를 끌어내리지 못하게 할 것이라고 노래한다.

25 When the song ended, _____ clapped enthusiastically.

노래가 끝났을 때, 전체 관중이 열광적으로 박수를 쳤다.

26 The second song that had _____ was "For Good."

나에게 큰 영향을 준 두 번째 노래는 'For Good(영원히)'이었다.

27 At the end of the musical, the two friends _____ different paths and say goodbye to each other.

뮤지컬의 마지막에, 두 친구는 다른 길을 선택해야 하고 서로에게 작별 인사를 해야 한다.

28 Elphaba decides to leave her home and asks Glinda _____ of Oz.

Elphaba는 그녀의 고향을 떠나기로 결정하고 Glinda에게 오즈의 사람들을 보호해 달라고 부탁한다.

29 The song moved me because Glinda and Elphaba explain that meeting each other has _____.

그 노래는 나를 감동시켰는데, Glinda와 Elphaba가 서로를 만난 것이 그들을 더 나은 쪽으로 바꿨다고 설명하기 때문이다.

30 It is a _____ that shows their strong friendship.

그것은 그들의 강한 우정을 보여 주는 진정으로 감동적인 순간이다.

31 The exciting story and beautiful songs of *Wicked* _____ beautiful visuals.

〈위키드〉의 흥미로운 이야기와 아름다운 노래는 아름다운 시각 정보와 동반된다.

32 In one scene, we see the people of Oz _____.

한 장면에서 우리는 오즈의 사람들이 독특한 옷을 입고 있는 것을 본다.

33 Furthermore, all kinds of tricks _____.

게다가, 모든 기교들이 나를 마법의 세계로 초대했다.

34 I really enjoyed _____ used in the performance.

나는 공연에 사용된 상징들을 알아채는 것을 정말 즐겼다.

35 For example, a huge dragon-shaped device _____ the stage.

예를 들어 거대한 용 모양의 장치가 무대 위에 걸려 있었다.

36 It _____ whenever Elphaba or Glinda made a choice.

그것은 Elphaba나 Glinda가 선택을 내릴 때마다 움직이는 것처럼 보였다.

37 I think _____ made the musical more exciting.

나는 이러한 시각적 효과들을 사용하는 것이 뮤지컬을 더 흥미롭게 만들었다고 생각한다.

38 It also has a strong plot that kept me engaged _____.

그것은 또한 시작부터 끝까지 나를 사로잡았던 탄탄한 줄거리 구성을 갖고 있다.

39 I _____ this show to anyone interested in musicals.

나는 뮤지컬에 관심이 있는 누구에게나 이 공연을 적극 추천한다.

40 You _____ the themes of friendship and personal change in a magical setting.

당신은 황홀한 무대 배경에서 우정과 개인의 변화라는 주제를 탐험할 수 있을 것이다.

♣ 다음 네모 안에서 옳은 것을 고르시오.

01   I had been | wanting / wanted | to see the musical *Wicked* for a long time.

02   It opened in 2003 on Broadway and | got / gotten | great reviews.

03   I finally got to see it | last / the last | weekend.

04   The musical is based | in / on | an imaginative story of two characters from the book *The Wizard of Oz*: Elphaba, the | weak / wicked | witch, and Glinda, the good witch.

05   It tells their background story and explains | how / who | they became known as wicked and good.

06 | That / What | impressed me the most was the theme of the musical.

07   It is about forming friendships, getting to know oneself, and | accepts / accepting | differences.

08   Elphaba was born with green skin and usually stays away | from / with | others.

09   Because of her | usual / unusual | appearance and cold personality, she has very few friends.

10   Meanwhile, Glinda has a very kind personality, | that / which | makes her quite popular.

11   At first, Elphaba and Glinda do not get | along / well |.

12   However, as they get to know and learn about each other, they become | close / closed | friends.

13   Elphaba has exceptional magical powers, and some other characters try to | make / take | advantage of this.

14   Glinda and Elphaba's friendship is continuously | challenging / challenged | in the story.

15   Every relationship has its | up / ups | and downs, so I could easily relate to the main characters.

16   Of course, I cannot | preview / review | a musical without talking about the songs.

17   "Defying Gravity" is the | more / most | famous song in the musical.

18   Elphaba used to | admire / admiring | a wizard, but one day she finds out that he has an evil plan and can't be trusted anymore.

19   She sings about her | destination / determination | to fight against him.

20   She shows her true powers and raises / rises into the air on her broom while singing this song.

21   She sings that she will not allow / let people bring her down anymore.

22   The second song that had a great impact / respect on me was "For Good."

23   At the end of the musical, the two friends have to choose different paths and say / says goodbye to each other.

24   Elphaba decides to leave her home and asks Glinda protect / to protect the people of Oz.

25   The song moved me because Glinda and Elphaba explain that meeting each other have / has changed them for the better.

26   It is a truly touching / touched moment that shows their strong friendship.

27   The exciting story and beautiful songs of *Wicked* are accompanied / accompanying by beautiful visuals.

28   In one scene, we see the people of Oz wearing / to wear unique clothes.

29   Furthermore, all kinds of tricks invited / visited me into the magical world.

30   I really enjoyed noticing / to notice the symbols used in the performance.

31   For example, a huge dragon-shaped device was hanging / hung above the stage.

32   It seemed to move whatever / whenever Elphaba or Glinda made a choice.

33   I think using these visible / visual effects made the musical more exciting.

34   It has great music and has / is visually impressive.

35   It also has a strong plot that kept me engaged at / from beginning to end.

36   I highly command / recommend this show to anyone interested in musicals.

37   You will be able explore / to explore the themes of friendship and personal change in a magical setting.

♣ 다음 밑줄 친 부분을 바르게 고쳐 쓰시오.

01   I had been wanting <u>seeing</u> the musical *Wicked* for a long time.

02   It opened in 2003 on Broadway and <u>gets</u> great reviews.

03   Everyone <u>recommend</u> it.

04   The musical <u>bases</u> on an imaginative story of two characters from the book *The Wizard of Oz*: Elphaba, the wicked witch, and Glinda, the good witch.

05   It tells their background story and explains how <u>did they become</u> known as wicked and good.

06   What <u>was impressed</u> me the most was the theme of the musical.

07   It is about forming friendships, <u>gets</u> to know oneself, and accepting differences.

08   Elphaba was born with green skin and usually <u>stay</u> away from others.

09   <u>Because</u> her unusual appearance and cold personality, she has very <u>a few</u> friends.

10   Meanwhile, Glinda has a very kind personality, <u>that</u> makes her quite popular.

11   However, as they get to know and learn about each other, they <u>became</u> close friends.

12   Elphaba has exceptional magical powers, and some other characters try to <u>make</u> advantage of this.

13   Nevertheless, <u>at</u> the end, their friendship wins.

14   Every relationship has its <u>up and down</u>, so I could easily relate to the main characters.

15   Of course, I <u>can</u> review a musical without talking about the songs.

16   *Wicked* has many great songs, but there are two <u>that especially like</u>.

17   "Defying Gravity" is <u>most famous</u> song in the musical.

18   Elphaba <u>is used to admire</u> a wizard, but one day she finds out that he has an evil plan and <u>can't trust</u> anymore.

19   She sings about her determination to fight <u>with</u> him.

20   She shows her true powers and <u>rise</u> into the air on her broom while <u>sings</u> this song.

21   She sings that she will not let people <u>to bring</u> her down anymore.

22   When the song ended, the entire audience <u>clap</u> enthusiastically.

23   The second song that <u>have</u> a great impact on me was "For Good."

24   At the end of the musical, the two friends <u>has to</u> choose different paths and say goodbye to each other.

25   Elphaba decides to leave her home and <u>ask</u> Glinda to protect the people of Oz.

26   The song moved me because Glinda and Elphaba <u>explains</u> that meeting each other <u>have</u> changed them for the better.

27   It is a <u>true</u> touching moment that shows their strong friendship.

28   The exciting story and beautiful songs of *Wicked* <u>accompanied</u> by beautiful visuals.

29   In one scene, we see the people of Oz <u>to wear</u> unique clothes.

30   I really enjoyed <u>notice</u> the symbols used in the performance.

31   For example, a huge <u>dragon shape</u> device was hanging above the stage.

32   It seemed <u>moving</u> whenever Elphaba or Glinda made a choice.

33   It has great music and <u>has</u> visually impressive.

34   It also has a strong plot that kept me <u>engaging</u> from beginning to end.

35   I highly recommend this show to <u>someone</u> interested in musicals.

36   You will <u>can</u> explore the themes of friendship and personal change in a magical setting.

[01~02] 다음 글을 읽고, 물음에 답하시오.

I had been wanting to see the musical *Wicked* for a long time. It opened in 2003 on Broadway and got great reviews. Everyone recommends it. I finally got to see it ① last weekend. The musical is based on an ② imaginative story of two characters from the book *The Wizard of Oz*: Elphaba, the wicked witch, and Glinda, the good witch. It tells their ③ background story and explains how they became known as wicked and good. What ④ impressed me the most was the theme of the musical. It is about forming friendships, getting to know oneself, and ⑤ ignoring differences.

01 밑줄 친 the musical *Wicked*에 관해 윗글의 내용과 일치하지 않는 것은?

① It first opened in 2003.
② It has received good reviews.
③ The story is based on *The Wizard of Oz*.
④ The main characters are two witches.
⑤ The visual effects impressed the writer the most.

02 윗글의 밑줄 친 부분 중 문맥상 낱말의 쓰임이 적절하지 않은 것은?

①   ②   ③   ④   ⑤

[03~04] 다음 글을 읽고, 물음에 답하시오.

The story begins in a magical place, the Land of Oz. In the musical, Elphaba and Glinda first meet at university. Elphaba was born with green skin and usually stays away from others. Because of her unusual appearance and cold personality, she has very few friends. (A), Glinda has a very kind personality, 이것은 그녀를 꽤나 인기 있게 만든다. At first, Elphaba and Glinda do not get along. However, as they get to know and learn about each other, they become close friends. Elphaba has exceptional magical powers, and some other characters try to take advantage of this. Glinda and Elphaba's friendship is continuously challenged in the story. (B), in the end, their friendship wins. Every relationship has its ups and downs, so I could easily relate to the main characters.

03 윗글의 빈칸 (A)와 (B)에 들어갈 말이 바르게 짝지어진 것은?

	(A)		(B)
①	However	···	Consequently
②	Meanwhile	···	Nevertheless
③	Furthermore	···	However
④	Therefore	···	Moreover
⑤	Nevertheless	···	Therefore

04 윗글의 밑줄 친 우리말과 일치하도록 에 맞게 영작하시오.

> **조건**
> 1. 관계대명사 which를 사용할 것
> 2. 다음 표현을 사용할 것: quite, popular

Glinda has a very kind personality, _____

_____ .

[05~06] 다음 글을 읽고, 물음에 답하시오.

Of course, I cannot review a musical without talking about the songs. Wicked has many great songs, but there are two that I especially like. "Defying Gravity" is the most famous song in the musical. It comes at a key turning point in the story. Elphaba used to admire a wizard, but one day she finds out that he has an evil plan and can't be trusted anymore. She sings about her determination to fight against him. She shows her true powers and rises into the air on her broom while singing this song. She sings that she will not let people bring her down anymore. Her powerful voice fascinated me. When the song ended, the entire audience clapped enthusiastically.

05 윗글의 내용과 일치하지 <u>않는</u> 것은?

① There are a lot of wonderful songs in the musical.
② The writer's favorite song comes at the end of the musical.
③ The wizard Elphaba admired was in fact an evil man.
④ Elphaba could fly with her broom.
⑤ Elphaba's song moved the audience.

06 윗글의 밑줄 친 this song이 가리키는 것을 글에서 찾아 쓰시오.

→ _____

[07~08] 다음 글을 읽고, 물음에 답하시오.

The second song that had a great impact on me was "For Good." At the end of the musical, the two friends have to choose different paths and say goodbye to each other. Elphaba decides (A) leaving / to leave her home and asks Glinda to protect the people of Oz. At this moment, they start to sing to each other. The song moved me because Glinda and Elphaba explain that meeting each other (B) have / has changed them for the better. It is a truly touching moment (C) that / when shows their strong friendship.

07 밑줄 친 "For Good"에 관해 윗글의 내용과 일치하는 것은?

① It was the writer's number-one song in the musical.
② It comes at the climax of the musical.
③ It was sung by Elphaba and Glinda.
④ Glinda says goodbye to Elphaba in the song.
⑤ It highlights Elphaba's strong will.

08 (A), (B), (C)의 각 네모 안에서 어법에 맞는 표현으로 가장 적절한 것은?

	(A)		(B)		(C)
①	leaving	…	have	…	that
②	leaving	…	have	…	when
③	leaving	…	has	…	that
④	to leave	…	has	…	when
⑤	to leave	…	has	…	that

[09~10] 다음 글을 읽고, 물음에 답하시오.

> The exciting story and beautiful songs of Wicked are accompanied by beautiful visuals.

> (A) For example, a huge dragon-shaped device was hanging above the stage. It seemed to move whenever Elphaba or Glinda made a choice.
>
> (B) First, the costumes were incredible. In one scene, we see the people of Oz wearing unique clothes. I couldn't believe the detail and beauty of the masks, wigs, and dresses.
>
> (C) Furthermore, all kinds of tricks invited me into the magical world. I really enjoyed noticing the symbols used in the performance.
>
> (D) I think using these visual effects made the musical more exciting.

09 주어진 문장 다음에 이어질 글의 순서로 가장 적절한 것은?

① (A) – (B) – (C) – (D)
② (B) – (C) – (A) – (D)
③ (B) – (D) – (C) – (A)
④ (C) – (A) – (B) – (D)
⑤ (C) – (B) – (A) – (D)

10 윗글의 주제로 가장 적절한 것은?

① the eye-catching visuals of the musical
② the most famous songs of the musical
③ ways the musical could improve
④ the themes of the musical
⑤ the main characters of the musical

[11~12] 다음 글을 읽고, 물음에 답하시오.

> In my opinion, the musical *Wicked* is an incredible work. It has great music and ① is visually impressive. It also has a strong plot that ② kept me engaged from beginning to end. I ③ highly recommend this show to anyone ④ interested in musicals. You will be ⑤ able explore the themes of friendship and personal change in a magical setting.

11 윗글의 목적으로 가장 적절한 것은?

① 뮤지컬 개봉을 홍보하려고
② 뮤지컬을 사람들에게 추천하려고
③ 우정과 자기 개발의 중요성을 강조하려고
④ 관객을 사로잡는 뮤지컬 제작을 요청하려고
⑤ 뮤지컬에 사용되는 음향과 특수 효과를 설명하려고

12 윗글의 밑줄 친 부분 중 어법상 틀린 것은?

①   ②   ③   ④   ⑤

[01~02] 다음 글을 읽고, 물음에 답하시오.

> **Host** Dr. Hill, let's start with a question about my experience last month. I worked out right after dinner and got a stomachache. Why did that happen?
>
> **Dr. Hill** Well, the problem is that you exercised too soon after eating. (A) This can cause various stomach issues. (B) When you eat, blood rushes to the digestive system to help break down the food and absorb its nutrients. (C) But when you start to exercise, blood moves from the digestive system to your muscles. (D) This happens in order to supply your muscles with the oxygen and nutrients they require. (E) So, whether you're lifting weights or going for a jog, you shouldn't do it with a stomach full of food.

01 글의 흐름으로 보아, 주어진 문장이 들어가기에 가장 적절한 곳은?

> As a result, the digestion process is paused until the blood returns.

① (A)　② (B)　③ (C)　④ (D)　⑤ (E)

02 윗글의 밑줄 친 질문에 대한 답을 요약할 때 빈칸 (A)와 (B)에 들어갈 말이 바르게 짝지어진 것은?

> The digestive system needs blood to break down ___(A)___ , but blood moves to the ___(B)___ when we start exercising.

	(A)		(B)
①	oxygen	…	stomach
②	muscles	…	oxygen
③	food	…	digestive system
④	nutrients	…	muscles
⑤	glucose	…	liver

[03~04] 다음 글을 읽고, 물음에 답하시오.

> **Host** I see. That makes sense. So, does that mean I should exercise on an empty stomach?
>
> **Dr. Hill** No, it doesn't. That can also be harmful and ① unpleasant. This is because the body needs energy to exercise. The fuel that provides this energy is glycogen. Carbohydrates in the food we eat are ② broken down into a kind of sugar called glucose. When this glucose is ③ stored in parts of the body, such as the muscles and the liver, it is called glycogen. This is why exercising on a completely empty stomach—such as when you first wake up in the morning—can be such a ④ challenge. Your blood sugar levels are low, and you don't have enough glycogen stored in your body. If you exercise on an empty stomach, you will most likely lack energy and feel unusually tired. There can also be more serious ⑤ causes. Some people end up suffering from nausea and headaches, and others even faint. This is because intense exercise uses up all the glycogen in your muscles.

03 윗글의 내용과 일치하지 <u>않는</u> 것은?

① 운동할 때 신체에 필요한 에너지를 공급하는 것은 글리코겐이다.
② 식품으로 섭취한 탄수화물은 글루코스로 분해된다.
③ 간과 근육에 저장되는 글리코겐을 글루코스라고 한다.
④ 저장된 글리코겐이 부족하면 혈당이 떨어지고 에너지가 부족하다.
⑤ 아침에 일어나자마자 운동을 하는 것은 바람직하지 않다.

04 윗글의 밑줄 친 부분 중 문맥상 낱말의 쓰임이 적절하지 <u>않은</u> 것은?

① ② ③ ④ ⑤

[05~06] 다음 글을 읽고, 물음에 답하시오.

> **Host** So, is it the loss of glycogen that causes us to have low levels of energy?
>
> **Dr. Hill** That's correct. For this reason, doctors recommend that people eat food containing carbohydrates within thirty minutes after working out. This replaces the muscle glycogen you have lost. Basically, you need between one and one and a half grams of carbohydrates for every kilogram you weigh. Let's do the math. If you weigh 60 kilograms, you should try to consume between 60 and 90 grams of carbohydrates after you exercise. This is equal to about one bowl of white rice or three bananas.

05 윗글의 밑줄 친 that과 쓰임이 같은 것은?

① It is strange that our team failed to get to the finals.
② It was your carelessness that ruined the plan.
③ They were so frightened that they couldn't speak anything.
④ We suggest that the actor publicly apologize.
⑤ Did you hear the news that she got married?

06 윗글의 내용과 일치하도록 다음 질문에 대한 답을 완성하여 쓰시오.

> How many grams of carbohydrates should an 80-kilogram person consume after exercising?

→ They should _____
_____ after exercising.

[07~08] 다음 글을 읽고, 물음에 답하시오.

> **Host** That's very interesting. But what about eating before we exercise? Can you explain how long ① should we wait after eating?
>
> **Dr. Hill** Well, as I said before, exercising right after you eat will cause feelings of discomfort. But, if you wait too long to exercise after eating, you'll suffer from a lack of energy. The best time to eat before you exercise ② varies from one to three hours. Basically, it depends on ⓐ several factors such as the type and amount of food as well as body size, age, and gender. The type of exercise also matters. For extremely active exercise like cycling, I suggest that ③ you wait between one and a half and three hours after eating a ④ moderate-sized meal. But for something more casual, such as golfing, waiting for one hour after a meal should be enough. Clearly, you can wait less after eating a snack.
>
> **Host** Thank you very much for this fascinating information, Dr. Hill. I'm sure ⑤ it will be very helpful for all of our viewers.

07 윗글의 밑줄 친 부분 중 어법상 틀린 것은?

①   ②   ③   ④   ⑤

08 윗글의 밑줄 친 ⓐ several factors로 언급되지 않은 것은?

① the amount of food
② weight and height
③ the type of exercise
④ the amount of sleep
⑤ age and gender

[09~10] 다음 글을 읽고, 물음에 답하시오.

Once someone learns how to ride a bike, the person will never forget how to do it. The same goes with other skills like eating with chopsticks or playing musical instruments. Once you learn the skill and get used to it, you can perform it without thinking about the necessary muscle movements. This long-lasting memory for certain skills is called muscle memory. Despite its name, it doesn't mean that _____.
Interestingly, muscle memory mostly develops in the brain. Different parts of the brain are used to perform a skill. When we practice a skill, these parts become strongly connected. This makes the skill easier to perform automatically. That's why professional musicians seem to play Mozart's songs so easily! Without muscle memory, this would be much harder.

09 윗글의 빈칸에 들어갈 말로 가장 적절한 것은?

① our body remembers certain skills
② we don't have to practice the skill
③ our muscles remember the skill
④ the brain plays a key role in learning skills
⑤ certain skills can be obtained automatically

10 윗글의 요지로 가장 적절한 것은?

① 음악가들은 연주 기술을 연마하기 위해 애쓴다.
② 특정 기술을 자동적으로 수행하게 하는 근육 기억은 실은 뇌의 작동에 의한 것이다.
③ 뇌의 다양한 부위가 관장하는 기능은 많이 알려져 있지 않다.
④ 장기 기억을 개발하기 위해서는 신체 활동과 악기 연주가 도움이 된다.
⑤ 근육 기억은 유년 시절부터 연마하는 것이 중요하다.

11 다음 글의 밑줄 친 부분 중 가리키는 내용이 나머지 넷과 다른 것은?

Space technology may not seem useful to the average person. But did you know that many of the items we use every day come from space technology? For example, ① the image sensors in modern cameras were originally developed to be used in space. However, ② they were easy to produce and didn't require much power, so companies started using ③ them in commercial products. These days, an updated version of ④ this technology can be found in many devices, including smartphones and video cameras. Look around you. What other ⑤ common items do you think come from space technology?

①   ②   ③   ④   ⑤

12 다음 글의 빈칸에 들어갈 말로 적절한 것을 <u>두 개</u> 고르면?

Recently, an artist used an artificial intelligence (AI) system to create the image above for an art contest. The image won first place in the digital arts category. This led to a controversy in the art community. Some people complained that the artist simply provided the system with basic instructions and let it do all the work. They felt this wasn't fair to the rest of the artists in the contest. However, _____.
Today, there are numerous AI programs that can create various forms of art including images, songs, and novels.

① there were concerns that AI would violate the copyright of artists
② some people believed human jobs would eventually be replaced by AI
③ some other people thought AI could not exceed human creativity
④ others worried AI would replace humans in more and more areas
⑤ there were also people who were excited by the potential of AI

[13~14] 다음 글을 읽고, 물음에 답하시오.

AI image generators create images based on our text requests. They do this by copying other images that were created by humans. The generators have the ability to analyze millions of images and their corresponding descriptions. This allows them (A) create / to create works of art in a short time based on the provided instructions.

Moreover, AI programs can mix the styles of existing images upon request. For example, you can blend a photograph of a cat with Johannes Vermeer's *Girl with a Pearl Earring*. These two images have (B) few / a few differences. However, the overall design, the eyes, and the scarf around the head (C) is / are clearly based on Vermeer's painting. A simple request was enough to create this complex and detailed image.

13 윗글의 주제로 가장 적절한 것은?

① making digital images with AI
② creativity and responsibility in the art world
③ blending masterpieces with digital images
④ role of AI in the music industry
⑤ image alysis technology

14 (A), (B), (C)의 각 네모 안에서 어법에 맞는 표현으로 가장 적절한 것은?

	(A)		(B)		(C)
①	create	···	few	···	is
②	create	···	a few	···	is
③	to create	···	few	···	is
④	to create	···	a few	···	are
⑤	to create	···	few	···	are

[15~16] 다음 글을 읽고, 물음에 답하시오.

인공 지능 프로그램은 미술 세계뿐만 아니라 음악 산업에서의 변화로도 이어질 수 있다. These programs are already able to compose songs, and they give you many options. ____(A)____, you can choose the style and key, such as C major or A minor. You can also set how long the song will be. Once you've entered the information, the program will produce a song that you can edit or use as it is. ____(B)____, computer-generated imagery (commonly known as CGI) has opened up new possibilities in the music industry. Virtual influencers with extremely realistic faces, bodies, and voices have already released several songs. Some of them have many followers on social media, just like human singers. These types of virtual musicians are able to speak and move realistically with the help of their human creators.

15 윗글의 밑줄 친 우리말과 일치하도록 조건에 맞게 영작하시오.

조건
1. not only ~ but also를 사용할 것
2. art, music이 포함되도록 할 것

→ AI programs may lead to changes _____

_____.

16 윗글의 빈칸 (A)와 (B)에 들어갈 말이 바르게 짝지어진 것은?

	(A)		(B)
①	In short	···	Therefore
②	In fact	···	Accordingly
③	As a result	···	However
④	For example	···	Furthermore
⑤	On the other hand	···	Consequently

Many AI programs are open to the public, ___(A)___ means they can be used freely and conveniently. However, these programs have sparked a debate over their impact on humans. Since AI has the potential to learn skills and perform them better than humans, some people view it as a threat. They worry that AI will replace humans in more and more areas. There are also concerns ___(B)___ AI may ⓐ imitate the styles of human artists without their consent. On the other hand, others think that AI cannot ⓑ exceed human imagination and that it is still dependent on human assistance. This is because the data that AI uses can have flaws or limitations. A dependence on imperfect data with little ⓒ diversity eventually limits the output of AI programs. Human imagination, on the other hand, ___(C)___.

What kind of future do you think lies ahead of us? Will more people use AI programs to boost their creativity and productivity? Or will people grow tired of the limitations of AI tools? AI provides many benefits and new opportunities. What we need to do is figure out how to use AI tools ⓓ ethically and think about how humans and AI can ⓔ collaborate.

17 윗글의 밑줄 친 부분에 대한 영어 뜻풀이가 바르지 않은 것은?

① ⓐ to copy the way something looks or behaves

② ⓑ to be greater than something in number or amount

③ ⓒ public disagreement about something

④ ⓓ in a way that follows moral beliefs

⑤ ⓔ to work together in order to achieve something

18 윗글의 빈칸 (A)와 (B)에 알맞은 말을 한 단어로 쓰시오.

(A) → _____

(B) → _____

19 윗글의 빈칸 (C)에 들어갈 말로 가장 적절한 것은?

① requires cooperation with AI

② has no limits or boundaries

③ needs instruction and correction

④ will finally imitate the output of AI

⑤ is imperfect and risky to depend on

The story begins in a magical place, the Land of Oz. In the musical, Elphaba and Glinda first meet at university. Elphaba was born with green skin and usually stays away from others. Because of her unusual appearance and cold personality, she has very few friends. Meanwhile, Glinda has a very kind personality, which makes her quite popular. At first, Elphaba and Glinda do not get along. However, as they get to know and learn about each other, they become close friends. Elphaba has exceptional magical powers, and some other characters try to take advantage of this. Glinda and Elphaba's friendship is continuously challenged in the story. Nevertheless, in the end, their friendship wins. Every relationship has its ups and downs, so I could easily relate to the main characters.

20 윗글의 목적으로 가장 적절한 것은?

① 관람한 뮤지컬에 관한 자신의 감상을 소개하기 위해

② 성향이 다른 사람 사이의 친분 형성이 어려운 이유를 설명하기 위해

③ 다양성을 존중하는 대학 문화 형성을 설득하기 위해

④ 뮤지컬 제작에서 주인공 선정의 어려움을 설명하기 위해

⑤ 제작에 참여한 뮤지컬의 관람을 홍보하기 위해

21 윗글의 내용과 일치하는 것은?

① 이야기의 제목은 'The Land of Oz'이다.

② Elphaba와 Glinda는 고등학교에서 처음 만났다.

③ Elphaba는 독특한 외모로 태어났지만 다정한 성품을 지녔다.

④ Elphaba와 Glinda는 만나자마자 친한 친구가 되었다.

⑤ Elphaba는 특별한 마법의 힘을 지니고 있었다.

[22~23] 다음 글을 읽고, 물음에 답하시오.

Of course, I cannot review a musical (A) with / without talking about the songs. *Wicked* has many great songs, but there are two that I especially like. "Defying Gravity" is the most famous song in the musical. It comes at a key turning point in the story. Elphaba used to admire a wizard, but one day she finds out that he has a(n) (B) evil / virtuous plan and can't be trusted anymore. She sings about her determination to fight against him. She shows her true powers and rises into the air on her broom _____. She sings that she will not let people bring her down (C) anymore / no more . Her powerful voice fascinated me. When the song ended, the entire audience clapped enthusiastically.

22 윗글의 빈칸에 들어갈 말로 가장 적절한 것은?

① as she looked into his eyes
② while singing this song
③ as if she were a bird
④ that was made from a magic tree
⑤ while shocking the audience

23 (A), (B), (C)의 각 네모 안에서 문맥에 맞는 낱말로 가장 적절한 것은?

	(A)		(B)		(C)
①	with	…	evil	…	anymore
②	with	…	virtuous	…	anymore
③	without	…	evil	…	anymore
④	without	…	virtuous	…	no more
⑤	without	…	evil	…	no more

[24~25] 다음 글을 읽고, 물음에 답하시오.

The exciting story and beautiful songs of Wicked are accompanied by beautiful visuals. First, the costumes were incredible. In one scene, we see the people of Oz wearing unique clothes. I couldn't believe the detail and beauty of the masks, wigs, and dresses. Furthermore, all kinds of tricks invited me into the magical world. I really enjoyed noticing the symbols used in the performance. For example, a huge dragon-shaped device was hanging above the stage. 그것은 Elphaba나 Glinda가 선택을 내릴 때마다 움직이는 것처럼 보였다. I think using these visual effects made the musical more exciting.

In my opinion, the musical *Wicked* is an incredible work. It has great music and is visually impressive. It also has a strong plot that kept me engaged from beginning to end. I highly recommend this show to anyone interested in musicals. You will be able to explore the themes of friendship and personal change in a magical setting.

24 윗글의 내용과 일치하지 <u>않는</u> 것은?

① 〈위키드〉는 이야기가 흥미롭고 노래가 아름답다.
② 오즈의 사람들은 독특한 의상을 입고 있다.
③ 정교하게 만든 가면과 가발에 필자는 감동되었다.
④ 거대한 용 모양의 장치가 무대 중앙에 놓여 있다.
⑤ 필자는 뮤지컬을 좋아하는 사람들에게 〈위키드〉를 추천한다.

25 윗글의 밑줄 친 우리말과 일치하도록 조건에 맞게 영작하시오.

> 조건
> 1. seem to를 사용할 것
> 2. whenever를 사용할 것
> 3. 다음 표현을 사용할 것: make a choice

→ _____

_____

NE 능률

어휘서의 표준,
대한민국 NO.1 어휘 학습서

1100 만부
대한민국 판매 1위

어원으로 쉽게 외우는 고등 어휘의 시작

능률 VOCA
어원편

BEIJING YULE VOCA
THE ORIGINAL
SINCE 1983

● 내신/수능/모의고사 빈출 어휘 수록
● 파생어 포함 총 **4000**여개 어휘 수록

NE능률 영어교육연구소 지음

워크북 제공 (별책)
휴대용 mini 능률VOCA 증정

무료 MP3 파일 제공
www.nebooks.co.kr

CC
CLASS CARD로
암기효과 UP!

교재구성
미리
보기

1 교육부 지정 주요 어휘 수록
교육부 지정 중고등 교과 어휘 및
EBS 교재들에 사용된 주요 기출 어휘 수록

2 풍부한 어휘 확장
각 어휘의 파생어, 유/반의어 수록과
어휘의 실제적 쓰임을 잘 보여주는 예문 제시로 어휘력 확장

3 체계적이고 완벽한 암기력 향상
암기 효과를 극대화 시켜주는 클래스 카드 QR과
워크북 및 휴대가 편리한 mini 능률 VOCA제공

BOOK LIST

고등

도/서/목/록

어휘 · 문법 · 구문

능률VOCA

대한민국 어휘서의 표준

어원편 Lite | 어원편 | 고교기본 | 고교필수 2000 |
수능완성 2200 | 숙어 | 고난도

GRAMMAR ZONE

대한민국 영문법 교재의 표준

입문 | 기초 | 기본 1 | 기본 2 | 종합 (각 Workbook 별매)

필히 통하는 시리즈

시험에 필히 통하는 고등 영문법과 서술형

필히 통하는 고등 영문법 기본편 | 실력편
필히 통하는 고등 서술형 기본편 | 실전편

문제로 마스터하는 고등영문법

고등학생을 위한 문법 연습의 길잡이

천문장

구문이 독해로 연결되는 해석 공식

입문 | 기본 | 완성

능률 기본 영어

최신 수능과 내신을 위한 고등 영어 입문서

내신
백신,

정답 및 해설

고등　기출문제집
Common
English 1

민병천

내신 백신

정답 및 해설

고등 기출문제집

Common English 1

민병천

LESSON 01 Getting to Know Yourself

교과서 어휘 익히기 .... pp. 8-9

STEP 1

01 영감을 주다, 격려하다	25 lecture
02 결함, 결점	26 attitude
03 A를 B보다 선호하다	27 slam
04 기분	28 aggressive
05 혼란스러운	29 independence
06 갈등, 분쟁	30 appropriate
07 조합, 결합	31 from time to time
08 ~을 다루다, 처리하다	32 proactive
09 영향을 미치다	33 fist
10 참여, 관계	34 instead of
11 중요하게, 상당히	35 verbally
12 성취하다, 이루다	36 strategy
13 강화하다, 심화시키다	37 physical
14 해결하다	38 violent
15 부당함, 불공평	39 recognize
16 ~으로 향하다	40 intense
17 영감을 주는, 고무적인	41 mention
18 특히, 특별히	42 sensitive
19 요인, 요소	43 in advance
20 꽉 쥐다	44 behavior
21 ~에 책임이 있다	45 focus on
22 정리하다	46 no longer
23 불리한 점	47 flushed
24 대처하다, 대응하다	48 adolenscent

STEP 2

A 01 ⓐ   02 ⓒ
B 01 ⓒ   02 ⓑ   03 ⓐ
C 01 possible   02 end
D 01 ⓒ   02 ⓐ   03 ⓑ

A draw는 '그리다, (주의를) 끌다, (돈을) 인출하다' 등의 뜻이 있다. 01에서는 '(주의를) 끌다'는 뜻으로, 02에서는 '(돈을) 인출하다'는 뜻으로 쓰였다.

B
01 deal with: ~을 다루다, 처리하다
02 focus on: ~에 집중하다
03 in advance: 미리, 사전에

C
01 possible reason: 가능성 있는 이유
02 end a relationship: 관계를 끝내다

D
01 independence(자립): ⓒ 자기 스스로를 돌볼 수 있는 자질
02 resolve(해결하다): ⓐ 문제나 어려움에 대한 해결책을 찾다
03 verbally(구두로): ⓑ 글이나 행동이 아닌 말로

교과서 핵심 대화문 .... pp. 10-11

Function 1 선호 표현하기
Check-Up ☇ ⓒ
Function 2 예시 들기
Check-Up ☇ ⓒ

교과서 기타 대화문 .... p. 12

Q1 T	Q2 music

교과서 핵심 대화문 익히기 .... p. 13

01 I prefer finding restaurants to finding a place to stay
02 ②
03 3-2-1-4-5

교과서 핵심 문법 .... pp. 14-17

POINT 1 주격 관계대명사

Q 1 that   2 who   3 that
Check-Up ☇
01 (1) who (2) which (3) which (4) which
02 (1) They need a person who[that] is good at programming.
(2) The movie which[that] my uncle recommended to me was wonderful.
(3) Helen Keller is a social educator whom[that] Dora admires the most.
(4) Megan is a veterinarian whose animal hospital is next to my office.
03 ①, ④
04 (1) that you are looking at were taken

(2) was given to the actor who[that] played the detective

(3) I'm looking for shoes which[that] go well

(4) the ring which he had given

01 (1) 선행사가 사람인 주격 관계대명사

(2) 선행사가 사물인 주격 관계대명사

(3), (4) 선행사가 사물인 목적격 관계대명사

02 (1) 선행사가 사람인 주격 관계대명사, (2) 선행사가 사물인 목적격 관계대명사, (3) 선행사가 사람인 목적격 관계대명사, (4) 선행사가 사람인 소유격 관계대명사를 사용하여 연결한다.

03 [보기]에서 that은 주격 관계대명사로 쓰인다.

①, ④ 주격 관계대명사

② 동사의 목적어절을 이끄는 접속사

③ 동격을 나타내는 접속사

⑤ 진주어절을 이끄는 접속사

04 (1) 관계사절의 them을 삭제

(2) 선행사 the actor 뒤에 관계대명사가 필요

(3) 선행사가 사물이므로 관계사는 which나 that

(4) 관계사절의 it을 삭제

POINT 2 It ~ to부정사

Q 1 It   2 to rely   3 for

Check-Up

01 (1) It is a great pleasure to walk my dog.

(2) It is never a waste of time to learn a new skill.

(3) it is more common to communicate via cell phones

(4) It was amazing to watch the sunset from the mountaintop.

02 (1) difficult for us to finish the project

(2) careless of you to lose your mother's ring

(3) important for children to learn from failure

(4) wonderful to travel around the world

03 ①

01 가주어 It을 주어 자리에 쓰고, 진주어인 to부정사구는 문장의 맨 뒤로 보낸다.

02 진주어인 to부정사의 의미상 주어를 나타낼 때는 일반적으로 「for+목적격」을 쓴다.

(2)의 careless와 같이 사람의 성질을 나타내는 형용사와 쓰일 때에는 「of+목적격」을 쓴다.

03 to부정사의 의미상 주어를 나타낼 때 보통 「for+목적격」을 쓰지만, 사람의 성격이나 성질을 나타내는 형용사 뒤에서는 「of+목적격」을 사용한다. ① foolish 뒤에서는 of를 써야 한다.

교과서 본문 익히기 ❶ .... pp. 24-26

01 find yourself suddenly feeling

02 the next moment, rolling your eyes at

03 are getting too upset

04 stress about everyday life

05 As a teen

06 a part that is responsible for

07 in development

08 lead you toward independence

09 At the same time, who you are

10 more sensitive to unfairness

11 with hormones

12 significantly affects

13 intensifies your strong emotions

14 It is natural, there is something wrong

15 Anger can

16 angry but open conversation

17 so that it does not turn into

18 stop yourself from

19 in a productive way

20 Ask yourself

21 better understand

22 How often

23 feel the most intense

24 anything in particular

25 focus on the causes

26 control my emotions

27 react and behave

28 how to deal with anger

29 behavior is a choice

30 The first step is

31 It is possible

32 increased heart rate

33 take action to reduce your anger

34 For example, before it gets too intense

35 the strategies mentioned above, proper coping skills for

36 Without the right coping skills

37 what is best for you, that come to your mind

38 advantages and disadvantages

39 many ways to solve a problem

40 that we all experience

41 By managing your anger, not the other way around

42 finding your true self

교과서 **본문 익히기 ②** ⋯⋯⋯⋯⋯⋯ pp. 27-29

01 feeling	02 rolling
03 upset	04 everyday
05 like	06 that, controlling
07 development	08 lead
09 who you are	10 sensitive
11 flowing	12 affects
13 intensifies	14 to feel
15 useful	16 resolve
17 so that	18 yourself
19 productive	20 questions
21 better	22 often
23 feel	24 directed
25 instead of	26 control
27 How	28 socially
29 choice	30 physical
31 in	32 increased
33 reduce	34 ending
35 mentioned	36 Without
37 what, writing	38 solutions
39 to solve	40 that
41 boss	42 taking

교과서 **본문 익히기 ③** ⋯⋯⋯⋯⋯⋯ pp. 30-32

01 yourself	02 slamming
03 are getting	04 that, controlling
05 in	06 lead, creativity
07 confused	08 more sensitive
09 intensifies	10 to feel, something
11 sometimes	12 but, between
13 is to manage, does not	14 from feeling
15 Rather	16 yourself
17 better understand	18 feel
19 instead of	20 how to
21 The first	22 It
23 flushed	24 take action
25 ending	26 may not, to find
27 becoming	28 taking, drawing, that
29 compare	30 to solve
31 that	32 By, not
33 taking	

교과서 **본문 외 지문 분석** ⋯⋯⋯⋯⋯⋯ p. 33

Q Telling jokes.
Check-Up ☙
01 make me unique
02 my interests
03 interested in
04 My daily habits
05 write about my feelings
06 helps me reduce
07 have a special talent
08 good at telling
09 make my classmates laugh

내신 **1등급 어휘 공략** ⋯⋯⋯⋯⋯⋯ pp. 34-35

01 ①	02 ⑤	03 ②	04 ③
05 ③	06 ②	07 ③	08 ①

01 (A) '(일단) ~하면'이라는 의미의 접속사 once가 적절하다.
(B) '영감을 주다, 동기를 부여하다'라는 의미의 동사 inspire가 알맞다.
(C) 앞문장의 one day와 함께 '하루는 ~, 또 하루는 …'이라는 구문이 되도록 another를 써야 한다.
오답 (A) since: ~ 이래로(접속사)
(B) perspire: 땀을 흘리다

02 자신이 이룬 성취들을 자축하는 행동은 자신감을 ⑤ '줄이는' 게 아니라 '키워줄' 것이므로, decrease 대신 increase를 써야 자연스러운 글이 된다.

03 십 대 때 뇌의 발달에 따른 변화가 일으키는 것으로는 ② '의존성'이 아닌 '독립성'이므로, independence를 써야 자연스럽다.

04 (A) from time to time: 때때로, 가끔
(B) '갈등을 해결하다'라는 의미이므로 resolve가 적절하다.
(C) '생산적인'이라는 뜻을 가진 productive가 문맥상 자연스럽다.
오답 (B) dissolve: 녹이다, 끝내다
(C) progressive: 진보적인

05 (A) '가장 강렬한 분노'라는 뜻이므로 intense가 알맞다.
(B) 해결책이 아닌 분노의 '원인'이라는 문맥에 맞게 causes가 적절하다.
(C) '행동하다'라는 뜻의 behave가 자연스럽다.
오답 (A) instant: 즉각적인
(B) effects: 결과
(C) behalf: 이익

06 ② 이어지는 내용(빨라진 심박수, 붉어진 얼굴, 꽉 쥔 주먹)은 '신체적' 표시이므로 mental이 아니라 physical을 써야 한다.

07 ③ '가능한 해결책'이란 뜻으로 possible을 써야 한다.

08 (A) compose: 작곡하다

(B) journal: 일기

(C) special: 특별한

오답 (A) comprise: 구성되다, 구성하다

(B) journey: 여행

(C) specific: 구체적인

내신 1등급 어법 공략
pp. 36-37

01 ①	02 ⑤	03 ⑤	04 ①
05 ③	06 ④	07 ⑤	08 ②

01 ① 선행사 things를 수식하는 주격 관계대명사절이므로 동사는 makes가 아닌 make가 되어야 한다.

오답 ② 「동사(make)+목적어(me)+목적격 보어(unique)」 구조이다.

③ help는 준사역동사로 목적격 보어 자리에 동사가 올 때 동사원형이나 to부정사로 쓸 수 있다.

④ be good at: ~을 잘하다

⑤ make는 사역동사로, 목적격 보어 자리에 동사원형을 쓴다.

02 (A) '~동안'이라는 기간을 나타내는 전치사는 for이다.

(B) loving의 의미상 주어가 you이므로 목적어로는 재귀대명사가 적절하다.

(C) inspire+목적어+to부정사: ~가 …하도록 영감을 주다

오답 (A) since는 '~부터'라는 의미로, 뒤에는 구체적인 때를 나타내는 말을 써야 한다.

03 (A) 선행사가 사물일 때의 주격 관계대명사는 which이다.

(B) 앞에 쓰인 independence, social engagement와 함께 toward의 목적어 형태가 되어야 하므로 명사를 써야 한다.

(C) 문장의 주어가 combination이므로 동사도 3인칭 단수에 맞는 intensifies가 알맞다.

오답 (C) 동사 바로 앞에 복수 형태인 factors가 있지만 of these factors는 combination을 꾸며 주는 전치사구이므로 주어는 combination이다.

04 ① 문장의 맨앞에 쓰인 It이 가주어이므로, 진주어 자리에는 to부정사 형태(to feel)가 알맞다.

05 ③ 진주어인 to부정사구(to recognize those signs in advance)를 대신하여 문장 앞에 쓰는 가주어는 It이다.

오답 ① how+to부정사: ~하는 방법

② 보어 역할을 하는 동명사

④ 「과거분사+명사」 형태이다.

⑤ try V-ing: ~해보다

06 (A) find의 목적격 보어로 쓰이고 있으므로 현재분사 형태가 알맞다.

(B) 선행사를 포함한 관계대명사 what이 알맞다.

(C) 전치사의 목적어로는 동명사를 써야 한다.

오답 (B) 접속사 that이 이끄는 명사절도 동사의 목적어가 될 수 있지만, 이때 that 뒤에는 완전한 절이 와야 한다.

07 (A) an emotion이 선행사이므로 사물을 선행사로 할 수 있는 관계대명사 that을 써야 한다.

(B) 전치사 by의 목적어이므로 동명사 형태가 적절하다.

(C) 앞에 쓰인 finding과 병렬 연결로 전치사 in의 목적어 역할을 하는 동명사가 알맞다.

오답 (A) whom은 사람을 선행사로 하는 목적격 관계대명사이다.

08 ② inspiring은 '영감을 주는'이라는 능동의 의미이고, inspired는 '영감을 받은'이라는 수동의 의미이다. 사람이 '영감을 받은' 것이므로 현재분사가 아닌 과거분사 형태(inspired)가 알맞다.

내신 1등급 실전 1회
pp. 38-41

01 ⑤	02 finding restaurants	03 ②
04 ⑤	05 ④	06 ⑤	07 ⑤
08 ④	09 ④		
10 ⓐ to feel angry from time to time ⓑ your anger		
11 ①	12 ④	13 ④	14 ⑤
15 ①			

01 ⑤ 엄마가 사진을 원할 거라고는 했지만 사진을 잘 찍는지는 알 수 없다.

오답 ① 남학생은 여학생의 남자 형제이다.

② 그들은 전주 여행 계획을 세우고 있다.

③ 그들은 엄마의 생신을 축하할 것이다.

④ 여학생은 숙소를 알아볼 것이다.

02 선호하는 것을 나타낼 때 prefer A to B의 표현을 쓴다. 앞에서 식당을 찾는 것과 머물 곳을 찾는 것 중 무엇을 하겠냐고 여학생이 물었고, 남학생의 말을 들은 후 여학생이 그럼 자신이 숙소를 찾겠다고 했으므로, 빈칸에 들어갈 말은 '식당을 찾는 것'이다.

03 주어진 문장의 It이 가리키는 것은 (B) 앞의 Self-love이다. 그러므로 주어진 문장은 (B) 자리에 들어가는 것이 가장 자연스럽다.

04 ⑤ 전치사 like의 목적어로 쓰이므로 동명사 형태인 not being late로 써야 한다.

05 (B) 직업에만 초점을 두면 그 직업을 갖게 된 후 더 이상 동기부여가 되지 않는다.

(C) 그러므로 '행동'을 꿈꾸어야 한다.

(A) 그러면 항상 추구해야 할 일이 있다.

오답 각 단락의 첫문장에 있는 연결어에 주의한다.

06 (A) 주어가 you이므로 목적어로는 '자기 자신'이라는 뜻의 재귀대명사 yourself를 써야 한다.

(B) '다음 순간에는'이라는 의미이므로 next가 적절하다.

(C) 부정적인 의미가 내포된 upset(속상해하는)이 알맞다.

오답 (B) one ~ the other는 '하나는 ~하고 나머지 하나는 …하다'라는 의미이다.

07 왕성한 뇌의 성장과 감정 변화, 호르몬 생성 등 다양한 요인이 십대의 감정 변화를 일으킨다고 설명하고 있으므로, 글의 주제는 ⑤ '왜 십 대들은 강렬한 감정이 생기는지'가 가장 적절하다.

오답 ① 언제 두뇌가 가장 많이 발달하는지

② 감정을 관할하는 뇌의 부위

③ 십 대들은 어떻게 문제를 극복하는지
④ 스트레스가 신체에 미치는 영향

08 선행사를 수식하는 주격 관계대명사로 쓰인 that은 ④이다.
오답 ① 목적어로 쓰인 명사절을 이끄는 접속사
②, ③ 동격의 명사절을 이끄는 접속사
⑤ so ~ that: 너무 ~해서 …하다

09 문장이 Rather(오히려)라는 말로 시작하므로 앞의 문장과 대조되는 내용이 필요하다.
④ '분노를 생산적인 방식으로 표현하다'가 가장 적절하다.
오답 ① 분노를 분출하다
② 분노를 증오로 바꾸다
③ 자신의 분노가 실제가 아니라고 말하다
⑤ 친구들과 열린 의사소통을 연습하다

10 ⓐ 가주어 역할을 하며 진짜 주어는 뒤에 나오는 to부정사구이다.
ⓑ 바로 앞에 쓰인 명사 your anger를 지칭한다.

11 분노를 다스리기 위해 당신은 우선 신체적 징후를 파악하고, 그것을 줄이기 위해 조치를 취해야 한다.

12 ⓓ reduce는 '줄이다'라는 뜻이지만, intensify는 '강화하다'라는 의미이다.
오답 ⓐ deal with: 다루다, manage: 관리하다
ⓑ choice: 선택, decision: 결정
ⓒ recognize: 인지하다, notice: 알아차리다
ⓔ intense: 치열한, fierce: 격렬한

13 ④ 분노는 우리 모두가 느끼는 감정이라고(Anger is an emotion that we all experience.) 했으므로, 일치하지 않는 진술이다.

14 (A) 문맥상 '~ 없이는'이라는 의미의 전치사 without이 필요하다.
(B) come to mind: (생각이) 떠오르다
(C) 방법을 나타내는 전치사 by가 적절하다.

15 (A) 선행사 a few things를 수식하는 주격 관계대명사 that이 알맞다.
(B) help는 준사역동사이므로 목적격 보어 자리에 오는 동사는 동사원형(reduce)이나 to부정사(to reduce) 형태로 써야 한다.
(C) 전치사 at의 목적어가 되는 동명사 형태가 적절하다.
오답 (A) what은 '~하는 것'이라는 의미로 선행사를 포함하는 관계대명사이다.

내신 1등급 실전 2회

pp. 42-45

01 ⑤	**02** ②	**03** ⑤	**04** ⓐ Self-love
ⓑ Your achievements		**05** ③	**06** ⑤
07 ②	**08** ①	**09** ④	**10** ③
11 ②	**12** ⑤	**13** ⑤	**14** ①
15 ①			

01 특정 직업으로 꿈 꾸지 말고 행동을 꿈꾸어야 삶에서 계속 지향할 것이 있다는 메시지의 글이므로 제목으로 가장 알맞은 것은 ⑤ '명사가 아니라 동사로 꿈을 꾸라'이다.

오답 ① 좋은 작가가 되기 위해 무엇을 해야 하는가?
② 다양한 직업이 당신을 기다리고 있다
③ 목표를 이루기 위해 계속 나아가라
④ 사람들에게 영감을 주어라, 세상에 영감을 주어라

02 (A) '그러니, 그러므로'의 의미가 있는 so나 therefore가 알맞은 연결어이다.
(B) '예를 들어'라는 의미의 for example이나 for instance가 적절하다.
오답 moreover, furthermore: 게다가, 더구나
on the contrary: 오히려, on the other hand: 반면
in other words: 다시 말해

03 자신을 사랑하는 방법으로 첫째, 자신의 재주와 능력을 떠올려 보고(①, ②, ③) 두 번째, 자신의 성취를 축하하라(④)고 했다.
⑤ '나는 위대한 무용가가 되고 싶다.'는 무관한 내용이다.
오답 ① 나는 우리 반에서 축구를 제일 잘한다.
② 나는 우리 집에 있는 것은 무엇이든 고칠 수 있다.
③ 나는 프로그래밍을 잘한다.
④ 나는 오늘 기타를 정말 열심히 연습해서 자랑스럽다.

04 ⓐ It은 앞문장의 Self-love를 가리키고, ⓑ They는 바로 앞에 쓰인 your achievements를 가리킨다.

05 (A) '책임이 있는'이라는 뜻의 responsible이 적절하다.
(B) lead A toward B: A를 B를 향해 이끌다
(C) '영향을 미치다'라는 뜻의 affects가 적절하다.
오답 (A) irresponsible: 무책임한 (C) effect: 영향, 결과

06 ⑤ 문제를 해결하고 감정을 통제하는 뇌의 부위가 계속 발전하는 단계라고 했다.
오답 ① lead you toward independence, social engagement, and creativity
② confused about who you are
③ sensitive to unfairness
④ flowing with hormones

07 단락의 마지막 부분에서 스스로에게 몇 가지 질문을 하면 자신의 화를 이해하는 데 도움이 될 거라 했으므로, 뒤에 이어지는 내용은 ② '자신의 화에 관해 스스로에게 할 질문'일 것이다.
오답 ① 화를 잘 다스릴 조언들
③ 화난 감정이 당신에게 미칠 영향
④ 화가 날 때 신체에 나타나는 징후
⑤ 화를 표현하는 것과 통제하는 것의 차이

08 ① 맨앞에 가주어 It이 쓰였으므로 진주어로 to부정사구(to feel)나 명사절(that you feel)을 써야 한다.
오답 ② something과 같은 부정대명사는 형용사가 뒤에서 꾸며준다.
③ so that: ~할 수 있도록
④ stop A from V-ing: A가 ~하는 것을 막다
⑤ better는 부사 well의 비교급으로 동사를 수식하고 있다.

09 ④ 나는 친구와 얘기하고 나면 화가 덜 난다.: 관련된 질문은 제시되어 있지 않다.
오답 ① 나는 매일 화가 나는 것 같다. → 첫 번째 질문의 답

② 나는 사람들이 약속을 지키지 않을 때 특히 화가 난다. → 두 번째 질문의 답

③ 나는 종종 남동생한테 화가 난다. → 세 번째 질문의 답

⑤ 나는 화가 나면 그 상황으로부터 벗어난다. → 여섯 번째 질문의 답

10 the other way around은 '반대 (상황)'이라는 뜻이다. 감정의 주도권을 갖는 것의 반대는 ④ '감정이 당신의 삶을 주도하다'이다.

오답 ① 당신의 기분이 완전히 당신의 통제 하에 있다

② 당신은 감정을 잘 관리할 수 있다

④ 당신은 분노에 압도되지 않는다

⑤ 당신은 쉽게 화내지 않게 스스로를 멈춘다

11 주어진 문장은 분노의 신체적 징후에 관한 이야기가 시작되는 것이므로 (B)에 들어가는 것이 자연스럽다. (B) 뒤에 오는 문장의 those signs는 주어진 문장의 the physical signs of anger를 가리킨다.

12 ⑤ '합의에 도달하기' 전에 대화를 끝내라는 내용은 자연스럽지 않다.

오답 ① 대화가 너무 격해지다

② 당신이 너무 격분하다

③ 당신이 이성을 잃다

④ 대화가 분쟁으로 변하다

13 (A) '언급된'이라는 수동의 의미이므로 과거분사가 알맞다.

(B) find의 목적격 보어로 쓰이는 현재분사가 알맞다.

(C) taking, drawing과 같은 동명사 형태가 알맞다.

14 자신의 관심사, 습관, 그리고 재능이 어떻게 자신을 특별하게 만드는가 설명하는 글이므로, 글의 주제는 ① '나를 특별하게 만드는 것들'이 가장 적절하다.

오답 ② 나를 행복하게 하는 특별한 재능

③ 일기 쓰기의 중요성

④ 스트레스를 줄이는 나만의 고유한 방법

⑤ 음악과 정신 건강

15 ① 이어지는 글의 흐름으로 보아 few(거의 없는)가 아니라 a few(몇 가지)가 알맞다.

내신 1등급 실전 3회
pp. 46-49

01 ⑤	**02** ④	**03** ①	**04** ④
05 ③	**06** Write down whatever comes to mind.		
07 ⑤	**08** ①	**09** ②	**10** ③
11 ①	**12** ④	**13** ②	**14** ②
15 (1) unique (2) talent			

01 주어진 문장은 '네가 수업을 더 즐긴다면 더 많이 배울 것이다'라는 의미이므로, 학생이 더 좋아하는 것이 무엇인지 묻고 답한 뒤 '음악 수업을 들으라'는 충고의 말 뒤인 (E)에 오는 것이 가장 자연스럽다.

02 대화에서 남학생의 희망 직업은 직접 언급되지 않았고, 진로를 생각해 컴퓨터 수업이 도움이 될 것 같다고 말하는 것으로 보아 ④ '남학생은 음악가가 되는 것을 고려하고 있다.'는 대화와 일치하지 않는다.

오답 ① 남학생은 Smith 선생님과 이야기하고 싶어 한다.

② 남학생은 음악과 컴퓨터 수업 중에서 선택해야 한다.

③ 남학생은 컴퓨터보다 음악에 더 관심이 있다.

⑤ Smith 선생님은 남학생이 음악 수업을 들어야 한다고 추천한다.

03 빈칸 뒤에 주어지는 예시가, '작가가 되고 싶다' 대신 '재미있는 이야기로 사람들에게 영감을 주고 싶다'라고 말하라는 것이므로, ① '단순히 직업 말고 행동을 꿈꾸라'가 알맞은 말이다.

오답 ② 보다 상세한 직업명을 생각하라

③ 직업을 바꾸기 위해 계획을 세우라

④ 가능한 한 빨리 꿈 꾸기 시작하라

⑤ 작가가 되기 위해 많은 책을 읽으라

04 ④ something과 to work의 관계는 '지향하며 일할 무언가'이므로 work with가 아니라 work towards가 적절하다.

05 ③ 자기애는 자신의 행복을 일순위로 두는 것이다. (It also means that you put your happiness first.)

06 whatever는 anything that의 의미이다.

07 빈칸에는 화가 났을 때 문을 세게 닫는 것과 유사한 행동이 들어가는 것이 자연스럽다.

⑤ '머리로 숫자를 세다'는 화가 났을 때의 동작으로 맞지 않다.

오답 ① 분노를 표출하다

② 책을 바닥에 던지다

③ 부모님에게 눈을 치켜뜨다

④ 형제들에게 소리를 지르다

08 (A) 빈칸이 포함된 문장과 앞의 문장이 서로 대조되는 관계이므로 역접의 의미를 가진 however가 적절하다.

(B) 앞문장에 덧붙여 부가되는 상황을 나타내는 furthermore가 알맞다.

오답 ② thus: 그래서, in addition: 게다가

③ therefore: 그래서, nevertheless: 그럼에도 불구하고

④ in consequence: 그 결과, on the other hand: 반면에

⑤ unfortunately: 불행하게도, in short: 요컨대

09 ② 화가 나는 것은 괜찮지만, 분노를 건강한 방식으로 표출하는 것이 중요하다.

오답 ① 자신의 분노에 관한 질문을 하는 것이 중요하다.

③ 분노는 친구들과 의사소통하는 강력한 방법이 될 수 있다.

④ 분노를 조절하는 것이 보다 나은 정신 건강을 위한 첫 번째 단계이다.

⑤ 분노는 어떤 식으로든 관리되어서는 안 되는 자연스러운 인간 감정이다.

10 from time to time: 때때로

stop A from V -ing: A가 ~하는 것을 막다

11 화가 났을 때 어떻게 그것을 인지하고 분노를 조절하는지 설명하는 글이므로, 글의 어조로는 ① '설명하는, 유익한'이 적절하다.

오답 ② 동정적인 ③ 회의적인 ④ 흥겨운 ⑤ 낙관적인

12 (A) 뒤에 쓰인 형용사 appropriate를 꾸며 주는 부사의 형태가 적절하다.

(B) 가주어 it이 앞에 쓰였으므로 진주어인 to부정사 형태로 와야 한다.

(C) taking과 함께 try의 목적어 역할을 하므로 동명사 형태가 적절하다.

13 첫 문장에 '위에서 언급한 전략(the strategies mentioned above)'이라는 표현이 나오므로, 이 글의 앞에는 ② '당신의 분노를 진정시킬 방법'이 설명되었을 것이다.

오답 ① 십 대의 분노를 유발하는 요인들
③ 화가 나는 것의 좋은 점
④ 당신이 화가 난 것을 의미하는 신체 징후
⑤ 감정을 관리하는 것의 중요성

14 ② 선행사 things를 꾸며 주는 주격 관계대명사 that이 적절하다. what은 선행사를 포함한 관계대명사이다.

15 나를 특별하게 만드는 세 가지는 나의 음악에 대한 관심, 일기를 쓰는 습관, 그리고 농담을 하는 나의 재능이다.

내신 1등급 수능형 고난도

01 ①	02 ⑤	03 ②	04 ①
05 ②	06 ⑤	07 ③	08 ④
09 ③	10 ④	11 ③	12 ③
13 ①	14 ②	15 ②	

[01-02] 해석

여러분은 무엇을 꿈꾸나요? 혹시 작가가 되고 싶다는 꿈을 꾸고 있을지도 모르겠군요. 하지만 단지 직함에만 초점을 맞춘다면, 그 목표를 달성한 후에는 공허함을 느낄 수도 있습니다. 대신, 여러분이 만들어 내고 싶은 영향을 꿈꿔보세요. 예를 들어, "작가가 되고 싶다"고 말하기보다는 "이야기를 들려주며 다른 사람들에게 영감을 주고 싶다"고 말하는 것입니다. 이런 접근법은 지속적인 목적 의식을 유지하도록 도와줍니다. 어떤 날에는 아이들을 위한 책을 쓰고, 다른 어떤 날에는 동기 부여 연설을 할 수도 있을 것입니다. 그렇다면, 여러분의 꿈은 무엇인가요?

01 무엇이 되는 것보다는 목적에 가치를 둔 꿈을 꾸는 것이 바람직하다는 내용이므로, 알맞은 주제는 ① '목적에 집중하는 목표 설정'이다.

오답 ② 꿈을 가지는 것의 중요성
③ 아이들에게 영감을 주는 이야기 쓰기
④ 최고의 직업을 고르는 방법
⑤ 공허감 극복을 위한 충고

02 (A) achieve a goal: 목표를 성취하다
(B) through: ~을 통하여
(C) motivational: 동기를 부여하는
오답 (A) arrive: 도착하다
(B) though: ~이긴 하지만
(C) monotonous: 단조로운

[03-04] 해석

동기 부여 연설가로서 저는 십대들이 종종 다른 사람들과 자신을 비교하며 자신의 결점을 부끄러워한다는 것을 발견했습니다. 여러분도 같은 문제를 겪고 있나요? 그렇다면 자기애를 실천하는 것이 중요합니다. 자기애란 자신이 사랑하는 사람들을 소중히 여기는 만큼 자신을 소중히 여기고, 자신의 행복을 우선으로 두는 것을 의미합니다. 자기애를 기르는 방법은 다음과 같습니다. 첫째, 자신의 기술과 재능을 되돌아보세요. 여러분은 자신이 얼마나 많은 기술과 재능을 가지고 있는지에 놀랄 것입니다. 둘째, 크고 작은 성취를 축하하세요. 이는 자신감을 높이고 위험을 감수할 수 있는 용기를 줄 것입니다. 자기애는 있는 그대로의 자신을 받아들이는 것을 의미한다는 것을 기억하세요.

03 ② to practice self-love가 진주어이므로 주어 자리에는 that이 아닌 가주어 it을 써야 한다.

오답 ① feel ashamed: 부끄럽게 여기다
③ as much as: 원급 비교
④ encourage+목적어+to부정사: ~에게 …하라고 용기를 북돋우다
⑤ as you are: 있는 그대로

04 문맥상 ① '당신이 얼마나 많은 기량과 재능을 가지고 있는지'에 놀라게 될 거라는 내용이 가장 자연스럽다.

오답 ② 당신이 왜 기량과 재능을 개발하지 않았는지
③ 어떤 기량과 재능을 개발할지
④ 당신의 기량과 재능을 어떻게 강화해야 할지
⑤ 새로운 기량과 재능을 어디에서 배울 수 있는지

[05-06] 해석

십 대인 당신은 성숙하다고 느낄 수 있지만, 실제로는 뇌가 아직 발달 중이다. 십 대 시절에는 문제를 해결하고 감정을 조절하는 역할을 하는 뇌의 부분이 여전히 성숙해지고 있다. 이러한 뇌의 변화는 독립심, 사회적 활동, 창의력을 촉진한다. 그러나 동시에 정체성에 대한 혼란을 초래하고 불공정함에 대한 민감도를 높일 수 있다. 또한, 호르몬의 변화는 기분에 상당한 영향을 미칠 수 있다. 이러한 요인들의 결합은 여러분의 강렬한 감정을 더욱 증폭시킬 수 있다.

05 ② 감정 통제에 관여하는 뇌 부위의 성장이 완료되는 것이 아니라, 여전히 성장하고 있다. (During your teenage years, the part that is responsible for solving problems and controlling emotions is still maturing.)

06 (A) the part를 꾸며 주는 형용사절을 이끄는 주격 관계대명사 that이 적절하다.
(B) 소유격 your 뒤에 오는 명사 sensitivity가 알맞은 형태이다.
(C) 주어 combination이 단수이므로 intensifies가 적절하다.

[07-08] 해석

당신은 때때로 화가 날 수 있다. 이것은 개인적인 결함을 나타내는 것이 아니다. 경우에 따라 화는 열린 의사소통같이 갈등을 해결하는 긍정적 방법을 가져오기도 한다. 핵심은 화가 공격성이나 폭력으로 변하지 않도록 관리하는 것이다. 이는 화를 억누르라는 의미가 아니다. 대신, 건설적으로 화를 표현하라. 자신의 감정을 되돌아보며 화가 나는 이유를 더 잘 이해하려고 노력하라.

07 ③을 제외한 나머지는 모두 '화가 나는 것은 자연스러운 일이다.'라는 의미이다.
③은 '화를 조절하는 것이 중요하다.'라는 뜻이다.

① 때때로 화가 날 수 있다.

② 화를 경험하는 것은 정상이다.

④ 화가 나는 것은 자연스럽다.

⑤ 당신이 화가 나는 것은 이상한 일이 아니다.

08 분노는 자연스러운 인간의 감정이며, 그것이 해롭게 변하는 것을 막기 위해 분노를 관리하는 것이 중요하다.

[09-10] 해석

스스로에게 자신의 분노에 관해 질문하라, 그러면 그것을 이해하는 데 도움이 될 것이다.

스스로에게 물어볼 질문들

√ 나는 얼마나 자주 화를 내는가?

√ 어떤 상황에서 내가 가장 화가 나는가?

√ 내가 화를 내는 특정한 사람이나 대상이 있는가?

√ 나는 화가 난 이유에 집중하는가, 아니면 해결책에 집중하는가?

√ 내가 화가 났을 때, 내 감정을 관리할 수 있는가?

√ 화가 날 때 나는 어떻게 행동하는가?

09 주어진 질문의 목적은 ③ '개인들이 자신의 분노를 이해하고 관리하는 데 도움을 주기 위해'이다.

오답 ① 화를 내는 것의 긍정적 측면을 설명하기 위해

② 개인들이 정신적 건강을 얻도록 지도하기 위해

④ 감정적 문제를 통제하는 다양한 방법을 제안하기 위해

⑤ 강렬한 감정을 유발하는 뇌의 특정 부위를 소개하기 위해

10 주어진 질문에서 ④ 분노의 강도를 묻고 있지는 않다.

오답 ① → 첫 번째 질문

② → 두 번째 질문

③ → 세 번째 질문

⑤ → 다섯 번째 질문

[11-12] 해석

화를 사회적으로 용인되는 방식으로 표현하는 법을 배우는 것이 중요하다. 화는 감정이지만, 행동은 선택이라는 것을 기억하라.

(B) 첫 번째 단계는 화가 났을 때 나타나는 신체적인 반응을 인식하는 것인데, 이러한 반응은 종종 미리 알아챌 수 있다.

(D) 이러한 반응에는 심박수 증가, 얼굴이 붉어짐, 주먹을 꽉 쥠 등이 포함된다.

(A) 이러한 신호를 인지했을 때, 화를 관리하기 위한 조치를 취하라.

(C) 예를 들어, 생각을 정리하기 위해 잠시 휴식을 취하거나, 대화가 격화되기 전에 대화를 끝낼 수 있다.

11 (B) 첫 번째 단계로, 화가 날 때 신체적 반응(physical reactions)를 인지하라고 한다.

(D) (B)에서 언급된 physical reactions를 구체적으로 예시 든다.

(A) (D)의 징후들을 인식한 후 조치를 취하라 하고,

(C) 그 조치를 예를 들어 설명한다.

12 ③ 앞문장을 부연 설명하며 콤마(,) 뒤에 쓰이는 계속적 용법의 관계대명사는 which이다. that은 계속적 용법으로 쓰지 않는다.

오답 ① 문장의 주어 역할을 하는 to부정사로, 앞에 가주어 It을 대신 쓰고 뒤에 쓰였다.

② 목적을 나타내는 부사적 용법의 to부정사이다.

④ take와 함께 조동사 could 뒤에 쓰인 동사원형이다.

⑤ '늘어난'이란 의미의 과거분사가 heart rate를 수식하고 있다.

[13-14] 해석

때로는 위에서 언급한 전략만으로는 충분하지 않을 수 있다. 따라서 자신의 특정 상황에 맞는 대처 기술을 찾아야 한다. 효과적인 대처 기술이 없으면 언어적이거나 심지어 신체적인 공격에 의존할 수 있다. 산책하기, 그림 그리기, 또는 일기 쓰기와 같은 다양한 전략을 탐구하여 자신에게 가장 잘 맞는 방법을 찾아보라. 또한, 문제에 대한 해결책을 브레인스토밍하고 그 장단점을 평가해 볼 수도 있다. 문제 해결 능력을 개발함으로써 분노에 의존하지 않고 문제를 해결할 수 있는 많은 방법이 있음을 깨닫게 될 것이다.

분노는 보편적인 감정이다. 분노를 효과적으로 관리함으로써 감정이 자신을 지배하지 않게 하고, 오히려 감정을 통제할 수 있다. 이것은 자기 발견과 삶의 주도권을 잡는 데 중요한 단계이다.

13 분노를 조절하는 다양한 방법을 시도하며 자신에게 맞는 방법을 찾는 것이 스스로를 파악하고 삶을 충만하게 하는 데 중요하다는 내용의 글이므로, ① '자기 자신만의 분노 조절 기술을 찾는 것이 중요하다.'가 요지로 가장 적절하다.

오답 ② 공격적인 말과 행동은 해롭다.

③ 분노를 다스리는 여러 기술이 있다.

④ 실외 활동은 당신의 화를 다스리는 좋은 방법이다.

⑤ 정신 건강을 위해 좋은 관계를 유지하라.

14 문맥상 '언어적이거나 신체적인 공격'이라는 표현이 적절하므로 ②는 mental이 아니라 physical을 써야 한다.

[15] 해석

나에게는 몇 가지 독특한 점이 있다. 친구들을 위해 음악을 작곡하는 것과 같은 나의 관심사가 나를 다른 사람들과 구분되게 만든다. 음악을 작곡할 수 있는 AI 프로그램이 있다. 감정을 일기에 기록하는 것과 같은 나의 일상적인 습관도 나를 독특하게 만든다. 이러한 습관은 스트레스를 관리하는 데 도움을 준다. 또한, 농담을 하고 다른 사람들을 웃게 만드는 나의 능력은 나를 돋보이게 하는 특별한 재능이다.

자신의 고유한 자질로 작곡과 같은 관심사, 일기 쓰기와 같은 일상의 습관, 사람들을 즐겁게 만드는 재능을 소개하는 글이다.

② '음악을 작곡할 수 있는 AI 프로그램이 있다.'는 글의 전체 흐름과 무관하다.

내신 1등급 서술형

pp. 54-56

01 ⓐ inspired

ⓑ doing

02 I want to inspire people by telling interesting stories.

03 loving yourself just like you love your friends and family, putting your happiness first

04 ⓐ whatever comes to mind

ⓑ how long the list is

ⓒ not being late for school

05 is a part that is responsible for solving problems and controlling your emotions

06 (A) (i)ndependence
(B) (s)ensitive
(C) (i)ntensifies

07 is natural to feel angry from time to time

08 your anger

09 Is my anger directed at anyone or anything in particular?

10 (A) with
(B) in

11 (1) an increased heart rate
(2) a flushed face
(3) the clenching of your fists

12 (1) ⓑ that[which]
(2) ⓕ laugh

13 (1) Coping
(2) developing

14 ⓐ that[which] come to your mind
ⓑ that[which] we all experience

01 ⓐ inspire는 '영감을 주다, 동기를 부여하다'라는 뜻이므로 I feel 뒤에는 '동기부여가 된'이라는 수동의 의미를 지닌 과거분사 형태를 써야 한다.
ⓒ 전치사 about의 목적어이므로 동명사 형태로 써야 한다.

02 전치사 by를 써서 '~하며'라는 방법을 나타낸다.

03 자기애는 당신이 당신의 친구와 가족을 사랑하듯 당신 자신을 사랑하는 것과 당신의 행복을 최우선으로 두는 것을 의미한다.

04 ⓐ whatever는 anything that이라는 의미의 복합관계사이므로

뒤에 that을 다시 쓰는 것은 바르지 않다.
ⓑ at의 목적어 역할을 하는 간접의문문이므로 평서문의 어순으로 써야 한다.
ⓒ 전치사 like의 목적어가 되기 위해 be를 동명사로 바꿔 써야 한다.

05 관계대명사절의 동사 are는 선행사이자 주어 역할을 하는 a part의 수에 맞춰 단수(is)로 바꿔야 하고, control은 solving과 함께 병렬 연결로 전치사 for의 목적어 역할을 하므로 동명사가 되어야 한다.

06 (A) 자신을 돌볼 능력이 되는 자질: 자립, 독립
(B) 쉽게 언짢고 불쾌하게 여기는: 예민한
(C) 무엇의 정도나 강도가 늘어나게 만들다: 강화하다

07 to부정사가 문장의 주어로 쓰일 때는 가주어 it을 주어 자리에 쓰고 to부정사를 뒤에 쓴다.

08 it은 앞에 반복적으로 쓰이고 있는 your anger를 가리킨다.

09 be directed at: ~을 향하다, in particular: 특별히

10 (A) deal with: ~을 다루다
(B) in advance: 미리

12 ⓑ 선행사가 사물(things)이므로 that이나 which를 써야 한다.
ⓕ 사역동사의 목적격 보어이므로 동사원형을 써야 한다.

13 분노는 정상적인 감정이지만, 그것을 효과적으로 관리하는 것이 중요하다. 산책이나 글쓰기 같은 극복의 기술은 화를 건강한 방법으로 다루는 데 도움이 된다. 문제 해결 기술을 개발함으로써 당신은 분노에 의존하지 않고 답을 찾을 수 있다.

14 ⓐ 주격 관계대명사를 쓰고, 동사는 선행사의 수에 맞게 복수형으로 쓴다.
ⓑ 목적격 관계대명사를 쓴다.

교과서 **어휘 익히기** ················· pp. 60-61

STEP 1

01 바꾸다, 교체하다	25 lost and found
02 시작하다, 개시하다	26 organic
03 보상	27 access
04 알아내다, 생각해 내다	28 opportunity
05 응시하다, 빤히 보다	29 disability
06 강조하다	30 investor
07 설치하다	31 be eager to
08 보호소	32 harvest
09 신이 난, 아주 기쁜	33 immediately
10 총액, 양	34 charity
11 약속하다	35 request
12 A를 B로 채우다	36 contribution
13 거의, 대략	37 ingredient
14 끌어들이다	38 potential
15 짧은 영상	39 raise
16 A를 B로 바꾸다	40 promotion
17 충족하다, 만족시키다	41 edit
18 유기하다	42 advantageous
19 (진행을) 추적하다	43 individual
20 입양하다	44 post
21 인상	45 application
22 퍼지다, 확산하다	46 calculation
23 최신 정보	47 progress
24 (서식을) 작성하다	48 crowdfunding

STEP 2

A 01 ⓑ 02 ⓒ
B 01 ⓑ 02 ⓐ 03 ⓑ
C 01 set 02 run
D 01 ⓒ 02 ⓐ 03 ⓑ

A raise는 '들어 올리다, (자금을) 모으다, 재배하다' 등의 뜻이 있다. 01은 '재배하다'라는 뜻으로 쓰였고, 02는 '들어 올리다'라는 뜻으로 쓰였다.

B
01 be eager to: ~을 하고 싶어 하다
02 fill out: 작성하다
03 figure out: 알아내다, 생각해 내다

C
01 set a record: 기록을 세우다
02 run a campaign: 캠페인을 진행하다

D
01 organic(유기농의): ⓒ 식용 식물을 기를 때 인공 화학물을 사용하지 않는
02 launch(개시하다): ⓐ 중요한 활동을 시작하다
03 commit(약속하다): ⓑ 무언가 혹은 누군가에게 당신의 시간, 노력, 또는 돈을 약속하다

교과서 **핵심 대화문** ················· pp. 62-63

Function 1 공감 표현하기
Check-Up ✓ ⓒ
Function 2 제안·권유하기
Check-Up ✓ ⓑ

교과서 **기타 대화문** ················· p. 64

Q1 elevator   Q2 T

교과서 **핵심 대화문 익히기** ················· p. 65

01 ④
02 5-1-3-2-4
03 adopted, shelter

교과서 **핵심 문법** ················· pp. 66-69

POINT 1 전치사+동명사

Q 1 making 2 Working 3 traveling
Check-Up ✓
01 (1) talking
   (2) Listening
   (3) appling
   (4) eating
   (5) taking
02 (1) Before leaving
   (2) after doing yoga
03 (1) is one of my favorite hobbies
   (2) is interested in learning a new language
   (3) forward to moving to a new city
   (4) After beginning our project / After we begin our project
   (5) were proud of performing / were proud to perform

01 (1), (3), (5) 전치사 뒤에 동사가 올 때는 동명사의 형태가 되어야 한다.
(2) 주어로 쓰이는 동명사
(4) 동사 avoid 뒤에 쓰이는 목적어는 동명사 형태이다.

02 before와 after는 전치사나 접속사로 모두 쓰이는 말이다. (1)과 (2) 모두 접속사로 쓰이고 있으므로 전치사 뒤에 동명사를 써서 같은 의미의 문장으로 바꿀 수 있다.

03 (1) 주어가 동명사일 때 동사는 단수로 쓴다.
(2) 전치사 (in) 뒤에 동사를 쓸 수 없으므로 동명사 형태로 바꿔야 한다.
(3) look forward to에서 to는 전치사이므로 뒤에 동명사를 써야 한다.
(4) after 뒤에는 (동)명사가 오거나 (전치사일 때) 「주어+동사」의 절이 와야 (접속사일 때) 한다.
(5) 전치사 (of) 뒤에 to부정사를 쓸 수 없으므로 동명사 형태로 바꿔야 한다. 또는 of를 없애고 proud to-V (~해서 자랑스럽다) 형태로 나타낼 수 있다.

POINT 2 목적격 보어로 쓰이는 to부정사

Q 1 to help   2 perform   3 to believe

Check-Up

01 (1) to accept
(2) call[calling]
(3) to walk
(4) feel
(5) to be

02 (1) wave[waving] his hand
(2) caused him to lose his fame
(3) felt the ground shake[shaking]
(4) helped me (to) speak English
(5) persuaded people to save energy

03 (1) clean, to clean
(2) to travel, travel
(3) burst, to burst

---

01 (2)는 지각동사로, 목적격 보어 자리에 원형부정사나 현재분사가 와야 하고 (4)는 사역동사로 목적격 보어 자리에 원형부정사가 들어가야 한다. 나머지는 목적격 보어 자리에 to부정사를 써야 한다.

02 (1), (3) 지각동사가 쓰일 때 목적격 보어 자리에는 원형부정사나 현재분사를 쓴다.
(2), (5) cause, persuade 같은 동사의 목적격 보어 자리에는 to부정사를 쓴다.
(4) help는 준사역동사로 목적격 보어로 to부정사나 원형부정사를 쓸 수 있다.

03 「동사+목적어+목적격 보어」 형태의 문장에서 목적격 보어 자리에 to부정사를 쓰는데, 사역동사(have, let, make)가 쓰였을 때에는 to부정사가 아닌 원형부정사를 써야 한다.

교과서 **본문 익히기 ❶** ····························· pp. 76-78

01 at the local market every weekend
02 to help them
03 had already sold
04 to make any more jam
05 stared out at the empty field
06 the perfect place for
07 could grow more
08 searching for a way
09 a way of raising money
10 to collect money
11 especially advantageous, can't attract big investors
12 direct rewards for their contribution
13 were thrilled
14 With the help of investors, a lot more strawberries
15 by sending them jars of organic jam
16 this plan in mind, to figure out
17 Before beginning your campaign
18 will it take to make
19 because your potential investors
20 Once your plan is complete
21 enough to complete
22 deciding on the amount
23 8-by-12-foot
24 cost approximately
25 Once it was built, within about four months
26 to turn the strawberries into
27 to cover all the costs
28 planned to run the campaign
29 when I filled out the form
30 In less than a week
31 For a successful crowdfunding
32 consider making
33 to get to know you
34 describe your situation
35 how important the product is
36 Don't forget to include
37 it is important to send
38 will be able to track
39 I was eager to make
40 To achieve this
41 how the strawberries were grown
42 with all-natural ingredients
43 where I wanted to put
44 on many social media sites
45 for word of our campaign
46 committed to supporting us
47 we have raised almost
48 seems like we might make

교과서 본문 익히기 ❷ ······················ pp. 79-81

01 organic	02 last
03 had	04 more
05 by, at	06 perfect
07 started	08 raising
09 These	10 advantageous, can't
11 rewards	12 thrilled
13 With, grow	14 by
15 the next	16 to plan
17 will it	18 potential
19 to set	20 fulfill
21 costs	22 foot
23 Once, within	24 to turn
25 set	26 run
27 excited, launch	28 accepted
29 making	30 to get
31 describe	32 how
33 to include	34 updates
35 Through, track	36 accepted, impression
37 how	38 ingredients
39 I wanted	40 posted
41 for	42 supporting
43 raised	44 might

교과서 본문 익히기 ❸ ······················ pp. 82-84

01 their, weekend	02 already sold
03 to make	04 stared
05 for	06 searching for
07 raising	08 collect
09 advantageous, that[which]	10 receive
11 them	12 a lot[much, far]
13 by sending them	14 With, figure out
15 beginning[you begin]	16 will it take
17 because	18 to set
19 fulfill	20 before
21 by	22 with, within about
23 a few, into	24 cover
25 to run	26 was accepted
27 is necessary	28 making
29 allows, learn	
30 how important the product is	
31 to include	32 to send
33 to track	34 was eager
35 how the strawberries were	36 with
37 where, asked	38 sites
39 to spread	40 Funding
41 supporting	42 have raised
43 seems	

교과서 본문 외 지문 분석 ······················ p. 85

Q F
Check-Up ❣
01 to participate in
02 During the event
03 planted some flowers
04 had contributed to
05 make our town a better place

내신 1등급 어휘 공략 ······················ pp. 86-87

01 ⑤	02 ④	03 ①	04 ⑤
05 ③	06 ⑤	07 ①	08 ⑤

01 (A) '신체적' 장애가 있는 학생들을 위해 엘리베이터를 설치하는 것이 적절하다.
(B) 시각장애인을 위해 표지판이 '제거되는' 것이 아니라 '개선되어 야' 하므로 improved가 알맞다.
(C) 칠판을 흑색에서 녹색으로 '바꾸는' 것이므로 replace가 적절 하다.
오답 (A) mental: 정신적인
(B) remove: 제거하다
(C) place: 놓다, 설치하다

02 ④ 큰 투자를 받기 어려운 개인이나 '작은' 기업에 크라우드펀딩이 효 과가 있다. 문맥상 small이 어울린다.

03 (A) thrilled: 아주 신난
(B) Moreover: 게다가, 더구나
(C) figure out: 알아내다, 생각해 내다
오답 (A) threatened: 위협을 느끼는
(B) Therefore: 그러므로
(C) find out: 발견하다

04 ⑤ 투자 규모를 정할 때 필요한 '비용'을 고려해야 하므로 incomes (수입)가 아니라 costs를 써야 한다.

05 (A) '대략'이라는 의미의 approximately가 알맞은 말이다.
(B) 비용을 '대는' 것이므로 cover가 적절하다.
(C) 지원서가 '받아들여진' 것이므로 accepted를 써야 한다.
오답 (A) appropriately: 알맞게, 적당히
(B) pay: 지불하다
(C) reject: 거절하다

06 ⑤ 투자자들에게 주기적으로 업데이트를 제공해야 하는 이유는 투자 자들이 캠페인의 '과정'을 따라갈 수 있기 때문이므로 result가 아니 라 progress가 들어가야 한다.
오답 result: 결과

07 ① 문맥상 투자자들에게 좋은 첫인상(first impression)을 주고 싶 었다는 의미이다.
오답 expression: 표현, 표정

08 (A) participate in: ~에 참가하다
(B) plant: (식물을) 심다
(C) contribute to: ~에 기여하다
오답 (C) attribute: ~의 결과로 보다

내신 1등급 어법 공략

01 ①	**02** ⑤	**03** ②	**04** ⑤
05 ②	**06** ②	**07** ④	**08** ④

01 ① 과거보다 앞선 일을 나타내야 하므로 대과거(had p.p.) 형태인 had already sold를 써야 한다.

02 (A) thrill은 '열광시키다'라는 뜻의 타동사이므로 수동태인 were thrilled가 알맞다.
(B) build와 함께 조동사 could에 걸리는 말이므로 동사원형 grow가 알맞다.
(C) be동사의 보어로 쓰이는 to부정사 to figure가 적절하다.

03 (A) '~하는 데에 (시간이) 걸리다'라는 의미의 구문에서는 주어 it을 쓴다.
(B) '~할 것을 기억하다'라는 의미가 되어야 하므로 to부정사 형태가 적절하다.
(C) 전치사 before의 목적어이므로 동명사 형태인 deciding이 알맞다.
오답 (B) remember 뒤에 동명사 목적어가 쓰이면 '~한 것을 기억하다'라는 의미이다.

04 ⑤ 신청서가 '받아들여지는' 것이므로 수동태인 was accepted가 알맞은 표현이다.

05 ② express의 목적어로 쓰인 간접의문문이므로 「의문사+주어+동사」의 어순인 how important the product is가 알맞다.
오답 ① 「allow+목적어+to부정사」 구문이다.
③ forget의 목적어로 to부정사가 쓰이면 '~할 것을 잊다'라는 의미이다.
④ 가주어 it이 주어 자리에 쓰이고 진주어인 to부정사는 문장의 뒤에 쓰였다.

06 (A) 전치사 without 뒤에는 목적어로 동명사 using을 써야 한다.
(B) 주절의 시제(explained)가 과거이므로, 목적어인 간접의문문도 과거시제(wanted)가 적절하다.
(C) to spread의 의미상 주어를 나타내므로 for가 적절하다.

07 (A) event가 '~라고 불리는' 것이므로 과거분사 called가 적절하다.
(B) 단락 전체의 시제가 과거이므로 planted가 적절하다.
(C) proud 뒤에 「주어+동사」로 된 절이 이어지므로 접속사 that을 써야 한다.
오답 (A) 분사가 형용사처럼 명사를 꾸며 줄 때 현재분사는 능동, 과거분사는 수동의 관계이다.

08 ④ 「동사(make)+목적어(words)+목적격 보어」 구조이므로, 목적격 보어 자리에 부사가 아닌 형용사가 쓰여야 하며, 의미상 비교급 형태(easier to see)가 적절하다.

내신 1등급 실전 1회

01 ④	**02** ③	**03** ③	
04 (1) an elevator (2) signs with voice guidance (3) greenboards			
05 ③	**06** ②	**07** ①	**08** ②
09 ⑤	**10** ④	**11** ④	**12** ④
13 ②			
14 It didn't take long for word of our campaign to spread.			
15 ⑤			

01 빈칸 다음에 여자가 동의하며 위치를 묻고 있으므로, 남자가 '장소에 가보라'고 조언했을 것이다. 문맥상 '분실물 보관소에 가보는 게 좋겠다'가 맞는 표현이다.
오답 ⑤도 장소에 가보라는 내용이지만, 남자가 '당신이 그것을 둔 장소에 가보세요'라고 말했는데, 여자가 그 장소의 위치를 묻는 것은 맞지 않다.

02 지난 주말에 참여한 행사를 소개하고, 거기서 자신이 한 일을 설명한 후에, 느꼈던 기분과 의견을 말하는 흐름이 자연스럽다. 주어진 문장은 After that으로 시작하며 참여한 활동을 설명하고 있으므로, 행사에서 한 일과 거기서 느낀 감정을 말하는 문장 사이인 (C)에 들어가는 것이 자연스럽다.

03 ③ 장애를 가진 학생들을 포함하여 모두가 쉽게 접근할 수 있는 학교를 만들기 위해 시설을 개선해야 한다는 내용이다.
오답 ② 낡은 엘리베이터를 바꾸는 것이 아니라, 엘리베이터를 설치해야 한다고 주장한다.

04 Lucy가 생각하는 세 가지 시설 변화는 엘리베이터를 설치하고, 표지판을 음성 안내가 있는 것으로 바꾸며, 흑색 칠판 대신 녹색 칠판을 사용하는 것이다.

05 빈 밭에 큰 온실을 지으면 ③ 더 많은 딸기를 재배할 수 있다.
오답 ① 내가 농사에 투자할 수 있다
② 그들이 과일잼 공장을 운영할 수 있다
④ 그들이 잼을 파는 것을 도울 수 있다
⑤ 아낌없는 투자자를 유치할 수 있다

06 ② 일손을 도와드리러 갔지만 이미 잼이 다 팔려서 실망했을 것이고, 빈 밭을 보다 온실을 지어 더 많은 딸기를 재배할 수 있다는 생각이 든 후에는 희망에 찼을 것이다.
오답 ① 걱정스러운 → 안도한
③ 흥분한 → 좌절한
④ 언짢은 → 즐거운
⑤ 자부심 있는 → 부끄러운

07 (A) 앞문장에 덧붙여 말을 이어가는 moreover(게다가)가 가장 자연스럽다.
(B) '(일단) 계획이 완료되면'이라는 의미의 때를 나타내는 접속사 once가 자연스럽다.
오답 ② 그런 이유로 - ~ 하기 전에
③ 그러므로 - ~때문에
④ 결과적으로 - ~ 때문에
⑤ 그렇지만 - ~하지 않으면

08 밑줄 친 sending은 전치사의 목적어로 쓰인 동명사이다.

② dancing은 문장에서 목적격 보어 역할을 하는 현재분사이다.

오답 ① 주어 역할을 하는 동명사

③ 동사의 목적어 역할을 하는 동명사

④, ⑤ 전치사의 목적어 역할을 하는 동명사

09 ⑤ 크라우드펀딩 캠페인 신청서를 작성한 지 일주일도 되지 않아 수락되어, 캠페인이 시작되었다.

오답 ① 온실의 크기는 가로 8피트, 세로 12피트이다.

② 온실에서 딸기를 재배하는 데에는 약 4개월이 걸린다.

③ 딸기잼 생산은 몇 주가 걸린다.

④ 캠페인 운영 기간은 3개월이다.

10 ④를 제외한 나머지는 모두 온실(greenhouse)을 가리킨다.

④ 「it take+시간+to부정사」 구문으로, '~하는 데에 (시간)이 걸리다'라는 의미이다.

11 성공적인 펀딩 캠페인을 위해 효과적인 홍보가 중요하다. 당신과 당신의 제품을 소개하는 영상을 만들어라. 또한 투자자들의 지원을 유지하기 위해 진행 상황에 대해 규칙적으로 정보를 전달하라.

12 (A) allow+목적어+to부정사: (목적어가) ~하도록 허락하다

(B) forget+to부정사: ~할 것을 잊다

(C) It is important+to부정사: ~하는 것이 중요하다 (It이 가주어, to부정사구가 진주어)

오답 forget의 목적어로 동명사를 쓰면 '(과거에) ~한 것을 잊다'라는 의미이다.

13 (A) '성취하다, 이루다'라는 뜻의 achieved가 적절하다.

(B) '~ 없이'라는 의미의 전치사는 without이다.

(C) '(기금을) 모으다'는 raise이다.

오답 (B) with using chemicals는 '화학물질을 사용하여'라는 의미가 된다.

(C) rise(-rose-risen)는 '오르다'라는 뜻의 자동사이다.

14 A가 ~하는 데 시간이 오래 걸리다: It takes long for A to-V

15 첫 투자자가 지원을 약속했을 때에는 ⑤ '뛸 듯이 기뻤을' 것이다.

오답 ① 나는 또다른 크라우드펀딩 캠페인을 시작했다

② 우리는 결과에 실망했다

③ 우리는 그에게 맛있는 잼을 보냈다

④ 우리는 서둘러 잼을 만들었다

내신 1등급 실전 2회

01 ③	**02** ④		

03 they had already sold all of their jam

04 ⑤	**05** ③	**06** ⑤	**07** ②
08 ⓐ beginning ⓑ deciding		**09** ④	**10** ④
11 ⑤	**12** ②	**13** ④	**14** highlighted
15 ①			

01 ③ 남학생이 무엇을 가르치고 싶냐고 묻자 여학생은 'Painting, of course.'라고 답하고 있다.

오답 ① → 두 사람은 자원봉사를 계획하고 있다.

② → 자원봉사의 내용이 아이들을 가르치는 것이지만, 두 사람의 장래 희망은 알 수 없다.

④ → 남학생은 무엇을 가르칠 수 있는지 모르겠다고 했다.

⑤ → 남학생이 'You're right! I'll do that.'이라고 했으므로 여학생의 충고를 받아들인 것이다.

02 ④ 동사 know의 목적어 역할을 하는 간접의문문이므로 「의문사+주어+동사」의 어순 (what I can teach)이 되어야 한다.

03 조부모님이 잼을 이미 모두 판 것은 필자가 조부모님을 방문한 것 이전에 일어난 일이므로, 대과거 형태(had p.p.)가 되어야 한다.

04 온실을 설치하는 완벽한 해결책은 바로 다음 문장에 언급된 ⑤ 크라우드펀딩 캠페인이다.

05 크라우드펀딩이 무엇인지 소개하는 글이다.

③ '성공적인 크라우드펀딩을 위해서는 홍보가 필요하다'는 어울리지 않는 문장이다.

06 마지막 문장에서 '다음 단계는 세부사항을 생각하는 것이다'라고 했으므로, ⑤ '투자를 받기 위한 구체적인 계획'이 이어질 것이다.

오답 ① 온실의 규모

② 특별한 유기농 잼 조리법

③ 투자자들에 대한 보상 방법

④ 투자자들의 개인 정보

07 (B)의 질문들이 주어진 문장의 details에 해당한다.

(C) This planning은 주어진 문장과 (B)를 가리킨다.

(A) 계획을 세운 다음에 구체적인 펀딩 목표를 세운다.

(D) It은 (A)의 funding goal을 가리킨다.

08 ⓐ와 ⓑ 모두 전치사 before 뒤에 쓰이고 있으므로 동명사 형태로 바꿔 써야 한다.

09 ④ 유기농 딸기잼의 가격이 얼마인지는 알 수 없다.

오답 ① 온실의 크기는? → 8×12피트

② 온실을 세우는 데 드는 예상 비용은? → 약 4000달러

③ 딸기 재배 기간은? → 4개월

⑤ 기금조성 캠페인의 기간은? → 3개월

10 ④ less than은 '~보다 적은'이라는 의미이므로 '일주일이 채 안 되어'는 in less than a week라고 나타낸다.

오답 ① 일주일 동안

③ 일주일 전에

③ 일주일 뒤에

⑤ 늦어도 일주일 전에

11 단락의 첫문장에서 주제를 말하고, 이어지는 문장들이 주제를 뒷받침하는 내용이다. 그러므로 글의 주제는 ⑤ '펀딩 캠페인을 홍보하는 방법'이 가장 적절하다.

오답 ① 크라우드펀딩이 무엇인지

② 크라우드펀딩의 계획 절차

③ 크라우드펀딩이 왜 중요한가

④ 펀딩 금액을 계산하는 방법

12 (A) '제품'이라는 뜻의 product가 적절하다.

(B) 지원에 대한 직접적인 요청을 '포함하다'라는 의미이므로 include

정답 및 해설 **15**

가 알맞다.

(C) '(진행을) 추적하다'라는 뜻의 track이 적절하다.

오답 (A) production: 생산, 제작

(B) exclude: 제외하다, 배제하다

(C) trick: 속임수; 속이다

13 주어진 문장에 나오는 clips(짧은 영상)에 대한 언급이 시작되는 문장 다음에 들어가야 한다. 또한 주어진 문장의 they는 바로 앞에 있는 my grandparents를 가리키므로 (D)에 들어가는 것이 가장 자연스럽다.

14 '무엇을 강조하거나 또는 사람들이 무엇을 인지하게 만들다'라는 뜻풀이에 해당하는 단어는 highlight(강조하다)이다.

15 ⓐ tell은 4형식 구조(동사+간접목적어+직접목적어)를 이루는 동사이다. → tell everyone

ⓔ 표지판이 '개선되는' 것이므로 수동태를 써야 한다. → should be improved

내신 1 등급 실전 3회
pp. 98-101

01 ④	02 ④	03 ③	04 ③
05 With this plan in mind		06 ①	07 ④
08 ④	09 ②	10 It was 5,000 dollars.	
11 ③	12 ②	13 ④	14 ③
15 (1) D (2) C (3) E			

01 반려동물을 유기하는 사람들에 대해 비판하는 내용의 대화이다. 주어진 말, '긍정적으로 생각해.'는 남학생이 유기동물 보호소에서 동물을 입양하는 행동을 확인한 후 그런 행동이 변화를 일으키고 있다는 말 앞(D)에 들어가는 것이 자연스럽다.

02 ④ 여학생이 Didn't you adopt your dog from the shelter?라고 말하자 I did.라고 답하고 있다.

오답 ① 반려동물 정책에 관해 화가 났다.

② 동물 보호소에서 자원봉사를 했다.

③ 친구들에게 자원봉사를 하라고 설득했다.

⑤ 동물 보호 활동에 참가했다.

03 ③ 온실을 짓는 데 얼마나 비용이 드는지는 글에 나와 있지 않다.

오답 ① 글쓴이의 조부모님이 지역 시장에서 판매하는 것은?

→ 유기농 잼

② 딸기 온실을 어디에 지을 수 있는가?

→ 집 뒤의 빈 들판

④ 딸기를 더 재배하기 위해 글쓴이는 어떻게 투자자를 모을까?

→ 크라우드펀딩

⑤ 크라우드펀딩이 누구에게 유리한가?

→ 개인이나 작은 기업

04 ⓒ raise는 '(기금을) 모으다'라는 뜻이지만, save는 '(돈을) 저축하다'라는 의미이다.

오답 ⓐ delicious: 아주 맛있는, tasty: 맛있는

ⓑ solution: 해결책, answer: 해답

ⓓ advantageous: 이로운, beneficial: 유익한

ⓔ reward: 보상, benefit: 이득

05 With는 '~한 채로'라는 표현을 이끄는 전치사이다.

06 봉사활동을 한 후, 이런 활동이 마을을 더 좋은 곳으로 변화시킨다고 생각하는 것으로 보아 ① 자부심을 느낄 것이다.

오답 ② 언짢은 ③ 지루한 ④ 좌절한 ⑤ 긴장한

07 캠페인을 시작하기 전 상세한 계획을 세우라는 내용의 글이므로 ④ '캠페인을 시작하기 전 고려할 것'이 가장 알맞은 제목이다.

오답 ① 생산 일정 정하기

② 누가 당신의 미래 투자자가 될 것인가?

③ 캠페인의 목적은 무엇인가?

⑤ 제품의 정확한 양 산출하기

08 (A) '~하는 데 (시간이) 걸리다'의 표현은 「It takes+(시간)+to부정사」 형태로 나타낸다.

(B) '잠재적인'이라는 의미의 potential이 알맞다.

(C) '보상'이라는 뜻의 rewards가 알맞다.

오답 (B) potent: 힘이 센

(C) loss: 손실, 손해

09 calculation은 '계산'이라는 뜻으로, 알맞은 영어 뜻풀이는 ② '총액을 정하기 위해 숫자를 사용하는 절차'이다.

오답 ① 어떤 일이 성공하도록 돕는 행위: contribution(기여)

③ 작물이 거둬들여지는 때: harvest(수확)

④ 제품 판매를 늘리기 위해 이뤄지는 행위: promotion(홍보)

⑤ 식물이 잘 자라도록 하기 위해 사용하는 물질: fertilizer(비료)

10 펀딩의 목표 금액은 얼마였나?:

We decided to set our funding goal at $5,000 to cover all the costs.에서 답을 찾을 수 있다.

오답 두 번째 문장에 등장하는 4,000달러는 8×12피트의 온실을 세우는 데 드는 비용이다.

11 ③ 지원에 대한 직접적인 요청을 하는 것을 피하라: Don't forget to include a direct request for support at the end.라고 말하고 있으므로 잘못된 진술이다.

오답 ① 영상을 만드는 것이 캠페인을 홍보하는 한 가지 방법이다.

② 당신 자신과 당신의 제품을 영상에서 소개할 수 있다.

④ 투자자들이 어떻게 캠페인이 진행되는지를 규칙적으로 알게 하라.

⑤ 투자자들에게 적어도 일주일에 한 번씩 최신 소식을 전하라.

12 (A) '~을 위해'라는 의미의 for가 알맞다.

(B) '~을 통해, ~으로'라는 의미의 수단을 나타내는 전치사 through가 적절하다.

13 ④ 새로 만든 온실을 소개하는 것이 아니라, 온실을 어디에 만들고 싶은지 소개하는 영상을 만들었다.

14 ③ 동사(explained)의 목적어 역할을 하는 간접의문문이므로 where I wanted라고 써야 한다.

15 (1) 표지판에 관한 설명이므로 (D)가 적절하다.

(2) 학교 어디든 쉽게 접근할 수 있게 도와주는 것은 엘리베이터이므로 (C)가 적절하다.

(3) 시력이 좋지 않은 사람들이 글자를 쉽게 읽을 수 있도록 도와주는 것은 녹색 칠판이므로 (E)의 위치가 적절하다.

01 ①	02 ④	03 ④	04 ②
05 ④	06 ③	07 ⑤	08 ②
09 ①	10 ④	11 ⑤	12 ②
13 ③	14 ⑤	15 ②	

01 해석

내 조부모님은 매주 주말 지역 시장에서 유기농 잼을 판매하신다. 지난 주말에 나는 그분들을 도우러 갔는데, 이미 다 팔려버렸다! 더 많은 잼을 만들기에는 딸기가 충분하지 않았다. 그날 밤, 나는 한 가지 아이디어를 떠올렸다. 조부모님 댁 뒤쪽에 있는 빈 땅이 더 큰 온실을 짓기에 딱 좋을 것 같았다. 거기에서 더 많은 딸기를 키울 수 있을 것이다! 그래서 나는 이를 실현할 방법을 찾아보기 시작했고, 크라우드펀딩 캠페인을 시작하기로 결정했다.

조부모님이 판매하는 유기농 잼의 매출을 올리기 위해 아이디어를 떠올리고 크라우드펀딩을 계획하므로 글의 어조는 ① '희망적인'이 가장 적절하다.

오답 ② 안도한 ③ 우울한 ④ 짜증난 ⑤ 동정적인

02 해석

크라우드펀딩은 사업이나 목적을 위해 자금을 모으는 방법이다. 오늘날 사람들은 온라인 플랫폼을 사용하여 자금을 모을 수 있다. 이는 큰 투자자를 끌어들이기 어려운 개인이나 소규모 사업체에 특히 유용하다. 캠페인이 성공하면, 기여자들은 자신들의 지원에 대한 직접적인 보상을 받게 된다.

크라우드펀딩이 개인이나 소규모 사업자에게 특히 도움이 된다는 말과 ④ '투자를 유치한 경험이 많은'이라는 말은 어울리지 않는다.

오답 ① 대형 투자자를 유치할 수 없는
② 대규모 투자를 끌어오기 위해 애쓰는
③ 대형 투자자를 만나는 데 어려움이 있기 때문에
⑤ 무엇을 시작할 대규모 자본이 없는

[03-04] 해석

나의 아이디어는 크라우드펀딩을 통해 큰 온실을 짓는 것이었다. 내가 아이디어를 공유했을 때 조부모님은 매우 흥분하셨다. 투자자들의 도움으로 더 큰 온실을 지을 수 있을 거였다. 그런 다음, 우리는 더 많은 딸기를 재배해 더 많은 잼을 만들 수 있을 것이었다. 다양한 종류의 유기농 잼이 직거래 장터에서 팔린다. 우리는 또한 우리의 유기농잼을 보내드림으로써 투자자들에게 답례할 수도 있을 것이었다. 그런 다음, 우리는 계획의 세부 사항을 생각해야 했다.

03 크라우드펀딩을 통해 온실을 만들어 딸기를 재배해 잼을 더 많이 만들기 위한 계획을 설명하는 글이므로, ④ '농산물 직거래 장터에서 여러 종류의 유기농 잼이 판매된다.'는 글의 흐름과 관계가 없다.

04 마지막 문장을 통해 이어질 내용이 ② '크라우드펀딩 계획의 세부 사항'임을 알 수 있다.

오답 ① 유기농 잼 조리법
③ 잼 판매를 위한 마케팅 전략
④ 가능한 투자자들에 대한 조사

⑤ 조부모님과의 의사소통

[05-06] 해석

캠페인을 시작하기 전에, 생산의 세부 사항을 신중히 계획해야 한다. 제작할 제품의 수량과 제작에 소요되는 시간을 결정하라. 이 계획은 매우 중요하다. 왜냐하면 잠재적인 투자자들이 명확한 일정을 보고 싶어 하기 때문이다. 계획이 완료되면, 자금 목표를 설정하라. 자금 목표는 프로젝트를 완료하고 투자자들에게 보상을 제공하기에 충분해야 한다. 필요한 모든 비용을 고려한 후 목표 금액을 결정하라.

05 주어진 문장의 주어 It은 (D) 앞의 a funding goal을 가리킨다.

06 크라우드펀딩을 시작하기에 앞서 생산 세부계획을 세우고 그 다음 여러 요소를 고려하여 펀딩 목표액을 정하라고 기술하고 있다.

[07-08] 해석

비용을 계산한 후, 우리는 8x12피트 크기의 온실을 짓기로 결정했으며, 그 비용은 약 4,000달러로 예상했다. 온실이 완공되면 딸기를 심을 수 있고, 약 4개월 후에 수확을 기대할 수 있었다. 그런 다음 딸기를 잼으로 만드는 데 몇 주가 걸릴 예정이었다. 우리는 모든 비용을 충당하기 위해 5,000달러를 자금 목표로 설정했고, 캠페인을 3개월 동안 진행하기로 계획했다. 캠페인을 시작하기 위해 양식을 제출했을 때 나는 정말 신이 났다. 일주일도 채 되지 않아 우리의 신청이 승인되었고, 자금이 들어오기 시작했다!

07 ⑤ 기금 조성 목표액은 5,000달러이다. (We set our funding goal at 5,000 dollars....)

08 ② 의미상 딸기를 잼으로 만드는 데에 '몇' 주가 걸린다는 뜻이므로, few가 아닌 a few를 써야 한다.
오답 ① estimate: 추산하다
④ submit: 제출하다
⑤ approve: 승인하다

[09-10] 해석

성공적인 크라우드펀딩 캠페인을 위해서는 홍보가 필수적이다. 동영상을 제작하는 것이 좋은 아이디어이다. 이를 통해 투자자들이 당신을 알고 당신의 제품에 대해 알 수 있다. 동영상에서는 당신의 상황을 명확히 설명하고, 제품을 보여 주라. 또한, 이 제품이 당신에게 얼마나 중요한지 강조하라. 마지막에는 직접적으로 지원을 요청하는 것을 잊지 마라. 캠페인 진행 중에는 투자자들에게 매주 업데이트를 보내는 것이 중요하다. 이렇게 하면 투자자들이 캠페인의 진행 상황을 확인할 수 있다.

09 이 글은 크라우드펀딩의 효과적인 홍보를 위해 비디오 제작과 투자자들에 대한 업데이트를 강조하고 있으므로, ① '비디오 마케팅과 투자자 의사소통'이 제목으로 가장 적절하다.
오답 ② 상황에 대한 규칙적 보고의 중요성
③ 투자자들로부터의 지속적 지원
④ 인상적인 제품의 전시
⑤ 인기 있는 크라우드펀딩 사이트

10 ⓐ it이 가리키는 것은 a crowdfunding campaign이고, ⓑ this가 가리키는 것은 앞문장의 creating a video이다.

우리의 신청이 승인된 후, 나는 투자자들에게 좋은 첫인상을 남기고 싶었다. 이를 위해, 나는 조부모님과 그분들의 잼에 대한 동영상을 제작했다. 동영상에서 나는 딸기가 어떻게 유기농으로 재배되었는지 강조했다. 또한, 조부모님께서 천연 재료로 잼을 만드는 장면을 동영상에 포함시켰다. 마지막으로, 새로운 온실을 어디에 지을 계획인지 설명하고 지원을 요청했다. 동영상을 편집한 후, 다양한 소셜 미디어 플랫폼에 공유했다. 우리의 캠페인 소식은 빠르게 퍼져나갔다.

우리 캠페인의 자금 조달은 천천히 시작되었다. 첫 번째 투자자가 지원을 약속했을 때, 나는 무척 기뻤다. 이제 6주가 지난 지금, 우리는 거의 2,500달러를 모금했다. 우리의 자금 목표를 달성할 수 있을 것 같다!

11 ⑤ 펀딩 개시 후 6주 경과한 시점에 2500달러를 모았으며, 펀딩 목표액에 도달할 수 있을 거라고 했다.

12 ② 동사 make가 문맥상 my grandparents를 꾸며 주는 (잼을 만드는 조부모님) 역할을 해야 하므로, 현재분사 형태인 making으로 써야 한다.

[13-14] 해석

좋은 아침입니다, 해피빌 고등학교 학생 여러분! 저는 2학년 루시입니다. 오늘 저는 중요한 메시지를 전하고자 합니다. 우리 학교의 장애인 편의시설을 개선해야 합니다. 이는 모두가 학교의 모든 공간을 이용할 수 있도록 하기 위해 중요합니다. 그렇다면 우리가 무엇을 할 수 있을까요? 첫째, 신체적 장애가 있는 사람들을 위해 엘리베이터를 설치해야 합니다. 이것은 학교의 모든 구역을 더 쉽게 접근할 수 있도록 만들어 줄 것입니다. 둘째, 시각장애인을 위한 모든 표지판을 개선해야 합니다. 음성 안내가 포함된 표지판은 매우 유용할 것입니다. 마지막으로, 모든 칠판을 녹색 칠판으로 교체해야 합니다. 이는 특히 시력이 약한 사람들에게 글씨를 더 잘 보이게 합니다. 이러한 변화를 이루기 위해 함께 노력합시다. 여러분의 도움으로 해피빌 고등학교는 모두를 환영하는 장소가 될 수 있습니다!

13 빈칸에는 '(신체적) 장애'를 의미하는 ③ disabilities가 가장 적절하다.
오답 ① 능력 ② 이로운 점 ④ 유사성 ⑤ 접근가능성

14 (A) '(시설을) 개선하다'라는 뜻의 improve가 알맞다.
(B) 다음 문장에서 '음성 안내가 있는 표지판'이라고 했으므로 '앞을 보지 못하는'이라는 뜻의 blind가 적절하다.
(C) 문맥상 '저시력'이라는 의미이므로 low가 적절하다.
오답 (A) approve: 승인하다
(B) deaf: 귀가 들리지 않는

[15] 해석

지난 주말, 내 동생과 나는 "우리 공원을 돕자"라는 커뮤니티 행사에 참여하기 위해 근처 공원에 갔다. 우리는 오래된 놀이터 기구를 페인트칠하고 연못 근처에 꽃을 심으며 공원을 보기 좋게 만들었다. 나는 우리 커뮤니티에 기여할 수 있어서 정말 좋았고, 이런 행사가 우리 마을을 정말로 발전시킨다고 생각한다.

(A) '~라고 불리는'이라는 뜻의 과거분사가 알맞다.

(B) painting과 함께 전치사 by의 목적어로 쓰이고 있으므로 동명사 형태가 적절하다.
(C) think의 목적어로 쓰이는 명사절에서 events가 주어, improve가 동사로 쓰이고 있다.

내신 1등급 서술형

pp. 106-108

01 ⓐ An elevator ⓑ Greenboards
02 (1) elevator
(2) voice
(3) welcoming
03 they had already sold all of their jam
04 (1) build
(2) strawberries
05 (A) (c)harity
(B) (a)dvantageous
06 ⓐ sending ⓑ to set
07 How many products will you make? /
How long will it take to make the product?
08 (1) It would take about four months.
(2) It would cost approximately 4,000 dollars.
(3) They would run the campaign for three months.
09 we decided on an 8-by-12-foot greenhouse
10 This allows investors to get to know you and learn about your product.
11 (1) a local park
(2) planted some flowers (around the pond)
12 how the strawberries were grown without using chemicals
13 우리 캠페인에 대한 소식이 퍼지는 데는 오래 걸리지 않았다.

01 ⓐ와 ⓑ 모두 바로 앞에 쓰인 말을 가리킨다.

02 엘리베이터, 음성 도움이 있는 표지판, 그리고 녹색 칠판과 같은 시설들이 해피빌 고등학교를 모두에게 보다 안락한 곳으로 만들 것이다.

03 조부모님을 도와드리러 갔던 것보다 조부모님이 딸기잼을 모두 판 것은 먼저 일어난 행동이므로 과거보다 앞서는 대과거(had p.p.) 형태로 써야 한다.

04 필자가 떠올린 아이디어는 '조부모님 집 뒤 공터에 온실을 지어 더 많은 딸기를 재배하는 것'이었다.

05 (A) 도움이 필요한 사람들을 돕는 공식 기구: 자선 단체
(B) 당신이 보다 더 성공적이 되도록 돕는: 유리한, 이로운

06 ⓐ 전치사 by의 목적어이므로 동명사 형태로 쓴다.
ⓒ '~할 것을 기억하다'라는 뜻이므로 to부정사 형태가 적절하다.
오답 ⓑ remember 뒤에 동명사 목적어를 쓰면 '(과거에) ~한 것을 기억하다'라는 뜻이 된다.

07 바로 뒤에 이어지는 문장들에서 구체적인 예시가 나온다.

08 (1) 딸기를 수확까지 재배하는 데 얼마나 걸리는가? → 약 4개월

(2) 온실 하나를 세우는 데 얼마나 들 것인가? → 대략 4,000달러

(3) 그들은 얼마나 오래 캠페인을 진행할 것인가? → 3개월

09 decide on은 '~을 정하다'라는 뜻이다. 무엇의 크기를 나타낼 때 전치사 by를 사용하여 '(가로) by (세로)'로 표현한다. 단위로 쓰이는 foot(피트)는 형용사처럼 greenhouse를 수식하여 단수 형태로 써야 한다.

10 「allow+목적어+to부정사」 구문을 활용하여 나타낸다.

11 (1) 장소: 지역의 공원

(2) 활동: 낡은 놀이터 시설 칠하기와 꽃 심기

12 how로 시작하는 간접의문문의 어순에 주의한다. without 뒤에는 동명사를 사용한다.

13 It take+(시간)+for A+to부정사: A가 ~하는 데에 (시간)이 걸리다

The True Treasure

교과서 본문 익히기 ❶ ···················· pp. 115–117

01 would go up to the top of a hill
02 stood a house
03 They shone at sunset
04 supposed that
05 have earned a holiday
06 learn something important
07 thanked his father, the house with the golden windows
08 His bare feet
09 seemed to be following him
10 stayed beside him
11 Before long, drink the clear water
12 as his mother had taught him to do
13 to a high green hill
14 for he could not see
15 was disappointed to find, there was no gold
16 asked him what he wanted
17 they are only glass
18 are not likely to have, better to see through
19 to sit down on the step, brought him a snack
20 her eyes were blue like the sky
21 which had a white star
22 about his own calf at home
23 as if they were now friends
24 he had mistaken
25 the wrong way
26 for yourself
27 could only be seen at sunset
28 just as the boy had seen before
29 recognized that it was
30 gave her his best pebble, that he had carried with him
31 promised to come again
32 in the light of the sunset
33 It was dark, just like he had seen
34 welcomed him warmly
35 had had a very good day
36 learned anything
37 windows of gold and diamond

교과서 본문 익히기 ❷ ···················· pp. 118–119

01 hard, look	02 with
03 disappeared	04 because
05 Take	06 bare
07 keeping	08 beside
09 drink	10 closed
11 disappointed	12 what
13 likely	14 him, of
15 modest, had seen	16 which
17 had	18 were
19 mistaken	20 wrong
21 for	22 sunset
23 had seen	24 recognized
25 stripe	26 to come
27 go	28 dark
29 had	

교과서 본문 익히기 ❸ ···················· pp. 120–121

01 look	02 stood a house
03 was	04 something important
05 left	06 feet
07 seemed to be following	08 drink
09 him to do	10 were closed
11 he wanted	12 they are
13 to see	14 brought
15 Although	16 which
17 like	18 as if
19 had them	20 yourself
21 be seen	22 that
23 had carried, one	24 what
25 go	26 It

내신 1등급 실전 공략 ·········· pp. 122–124

01 ⑤   02 On this far hill stood a house with windows of gold and diamond.   03 ③   04 ⑤
05 ⑤   06 ④   07 ④   08 ⑤
09 ④   10 ①
11 stood in the light of the sunset and watched him go
12 ②

01 글의 마지막 부분에 황금 창이 있는 집을 찾기 위해 집을 떠났다고 했으므로, 바로 이어지는 내용은 ⑤ '황금 창으로 된 집을 향한 소년의 여정'이 가장 적절하다.
오답 ① 소년의 부모가 걱정한 것

② 소년과 그의 부모의 관계

③ 소년이 배워야 할 교훈

④ 황금 창이 있는 집의 비밀

02 On this far hill이라는 부사구를 문장 앞에 써서 강조할 때에는 「주어+동사」의 어순을 바꾸어(도치) 쓴다.

03 홀로 길을 떠나는 소년의 발자국이 길동무를 해주고 그림자가 함께 춤추는 듯하고, 냇가에 앉아 빵을 먹을 때에는 새들에게 나눠주는 모습이 ③ 평화롭다.

오답 ① 슬프다 ② 활기차다 ④ 재미있다 ⑤ 공포스럽다

04 소년은 해변에서 걷기를 즐겼다. 그는 발자국을 모래에 남기고 그림자와 동반했다. 빵을 먹은 후에 새들에게 먹이고 자신의 여정을 이어갔다.

05 언덕 위에서 본 황금 창문을 직접 보러 찾아왔지만, 창문이 유리로 된 것을 확인했으므로 가장 알맞은 심경은 ⑤ '실망한'일 것이다.

오답 ① 기쁜 ② 놀란 ③ 분노한 ④ 자랑스러운

06 (A) '그가 무엇을 원하는지'라는 의미의 간접의문문이므로 what이 적절하다.

(B) better를 수식하는 부사적 용법의 to부정사가 적절하다.

(C) told, brought와 함께 동사로 쓰이고 있으므로 과거시제가 적절하다.

오답 (A) if는 의문사가 없는 의문문이 간접의문문으로 쓰일 때 사용하는 접속사이다.

07 ④ 마치 이제 친구인 것처럼 느껴졌다 했으므로 '소년과 소녀가 친구가 되었다.'가 일치하는 내용이다.

오답 ① brown eyes → blue eyes

② red → black

③ a white head → white feet

⑤ was curious → knew all

08 ⑤ '어떤 집이 (그것들을) 가지고 있는지'라는 의미이므로 접속사 that이 아니라 간접의문문을 이끄는 의문사 which가 적절하다.

09 ④ 두 사람이 높은 곳에 올랐을 때 소년은 예전에 자신이 보아온 것처럼(just as the boy had seen before) 멀리 떨어진 황금 창문의 집을 보았다.

10 ⓐ는 소녀를 가리키고 ⓑ~ⓔ는 소년을 가리킨다.

11 동사의 시제는 과거시제로 나타내고, 지각동사 watch 뒤의 목적격 보어는 동사원형을 쓴다.

12 황금 창문이 먼 곳에 있지 않고 자신의 집에 있었다는 깨달음을 얻었으므로 ② '우리 가정이 다른 사람들보다 돈이 훨씬 많다'는 관계가 없다.

오답 ① 우리집이 세상에서 가장 소중한 곳이다

③ 우리집이 황금과 다이아몬드 창문을 가지고 있다

④ 황금 창문을 가진 곳은 없다

⑤ 중요한 것은 먼 곳에 있지 않다

01 ①	**02** ②	**03** ④	**04** ②
05 ③			

06 It is natural to feel angry from time to time.

07 ①	**08** ⑤	**09** ③	**10** ④
11 ⑤	**12** ⑤	**13** ②	**14** ④

15 ⓐ (c)harity ⓑ (a)dvantageous

16 ①

17 allows investors to get to know you and (to) learn

18 ④	**19** ⑤	**20** ③

21 stood a house with windows of gold and diamond

22 ②	**23** ④	**24** ③

25 Our house has windows of gold and diamond.

01 십 대들이 자기애를 가지는 것이 중요하며, 그를 위한 구체적인 방법을 소개하는 글이므로 ①이 글의 요지로 가장 적절하다.

02 like 앞에 '작은 것들이 될 수도 있다'고 했으므로, 작은 성취의 예시가 될 만한 것이 빈칸에 적절하다.

② '전국 수영 대회에서 우승하는 것'은 작은 성취의 예로 부적절하다.

오답 ① 오늘 아침 학교에 늦지 않은 것

③ 영어 수업 때 발표를 한 것

④ 체육 시간에 골을 넣은 것

⑤ 쿠키 굽는 법을 배운 것

03 선행사를 수식하는 주격 관계대명사로 쓰인 that은 ④이다.

오답 ① 문장의 진주어 역할을 하는 명사절을 이끄는 접속사

② 목적어로 쓰인 명사절을 이끄는 접속사

③ so ~ that: 너무 ~해서 …하다

⑤ It ~ that 강조 구문

04 독립적인 성향이 강화된다고 했으므로(your brain lead you toward independence) ②는 맞지 않은 진술이다.

05 화가 나는 것은 자연스러운 일이고 화를 내는 것이 유용할 때도 있지만, 화를 생산적으로 표현하는 것이 중요하다는 내용의 글이다.

③ '신체적 신호가 나타나면 분노를 줄이기 위해 조치를 취하라.'라는 문장은 글의 전체 흐름과 관계가 없다.

06 To부정사가 문장의 주어로 쓰일 때 주어 자리에 보통 가주어 It을 쓰고 to부정사구는 문장의 뒤로 보낸다.

07 이 글은 화를 내는 상황에 대해 스스로에게 질문을 하여 파악하고, 화가 날 때 사회적으로 적절한 방식으로 표현하고 조절하는 방법을 설명하는 글이다.

08 ⑤ 내 친구 Tony가 주로 나에게 화를 낸다: 누가 나에게 화를 내는지에 관한 질문은 없다.

오답 ① 일주일에 두 번. → 첫 번째 질문에 대한 답

② 사람들이 내 말을 듣지 않을 때. → 두 번째 질문에 대한 답

③ 그렇다, 나는 보통 부모님에게 화를 낸다. → 세 번째 질문에 대한 답

④ 아니다, 나는 분노를 조절할 수 없다. → 다섯 번째 질문에 대한 답

09 빈칸 뒤 For example로 시작하는 문장에서 구체적인 사례를 설명

하는데 그것은 '분노를 줄이기 위한 조치'에 해당한다. 그러므로 빈칸에는 ③ '분노를 줄일 조치를 취하라'가 가장 적절한 말이다.

오답 ① 가서 의사를 만나라
② 그것은 당신이 화가 났다는 뜻이다
④ 분노의 신체적 증상을 인지하라
⑤ 그것들은 심각한 영향을 미칠 수 있다

10 첫 문장에 '위에서 언급한 전략(the strategies mentions above)'이라는 표현이 나오므로, 이 글의 앞에는 ④ '분노를 가라앉히는 데 도움이 되는 조치'가 설명되었을 것이다.

오답 ① 화가 나는 것의 긍정적 측면
② 십 대들이 쉽게 화가 나는 이유
③ 분노의 감정에 수반되는 신체적 징후들
⑤ 감정을 통제하는 것이 중요한 이유

11 (A) discover의 목적어 역할을 하는 간접의문문을 이끄는 의문사 what을 써야 한다.
(B) 선행사 emotions를 수식하는 목적격 관계대명사 that이 적합하다.
(C) finding과 함께 전치사 in의 목적어 역할을 하는 동명사가 적절하다.

오답 (B) who는 사람을 선행사로 하는 주격 관계대명사이다.

12 학교의 모든 구성원이 환영받을 수 있는 환경을 조성하기 위해 구체적인 개선책을 제안하고 있으므로 필자의 어조는 ⑤ '설득하는' 어조이다.

오답 ① 재미있는 ② 비판적인 ③ 정보를 전달하는 ④후회하는

13 주어진 문장의 this는 의미상 앞에 쓰인 엘리베이터(an elevator)를 가리키므로 (B)에 들어가는 것이 가장 자연스럽다.

14 ④ 필자는 조부모님이 더 많은 딸기를 재배할 온실을 세우는 데 필요한 투자를 모으기 위해 크라우드펀딩을 계획한다.

오답 ① → 도와드리러 갔지만 잼이 다 팔렸다.
② → 잼을 만들 충분한 딸기를 재배하지 않는다.
③ → 조부모님 집 뒤에는 빈 밭이 있다.
⑤ → 크라우드펀딩은 개인이나 작은 기업에 유리하다.

15 ⓐ 도움이 필요한 사람들을 돕는 공식 기구: charity(자선 단체)
ⓑ 당신이 더 성공적으로 되도록 돕는: advantageous(유리한)

16 ① 온실의 크기는 8×12피트이다.

17 「allow+목적어+to부정사」 구문을 사용한다, get to know: 알게 되다

18 ④ Funding for our campaign started slowly.라고 말한 것으로 보아, 영상을 올리자마자 많은 투자를 유치했다고 보기는 어렵다.

19 (A) '포함했다'는 의미의 included가 적절하다.
(B) '(소셜 미디어에) 게시하다'라는 의미의 동사는 post이다.
(C) '(기금을) 조성하다'라는 의미의 동사는 raise이다.

오답 (A) exclude: 배제하다
(B) pose: (문제를) 제기하다
(C) rise: 일어나다

20 ③ 소년의 아버지는 소년이 착하게 일해서 하루 휴가를 주겠다(You have been a good boy and have earned a holiday.)고 했다.

오답 ① → 하루의 일을 마치고 언덕에 올랐다.
② → 일몰 시간에 잠시 반짝였지만 빛은 이내 사라졌다.
④ → 황금 창문이 있는 집을 찾으러 떠났다.
⑤ → 어머니와 입맞춤을 하고 헤어졌지만, 어머니가 울었는지는 알 수 없다.

21 On this far hill이라는 부사구를 문장 앞에 써서 강조할 때에는 「주어+동사」의 어순을 바꾸어(도치) 쓴다.

22 ② her는 여자 농부를 가리키고, 나머지 넷은 그녀의 딸인 소녀를 가리킨다.

23 ④ 소녀가 키우는 송아지의 나이가 몇 살인지는 언급되지 않았다.

오답 ① → 소년과 동갑이다.
② → 금발이다.
③ → 검정색이고 이마에 별 모양이 있다.
⑤ → 모든 것을 알고 있다.

24 ③ 소녀: 네가 다시 올 때까지 기다릴게. → 소년이 다시 오겠다는 약속을 했다.

오답 ① 소년: 이제 집에 가야겠다.
② 소년: 네게 내가 좋아하는 조약돌을 줄게.
④ 소년의 어머니: 오늘 하루 어땠니?
⑤ 소년의 아버지: 네 여행에서 어떤 교훈을 배웠니?

25 '그가 배운(깨달은) 것'은 글의 마지막, 아버지의 질문에 답하는 말에 나와 있다.

교과서 **어휘 익히기** ···················· pp. 134-135

STEP 1

01 흡수하다	25 digestive
02 결과	26 pause
03 탄수화물	27 break down
04 ~에 익숙해지다	28 nutrient
05 대신하다, 대체하다	29 weigh
06 메스꺼움	30 immune system
07 A에게 B를 공급하다	31 oxygen
08 완전히, 전적으로	32 faint
09 해로운	33 active
10 기본적으로	34 suffer from
11 운동하다	35 long-lasting
12 ~이 함유되어 있다	36 recommend
13 중간의, 보통의	37 automatically
14 먹다, 마시다	38 cut down on
15 다 써 버리다	39 dizzy
16 중요하다	40 liver
17 막다, 예방하다	41 diet
18 제공하다	42 extremely
19 감사하는	43 muscle
20 매력적인, 흥미로운	44 despite
21 일상적인	45 sugary
22 연료	46 store
23 서로 다르다	47 supply
24 대단히, 비정상적으로	48 discomfort

STEP 2

A 01 ⓒ   02 ⓐ
B 01 ⓐ   02 ⓒ   03 ⓐ
C 01 caused   02 lack
D 01 ⓑ   02 ⓐ   03 ⓒ

A

01 store: 저장하다
02 work out: 운동하다

B

01 break down: 분해하다
02 use up: 소진하다, 다 써 버리다
03 suffer from: ~으로 고통받다

C

01 cause an accident: 사고를 일으키다
02 lack confidence: 자신감이 부족하다

D

01 absorb(흡수하다): 표면이나 주위 공간으로부터 액체나 기체를 흡수하다
02 pause(잠시 멈추다): 짧은 시간 동안 무언가 하는 것을 멈추다
03 faint(실신하다): 뇌로 충분한 혈액이 공급되지 않아 의식을 잃다

교과서 **핵심 대화문** ···················· pp. 136-137

Function 1 궁금증 표현하기
Check-Up ✔ ⓑ
Function 2 알거나 모름 표현하기
Check-Up ✔ ⓒ

교과서 **기타 대화문** ···················· p.138

Q1 F   Q2 diet

교과서 **핵심 대화문 익히기** ···················· p. 139

01 2-1-5-3-4
02 2.5 mg of caffeine per kilogram of body weight
03 ⑤

교과서 **핵심 문법** ···················· pp. 140-143

POINT 1 목적어 역할을 하는 that절의 「(should)+동사원형」

Q 1 has   2 provide   3 see
Check-Up ✔
01 (1) X (2) O (3) X (4) O (5) X
02 (1) insisted that she get a refund
   (2) recommended that you eat less meat
   (3) suggested that the actor grow out his hair
   (4) required that the school take care of every kid
   (5) we check out every detail before making decisions
03 (1) proposed that the students (should) wear school uniforms
   (2) suggest (that) Brian (should) publish his amazing story
   (3) recommended that he (should) practice piano every day
   (4) requires that she (should) turn off her cell phone

01 (1), (5) 의무와 필요를 나타내는 should

(2), (4) 요구와 주장을 나타내는 동사의 목적어절에 쓰인 should는 생략할 수 있다.

(3) should have+p.p.: ~해야 했는데 (과거에 하지 못한 일에 대한 유감)

02 요구나 주장을 나타내는 동사의 목적어 역할을 하는 that절에서는 동사를 동사원형 형태로 쓴다.

03 요구나 주장을 나타내는 propose, suggest, recommend, require 등의 동사 뒤에 목적어로 오는 that절에서는 동사가 「(should+)동사원형」의 형태이다.

(POINT 2) 간접의문문

Q 1 who broke 2 if 3 how we can

Check-Up

01 (1) what (2) how often (3) when (4) why

02 (1) We want to know where his house is.

(2) I'd like to find out who entered the room at that time.

(3) They can't be sure if[whether] the dog is abandoned.

(4) Let's discuss how we can deal with this problem.

(5) Tell me if[whether] you believe the news.

03 (1) what time the concert starts

(2) why the soccer match was canceled

(3) if[whether] I passed the exam

(4) what caused the accident

01 (1) 내가 무엇을 사야 하는지

(2) 우리가 얼마나 자주 운동하는지

(3) 내 기차가 언제 도착하는지

(4) 왜 친환경 제품이 중요한지

02 의문문이 동사의 목적어로 쓰이는 간접의문문이 될 때에는 「주어+동사」의 어순으로 써야 한다. 의문사가 있는 의문문은 의문사가 접속사 역할을 하고, 의문사가 없을 때에는 접속사 if나 whether를 써서 연결해야 한다.

03 (1) (2) 간접의문문은 의문문의 어순이 아니라 「주어+동사」의 어순으로 써야 한다.

(3) 의문사가 없는 의문문이 간접의문문으로 쓰일 때에는 접속사로 if나 whether를 사용한다.

(4) 의문사가 주어인 간접의문문이므로 「의문사+동사」의 형태가 되어야 한다.

06 Why did

07 that you exercised

08 This can cause

09 When you eat, to help break down

10 from the digestive system

11 oxygen and nutrients they require

12 As a result

13 with a stomach full of food

14 That makes sense

15 does that mean

16 harmful and unpleasant

17 This is because

18 that provides this energy

19 are broken down, called glucose

20 such as the muscles and the live

21 This is why, can be such a challenge

22 stored in your body

23 you will most likely lack

24 more serious outcomes

25 end up suffering from

26 intense exercise uses up

27 that causes us to have

28 that people eat food, within thirty minutes

29 replaces the muscle glycogen

30 between one and one and a half

31 do the math

32 If you weigh 60 kilograms, after you exercise

33 equal to

34 what about eating

35 how long we should wait

36 will cause feelings of discomfort

37 wait too long to exercise

38 The best time to eat

39 depends on several factors, as well as

40 also matters

41 I suggest that you wait, a moderate-sized meal

42 waiting for one hour after a meal

43 can wait less

44 for this fascinating information

45 I'm sure

교과서 본문 익히기 ❶ ·················· pp. 150-152

01 back to

02 going to be

03 some useful tips

04 start with a question

05 right after dinner

교과서 본문 익히기 ❷ ·················· pp. 153-155

01 talking	**02** last
03 right	**04** that
05 cause	**06** digestive, absorb
07 muscles	**08** supply, they
09 paused	**10** going, full

11 sense　　　　　　　　12 I should

13 unpleasant　　　　　14 because

15 are, called　　　　　16 is stored

17 why, such as　　　　18 low

19 exercise　　　　　　20 more

21 suffering, others　　22 intense

23 it, to have　　　　　24 eat, within

25 lost　　　　　　　　26 between, weigh

27 consume　　　　　　28 equal

29 about　　　　　　　30 we should

31 as, discomfort　　　32 from

33 varies　　　　　　　34 such as

35 active, and　　　　　36 waiting

37 fascinating　　　　　38 sure

교과서 본문 익히기 ❸ ·········· pp. 156-158

01 to be talking　　　　02 share

03 let's　　　　　　　　04 got

05 eating　　　　　　　06 cause

07 absorb

08 moves from the digestive system

09 with, they require　10 returns

11 whether, of　　　　12 sense

13 does　　　　　　　　14 unpleasant

15 to exercise　　　　　16 provides

17 are broken down, called　18 it is

19 completely, such　　20 stored

21 likely　　　　　　　22 more serious

23 suffering, others　　24 because

25 causes us to have　　26 containing

27 have lost　　　　　　28 between, kilogram

29 weigh, and　　　　　30 to

31 we should　　　　　32 exercising

33 from　　　　　　　　34 varies

35 as well as　　　　　36 matters

37 moderate-sized　　　38 waiting

39 less　　　　　　　　40 (that) it

교과서 본문 외 지문 분석 ·········· p. 159

Q T

Check-Up 🐰

01 too many things to do

02 to help you relieve

03 to think of

04 much better than before

05 what you're grateful for

06 will be able to focus

07 remember to ask

내신 1등급 어휘 공략　　　　pp. 160-161

01 ⑤	02 ⑤	03 ③	04 ③
05 ②	06 ②	07 ③	08 ⑤

01 ⑤ 근육 기억은 기술을 자동적으로 수행하는 것을 '쉽게(easier)' 만들어준다.

02 ⑤ 진행자가 식사 직후에 운동을 했다(I worked out right after dinner)고 했으므로 late가 아닌 soon을 써야 한다.
　오답 ① talk about: ~에 관해 이야기하다
　② start with: ~으로 시작하다
　③ last month: 지난달
　④ work out: 운동하다(= exercise)

03 (A) absorb: 흡수하다
　(B) pause: 잠시 멈추다
　(C) full: 가득 찬
　오답 (A) observe: 준수하다, 관찰하다
　(B) pose: 자세를 취하다
　(C) filled: 가득 찬 (with와 함께 쓰인다.)

04 ③ 이 에너지를 '소비하는' 게 아니라 '공급하는(provides)' 연료가 글리코겐이다.

05 (A) 이어지는 말로 '아침에 일어나자마자'라고 예를 들고 있으므로, '빈'이라는 뜻의 empty가 적절하다.
　(B) 문맥상 '평소와 달리'라는 의미의 단어가 어울리므로 unusually를 써야 한다.
　(C) 메스꺼움, 두통 등의 증상을 겪는 이유가 글리코겐을 모두 써버려서 이므로, because가 적절하다.
　오답 (A) full: 배가 부른
　(B) usually: 보통
　(C) why를 쓰면 why 뒤의 문장이 앞에 있는 문장의 결과를 나타낸다.

06 (A) replace: 대신하다, 대체하다
　(B) weigh: 무게가 나가다
　(C) equal to: ~과 (수량이) 동등한
　오답 (A) place: 놓다, 두다
　(B) 문맥상 동사가 필요하다. weight는 '무게'라는 뜻의 명사이다.

07 ③ 문맥상 '자전거 타기와 같은 활동적인 운동'이라는 의미이므로, light가 아니라 active, energetic 등의 단어가 적절하다.
　오답 light exercise: 가벼운 운동, 쉬운 운동

08 (A) relieve: 완화하다, 없애다
　(B) be grateful for: ~에 감사하다

(C) overwhelm: 압도하다

오답 (A) release: 놓아주다, 배포하다

(B) regretful: 후회하는

(C) overjoy: 매우 기쁘게 하다

01 ③	02 ②	03 ⑤	04 ②
05 ⑤	06 ①	07 ①	08 ⑤

01 ③ 주어(This long-lasting memory)가 단수이므로, 동사도 is called가 되어야 한다.

02 (A) let's+동사원형: (우리) ~하자

(B) worked out과 함께 쓰이는 문장의 동사이므로 과거형 got이 알맞다.

(C) 문장의 보어 역할을 하는 명사절을 이끄는 that이 알맞다.

03 (A) break와 함께 help 뒤에 쓰이는 동사원형이다.

(B) 앞에 쓰인 muscles를 가리키는 것이므로 they가 적절하다.

(C) 뒤에 있는 or와 함께 '~이든 아니든'이라는 의미로 쓰이고 있는 whether가 알맞다.

04 (A) 선행사 the fuel을 수식하는 관계대명사 that이 적절하다.

(B) 주어가 carbohydrates이므로, 복수 형태인 are가 알맞다.

(C) '글루코스라고 불리는'이라는 뜻이므로 수동의 의미가 있는 과거분사가 적절하다.

오답 (A) 관계대명사 what은 선행사를 포함하여(the thing which) 명사절을 이끈다.

05 (A) it(this glucose)이 '불리는' 것이므로 수동태인 is called가 알맞다.

(B) '저장된'이라는 의미의 과거분사 stored가 알맞다.

(C) 동사 end up의 목적어 역할을 하므로 동명사 형태 suffering이 알맞다.

06 ① cause의 목적격 보어로 동사가 쓰이기 위해서는 to부정사(to have)를 써야 한다.

오답 ② recommend의 목적어로 쓰이는 명사절에서는 동사가 동사원형 형태이며, 이때 조동사 should가 생략된 것이다.

③, ④ 모두 목적격 관계대명사절로, 관계대명사가 생략되어 있다.

⑤ try의 목적어 역할을 하는 to부정사이다.

07 ① explain의 목적어로 쓰이는 간접의문문이므로, 평서문의 어순(we should wait)이 되어야 한다.

08 (A) 비교급(better)을 강조할 때는 much를 쓴다.

(B) write down의 목적어 역할을 하는 명사절이 필요하므로 선행사를 포함하는 관계대명사 what이 알맞다.

(C) '~할 것을 기억하라'라는 뜻이므로 to부정사가 적절하다.

오답 remember나 forget의 목적어로 동명사를 쓰면 '(과거에) ~한 것을 기억하다/잊다'라는 의미이다.

01 ⑤	02 ②	03 ⑤	04 ①
05 ⑤	06 ④	07 ③	08 empty
09 ④	10 outcome	11 ④	12 50, 75
13 ④	14 ⑤	15 ⑤	

01 ⑤ 선생님은 영상을 볼 수 있는 웹사이트를 추천해주겠다고 했지만, 자신이 영상을 촬영했는지는 알 수 없다.

02 (A) '어떻게'라는 의미의 의문부사인 how가 알맞다.

(B) allow+목적어+to부정사: (목적어)가 ~하는 것을 허락하다

(C) 사역동사 let의 목적격 보어로 쓰이고 있으므로 동사원형(know)이 알맞은 형태이다.

03 주어진 문장의 these parts가 가리키는 것은 (E) 앞에 있는 문장의 different parts of the brain이다.

04 근육 기억은 습득한 기술을 자동적으로 행하도록 해주는 것이므로, 빈칸에는 음악가들이 '모차르트의 음악을 그토록 쉽게 연주하다'가 적절하다.

오답 ② 어려서 교향곡을 작곡하다

③ 항상 악기를 연습하다

④ 노래를 배우는 데 어려움이 있다

⑤ 그들의 근육을 강화하다

05 호스트가 지난달 저녁을 먹은 직후 운동을 하고 복통을 느꼈던 경험을 이야기하며 왜 그런지 묻자, Hill박사가 우리 몸에서 일어나는 현상을 설명하고 있다. 그러므로 글의 주제는 ⑤ '식사를 한 직후 운동을 하면 불편한 이유'가 가장 알맞다.

오답 ① 식전과 식후 운동의 차이

② 근육이 제대로 기능하는 데 필요한 영양소

③ 운동하러 가기 가장 좋은 때

④ 혈액이 소화계의 작동을 돕는 방법

06 (A) 앞문장(식사를 하면 혈액이 소화계로 모여든다)과 빈칸 뒤의 문장(운동하기 시작하면 혈액이 소화계에서 근육으로 이동한다)은 대조되는 상황이므로 역접을 나타내는 접속사가 필요하다.

(B) 빈칸 뒤의 문장은 앞의 문장들의 결과를 설명하는 내용이므로 As a result(그 결과)가 적절하다.

07 (C) 호스트의 질문에 답을 하고 → (A) (C)에서 언급한 에너지를 공급하는 연료인 글리코겐을 소개하고, 그 전단계인 글루코스를 설명한 후 → (D) 글루코스가 글리코겐으로 변환되는 것을 설명하며 → (B) 공복에 운동하는 것이 위험함을 다시 한 번 얘기하는 순서가 자연스럽다.

08 질문과 답변의 주제가 '공복에 하는 운동이 적절한가?'이고, 빈칸에 such as ...로 소개하는 예시도 '아침에 일어나서 바로'라고 되어 있으므로 빈칸에 알맞은 말은 empty이다.

09 ④ 구역감과 두통이 있는 사람은 아침 일찍 운동해야 한다. → 공복에 운동하면 심할 경우 구역감과 두통이 올 수 있다고 했지만, 아침 일찍 운동해야 한다는 말은 본문에 언급되지 않았다.

오답 ① 글리코겐은 간과 근육에 저장되어 있다.

② 위가 비면 혈당치가 떨어진다.

③ 공복에 운동하는 것은 피로를 유발한다.
⑤ 운동하는 동안 근육에 있는 에너지를 써버린다.

10 outcome(결과): 행동이나 사건의 결과 또는 영향

11 본문의 that은 It ~ that 강조 구문으로 쓰이고 있다. ④의 that도 강조 구문이다.
오답 ① 진주어인 명사절을 이끄는 접속사
② so ~ that: 너무 ~해서 …하다
③ recommend의 목적어인 명사절을 이끄는 접속사
⑤ the news와 동격의 명사절을 이끄는 접속사

12 운동 후에는 손실된 글리코겐을 보충하기 위해 체중 1kg당 1~1.5g 사이의 탄수화물을 섭취해야 한다. 체중이 50kg이면 50~75g의 탄수화물을 섭취해야 한다.

13 Q: 운동 전 식사하기에 적절한 시간을 결정하는 것은 무엇인가?
④ 혈당치는 윗글에서 언급되어 있지 않다.
오답 ① 연령, ② 체중, ③ 섭취한 음식의 종류, ⑤ 운동의 종류가 영향을 미친다고 언급되었다.

14 ⑤ 문장의 주어 역할을 하므로 동명사 형태인 waiting으로 바꿔야 한다.

15 스트레스를 관리하는 데 두 가지 유용한 팁이 있다. 그것들은 좋아하는 사람이나 장소에 관해 생각하며 기분을 전환하는 것과, 감사한 일들을 적으며 긍정적인 것에 집중하는 것이다. 친구나 가족에게서 도움을 찾는 것 또한 중요하다.

내신 1등급 실전 2회

pp. 168-171

01 ④	**02** ⑤	**03** ④	**04** brain
05 ①	**06** ⑤	**07** ④	**08** ③
09 ④	**10** ⑤	**11** ⑤	

12 Doctors recommend that people eat food

13 ②	**14** ③

15 Can you explain how long we should wait after eating?

01 ④ 남학생의 카페인 일일 권장량은 150mg이지만, 매일 카페인 120mg이 든 에너지 음료 2병을 마셨으니 실제로는 240mg을 섭취하고 있다.

02 남학생이 과도하게 에너지 음료를 마시고 있다고 말하고 카페인의 일일 권장 섭취량을 알려주고 있으므로, 빈칸에는 ⑤ '너는 에너지 음료를 줄여야 할 것 같아.'라는 충고의 말이 가장 자연스럽다.
오답 ① 카페인의 일일 권장 섭취량은 너무 높다.
② 잠을 잘 자고 싶다면 규칙적으로 운동을 해라.
③ 건강을 유지하기 위해 너는 채소를 더 먹어야 한다.
④ 너는 매일 에너지 음료를 두 병씩 마신다.

03 주어진 글에 이어 (C) muscle memory에 대해 소개한 후 → (B) 그 이름에도 불구하고 실은 뇌와 관련되어 있다고 말하며 → (A) 뇌의 여러 부위가 함께 사용되어 기술을 익히도록 도와준다고 한 뒤 →

(D) 결론 문장으로 이어지고 있다.

04 근육 기억은 자전거 타기와 같은 특정한 기술에 관해 오래 지속되는 기억이다. 그것은 주로 근육이 아닌 뇌의 기능이다. 우리가 기술을 익히면 우리 뇌의 여러 부위가 강력하게 연결되어 자동적으로 수행하는 것을 쉽게 만든다.

05 질문 뒤에 이어지는 답변은 음식을 먹은 직후 운동할 때 혈액의 이동과 그로 인한 결과에 관해 설명하는 것이므로 빈칸에는 ① '저녁을 먹은 직후 (운동했고) 복통이 있었다'가 가장 적절하다.
오답 ② 공복에 (운동했고) 불편함을 느꼈다
③ 식사를 한 후 2시간 뒤에 (운동했고) 활기차게 느꼈다
④ 친한 친구들과 (운동했고) 언쟁이 있었다
⑤ 학교 체육관에서 (운동했고) 다리가 부러졌다

06 nutrient(영양소)의 적절한 영어 뜻풀이는 ⑤ '생물이 생존하기 위해 필요한 물질'이다.
오답 ① 당신이 보통 먹는 음식의 종류: 식단(diet)
② 행위나 사건의 결과 또는 영향: 결과(outcome)
③ 토하고 싶은 불쾌한 기분: 메스꺼움(nausea)
④ 크기나 양이 평균적이고 너무 많지 않은: 보통의(moderate)

07 ④ 신체 조직에 저장되는 당을 글리코겐이라고 부른다.

08 (A) 빈칸 뒤 절의 내용이 This(앞문장)의 이유이므로 빈칸에는 because가 적절하다.
(B) This(앞문장)가 빈칸 뒤 절의 내용의 이유이므로 why가 적절하다.

09 음식을 섭취하지 않으면 혈당이 떨어지고 저장된 글리코겐이 부족해진다. 그러므로 공복에 운동을 하면 ④ '에너지가 부족하고 유난히 피곤하게 느낄' 가능성이 높다.
오답 ① 근육과 간에 글리코겐을 저장하다
② 배가 부르고 무엇을 먹고 싶지 않다
③ 활기차게 느끼고 역동적으로 운동하다
⑤ 신체에서 더 많은 에너지를 생산하다

10 (A) store는 '저장하다'라는 뜻의 타동사이다. 글루코스가 '저장되는' 것이므로 수동태 is stored를 써야 한다.
(B) such a 뒤에 명사 형태로 와야 하므로 challenge가 알맞다.
(C) some ~ others: 일부는 ~하고, 또 다른 일부는 …하다

11 체중이 60kg인 사람은 운동 후 60~90g의 탄수화물을 섭취해야 하는데, 그것은 쌀밥 한 공기 또는 바나나 3개와 비슷한 양이다.
⑤ 쌀밥 한 공기와 바나나 3개를 모두 먹는다는 진술은 맞지 않다.
오답 ① 글리코겐 손실은 에너지 부족으로 이어진다.
② 근육 글리코겐을 복구하기 위해 탄수화물이 든 음식을 먹어야 한다.
③ 운동 후 30분 이내에 음식을 먹는 것이 필요하다.
④ 우리는 체중 1kg당 1g의 탄수화물을 먹어야 한다.

12 동사 recommend 뒤에 접속사 that이 이끄는 절이 목적어로 쓰이면 명사절에서 동사는 should가 생략된 동사원형으로 나타낸다.

13 음식을 먹은 직후에 운동하면 불편함을 느끼고, 너무 오래 지나 운동하면 에너지 부족으로 고생한다. (B) '운동하기 전 음식을 먹을 가장 좋은 시간은 1시간에서 3시간으로 다르다.'
(B) 뒤에 쓰인 문장의 주어 it은 주어진 문장의 the best time을 가리킨다.

14 운동 전 식사 시간을 결정할 때는 ① 성별과 나이, ② 신체 크기, ④ 먹은 음식의 종류, ⑤ 운동의 유형 등을 고려해야 한다.

15 how로 시작하는 절은 explain의 목적어로 쓰이는 간접의문문이다. 간접의문문은 평서문의 어순(주어+동사)이 되어야 한다.

내신 **1**등급 **실전 3회**   pp. 172-175

01 ④	02 ②	03 ①	04 ④
05 ④	06 ③	07 ③, ④	08 ③
09 ③	10 ①	11 ④	
12 ⓑ what you did		13 ②	
14 ⓐ varies ⓑ wait		15 ①	

01 자신이 카페인 일일 권장 섭취량보다 더 많이 마시고 있다는 사실을 여학생으로부터 듣고 놀라고 있으므로 ④ '나는 하루에 에너지 음료를 두 병 마셨다'는 대화의 흐름상 자연스럽지 않다.

오답 ① 내가 그렇게 많은 카페인을 마시고 있었다
② 내가 많은 양의 카페인을 섭취해왔다
③ 에너지 음료 때문에 내가 잠을 못 잤다
⑤ 에너지 음료 한 병에 카페인 120mg이 들어 있다

02 (A) '추천된, 권장된'이라는 수동의 의미가 있는 과거분사 형태가 알맞다.
(B) 주어 each에 알맞은 동사는 contains이다.
(C) '오늘부터 시작하여'라는 의미의 분사구문 형태가 알맞다.
오답 (B) 바로 앞에 쓰인 drinks로 인해 contain을 쓰지 않도록 주의한다.

03 muscle memory가 무엇이고, 어느 신체 기관이 작동하는지를 설명하는 글이다.
오답 ② 근육을 강화하는 방법
③ 음악가들이 지닌 특별한 기술
④ 비범한 재주를 가진 사람들
⑤ 동작에 관여하는 뇌의 부위

04 (A) '~에도 불구하고'라는 의미의 전치사 despite가 알맞다.
(B) '~이 없다면'이라는 뜻의 전치사 without이 필요하다.
오답 ② Through: ~을 통하여
③ But for: ~이 없다면

05 ④ 소화계에서 잠깐 멈추는 것은 음식을 분해하는 데 도움이 된다.
→ 혈액이 소화계에서 근육으로 이동해서 소화 과정이 중단되면 소화 관련 문제가 생긴다.
오답 ① 식후 너무 빨리 운동을 하면 소화 문제를 일으킬 수 있다.
② 식사를 하면 혈액이 소화계로 이동한다.
③ 운동하기 시작하면 혈액이 근육으로 이동한다.
⑤ 배가 부른 채로 운동을 하는 것은 권장되지 않는다.

06 ⓐ its: 혈액이 소화계로 이동하여 음식을 분해하고 '그것의' 영양소를 흡수하도록 돕는다고 했으므로 그것은 '음식'을 가리킨다.

ⓑ they: 근육에 '그것'이 필요로 하는 산소와 영양분을 공급하도록 돕는다고 했으므로, '그것'은 '근육'을 말한다.

07 ③ 아침에 일어난 직후에 글리코겐 수치가 높다.
→ 글리코겐은 탄수화물을 분해해서 만들어지는 당(글루코스)이 간이나 근육에 축적된 것이므로, 사실과 맞지 않은 진술이다.
④ 더 많은 탄수화물을 먹을수록 우리 근육은 더 잘 작동할 것이다.
→ 탄수화물이 근육의 기능에 중요하기는 하지만 더 많이 먹을수록 좋다는 말은 없다.
오답 ① 글리코겐은 우리 몸에 필수적인 화학물질이다.
② 우리가 먹는 음식은 글루코스라고 불리는 일종의 당으로 분해된다.
⑤ 근육에 에너지가 필요하기 때문에 공복에 운동하는 것은 좋지 않다.

08 ③ 수동의 의미(~라고 불리는)로 쓰이므로 과거분사 called가 알맞은 형태이다.
오답 ⓐ 선행사 the fuel이 주어이므로 provides가 알맞다.
ⓑ 과거분사 형태인 broken을 써야 한다.
ⓓ 주어 역할을 하는 동명사 형태가 필요하다.
ⓔ when이 이끄는 절의 동사이다.

09 공복에 운동을 할 때 글리코겐 부족으로 인해 여러 신체 이상 반응이 나온다는 흐름의 글이다. ③은 탄수화물의 권장 섭취량을 서술한 문장으로, 글의 흐름과 어울리지 않는다.

10 공복에 운동하는 것은 낮은 혈당과 불충분한 글리코겐 저장 때문에 위험할 수 있다. 이것은 피로, 구토, 두통, 심지어는 기절까지 이어질 수 있다.

11 ④ 문맥상 체중이 60kg이라면 운동 후 60에서 90g의 탄수화물을 '섭취해야' 하므로, use up이 아니라 consume, eat, have 등을 써야 한다.

12 ⓑ 전치사 about의 목적어 역할을 하는 간접의문문이므로 평서문(주어+동사)의 어순으로 써야 한다.

13 글의 요지로 가장 알맞은 것은 ② '식사와 운동 사이에 일정한 시간이 필요하다'이다.
오답 ① 자신에게 가장 적합한 운동을 택하라.
③ 공복에 운동하는 것은 불편함을 초래한다.
④ 운동하기 전에 든든한 식사보다는 간식을 먹어라.
⑤ 식사를 한 후 적어도 4시간 후에 운동하는 것을 권한다.

14 ⓐ 주어가 the best time이므로 3인칭 단수 현재형이 적절하다.
ⓑ suggest의 목적어로 쓰이는 that절에서는 동사 앞에 should가 생략된 것으로 봐 동사원형을 쓴다.

15 감사하는 일을 적어보면 ① '긍정적인 일들'에 더 집중할 수 있을 것이다.
오답 ② 부정적인 측면
③ 가능한 이유
④ 위대한 도전
⑤ 잠재적 위험

01 ⑤	02 ⑤	03 ①	04 ⑤
05 ①	06 ④	07 ⑤	08 ④
09 ④	10 ①	11 ④	12 ①
13 ③	14 ②	15 ③	

[01-02] 해석

> 진행자: 〈오늘의 건강〉으로 돌아오신 걸 환영합니다. 오늘 우리는 운동에 대해 이야기해 보겠습니다. Victoria Hill 박사님이 유용한 팁을 공유해 주시기 위해 이 자리에 계십니다. 그럼, Hill 박사님, 지난달 제게 일어났던 일에 관한 질문으로 시작하겠습니다. 저는 저녁 식사 후 바로 운동을 했는데, 배가 아팠습니다. 왜 그런 일이 일어났을까요?
>
> Hill 박사: 문제는 식사 후 너무 빨리 운동을 했다는 점입니다. 이는 다양한 위장 문제를 일으킬 수 있습니다. 음식을 먹으면 혈액이 소화기관으로 흐르며 음식을 분해하고 영양소를 흡수하는 것을 돕습니다. 그러나 운동을 시작하면 혈액이 소화기관에서 근육으로 이동하여 산소와 영양소를 공급합니다. 이로 인해 소화 과정이 혈액이 다시 돌아올 때까지 멈추게 됩니다. 따라서, 역기를 들든 달리기를 하든, 배가 부른 상태에서 운동하는 것은 피하는 것이 좋습니다.

01 Dr. Hill이 말하는 핵심으로 알맞은 것은 ⑤ '식사 직후에 운동하는 것은 불편함을 유발할 수 있다.'이다.

> 오답 ① 혈액은 신체를 순환하며 산소를 운반한다.
> ② 역기 들기와 달리기가 십 대에게 최고의 운동이다.
> ③ 운동을 하면 여러 위장 문제가 있다.
> ④ 소화계가 영양분을 분해하는 데에 혈액이 필요하다.

02 ⑤ ⓔ it은 가주어로, 뒤에 이어지는 **to avoid exercising on a full stomach**을 가리킨다.

[03-04] 해석

> 몸은 운동을 위해 에너지가 필요하며, 이 에너지원은 글리코겐입니다. <u>우리가 섭취하는 음식 속 탄수화물은 글루코스(포도당)라는 형태의 당으로 분해됩니다.</u> 이 글루코스가 근육이나 간과 같은 신체 부위에 저장되면 이를 글리코겐이라고 부릅니다. 이런 이유로, 아침 일찍 완전히 빈속에 운동하는 것이 매우 어려울 수 있습니다. 혈당 수치가 낮고, 몸에 저장된 글리코겐이 충분하지 않기 때문입니다. 빈속에 운동을 하면 에너지가 부족하고 비정상적으로 피곤함을 느낄 가능성이 높습니다.

03 주어진 문장은 글루코스를 설명하고 있다. (A) 앞에서 글리코겐을 설명하고, (A) 뒤에서 글루코스와 글리코겐의 관계를 설명하므로, 주어진 문장이 (A)에 들어가는 것이 가장 자연스럽다.

04 ⑤ 운동은 당신의 몸에 글리코겐을 저장하는 데 도움이 된다. → 운동을 하는 데에 글리코겐이 필요하다.

> 오답 ① 당신의 몸은 운동하기 위해 에너지가 필요하다.
> ② 글리코겐은 당신의 몸에서 연료의 역할을 한다.
> ③ 글리코겐은 근육과 간에 저장된다.
> ④ 아침 식사 전에 당신의 몸에는 글리코겐이 많지 않다.

[05-06] 해석

> 진행자: 그렇다면 글리코겐의 소모가 에너지 부족의 원인인가요?
>
> Hill 박사: 맞습니다. 이런 이유로 의사들은 운동 후 30분 이내에 탄수화물이 포함된 음식을 섭취할 것을 권장합니다. 이렇게 하면 소모된 근육 글리코겐을 보충할 수 있습니다. 기본적으로 체중 1킬로그램당 약 1~1.5그램의 탄수화물이 필요합니다. 계산해 보죠. 체중이 50킬로그램이라면, 운동 후 <u>50~75그램의 탄수화물</u>을 섭취해야 합니다. 이는 대략 흰쌀밥 한 공기나 바나나 세 개에 해당합니다.

05 ① It ~ that 강조구문으로 what이 아닌 that을 써야 한다.

06 체중 1kg당 1~1.5g의 탄수화물을 섭취하라고 했으므로, 50kg의 체중인 사람은 ④ '50에서 75g 사이의 탄수화물'을 섭취하는 것이 맞다.

> 오답 ① 약 90g의 탄수화물
> ② 약 두 개의 사과와 오렌지 하나
> ③ 가능한 한 많은 탄수화물
> ⑤ 60에서 90g까지의 탄수화물

[07-08] 해석

> 진행자: 정말 흥미롭네요. 그렇다면 운동 전에 식사하는 것은 어떨까요? 식사 후 얼마나 기다려야 할지 설명해 주실 수 있나요?
>
> Hill 박사: 음, 앞서 말씀드렸듯이, 식사 직후에 운동을 하면 불편함을 초래할 수 있습니다. 하지만 식사 후 너무 오래 기다리고 운동을 하면 에너지가 부족할 수 있습니다. 운동 전 최적의 식사 시간은 1시간에서 3시간 사이로 다양합니다. 이는 음식의 종류와 양, 신체 크기, 나이, 성별과 같은 여러 요인에 따라 달라집니다. 운동의 종류 또한 중요합니다. 자전거 타기와 같은 격렬한 운동의 경우, 중간 크기의 식사를 한 후 1시간 반에서 3시간 정도 기다리는 것을 권장합니다. 하지만 골프처럼 덜 격렬한 운동의 경우, 식사 후 1시간만 기다려도 충분합니다. 물론, 간단한 간식을 먹은 후에는 더 적게 기다려도 됩니다.
>
> 진행자: 이 귀중한 정보를 제공해 주셔서 정말 감사합니다, Hill 박사님. 이 정보가 모든 시청자들에게 매우 유용할 것이라고 확신합니다.

07 ⑤ 골프와 같은 가벼운 운동은 식후 1시간 정도가 적절하다.

08 (A) 주어가 동명사(waiting)이므로 동사는 단수 형태인 leads가 적절하다.

> (B) 동사 recommend의 목적어로 쓰이므로 동명사 형태가 알맞다.
>
> (C) 전치사 뒤에 목적어 역할을 하는 동명사 형태로 써야 한다.

[09-10] 해석

> 할 일이 너무 많아서 종종 압도감을 느끼나요? 그렇다면 스트레스를 줄이는 데 도움이 될 몇 가지 팁을 소개합니다. 첫째, 여러분이 가장 좋아하는 사람이나 장소를 떠올려 보세요. 이렇게 하면 기분이 훨씬 나아질 수 있습니다. 둘째, 감사하는 것들을 적어보세요. <u>작가들은 독자들이 이해하기 쉬운 이미지를 만들기 위해 은유를 사용합니다.</u> 삶의 긍정적인 면에 더 집중할 수 있게 될 것입니다. 스트레스를 받을 때는 항상 친구나 가족에게 도움을 요청하는 것을 잊지 마세요.

09 스트레스를 줄이는 방법 두 가지를 소개하는 글로, 좋아하는 사람이나 장소를 떠 올리고 감사하는 일을 써 보라는 내용이다. ④ '작가들은 독자들이 이해하기 쉬운 이미지를 만들기 위해 은유를 사용한다'는 글의 흐름과 관계가 없다.

10 스트레스를 해소하는 방법 두 가지를 소개하는 글이므로 제목으로는 ① '당신의 정신 건강을 유지하는 방법'이 가장 알맞다.
오답 ② 스트레스는 당신의 몸과 영혼을 해친다
③ 항상 다른 사람들에게 감사하라
④ 당신이 제일 좋아하는 장소는 어디인가?
⑤ 긍정적 사고를 위한 조언

[11-12] 해석

> B: 나는 요즘 잠을 잘 못 자고 낮에는 때로는 어지럽기도 해.
> G: 아마도 네가 에너지 음료를 너무 많이 마셔서 그럴 거야. 너는 카페인의 일일 권장량을 인지하고 있니?
> B: 아니, 그렇지 않아. 하지만 나는 하루에 두 병밖에 안 마셔.
> G: 음, 체중 1kg당 2.5mg의 카페인만으로도 충분해.
> B: 그건 몰랐어. 그럴 경우 나는 하루에 약 150mg의 카페인만 마셔야 하네.
> G: 그런데 에너지 음료 한 병에는 120mg이 들어있어.
> B: 세상에! 나는 내가 그렇게 많은 카페인을 마시고 있는지 몰랐어.
> G: 내 생각에 네가 에너지 음료를 줄여야 할 것 같아.
> B: 네 말이 맞아. 내일부터 시작해서 나는 하루에 한 병만 마시겠어.

11 ④ 에너지 음료 한 병에는 120mg의 카페인이 들어있고, 남학생이 150mg을 섭취하고 있었다.
오답 ① 남학생은 수면 장애가 있다.
② 남학생은 하루에 에너지 음료 두 병을 마신다.
③ 남학생의 체중은 60kg이다.
⑤ 여학생은 남학생이 에너지 음료를 덜 마셔야 한다고 권한다.

12 ① '잠을 잘 못 자고, 때때로 낮에 ~하다'에 alert(기민한, 초롱초롱한)는 어울리지 않는 말이다. '어지럽다'는 의미의 dizzy가 들어가야 자연스럽다.

[13-15] 해석

> 누군가 자전거 타는 법을 배우면 그 기술을 절대 잊지 않는다고 한다. 젓가락을 사용하는 것이나 악기를 연주하는 것 같은 다른 기술도 마찬가지이다. 어떤 기술을 배우고 연습한 후에는 근육의 움직임을 의식적으로 생각하지 않고도 할 수 있게 된다. 이러한 특정 기술에 대한 오래 지속되는 기억을 근육 기억이라고 부른다. 이름과 달리, 기술을 기억하는 것은 우리의 근육이 아니다. 근육 기억은 실은 주로 뇌에서 발달한다. 기술을 수행하는 데는 뇌의 여러 부분이 관여한다. 우리가 기술을 연습할 때, 이러한 부분들이 강하게 연결되어 자동적으로 수행하는 것이 더 쉬워진다. 이것이 왜 전문 음악가들이 모차르트의 곡을 그렇게 쉽게 연주할 수 있는지를 설명한다! 근육 기억이 없다면, 이는 훨씬 더 어려울 것이다.

13 ③ 그것을 습득하는 데에는 근육이 중요한 역할을 한다. → 이름이 근육 기억이지만 실제로는 뇌의 여러 부위가 작동하는 것이다.
오답 ① 그것은 자전거 타기나 악기 연주를 배우는 것에 관여한다.
② 그것 덕에 우리는 의식적으로 동작을 생각하지 않으며 기술을 쓸

수 있다.
④ 그것을 개발하기 위해 연습이 필요하다.
⑤ 음악가들이 모차르트의 음악을 쉽게 연주하는 것이 그 예이다.

14 빈칸 뒤의 내용, '기술을 기억하는 것은 근육이 아니다'와 어울리는 말은 ① '이름에도 불구하고'이다.
오답 ② 기술 때문에
③ 장기 기억 덕분에
④ 이름에서 짐작할 수 있듯이
⑤ 근육의 동작이 관여하는 이상

15 (A) 문맥상 '의식적으로 생각하지 않고도'라는 뜻이므로 consciously가 적절하다.
(B) 앞문장에서 뇌의 여러 부위가 기술을 수행하는 데 관여한다고 했으므로 '연관되어 있다'는 의미의 connected가 알맞다.
(C) 근육 기억이 없다면 훨씬 '어려울(difficult)' 것이다.
오답 (A) automatically: 자동적으로
(C) efficient: 효율적인

내신 1등급 서술형

01 (1) is long-lasting memory for certain skills
(2) mostly develops in (different parts of) the brain
02 ⓐ playing
ⓑ thinking
ⓒ are used
03 exercised
04 with
05 (1) broken down
(2) glycogen
06 ⓐ why → because
ⓑ possess → lack
07 faint
08 is it the loss of glycogen that causes us to have low levels of energy
09 60 and 90
10 Can you explain how long we should wait after eating[we eat]?
11 (1) type and amount of food
(2) body size[age, gender]
(3) the type of exercise
12 I suggest that you wait between one and a half and three hours
13 to ask your friends or family for help when you're overwhelmed with stress

01 (1) 근육 기억은 무엇인가? → 그것은 특정 기술에 관해 오랜 시간 지속되는 기억이다.
(2) 근육 기억은 어디에서 발달하는가? → 대부분 뇌(의 여러 부분)에서 발달한다.

02 ⓐ 앞에 있는 eating과 함께 병렬 연결로 전치사 like의 목적어 역할을 하므로 동명사 형태가 알맞다.
ⓑ 전치사 without의 목적어이므로 동명사 형태로 써야 한다.
ⓒ 주어가 different parts of the brain이므로 수동태로 써야 한다. 이때 동사의 수는 parts에 맞춰 are로 써야 한다.

03 work out과 바꿔 쓸 수 있는 말은 exercise이다.

04 supply A with B: A에게 B를 공급하다
with a stomach full of food: 배가 음식으로 꽉 찬 채로

05 우리가 음식을 먹으면 음식에 든 탄수화물을 섭취한다. 탄수화물은 글루코스(포도당)로 <u>분해된다</u>. 근육과 간에 저장된 글루코스는 <u>글리코겐</u>이라고 불린다.

06 ⓐ 우리 몸이 운동할 에너지를 필요로 하기 "때문에" 빈속에 운동하는 것이 해롭고 불편한 것이다.
ⓑ 빈속에 운동을 하면 에너지가 "부족하고" 피곤할 것이다.
오답 ⓐ This is why: why 이하에 결과에 해당하는 내용이 온다.
ⓑ possess: 소유하다

07 faint(실신하다): 충분한 혈액이 뇌에 공급되지 않아 의식을 잃다

08 It is ~ that 구문을 활용하여 주어, the loss of glycogen을 강조하는 문장으로 바꾼 뒤, 의문문이므로 it과 is의 순서를 바꾼다.

09 체중 1kg당 1~1.5g의 탄수화물을 섭취하라 권장하므로, 체중이 60kg인 사람은 60~90g을 섭취하는 것이 맞다.

10 how가 이끄는 의문문이 explain의 목적어로 쓰이고 있으므로 「주어＋동사」 어순이 되어야 한다. 그리고 after 뒤에는 동명사(전치사일 때)나 「주어＋동사」의 절(접속사일 때)이이어져야 한다.

11 식후 운동 시간을 정하는 요인으로 글에서 언급된 것은 type and amount of food(음식의 종류와 양), body size(체격), age(나이), gender(성별), the type of exercise(운동의 종류)이다.

12 suggest 뒤에 접속사 that이 이끄는 명사절에서는 동사가 원형으로 쓰인다.
1시간 30분에서 3시간 사이: between one and a half and three hours

13 remember to-V: ~할 것을 기억하다, ask ~ for help: ~에게 도움을 청하다, be overwhelmend with: ~에 압도되다

교과서 **어휘 익히기** ···························· pp. 186-187

STEP 1

01 촉발하다	25 artificial intelligence
02 가상의	26 imagination
03 지시, 설명	27 industry
04 협력하다	28 fire extinguisher
05 결국에, 결과적으로	29 overall
06 역사적 인물	30 imitate
07 ~으로 이어지다	31 output
08 넘어서다	32 landscape
09 조합하다, 섞다	33 ethically
10 영향	34 description
11 가상 현실	35 compose
12 논란	36 rest
13 사실적인, 실제 그대로의	37 diversity
14 기존의, 현존하는	38 complex
15 초상화	39 assistance
16 전투, 투쟁	40 originally
17 많은	41 consent
18 경계, 한계	42 analyze
19 애플리케이션	43 complain
20 한계	44 fair
21 보통의, 일반적인	45 ability
22 발생기	46 commercial
23 설치하다	47 take over
24 생각해 내다	48 category

STEP 2

A 01 ⓒ   02 ⓑ
B 01 ⓑ   02 ⓒ   03 ⓐ
C 01 analyzing 02 boost
D 01 ⓒ   02 ⓑ   03 ⓐ

A compose는 '구성하다, (마음을) 가다듬다, 작곡하다' 등의 뜻이 있다. 01 문장에서는 '구성하다'는 뜻으로 쓰였고, 02에서는 '작곡하다'는 뜻으로 쓰였다.

B
01 lead to: ~으로 이어지다
02 be dependent on: ~에 의존하다
03 be based on: ~을 기반으로 하다

C
01 analyze an effect: 효과를 분석하다
02 boost economy: 경제를 활성화하다

D
01 virtual(가상의): 컴퓨터 소프트웨어나 인터넷에서 만들어져 존재하는
02 exceed(넘어서다): 무엇의 수량보다 더 크다
03 collaborate(협력하다): 무언가를 성취하기 위해 함께 일하다

교과서 **핵심 대화문** ···························· pp.188-189

Function 1 기대 표현하기
Check-Up ✓ ⓒ
Function 2 설명 요청하기
Check-Up ✓ Could you explain how

교과서 **기타 대화문** ···························· p. 190

Q1 T   Q2 AI program

교과서 **핵심 대화문 익히기** ···························· p. 191

01 I'm looking forward to asking the general
02 1-3-2-4
03 self-portrait, AI

교과서 **핵심 문법** ···························· pp. 192-195

POINT 1 not only A but also B

Q 1 standing   2 nor   3 need
Check-Up ✓
01 (1) educational
   (2) directed
   (3) reading
   (4) physically
02 (1) dancing as well as singing
   (2) both helpful advice and
   (3) neither take pictures nor
   (4) either under the bed or
03 (1) Both the boy and his mother seem shocked
   (2) was neither correct nor trustworthy
   (3) either taking the exams or submitting
   (4) not only rescued the cat but also brought it

02 (1) A뿐 아니라 B도: B as well as A

(2) A와 B 둘 다: both A and B

(3) A도 B도 아닌: neither A nor B

(4) A 또는 B: either A or B

03 (1) both A and B는 복수 취급한다. seems → seem

(2) neither A nor B 구문이므로 or → nor

(3) either A or B의 A와 B 자리에는 어법상 대등한 성격의 표현을 써야 한다. to submit → submitting

(4) not only ~ but also에서 also는 생략할 수 있지만 but은 생략할 수 없다. also → but (also)

(POINT 2) 동격의 접속사 that

> **Q** 1 that   2 that   3 that
>
> **Check-Up ᱺ**
>
> **01** (1) the conclusion that they should take the bus
>
> (2) that Judy published the book
>
> (3) that holds a special exhibition
>
> **02** (1) the fact that the best-seller writer lives
>
> (2) the conclusion that his judgment was unfair
>
> (3) a belief that we will win the race
>
> **03** ②

01 (1) the conclusion과 동격 관계의 절을 이끄는 접속사 that

(2) 가주어 it이 문장의 맨앞에 쓰이고, 진주어 Judy ....를 이끄는 접속사 that

(3) the museum을 꾸며 주는 형용사절을 이끄는 관계대명사 that

02 fact, conclusion, belief와 같은 명사 뒤에 that이 이끄는 절이 쓰이면 동격을 나타낼 수 있다. 이때 that이 이끄는 절은 완전한 문장으로 써야 한다.

03 ⓐ와 ⓓ는 동격의 명사절을 이끄는 접속사,ⓑ와 ⓕ는 형용사절을 이끄는 관계대명사, ⓒ와 ⓔ는 동사의 목적어로 쓰이는 명사절을 이끄는 접속사이다.

교과서 **본문 익히기 ❶** ················· pp. 202-204

01 an artist used, for an art contest

02 won first place

03 led to a controversy

04 complained that, let it do all the work

05 this wasn't fair

06 by the potential of AI

07 that can create, including images, songs

08 based on our text requests

09 by copying other images

10 have the ability, corresponding descriptions

11 in a short time

12 the styles of existing images

13 blend a photograph of a cat

14 a few differences

15 are clearly based on

16 enough to create

17 not only in the art world

18 able to compose songs

19 For example

20 also set how long

21 Once you've entered, that you can edit or use

22 has opened up new possibilities

23 have already released

24 just like human singers

25 virtual musicians, their human creators

26 are open to the public

27 over the impact on humans

28 the potential to learn skills, view it as a threat

29 AI will replace humans

30 imitate the styles

31 On the other hand, it is still dependent on

32 that AI uses

33 imperfect data with little diversity

34 has no limits or boundaries

35 lies ahead of us

36 to boost their creativity

37 grow tired of

38 new opportunities

39 how to use AI tools ethically

교과서 **본문 익히기 ❷** ················· pp. 205-207

01 intelligence	**02** do
03 rest	**04** excited
05 including	**06** on
07 humans	**08** corresponding
09 to create	**10** Moreover, upon
11 few	**12** overall, are
13 enough	**14** not only
15 compose, you	**16** key
17 long	**18** Once, as
19 computer-generated	**20** Virtual, released
21 human	**22** creators
23 which	**24** However, over
25 perform, view	**26** replace
27 that, without	**28** hand, dependent
29 flaws	**30** little
31 has	**32** lies
33 boost	**34** grow
35 out, how	

교과서 본문 익히기 ❸ ····· pp. 208-210

01 create	**02** won
03 led to	**04** with basic instructions
05 wasn't	**06** were excited
07 there are	**08** were created
09 millions of	**10** to create
11 upon request	**12** with
13 differences	**14** are clearly based
15 to create	**16** in the music industry
17 they give	**18** such as
19 the song will be	**20** you can edit
21 commonly known	**22** have already released
23 just like	**24** move
25 freely and conveniently	**26** their impact
27 as a threat	**28** more and more
29 that, without	**30** others think, that
31 because	**32** limits
33 no	**34** do you think
35 grow tired of	**36** humans and AI can

교과서 본문 외 지문 분석 ············· p. 211

Q T
Check-Up ☘

01 take over human work
02 in many roles
03 There are two reasons
04 more productively than
05 in a shorter amount of time
06 that humans cannot reach
07 can reduce the risk
08 For these reasons

내신 1등급 어휘 공략 pp. 212-213

01 ③	**02** ⑤	**03** ④	**04** ①
05 ⑤	**06** ④	**07** ④	**08** ⑤

01 (A) 우주 기술이 보통의 사람들에게는 '유용해' 보이지 않을지도 모른다.
(B) 이미지 센서가 생산하기 '쉽고' 전력이 많이 소모되지 않으면서 기업들이 상업용 제품에 사용하기 시작했다.
(C) 오늘날에 이 기술의 '최신' 버전이 여러 장치에서 발견된다.
오답 (A) useless: 쓸모없는
(B) hard: 어려운
(C) outdated: 구식의, 낡은

02 ⑤ '~을 포함하여'라는 뜻의 전치사 including을 써야 한다. except 는 '~을 제외하고'라는 뜻이다.

03 (A) copy: 복사하다
(B) millions of: 수백만의 ~
(C) instruction: 지시, 설명
오답 (A) coping: cope(대처하다)의 동명사형
(B) '수백만의'라는 의미의 표현은 millions of로, 복수형으로 나타낸다.
(C) construction: 건축, 건설

04 ① upon request: 요청에 따라, 요청이 있으면
오답 ② for example: 예를 들면
③ blend A with B: A와 B를 혼합하다
④ around: ~ 둘레에
⑤ based on: ~에 근거하여

05 ⑤ 문맥상 '사실적인 얼굴, 신체, 목소리를 가진 가상의 인플루언서'라는 표현이 적절하므로, artificial이 아닌 realistic으로 써야 한다.

06 ④ '동의 없이'라는 표현이 문맥상 적절하므로, content가 아닌 consent를 써야 한다.
오답 content: 내용, 내용물

07 (A) '놓여 있다'라는 뜻의 자동사이므로 lies가 알맞다.
(B) '생산성'이라는 의미의 productivity가 적절하다.
(C) 뒤에 있는 out과 함께 '생각해내다, 알아내다'라는 의미를 갖는 figure가 알맞다.
오답 (A) lay: 놓다, 두다
(B) production: 생산
(C) consider: 고려하다

08 (A) take over: 인계하다, 장악하다
(B) in a shorter amount of time: 더 짧은 시간 안에
(C) risk of accident: 사고 위험
오답 (A) take up: 차지하다, 쓰다

내신 1등급 어법 공략 pp. 214-215

01 ③	**02** ④	**03** ④	**04** ①
05 ④	**06** ③	**07** ⑤	**08** ②

01 ③ 사역동사 let의 목적격 보어이므로 to부정사가 아닌 동사원형(do)을 써야 한다.
오답 ① 목적을 나타내는 to부정사의 부사적 용법
② 목적어로 쓰이는 명사절을 이끄는 접속사
④ 사람들(people)이 흥분되는 것이므로 수동태
⑤ 주격관계대명사

02 (A) 전치사 by의 목적어 역할을 하는 동명사 형태가 적절하다.
(B) other images가 선행사이자 주어이므로 수동태가 알맞다.
(C) allow+목적어+to부정사: (목적어)가 ~하도록 허락하다

03 (A) '현존하는'이라는 의미의 현재분사가 적절하다.

(B) 뒤에 이어지는 내용으로 미루어 '몇몇 차이가 있다'는 뜻이므로 a few가 알맞다.

(C) enough+to부정사: ~하기에 충분한

오답 (B) few: '거의 없는'이라는 의미로 부정의 뜻을 가진다.

04 not only A but also B에서 A와 B는 구조적으로 동등해야 하므로, ① the music industry는 but 앞의 in the art world처럼 전치사구(in the music industry) 형태가 되어야 한다.

오답 ② 수여동사 give의 간접목적어(you)와 직접목적어(many options)이다.

③ set의 목적어로 쓰이는 간접의문문에서 「주어+동사」의 어순으로 바르게 쓰였다.

④ as it is: 그대로

⑤ 현재완료 문장으로, 주어(Virtual influencers)에 맞게 have가 쓰였다.

05 ④ concerns와 이어지는 절은 동격 관계이므로, 관계대명사 which가 아닌 접속사 that이 쓰여야 한다.

오답 ① 콤마 뒤에 쓰이는 관계대명사 which는 앞문장을 부연 설명하는 계속적 용법이다.

② potential을 꾸며 주는 형용사적 용법의 to부정사이다.

③ view A as B: A를 B로 여기다

⑤ that은 앞에 쓰인 동사 think의 두 번째 목적어가 되는 명사절을 이끄는 접속사이다.

06 (A) people을 가리키고 있으므로 their가 알맞다.

(B) 선행사를 포함하는 관계대명사 what이 적절하다.

(C) figure out과 함께 is의 보어 역할을 하고 있으므로 think가 적절하다.

07 (A) 주어가 two reasons이므로 동사는 are이다.

(B) 선행사 places가 관계사절의 동사인 reach의 목적어 역할을 하므로, 목적격 관계대명사가 적절하다.

(C) 문장 마지막의 부사구 in the future로 보아 미래시제가 알맞다.

오답 (B) 관계부사 where는 in which의 뜻으로, 관계부사 이고 는 절에서 선행사는 부사구의 일부로 쓰인다. e.g. the place where you work (= the place that you work in)

08 ② to부정사의 의미상 주어가 the image sensors이므로 수동태인 to be used로 써야 한다.

내신 1등급 실전 1회

01 ②	02 ⑤	03 ③	04 ③
05 ③	06 ④	07 ⑤	08 ④
09 ④	10 ②	11 ⑤	12 ①
13 ④	14 ①	15 ①	

01 ② 여학생은 2차 세계대전에 관해 알고 싶어 한다. → 여학생은 노량 해전에 대해 이순신장군과 얘기하고 싶어 한다.

오답 ① 여학생은 역사적 인물과 얘기하고 있다.

③ 여학생은 그 인물에게 교전 당시의 감정에 관해 물어볼 계획이다.

④ 남학생은 여학생이 사용중인 앱을 설치할 계획이다.

⑤ 남학생은 Marie Curie와 얘기하고 싶어 한다.

02 '~할 것을 고대하다'라고 기대를 나타내는 표현은 look forward to 뒤에 명사나 동명사를 써서 나타낸다.

03 우주에서 사용된 기술이 일상생활에 사용되고 있는 예시를 두 개 소개하고 있으므로, 글의 주제는 ③ '일상에 사용되는 우주 기술'이 적절하다.

오답 ① 동결 건조 식품의 종류

② 최신의 우주 기술들

④ 우주 기술을 둘러싼 국제 경쟁

⑤ 이미지 센서가 내장된 상업 제품들

04 우주 기술이 상용화된 예시로 이미지 센서를 소개하며, 처음에는 우주에서 사용되도록 개발되었지만 → 생산하기 쉽고 전력이 많이 필요치 않아 기업들이 상업 제품으로 개발하게 되었고 → 오늘날에는 스마트폰이나 비디오 카메라 같은 다양한 장비에 이 기술이 사용되고 있다.

05 this가 가리키는 것은 앞의 내용(미술 대회에 한 화가가 AI를 사용한 그림을 그렸고 그것이 수상했다)이다.

오답 ① 많은 AI 프로그램들이 노래와 소설을 만들고 있다.

② 대부분의 화가들이 AI를 사용하여 작품을 만든다.

④ 일부 사람들은 AI의 사용을 환영했다.

⑤ 그 화가는 AI에게 지시를 내렸다.

06 (A) 목적어(it) 뒤에 목적격 보어로 동사원형(do)이 쓰이고 있으므로 사역동사 let이 알맞다.

(B) 주어가 people로 복수이므로 were가 알맞다.

(C) '포함하는'이라는 능동의 뜻이므로 현재분사 including이 적절하다. 이때 including은 전치사처럼 쓰인다.

07 AI를 이용한 이미지 생성에 관한 글이므로 ⑤ 'AI의 도움으로 디지털 이미지 생성하기'가 가장 알맞은 제목이다.

오답 ② 'AI의 미래: AI의 창조적 천재성'도 가능한 제목이지만, 구체적으로 미술 분야와 관련된 내용을 다룬 단락이므로 ⑤가 더 적절하다.

① AI와 인간 예술가들의 협업

③ 디지털 시대에 AI의 한계

④ AI 예술의 윤리적 함의

08 (A) 앞 단락에 더해 부가되는 설명을 하고 있으므로 '게다가'라는 의미의 Moreover가 적절하다.

(B) 앞뒤의 문장이 역접 관계이므로, '하지만'이라는 뜻의 However가 알맞다.

오답 ① Therefore: 그러므로, In short: 요컨대

② Accordingly: 그런 이유로

③ Consequently: 결과적으로, On the other hand: 반면에

⑤ In fact: 사실

09 음악 산업에서의 변화로는 작곡 능력이 있는 AI 프로그램과 컴퓨터로 생성된 가상의 인플루언서 등이 언급되고 있다. ④는 이러한 변화에 해당하지 않는다.

10 ② set의 목적어로 쓰이는 간접의문문이므로 the song will be가 어법상 적절하다.

정답 및 해설 **35**

11 ⓔ assistance는 '도움, 지원'이라는 뜻이지만, direction은 '지시'라는 의미이다.

오답 ⓐ impact: 영향, 충격, influence: 영향

ⓑ view: 간주하다, consider: 고려하다

ⓒ concern: 염려, worry: 걱정

ⓓ consent: 동의, agreement: 합의

12 on the other hand 앞에 언급된 내용은 'AI가 내놓는 결과물은 제한적일 수 밖에 없다'는 것이므로, 그와 대조하여 인간의 상상력은 ① '한계나 경계가 없다'가 가장 적절하다.

오답 ② 지시와 교정이 필요하다

③ 불완전하고 의존하기에 위험하다

④ 결국 AI의 결과물을 모방할 것이다

⑤ AI와의 협력이 필요하다

13 AI 프로그램들이 대중에게 접근 가능하지만 인간에게 미치는 영향에 관한 우려를 야기한다. 일부 사람들은 AI가 여러 분야에서 인간을 대체할 거라고 우려하는 한편 다른 어떤 사람들은 AI가 불완전한 데이터에 의존하며 제한적일 수밖에 없다고 믿는다.

14 AI가 상용될 미래 세상은 당신의 손에 달려있다며 윤리적으로 AI를 사용할 방법과 인류가 AI와 협력할 방법을 찾아야 한다고 ① 설득하고 있다.

오답 ② 비관적인 ③ 재미있는 ④ 긍정적인 ⑤ 회의적인

15 로봇이 인간의 일을 대체할 수 있다고 필자가 생각하는 두 가지 이유는 로봇이 인간보다 생산적으로 일할 수 있고 위험한 장소에서도 일할 수 있다는 것이므로, ① '로봇은 위험한 환경에서 일할 수 있다'가 알맞은 이유이다.

오답 ② 로봇은 결함과 제한된 상상력이 있다.

③ 로봇은 인간 작업자와 협력할 수 있다.

④ 로봇은 인간보다 더 지능이 좋다.

⑤ 로봇은 인간의 지시 하에 일을 한다.

내신 1등급 실전 2회　　　　　pp. 220-223

01 (1) VR (2) extinguisher	**02** ①	**03** ②
04 ④	**05** ④	**06** controversy
07 ⑤	**08** ④	

09 in the music industry as well as in the art world

10 ②	**11** ⑤	**12** ②	**13** ⑤
14 ③	**15** ③		

01 오늘 학교에서 소방 훈련이 있을 것이다. VR 장비를 이용하여 학생들은 실재 화재 상황을 체험하고 소화기를 사용하는 법을 배울 것이다.

02 (A) 동사 hurt의 과거형은 hurt이다.

(B) '어떻게 작동하는지'이므로 how를 쓴다.

(C) what이 이끄는 절이 experience의 목적어 역할을 하는 간접 의문문이므로 「주어+동사」의 어순으로 쓴다.

03 본래 우주에서의 사용을 위해 개발된 '또 다른' 기술인 동결 건조를 소개하며 글이 시작되고 있으므로, 이 글 앞에는 ② '우주 기술로부터

유래한 일상의 제품'이 가장 적절하다.

오답 ① 음식 산업에 동결 건조 제품이 미친 영향

③ 우주 기술 개발의 이유

④ 우주 기술의 발전

⑤ 동결 건조와 우주에서의 생활

04 빈칸 앞에서는 우리가 오늘날 사용하는 많은 제품이 우주 기술에서 비롯되었다고 했고, 빈칸 뒤에서는 현대 카메라의 이미지 센서가 원래 우주에서 사용되기 위해 개발되었다고 했으므로 ④ '예를 들어'가 가장 적절한 말이다.

오답 ① 유사하게 ② 요건대 ③ 게다가 ⑤ 다시 말해

05 주어진 문장은 역접을 나타내는 however로 시작하며 AI에 긍정적인 사람들도 있다고 진술하고 있으므로, AI에 반대하는 입장을 가진 사람들에 관한 문장 뒤인 (D)에 오는 것이 자연스럽다.

06 '무엇에 관한 공적 불일치'라는 뜻풀이에 해당하는 단어는 controversy(논란)이다.

07 ⑤ 마지막 문장에서 '간단한 요청이면 충분하다(a simple request was enough)'고 했으므로, 알맞은 진술이 아니다.

08 ④ '요청하는대로, 요청에 따라'라는 의미가 되기 위해서는 on request 또는 upon request라고 써야 한다.

오답 ① based on: ~에 기반하여

② by: ~으로 (수단이나 방법)

③ in a short time: 짧은 시간 내에

⑤ blend A with B: A를 B와 혼합하다

09 not only A but also B(A뿐만 아니라 B도)는 B as well as A와 같은 의미이다. 이때 A 위치에 오는 말과 B 위치에 오는 말의 순서가 다름에 주의한다.

10 바로 앞문장의 주어로 쓰인 가상 인플루언서들을 가리킨다.

11 ⑤ AI에 대해 우려하지 않는 입장의 사람들은 AI가 인간의 상상력에 미치지 못하고 인간의 도움이 있어야만 작동한다고 믿는다.

12 주어진 문장과 ②의 that은 모두 앞에 쓰인 명사와 동격을 이루는 절을 이끄는 접속사이다.

오답 ①, ③, ④ 동사의 목적어 역할을 하는 명사절을 이끄는 접속사

⑤ 앞에 쓰인 명사를 꾸며 주는 형용사절을 이끄는 관계대명사

13 우리가 윤리적으로 AI를 사용할 방법과 함께 고민해야 할 것으로 ⑤ '세상을 AI의 위협에서 지키는 방법들'은 적절하지 않다.

오답 ① AI의 사회적 영향

② AI 시대에 인간의 역할

③ 인간과 AI가 어떻게 협력할 수 있는지

④ AI가 주도하는 세상에서 일의 미래

14 지문의 필자는 로봇이 보다 생산적으로 일하고 위험한 곳에서도 일할 수 있기 때문에 인간의 일을 대체할 것이라 주장한다. 이와 가장 유사한 주장은 ③ '로봇은 어렵고 위험한 상황에서 더 잘 일한다'이다.

오답 ① 로봇 때문에 점점 더 많은 사람들이 직업을 잃을 것이다.

② 예술과 교육 분야에서 로봇은 인간을 대체할 수 없다.

④ 작업장에서 로봇을 사용하는 것은 비용이 더 많이 든다.

⑤ 로봇은 작업시 인간을 잘 보조한다.

15 ③ 다음에 이어지는 문장에서 더 짧은 시간에 더 많이 생산한다고 설명하는 것으로 보아, 로봇이 더 '창의적으로' 일하는 것이 아니라 더 '생산적으로(productively)' 일하는 것이다.

01 ②	02 ⑤	03 ①	04 ①
05 ⑤	06 ⓐ were ⓑ do		07 ⑤
08 ②	09 ⑤	10 ③	11 ②
12 ③	13 ③	14 ⑤	
15 (1) replace (2) dangerous			

01 AI로 그린 여학생의 초상화를 보며 그린 방법을 묻고 답하는 대화이므로, 대화의 주제로는 ② '이미지를 만드는 AI 프로그램'이 가장 적절하다.

오답 ① 화가와 그 작품으로 인기 있는 웹사이트
③ 초상화를 그리는 데 필요한 기술
④ 친구들과 사진 찍기
⑤ 친구의 초상화 그리기

02 ⓐ~ⓓ는 AI가 그려준 여학생의 초상화를 가리키고, ⓔ it은 사이트에 공유한 여학생의 사진을 가리킨다.

03 이미지 센서에 이어 동결 건조 기술은 ① '본래 우주에서 사용되기 위해 개발된' 기술이다.

오답 ② 짧은 시간 안에 생산하기 쉬운
③ 음식 산업에서 혁명적인
④ 쉽게 조리되고 준비되는
⑤ 우리 일상 생활에 유용한

04 ① that이 이끄는 절에서 주어는 many of the items이므로 동사는 복수형(come)이 자연스럽다. we use every day는 items를 꾸며 주는 관계대명사절이다.

05 (D)의 This는 AI가 그린 그림이 대회에서 수상한 것을 가리킨다.
(B)는 (D)에 언급된 controversy의 구체적인 내용이 시작되는 문장이다.
(C)의 they는 (B)에 나온 some people을 가리킨다.
(A)는 AI 그림에 반대하는 앞의 내용과 역접되는 내용을 소개하는 문장이다.

06 ⓐ 과거시제이고, 뒤에 있는 주어가 people로 복수이므로 were가 알맞다.
ⓑ 사역동사 let의 목적격 보어로 쓰이므로 동사원형 do가 알맞다.

07 두 그림 중 하나는 Johannes Vermeer의 작품이고, 다른 하나는 AI가 그의 그림과 고양이 이미지를 합성한 그림이므로 ⑤ 'Johannes Vermeer가 이미지를 만들기 위해 AI 프로그램을 이용했다'는 바르지 않은 진술이다.

오답 ① 이것들은 Johannes Vermeer의 그림과 AI 프로그램이 만든 이미지이다.
② 고양이 사진이 이것들 중 하나를 만드는 데에 사용되었다.
③ 두 이미지는 많은 유사성을 지녔다.
④ 그림 속 소녀는 스카프를 매고 있다.

08 (A) '상응하는'이라는 의미의 corresponding이 적절하다.
(B) '섞다'라는 의미의 mix가 알맞다.
(C) '전반적인'이라는 의미의 overall이 적합하다.

오답 (A) responding: 응답하는
(B) fix: 고치다
(C) partial: 부분적인

09 ⑤ 가상 음악가들은 실제 같은 외모와 목소리를 지녔고, 사실적으로 말하고 행동한다고 했으며, 인간 음악가와 어떤 차이가 있는지를 언급하고 있지는 않다.

오답 ① → 장르, 조성, 길이
② → 정보를 입력
③ → 가상 인플루언서를 만들어냄
④ → 노래를 발매하고 소셜 미디어에서 팔로워 보유

10 (A) '(일단) ~하면'이라는 뜻의 once가 적절하다.
(B) '더욱이, 게다가'라는 뜻의 Furthermore나 moreover가 적절하다.

오답 ② while: ~하는 동안, ~인데 반해, moreover: 게다가
④ since: ~인 이상, ~ 이래로, whereas: 반면
⑤ for: 왜냐하면, in short: 요컨대

11 AI가 인류에 위협이 될 거라 여기는 입장과 AI가 인간의 창의성을 뛰어넘지 못할 거라고 여기는 입장을 소개하고 있으므로, 가장 적절한 주제는 ② 'AI가 인간에게 미치는 영향에 관한 논쟁'이다.

오답 ① 미술과 음악 산업에서 AI의 미래
③ AI 시대의 윤리적 문제
④ AI와 미래의 직업들
⑤ AI와 인간의 창의성

12 (A) 앞문장을 부연설명하는 계속적 용법의 관계대명사는 which이다.
(B) 앞에 to가 생략된 채 learn과 함께 부정사로 쓰이고 있으므로 동사원형 형태가 알맞다.
(C) 명사 concerns와 동격의 명사절을 이끄는 접속사 that이 적절하다.

13 AI와 함께 하는 세상의 모습은 우리가 어떤 자세를 취할 것이냐에 따라 달라질 거라는 주장의 글이다. ③ 'AI 프로그램은 요청에 따라 기존 이미지의 풍을 섞을 수 있다'는 글의 흐름과 무관한 문장이다.

14 주어진 영어 뜻풀이는 '무언가를 이루기 위해 함께 일하다'이므로 이에 해당하는 단어는 ⑤ '협력하다'이다.

15 로봇은 탁월한 생산성과 <u>위험한</u> 조건에서 일할 수 있는 능력으로 인해 미래에 인간 노동자를 <u>대체할</u> 듯하다.

01 ①	02 ③	03 ②	04 ②
05 ④	06 ③	07 ③	08 ⑤
09 ②	10 ②	11 ⑤	12 ⑤
13 ③	14 ②	15 ④	

위 이미지는 최근 한 예술가가 인공지능(AI) 기술을 사용하여 미술 대회에 출품하기 위해 제작한 것이다. 디지털 예술 분야에서 이 그림은 1위를 차지했다. 그 결과에 관해 예술계는 분열되었다. 일부 사람들은 예술가가 시스템에 기본적인 지시만 내리고 모든 작업을 AI에 맡겼다며 불만을 표출했다. 그들은 이것이 다른 참가자들에게 불공정하다고 생각했다. 반면에, 일부는 AI의 가능성에 대해 매우 고무되었다. 오늘날 많은 AI 프로그램이 소설, 노래, 사진 등 다양한 예술 작품을 제작할 수 있는 능력을 가지고 있다.

01 미술을 시작으로 예술 영역에 인공지능을 사용하기 시작하며 발생하는 논쟁을 소개하고 있으므로 가장 적절한 주제는 ① '예술 분야에 인공지능의 등장'이다.

오답 ② 디지털 시대에 우리가 직면하는 위협

③ 미술 대회에서 심사 절차

④ 디지털 사생활을 둘러싼 찬반 의견

⑤ 인공지능 프로그램과 관련된 이슈들

02 (A) 동사 뒤 간접목적어(the system)와 직접목적어(basic instructions)가 쓰이고 있으므로 gave가 알맞다.

(B) 동사 believed의 목적어 역할을 하는 명사절을 이끄는 접속사 that이 적절하다.

(C) 주어(many AI programs)가 복수이므로 are가 알맞다.

오답 (A) provide가 답이 되려면 provide A with B(A에게 B를 공급하다) 형태로 써야 한다.

(B) what은 선행사를 포함하는 관계대명사이다.

AI 이미지 생성기는 우리가 입력한 텍스트 명령을 사용하여 이미지를 생성한다. 이들은 다른 사람이 만든 이미지를 모방하여 작업을 수행한다. 생성기는 수백만 개의 사진과 그에 첨부된 캡션을 분석할 수 있다. 이를 통해 주어진 지침에 따라 빠르게 예술 작품을 만들어낼 수 있다.

또한, AI 시스템은 요청에 따라 기존 사진들의 스타일을 혼합할 수도 있다. 예를 들어, 요하네스 베르메르의 〈진주 귀걸이를 한 소녀〉와 고양이 사진을 결합할 수 있다. 이 두 그림 사이에는 몇 가지 차이가 있지만, 베르메르의 그림이 전체적인 패턴, 눈, 그리고 머리에 두른 스카프에 영감을 준 것이 분명하다. 이처럼 세밀하고 아름다운 작품을 만들어내는 데 필요한 것은 단순한 요청 한 가지뿐이었다.

03 ② 수많은 사진과 사진 설명을 분석할 수 있기 때문에 예술 작품을 빨리 만들어낼 수(This enables them to quickly produce artwork) 있다.

04 ⓐ '그것들(사진들)에 함께 있는 사진 설명'이란 뜻이므로, them이 가리키는 것은 the photos이다.

ⓑ this가 가리키는 것은 앞문장이다. 이미지 생성기가 사진과 캡션을 분석하는 것이 그것들(생성기들)이 빨리 미술 작품을 만들 수 있도록 한다는 뜻이므로, them은 generators를 가리킨다.

AI 프로그램은 미술 세계뿐만 아니라 음악 산업도 혁신할 잠재력을 가지고 있다. 이미 멜로디를 작곡할 수 있는 많은 선택지가 존재한다. 예를 들어, 만들고 싶은 곡의 키와 스타일을 선택할 수 있고, 곡의 길이도 지정할 수 있다. 데이터를 입력하면, 애플리케이션이 곡을 생성하며, 이를 수정하거나 그대로 사용할 수 있다. 게다가, 컴퓨터 생성 이미지(CGI)는 음악 산업에서도 새로운 기회를 창출하고 있다. 이미 놀랍도록 현실적인 목소리를 가진 가상 인플루언서들이 만든 여러 곡이 존재한다. 그들 중 일부는 실제 가수처럼 큰 소셜 미디어 팔로워를 보유하고 있다. 이러한 가상 음악가들은 인간 디자이너들의 도움을 받아 현실적인 움직임과 말하기를 구현할 수 있다.

05 (A) 앞문장 a lot of options의 구체적 예를 들고 있으므로 for example이나 for instance가 적절하다.

(B) 음악 산업에서 AI의 역할을 추가적으로 설명하고 있으므로 Moreover, Furthermore, In addition 등의 연결어가 자연스럽다.

오답 ① Nevertheless: 그럼에도 불구하고

② in short: 요컨대

③ therefore: 그러므로

⑤ on the other hand: 반면에

06 ③ either A or B(A 또는 B)로 표현한다.

오답 ① B as well as A: A뿐 아니라 B도

② after는 접속사나 전치사로 쓰일 수 있고, 여기서는 뒤에 「주어+동사」가 이어지는 접속사로 쓰였다.

④ a number of+복수명사: 많은 ~

많은 AI 도구가 공개적으로 이용 가능하여 쉽게 접근할 수 있다. 그러나 AI의 능력이 점점 향상됨에 따라 인간에게 미치는 영향에 대한 우려가 제기되고 있다. 일부 사람들은 AI가 다양한 작업에서 인간의 능력을 능가하여 일자리 상실을 초래할 수 있다고 걱정한다. 또한 AI가 인간 예술가들의 스타일을 허락 없이 모방하는 것에 대한 우려도 있다. 반면에, 다른 사람들은 AI가 인간이 생성한 데이터에 의존하기 때문에 결함이 있거나 편향될 수 있다고 주장한다. 이들은 인간의 상상력이 AI보다 뛰어나고 제한이 없다고 믿는다.

07 There are also concerns ...로 시작하므로, 주어진 문장은 AI에 관해 추가적으로 우려하는 입장을 나타낸다. 그러므로 AI에 대한 우려의 입장을 나타낸 문장 뒤, 그리고 그에 반대되는 입장을 나타내는 문장의 앞인 (C)가 알맞은 위치이다.

08 ⓐ~ⓓ는 AI tools를 가리키는 반면, ⓔ는 Others를 의미한다.

우리 앞에 어떤 미래가 펼쳐질 것이라고 생각하는가? AI가 창의성과 효율성을 높이는 일반적인 도구가 될까? AI가 생성한 그림은 점점 많은 인기를 얻고 있다. 아니면 사람들이 AI 도구의 한계에 지쳐갈까? AI는 많은 이점을 제공한다. 그러나 그 윤리적 영향을 고려하고, 인간과 AI가 효과적으로 협력할 방법을 모색하는 것이 중요하다.

09 AI가 본격화될 미래에 대한 기대와 우려가 있으며, 그에 대한 여러

대비가 필요하다는 내용의 글이다. ② AI에 의한 예술 창작이 점점 대중화되고 있다는 문장은 글의 흐름과 어울리지 않는다.

10 (A) 동사 lie(s)의 주어는 what kind of future이므로 단수 형태인 lies가 맞다.
(B) '지친'이라는 수동의 의미이므로 과거분사가 적절하다.
(C) to부정사(to work)의 의미상 주어를 나타내는 전치사 for가 알맞다.

[11-12] 해석

AI 기술이 발전함에 따라, 로봇이 인간 노동자를 대체할까?
(D) 나는 두 가지 이유 때문에 그렇게 생각한다. 첫째, 로봇은 더 효율적으로 작업하여 짧은 시간에 더 많은 생산을 할 수 있다.
(C) 또한, 로봇은 인간보다 더 안전하게 작업할 수 있다.
(A) 로봇은 인간이 할 수 없는 위험한 작업을 처리할 수 있다.
(B) 이러한 이유로, 나는 로봇이 점점 더 직장에서 보편화될 것이라고 생각한다.

11 (D) 주어진 문장의 질문에 대한 답을 하며 첫 번째 이유를 설명하고 → (C) 두 번째 이유를 말하며 → (A) 그 내용을 부연설명하고 → (B) 다시 한 번 자신의 의견을 말하며 글을 마무리한다.

12 ⑤ 로봇이 더 효과적으로(more efficiently) 일한다고 했으므로 producing more in less time이 맞는 표현이다.

[13-15] 해석

일반 사람들에게는 우주 기술이 실용적으로 보이지 않을 수 있다. 하지만 우리가 일상적으로 사용하는 많은 것들이 우주 기술의 산물이라는 사실을 알고 있는가? 예를 들어, 현대 카메라의 이미지 센서는 처음에는 우주 여행을 염두에 두고 만들어졌다. 그러나 이 기술은 제작이 간단하고 전력을 적게 소모한다는 이유로 상업용 제품에 활용되기 시작했다. 오늘날에는 휴대전화나 비디오 카메라와 같은 많은 기기들이 이 기술의 업그레이드된 버전을 사용하고 있다. 우주에서 사용하기 위해 처음 개발된 또 하나의 기술은 동결 건조 기술이다. 이 기술은 우주비행사들이 준비하기 쉽고 오래 보존되는 음식을 먹을 수 있도록 해주었다. 그러나 이제는 동네 상점에서도 동결 건조 과일이나 수프와 같은 제품을 구입할 수 있다! 이것은 우주 기술이 우리 모두에게 혜택을 준 두 가지 예에 불과하다.

13 우주에서의 사용을 목적으로 개발된 기술들이 상용화된 것을 두 가지 사례를 들어 설명하고 있다. 그러므로 요지로는 ③ '우주 기술이 일상 생활에 큰 영향을 미쳐왔다.'가 가장 적절하다.
오답 ① 점점 더 많은 국가들이 우주 경쟁에 참가하고 있다.
② 식료품점의 제품들은 우주 여행을 위해 원래 개발되었다.
④ 우주 기술은 모든 이의 이익을 위해 책임있게 사용되어야 한다.
⑤ 이미지 센서는 현대 카메라와 휴대전화에서 광범위하게 사용된다.

14 우리가 매일 사용하는 많은 것들이 '우주에서 사용하기 위해 개발된 것'을 알고 있는지 묻고 있으므로 ② '지역 식료품점의 선반에 있는지'는 빈칸에 들어갈 말로 어색하다.
오답 ① 우주 기술의 산물
③ 애초에 우주에서 사용될 의도였다
④ 우주 여행의 목적으로 만들어졌다

15 (A) 문맥상 '~을 염두에 두고'라는 뜻이므로 mind가 적절하다.
(B) power는 셀 수 없는 명사이므로 little을 쓴다.
(C) '원래' 우주에서 사용하기 위해 개발된 것이므로 initially가 적절하다.
오답 (B) few: (수가) 적은
(C) consequently: 결과적으로

내신 **1**등급 서술형   pp. 232-234

01 ⓐ to be used
    ⓑ using[to use]
02 image sensors and freeze-drying
03 (1) They were easy to produce and didn't require much power.
     (2) (Freeze-dried) Soups and fruit can be found.
04 (A) (c)ontroversy
     (B) (n)umerous
05 This allows them to create works of art in a short time based on the provided instructions.
06 (A) with
     (B) on
07 changes not only in the art world but also in the music industry
08 artificial → realistic
09 There are also concerns that AI may imitate the styles of human artists without their consent.
10 (1) imperfect
     (2) imagination
11 think about how humans and AI[AI and humans] can collaborate
12 (1) productively
     (2) dangerous

01 ⓐ 이미지 센서가 '사용되는' 것이므로 수동태가 적절하다.
     ⓑ start의 목적어이므로 동명사나 to부정사 형태가 적절하다.

02 예시로 든 두 가지 우주 기술은 이미지 센서와 동결 건조이다.

03 (1) 무엇이 이미지 센서를 상업적으로 유용하게 만들었는가?
     → 그것들은 생산하기 쉽고 많은 전력을 필요로 하지 않는다.
     (2) 어떤 종류의 동결 건조 음식을 지역 상점에서 찾을 수 있나?
     → (동결 건조된) 수프와 과일을 찾을 수 있다.

04 (A) 무엇에 관한 공적 불일치: controversy(논쟁, 논란)
     (B) 수가 많은: numerous(많은)

05 create는 문장의 목적격 보어로 to부정사 형태가 되어야 한다. providing이 수식하는 instructions와 수동 관계(제공되는 지시)이므로 현재분사가 아닌 과거분사 형태로 써야 한다.

06 (A) blend A with B: A를 B와 혼합하다
     (B) be based on: ~에 기반하다

07 not only A but also B: A뿐만 아니라 B도, 이때 의미상 A와 B의 자리에 전치사구를 써야 한다.

08 컴퓨터 생성 이미지(CGI) 덕에 '사실적인' 얼굴, 몸, 목소리를 가진 가상 인플루언서가 등장했다.

오답 artificial: 인공의

09 concerns 뒤의 절은 concerns의 내용을 설명하며 동격의 관계를 이루므로 앞에 관계대명사 which가 아닌 접속사 that이 필요하다.

10 그들은 AI가 불완전한 데이터에 의해 제한되고 인간의 상상력을 능가하지 못할 거라 믿는다.

11 how가 이끄는 간접의문문이 think about의 목적어가 되도록 문장을 구성한다.

12 로봇이 인간의 역할을 대신할 거라 필자가 생각하는 두 가지 이유는 첫째, 로봇이 인간보다 더 생산적으로 일할 수 있고, 둘째, 로봇이 위험한 장소에서 일할 수 있기 때문이다.

Ready to Be Wicked

교과서 본문 익히기 ❶ ·················· pp. 241-243

01 wanted to see
02 got great reviews
03 Everyone recommends, last weekend
04 is based on, the wicked witch
05 known as wicked and good
06 What impressed me the most
07 getting to know oneself
08 in a magical place
09 born with green skin
10 she has very few friends
11 which makes her quite popular
12 as they get to know
13 take advantage of
14 is continuously challenged
15 in the end
16 ups and downs
17 without talking about
18 that I especially like
19 the most famous song
20 at a key turning point
21 used to admire, can't be trusted anymore
22 to fight against him
23 rises into the air
24 let people bring her down anymore
25 the entire audience
26 a great impact on me
27 have to choose
28 to protect the people
29 changed them for the better
30 truly touching moment
31 are accompanied by
32 wearing unique clothes
33 invited me into the magical world
34 noticing the symbols
35 was hanging above
36 seemed to move
37 using these visual effects
38 from beginning to end
39 highly recommend
40 will be able to explore

교과서 본문 익히기 ❷ ·················· pp. 244-245

01 wanting	02 got
03 last	04 on, wicked
05 how	06 What
07 accepting	08 from
09 unusual	10 which
11 along	12 close
13 take	14 challenged
15 ups	16 review
17 most	18 admire
19 determination	20 rises
21 let	22 impact
23 say	24 to protect
25 has	26 touching
27 accompanied	28 wearing
29 invited	30 noticing
31 hanging	32 whenever
33 visual	34 is
35 from	36 recommend
37 to explore	

교과서 본문 익히기 ❸ ·················· pp. 246-247

01 to see	02 got
03 recommends	04 is based
05 they became	06 impressed
07 getting	08 stays
09 Because of, few	10 which
11 become	12 take
13 in	14 ups and downs
15 cannot	16 that I especially like
17 the most famous	18 used to, can't be trusted
19 against	20 rises, singing
21 bring	22 clapped
23 had	24 have to
25 asks	26 explain, has
27 truly	28 are accompanied
29 wearing[wear]	30 noticing
31 dragon-shaped	32 to move
33 is	34 engaged
35 anyone	36 be able to

01 ⑤	02 ⑤	03 ②
04 which makes her quite popular		05 ②
06 "Defying Gravity"	07 ③	08 ⑤
09 ②	10 ①	11 ②	12 ⑤

01 ⑤ 필자에게 가장 감명을 준 것은 뮤지컬의 주제(the theme of the musical)이었다.

오답 ① 2003년에 처음 시작했다.

② 훌륭한 리뷰를 받아왔다.

③ 이야기는 〈오즈의 마법사〉에 기반한다.

④ 주요 등장인물은 두 마녀이다.

⑤ 시각 장치가 필자에게 가장 인상적이었다.

02 ⑤ '우정을 쌓고 자신을 알게 되는 것'과 같은 맥락의 말은 '차이를 무시하다'가 아니라 '차이를 받아들이다'이므로, ignoring을 accepting으로 바꿔야 자연스럽다.

03 (A) 빈칸 앞뒤 문장이 대조되는 내용이므로 '한편, 반면'이라는 뜻의 Meanwhile이 적절하다.

(B) '둘의 우정이 끊임 없이 도전받았으나 결국 승리했다'는 내용이므로 가운데 들어갈 말은 '그럼에도 불구하고'라는 뜻의 Nevertheless이다.

오답 ① 하지만 - 결과적으로

③ 게다가 - 하지만

④ 그러므로 - 더욱이

⑤ 그럼에도 불구하고 - 그러므로

04 계속적 용법의 관계대명사 which는 앞 문장의 내용 전체를 가리킨다.

05 ② 필자가 제일 좋아하는 노래 'Defying Gravity'는 뮤지컬의 전환점에(at a key turning point) 등장한다.

오답 ① 뮤지컬에는 멋진 노래들이 많이 있다.

③ Elphaba가 존경했던 마법사는 사실은 사악한 사람이었다.

④ Elphaba는 빗자루로 날 수 있었다.

⑤ Elphaba의 노래는 관객들에게 감동을 주었다.

06 뮤지컬에서 가장 유명한 곡이자 필자가 가장 좋아하는 곡인 'Defying Gravity'를 가리킨다.

07 ③ Elphaba와 Glinda가 서로에게 노래를 불러주었다고 했으므로 알맞은 진술이다.

오답 ① 그것은 필자에게 최고의 뮤지컬 노래였다.

② 그것은 뮤지컬의 절정에 등장한다.

④ Glinda는 노래에서 Elphaba에게 작별을 고한다.

⑤ 그것은 Elphaba의 강한 의지를 강조한다.

08 (A) decide의 목적어로 동명사를 쓰지 않고 to부정사를 쓴다.

(B) 동명사(meeting)가 주어일 때 동사는 단수 형태를 쓴다.

(C) 주격 관계대명사 that이 적절하다.

09 (B) 시각 장치의 첫 번째로 의상을 이야기하고 → (C) 덧붙여 기교와 상징을 이야기하며 → (A) 그 예시로 용 모양 장치를 설명한 후 → (D) 결론을 내리고 있다.

10 독특한 의상, 무대장치가 뮤지컬을 흥미롭게 만든다는 내용이므로 ① '뮤지컬의 눈을 사로잡는 시각 장치들'이 글의 주제이다.

오답 ② 뮤지컬의 가장 유명한 노래들

③ 뮤지컬이 더 좋아지는 방법들

④ 뮤지컬의 주제들

⑤ 뮤지컬의 주요 등장인물

11 글 중간에 글의 목적이 되는 문장이 나온다. 뮤지컬에 관심이 있는 사람들에게 이 공연을 추천한다.(I highly recommend this show to anyone interested in musical.)

12 ⑤ able to explore로 표현해야 한다.

01 ⑤	**02** ④	**03** ③	**04** ⑤
05 ②			

06 consume between 80-120 grams of carbohydrates

07 ①	**08** ④	**09** ②	**10** ②
11 ⑤	**12** ③, ⑤	**13** ①	**14** ④

15 not only in the art world but also in the music industry

16 ④	**17** ③	**18** (A) which (B) that	
19 ②	**20** ①	**21** ⑤	**22** ②
23 ③	**24** ④		

25 It seemed to move whenever Elphaba or Glinda made a choice.

01 주어진 문장의 As a result에 해당하는 내용은 혈액이 소화계에서 근육으로 이동하는 것을 가리키므로 (E)에 들어가는 것이 가장 자연스럽다.

02 소화계는 <u>영양분을 분해하기 위해</u> 혈액이 필요하지만, 우리가 운동을 시작하면 혈액이 <u>근육으로</u> 이동한다.

03 ③ 간과 근육에 저장되는 글루코스를 글리코겐이라고 한다. (When this glucose is stored in parts of the body, such as the muscles and the liver, it is called glycogen.)

04 공복에 운동할 때 생기는 문제를 설명하는 문장에 이어지는 문장이다. 구토, 두통, 실신 등의 더 심각한 '결과(outcomes)'가 생길 수도 있다고 서술해야 자연스럽다.

05 본문과 ②에 쓰인 that은 It ~ that 강조 구문으로 쓰인다.
오답 ① 진주어인 명사절을 이끄는 접속사
③ so ~ that 구문에 쓰이는 부사절을 이끄는 접속사
④ suggest의 목적어로 쓰이는 명사절을 이끄는 접속사
⑤ news와 동격의 명사절을 이끄는 접속사

06 체중 1kg당 1~1.5g의 탄수화물을 섭취하라고 했으므로, 체중이 80kg인 사람은 80~120g의 탄수화물을 섭취해야 한다.

07 ① how 이하가 explain의 목적어로 쓰이는 간접의문문이므로, 「주어+동사」의 어순(we should wait)이 되어야 한다.

08 식후 운동 시간을 결정하는 요인으로는 음식의 종류와 양, 체격, 나이, 성별, 운동의 종류가 언급되었지만, ④ 수면의 양은 언급되지 않았다.
오답 ① 음식의 양
② 체중과 신장
③ 운동의 종류
⑤ 나이와 성별

09 Despite(~에도 불구하고)로 문장이 시작하고, 뒤에 이어지는 내용도 근육 기억의 발달에 뇌가 주로 역할을 한다고 했으므로, 빈칸에는 ③ '우리의 근육이 기술을 기억한다'가 적절하다.
오답 ① 우리 신체가 특정한 기술을 기억한다
② 우리는 기술을 연습할 필요가 없다
④ 두뇌는 기술을 익히는 데에 핵심적인 역할을 한다
⑤ 특정한 기술은 자동적으로 습득된다

10 젓가락 사용이나 악기 연주 같은 특정한 기술을 자동적으로 수행하는 장기 기억을 '근육 기억'이라 하는데, 이것은 두뇌의 여러 부위가 함께 작동하며 기술을 수행하는 것이다.

11 ①~④는 모두 이미지 센서를 가리키지만, ⑤ '흔한 물건들'은 이미지 센서와 다르다.

12 however 앞에서는 AI의 등장에 불만과 우려의 입장을 가진 사람들이 있다고 했으므로, 빈칸에는 이와 대조되는 입장을 소개하는 내용이 들어가야 한다.
③ 어떤 다른 사람들은 AI가 인간의 창의성을 능가하지 못할 거라 생각했다
⑤ AI의 잠재력에 흥분한 사람들도 있었다
오답 ① AI가 예술가의 저작권을 침해할 거란 우려가 있었다
② 어떤 사람들은 인간의 직업이 결국 AI에 의해 대체될 거라 믿었다
④ 다른 사람들은 점점 더 많은 영역에서 AI가 인간을 대체할 거라 걱정했다

13 AI를 이용한 이미지 생성이 도달한 수준에 관해 설명하는 글이므로 ① 'AI를 이용한 디지털 이미지 생성'이 글의 주제로 가장 적합하다.
오답 ② 미술계에서의 창의성과 책임
③ 명작과 디지털 이미지의 혼합
④ 음악 산업에서 AI의 역할
⑤ 이미지 분석 기술

14 (A) allow+목적어+to-V: ~가 …하도록 허락하다
(B) 문맥상 '몇 가지의'라는 표현이 적절하므로 a few를 써야 한다.
(C) 주어가 the overall design, the eyes, and the scarf around the head이므로 복수의 동사를 써야 한다.

15 not only A but also B: A뿐만 아니라 B도, 이때 A와 B는 대등한 형태로 써야 하며 의미상 전치사구를 써야 한다.

16 (A) many options의 구체적인 사례를 설명하고 있으므로 빈칸에는 '예를 들어'라는 뜻의 for example이 적절하다.
(B) AI를 통해 작곡을 하고, 더 나아가 CGI를 이용한 가상 인플루언서까지 등장하고 있다고 진술하고 있으므로 빈칸에는 '게다가, 더구나'라는 뜻의 furthermore나 moreover가 적절하다.
오답 ① In short: 요컨대, Therefore: 그러므로
② In fact: 사실, Accordingly: 그런 이유로
③ As a result: 그 결과
⑤ On the other hand: 반면에, Consequently: 결과적으로

17 ⓒ diversity는 '다양성'이라는 뜻이지만, 영어 뜻풀이는 controversy (논쟁)에 관한 것이다.
오답 diversity: the state having different things or people together in a group (한 집단 내에 다른 것들이나 사람들이 함께 있는 상태)
① ⓐ imitate(모방하다): 무엇이 보이거나 행동하는 것을 따라 하다
② ⓑ exceed(넘어서다): 수나 양으로 무엇보다 더 크다
④ ⓓ ethically(윤리적으로): 도덕적 믿음을 따르는 방식으로
⑤ ⓔ collaborate(협력하다): 무엇을 이루기 위해 함께 일하다

18 (A) 계속적 용법의 관계대명사 which를 써야 한다.
(B) concerns와 동격의 명사절을 이끄는 접속사 that을 써야 한다.

19 on the other hand 앞에 언급된 내용은 AI가 내놓는 결과물은 제

한적일 수 밖에 없다는 것이므로, 그와 반대되는 인간의 상상력은 ② '한계나 경계가 없다'가 가장 적절하다.

오답 ① AI와의 협력이 필요하다

③ 지시와 교정이 필요하다

④ 결국 AI의 결과물을 모방할 것이다

⑤ 불완전하고 의존하기에 위험하다

20 뮤지컬의 이야기 구조를 설명하고 글의 마지막에서 그에 대한 자신의 감상을 말하고 있으므로, 이 글은 뮤지컬 감상평이다.

21 ⑤ Elphaba has exceptional magical powers.라고 했으므로 알맞은 진술이다.

오답 ① → 오즈의 나라는 이야기의 공간적 배경이다.

② → 대학교에서 처음 만났다.

③ → 차가운 성격(cold personality)를 가졌다.

④ → 처음에는 잘 지내지 못했다.

22 뮤지컬에서 가장 인기있는 노래를 소개하며, 주인공이 노래를 부르게 되는 상황을 설명하고 있으므로 빈칸에는 '노래를 부르며'가 들어

가는 것이 가장 자연스럽다.

오답 ① 그의 눈을 바라보며

③ 마치 그녀가 새인 듯이

④ 마법의 나무로 만든

⑤ 관객을 충격에 빠뜨리며

23 (A) cannot ~ without ...: …없이 ~할 수 없다

(B) '더 이상 신뢰할 수 없다'와 호응하는 말은 '사악한 계획을 가졌다'이므로, evil이 적절하다.

(C) not ~ anymore: 더이상 ~ 아닌

오답 (B) virtuous: 도덕적인, 고결한

(C) no more: 그 이상 ~ 않다

24 ④ 거대한 용 모양의 장치는 무대 위에(above the stage) 걸려 있다

25 It seem to-V: ~하는 것처럼 보이다, whenever: ~할 때마다

독해

READING EXPERT
중고등 대상 7단계 원서 독해 교재
Level 1 | Level 2 | Level 3 | Level 4 | Level 5 |
Advanced 1 | Advanced 2

기강 잡고
기본을 강하게 잡아주는 고등영어
독해 잡는 필수 문법 | 기초 잡는 유형 독해

빠른 독해를 위한 바른 선택
기초세우기 | 구문독해 | 유형독해 | 수능실전

The 상승
독해 기본기에서 수능 실전 대비까지
직독직해편 | 문법독해편 | 구문편 |
수능유형편 | 어법·어휘+유형편

수능

맞수
맞춤형 수능영어 단기특강 시리즈
구문독해 기본편 | 실전편
수능유형 기본편 | 실전편
수능문법어법 기본편 | 실전편
수능듣기 기본편 | 실전편
빈칸추론

핵심만 콕 찍어주는 수능유형 필독서
독해 기본 | 독해 실력 | 듣기

특급
수능 1등급 만드는 특급 시리즈
독해 유형별 모의고사 | 듣기 실전 모의고사 24회 |
어법 | 빈칸추론 | 수능·EBS 기출 VOCA

얇빠 얇고 빠른 미니 모의고사 10+2회
수능 핵심유형들만 모아 얇게! 회당 10문항으로 빠르게!
입문 | 기본 | 실전

수능만만
만만한 수능영어 모의고사
기본 영어듣기 20회 | 기본 영어듣기 35회+5회 |
기본 영어독해 10+1회 | 기본 문법·어법·어휘 150제 |
영어듣기 20회 | 영어듣기 35회 |
영어독해 20회 | 어법·어휘 228제

지은이

민 병 천	現 서울대학교 영어교육과 교수	주 용 균	現 과천여자고등학교 교사	김 민 준	現 운정고등학교 교사
이 지 현	現 인창중학교 교사	고 경 욱	現 신성고등학교 교사	조 은 영	現 ㈜NE능률 교과서개발연구소
송 민 아	前 ㈜NE능률 교과서개발연구소				

고등　기출문제집

내신백신
Common English 1　

펴 낸 날	2025년 3월 1일 (초판 1쇄)
펴 낸 이	주민홍
펴 낸 곳	(주)NE능률

개 발 책 임	김지현
영 문 교 열	Curtis Thompson, Alison Li, Courtenay Parker
디자인책임	오영숙
디 자 인	안훈정, 오솔길
제 작 책 임	한성일

등 록 번 호	제1-68호
I S B N	979-11-253-4960-0

대 표 전 화	02 2014 7114
홈 페 이 지	www.neungyule.com
주 　 소	서울시 마포구 월드컵북로 396(상암동) 누리꿈스퀘어 비즈니스타워 10층